Linda

Rick Steves®

ISTANBUL

By Lale Surmen Aran & Tankut Aran

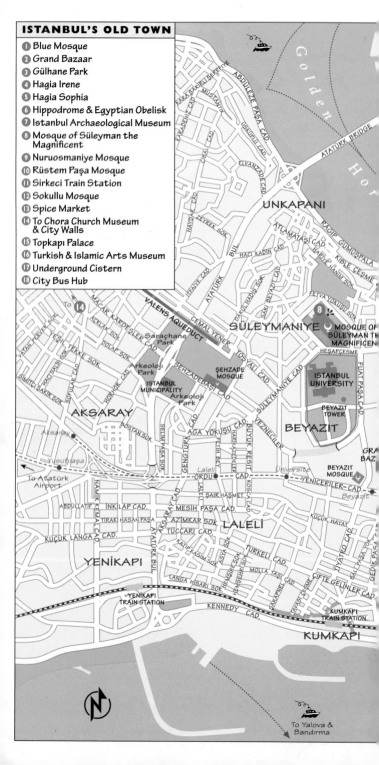

ISTANBUL'S OLD TOWN

1. Blue Mosque
2. Grand Bazaar
3. Gülhane Park
4. Hagia Irene
5. Hagia Sophia
6. Hippodrome & Egyptian Obelisk
7. Istanbul Archaeological Museum
8. Mosque of Süleyman the Magnificent
9. Nuruosmaniye Mosque
10. Rüstem Paşa Mosque
11. Sirkeci Train Station
12. Sokullu Mosque
13. Spice Market
14. To Chora Church Museum & City Walls
15. Topkapı Palace
16. Turkish & Islamic Arts Museum
17. Underground Cistern
18. City Bus Hub

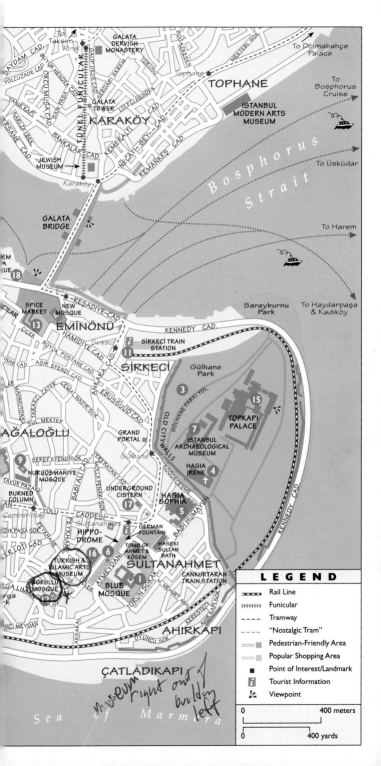

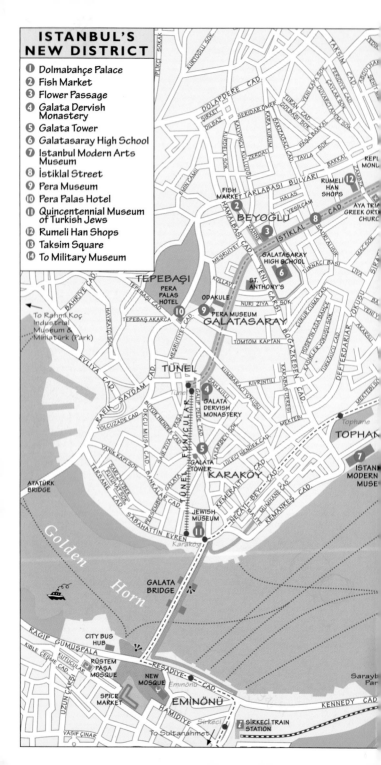

ISTANBUL'S
NEW DISTRICT

1. Dolmabahçe Palace
2. Fish Market
3. Flower Passage
4. Galata Dervish Monastery
5. Galata Tower
6. Galatasaray High School
7. Istanbul Modern Arts Museum
8. İstiklal Street
9. Pera Museum
10. Pera Palas Hotel
11. Quincentennial Museum of Turkish Jews
12. Rumeli Han Shops
13. Taksim Square
14. To Military Museum

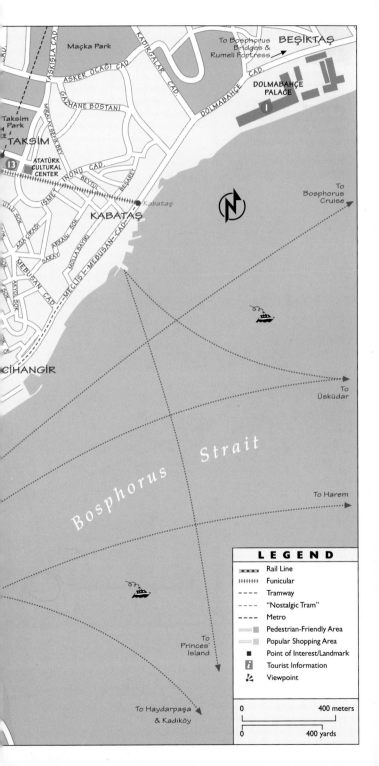

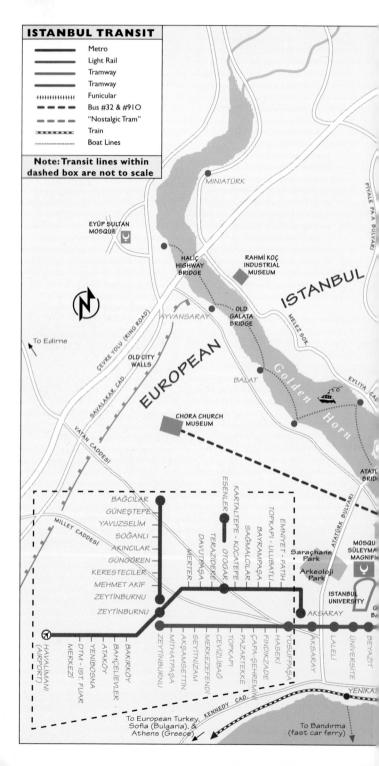

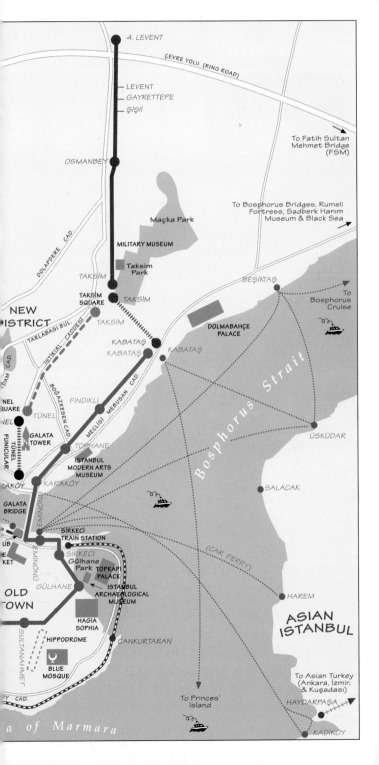

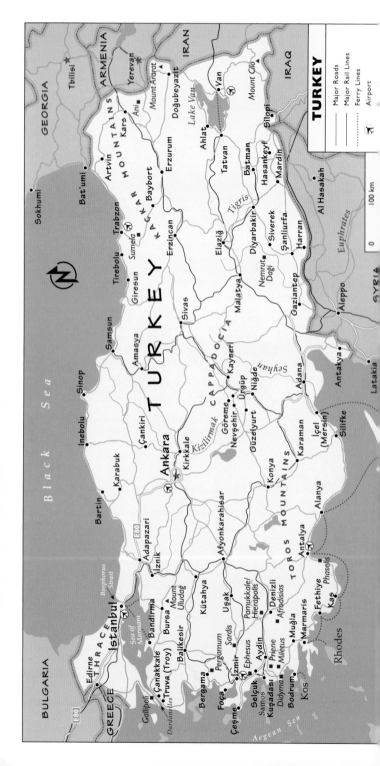

Rick Steves'

ISTANBUL

By Lale Surmen Aran & Tankut Aran

AVALON
TRAVEL

CONTENTS

INTRODUCTION

Walk in the footsteps of Roman emperors and Ottoman sultans. Explore some of the world's greatest monuments, their names etched in history: Hagia Sophia, the Blue Mosque, Topkapı Palace. Bargain-hunt your way through a twisted warren of lanes in the Grand Bazaar—the world's oldest shopping mall—pausing to sip tea with a merchant. Set sail on the Golden Horn, and take in a spine-tingling skyline bristling with minarets. Inhale the apple-flavored smoke from a water pipe as you listen to the strains of exotic music. And enjoy meeting some of the planet's friendliest people, whether you're chatting with a fisherman on a bustling bridge, haggling for a carpet, learning about Islam from a peace-loving Muslim, or playing backgammon with a grizzled old Turk.

Istanbul is one of the world's great cities, period. For millennia, this point where Europe meets Asia has been the crossroads of civilization. Few places on earth have seen more history than this sprawling metropolis on the Bosphorus. Once called Byzantium, then Constantinople, Istanbul boasts the opulent trappings of an epic past—from the Byzantine emperors and the Ottoman sultans of the distant ages, to the modern Republic-builders and "Eurocrats" of our own time. And, as the biggest city of a moderate Muslim nation, Istanbul also offers the inquisitive traveler a unique opportunity to grapple with the rich and inspiring Islamic faith: hear the eerie wail of the call to prayer echo across the rooftops, poke into a neighborhood mosque, and watch a Dervish whirl in prayer.

Turkey has long been the most exciting and inviting cultural detour from Europe. And as their nation starts down the long and winding road to European Union membership, the Turks are more Western-facing and welcoming than ever. Now's the time to visit.

About This Book

Rick Steves' Istanbul is a personal tour guide in your pocket. Better yet, it's actually two tour guides in your pocket: The authors of this book are Lale Surmen Aran and Tankut Aran, who have been guiding Rick Steves' tours in Turkey for more than a decade. As Turkish natives and residents of Istanbul, Lale and Tankut give you an insightful, knowledgeable look at this exciting and complex destination. While Rick is not a co-author, he is committed to the quality of this book and contributed to this update by personally visiting nearly every sight covered in this book.

Here's what you'll find in the following chapters:

Orientation includes a verbal map of Istanbul, tourist information, specifics on public transportation, and other helpful hints. The "Planning Your Time" section suggests a day-to-day schedule for how to best use your limited time.

Sights provides a succinct overview of the most important sights, arranged by neighborhood, with ratings:

▲▲▲—Don't miss.
▲▲—Try hard to see.
▲—Worthwhile if you can make it.
No rating—Worth knowing about.

The **Self-Guided Walks** cover Istanbul's most intriguing neighborhoods: the historic core of the city, the back streets of the Old Town, the Golden Horn, and the New District.

The **Self-Guided Tours** lead you through Istanbul's most fascinating museums and sights: Hagia Sophia, Topkapı Palace, Istanbul Archaeological Museum, the Turkish and Islamic Arts Museum, the Grand Bazaar, the Mosque of Süleyman the Magnificent, the Chora Church Museum, and the City Walls. And to help you see more than Istanbul, we've narrated the cruise along the Bosphorus Strait.

Experiences prepares you to dive into Turkish culture, whether visiting a mosque or Turkish bath, sipping Turkish coffee, trying a water pipe *(nargile),* or playing backgammon.

Sleeping describes our favorite hotels, from budget deals to cushy splurges.

Eating serves up a range of options, from inexpensive kebab stops to elegant seafood restaurants, clustered by neighborhood.

Shopping gives you tips for shopping painlessly and enjoyably, without letting it overwhelm your vacation or ruin your budget. Read up on Istanbul's great marketplaces, where you can find textiles, tiles, ceramics, jewelry, and (of course) carpets.

Entertainment is your guide to events, low-key evening fun, and lively nightlife.

Transportation Connections lays the groundwork for your smooth arrival and departure, with detailed information on

⤓	Viewpoint	✈	Airport	▭▭▭	Pedestrian Zone
➤	Entry Point	ⓣ	Taxi Stand	o⊦⊦⊦⊦⊦⊦o	Funicular
𝒊	Tourist Info	Ⓜ	Metro Stop	------	Railway
WC	Restroom	Ⓣ	Tram Stop	⊦——⊦	Tram Line
⛫	Castle	Ⓑ	Bus Stop	▥▥▥▥▥	Stairs
⛪	Church	⚓	Boat Stop	- - - -	Trail
☪	Mosque	Ⓟ	Parking	)▥▥▥▥(	Tunnel

Use this legend to help you navigate the maps in this book.

Atatürk Airport and Istanbul's two train stations.

Turkish History and Culture introduces you to some of the key people and events in this nation's complicated past, making your sightseeing more meaningful. The language tips and glossary of terms will come in handy.

Understanding Islam covers the basics of one of the world's most widely practiced religions.

The **appendix** is a traveler's tool kit, with a handy packing checklist, recommended books and films, instructions on how to use the telephone, useful phone numbers, a climate chart, festival list, hotel reservation form, and Turkish survival phrases.

Throughout this book, when you see a ✪ in a listing, it means that the sight is covered in more detail in one of the self-guided tours (a page number will tell you where to find more information).

Browse through this book and select your favorite sights. Then have a great trip! Traveling like a temporary local—and taking advantage of the information here—you'll get the absolute most out of every mile, minute, and lira. As you visit places we know and love, we're happy you'll be meeting some of our favorite Turkish people.

PLANNING

Trip Costs

Five components make up your trip costs: airfare, surface transportation, room and board, sightseeing and entertainment, and shopping and miscellany.

Airfare: A basic round-trip flight from the US to Istanbul costs $700 to $1,500, depending on where you fly from and when (cheaper in winter). Turkish Airlines has direct flights to Istanbul three days a week from Chicago; direct flights between New York City and Istanbul run at least once daily on Turkish, American, and Delta. Direct daily flights also link Istanbul to these major European hubs: Amsterdam, Athens, Barcelona, Berlin, Brussels, Copenhagen, Frankfurt, London, Munich, Paris, Rome, and

Merhaba (Hello) From Rick Steves

I love Istanbul. When I was in my twenties, I finished six or seven trips in a row here. I didn't plan to...it was just the sub-conscious cherry on top of every European adventure. And since before the first Gulf War, my company has been taking tour groups to Istanbul, turning people on to one of this planet's most exciting cities. Today, a visit to Istanbul is more important than ever: It's a city that's 99 percent Muslim, and still welcoming to outsiders and eager to connect with the

West. I am personally committed to the notion that without visiting a place such as Istanbul, we cannot hope to understand the dynamics of a faith and a region that will be in our headlines for the foreseeable future.

In short, Istanbul is an essential destination that certainly merits a top-notch guidebook. And, selfishly, I'd love to write that guidebook. But you deserve the expertise of locals to guide you through this rich, complex, and fast-changing metropolis.

I've worked with this book's authors, Lale Surmen Aran and Tankut Aran, for more than a decade as tour guides. I believe they know their hometown better than any non-Turk ever could. And, after a lifetime of tour guiding, they relate well to Americans and understand their needs and concerns. They know how to present their city in a way that's inspiring rather than tiring.

A while ago, Lale and Tankut told me of their powerful desire to share Istanbul with more Americans than can squeeze

Venice. If your visit to Istanbul is part of a longer European trip, consider saving time and money by flying "open jaw" (flying into one city and out of another).

Surface Transportation: You'll spend most of your time in Istanbul doing your sightseeing on foot, because distances between most attractions are short. You can reach far-flung sights with Istanbul's affordable trams, light rail, funicular, Metro, ferries, and buses. Allow $15–20 per person per week for public transportation (each individual trip costs a little less than a dollar). It's cheap to treat yourself to a cab—$5–15 will cover the cost of connecting virtually any two sights listed in this book. From the airport, a taxi ride to your hotel in the Old Town or New District will total $25–45 (some hotels offer free airport transfers—see page 271).

Room and Board: You can thrive in Istanbul on an average of into their tour buses. I knew they were right. And so, you hold in your hands the first "Rick Steves" book that I didn't actually author. It was a big step for me, and not one I took lightly—I know that people who enjoy my guidebooks have high expectations. But because of Lale and Tankut's fine work and deep knowledge, I was confident they would do a good job of writing a book that would be an invaluable tool for my traveling readers. They did and it is.

Before the first edition was printed, Cameron Hewitt (co-author of my Eastern Europe and Croatia & Slovenia guidebooks) traveled to Istanbul from our office with Lale and Tan's work and shaped it to my readers' unique needs. And for the next edition, I spent a busy week in Istanbul, giving the guidebook a thorough shakedown and visiting nearly every covered sight.

I came home from that trip thankful for Lale and Tankut's passion for sharing their city with our readers, appreciative of Cameron's expert editing, satisfied that we have produced the best book available on Istanbul, and newly enthused about what is one of the world's most vibrant and fascinating cultural capitals.

I hope this guidebook helps you have the time of your life exploring Istanbul.

Happy travels,

Rick

$110 per person a day for room and board. A $110-a-day budget per person allows $15 for lunch, $20 for dinner, and $75 for lodging (based on two people splitting the cost of a $150 double room that includes breakfast). Students and tightwads eat and sleep for $40 a day ($20 per hostel bed, $20 for meals).

Sightseeing and Entertainment: Some attractions, such as mosques and markets, are free. At museums and sights, fees range from $2–14. Figure an average of $14 per major sight (Hagia Sophia-$14, Topkapı Palace-$14, Turkish and Islamic Arts Museum-$6.50) and $2 for minor ones. Note that at Topkapı Palace ($14), you'll pay an additional $10 to see the Harem. Concerts at the Atatürk Cultural Center can run as low as $10; for less than $35, you can see Dervishes whirl. An overall average of $20–30 a day works for most. Don't skimp here. After all, this category is

Major Holidays and Weekends

Popular places are even busier on weekends, and holidays can bring many businesses to a grinding halt. Plan ahead and reserve your accommodations and any major transportation well in advance.

Mark these dates in red on your travel calendar: **Easter** (both Western and Orthodox Easter fall on April 4 in 2010), **Turkey Grand Prix** Formula 1 car race (likely April 23-25 in 2010; hotel prices skyrocket and rooms go fast), **Ascension Day** (both Western and Orthodox Ascension fall on May 13 in 2010), **Christmas, December 26,** and **New Year's Day.**

Surprisingly, major Christian holidays are busy times in Muslim Turkey because Europeans flock here when they have time off. Be sure to book rooms far ahead if you're traveling any time around Easter (including the week before and after) or Christmas (roughly Dec 18–Jan 2 every year).

Istanbul hotels generally don't fill up for Muslim festivals (listed on page 356 in the appendix), when many people travel outside of the city. On religious festival days, avoid public transportation because it's free (or discounted) and packed with locals visiting their families and heading out to parks, fairs, and theaters. Streets are crowded—it's a great time for people-watching.

the driving force behind your trip—you came to sightsee, enjoy, and experience Istanbul.

Shopping and Miscellany: Figure $2–3 per ice-cream cone, coffee, and soft drink. Shopping can vary in cost from nearly nothing to a small fortune. Good budget travelers find that this category has little to do with assembling a trip full of lifelong and wonderful memories.

When to Go

Istanbul has a moderate climate year-round. It is generally hot and humid from mid-July to mid-August, and it can snow during January and February. The peak-season months (with the best weather) are from mid-April to June and September to October. During the off-season, you can generally find better deals and smaller crowds; the weather is usually good; and all the sights are open. Note that weather conditions can change throughout the day—especially in spring and fall—but extremes are rare. Summer temperatures generally range from 65–85 degrees Fahrenheit (42–60 degrees in winter). Temperatures below freezing and above 90 degrees make headlines. For more information, refer to the climate chart in the appendix; for daily weather, go to www.meteor.gov.tr.

Keep in mind that prices in Istanbul are higher in early August (for the Turkey Grand Prix) and around Christmas and New Year's. During the holidays, you'll see lots of vacationing Europeans, mostly from Spain, Italy, and France.

Travel Smart

Your trip to Istanbul is like a complex play—easier to follow and really appreciate on a second viewing. While no one does the same trip twice to gain that advantage, reading this book in its entirety before your trip accomplishes much the same thing.

Design an itinerary that enables you to visit the various sights at the best possible times. As you read this book, make note of festivals, colorful market days, and when sights are closed.

If you have only a few days for Istanbul, remember that most of the city's museums are closed on Monday, and the Grand Bazaar and Spice Market are closed on Sunday. For a complete list of closed days, see the "Daily Reminder" on page 22.

Saturdays in Turkey are virtually weekdays with earlier closing hours. Sundays have the same pros and cons as they do for travelers in the US—sights are generally open but may have more limited hours, shops and banks are closed, city traffic is light, and public transportation options are fewer.

Be sure to mix intense and relaxed periods in your itinerary. Every trip (and every traveler) needs at least a few slack days. Pace yourself. Assume you will return.

Plan ahead for banking, laundry, and picnics. Get online at Internet cafés or your hotel to research transportation connections, confirm events, check the weather, and get directions. Buy a phone card (or carry a mobile phone) and use it for making restaurant reservations and double-checking hours of out-of-the-way sights.

Connect with the culture. Set up your own quest for the best mosque, kebab, or Turkish coffee. Slow down and be open to unexpected experiences. Enjoy the friendliness of the Turkish people. Ask questions—most locals are eager to point you in their idea of the right direction. Keep a notepad in your pocket for organizing your thoughts. Wear your money belt, familiarize yourself with the local currency, and learn a simple formula to quickly estimate rough prices in dollars. Those who expect to travel smart, do.

PRACTICALITIES

Red Tape: Currently, American and Canadian citizens need a passport and a visa, but no shots, to travel in Turkey. You're required to buy the three-month visa (a sticker that's affixed to a page of your passport) when you enter the country at a border or

Know Before You Go

Your trip is more likely to go smoothly if you plan ahead. Check this list of things to arrange while you're still at home.

Be sure that your **passport** is valid at least six months after your ticketed date of return to the US. If you need to get or renew a passport, it can take up to two months (for more on passports, see www.travel.state.gov). You'll also need a **visa** to travel in Turkey—you can buy it when you enter the country (see "Practicalities—Red Tape," on page 7).

Book your rooms in advance if you'll be traveling during peak season (mid-April–June and Sept–Oct) or around any major holidays or events (see "Major Holidays and Weekends," on page 6), and definitely for your first night.

Call your **debit and credit card companies** to let them know the countries you'll be visiting, so that they'll accept (and not deny) your international charges. Confirm your daily withdrawal limit; consider asking to have it raised so you can take out more cash at each ATM stop. Ask about international transaction fees.

Since **airline carry-on restrictions** are always changing, visit the Transportation Security Administration's website (www.tsa.gov/travelers) for an up-to-date list of what you can bring on the plane with you...and what you have to check. Remember to arrive with plenty of time to get through security.

airport. At Atatürk Airport, you'll see the window to buy your visa before you get to the passport-control checkpoint. You'll pay in cash, and exact change (in US dollars) is required: US citizens pay $20, while Canadians pay $60—in US dollars, not Canadian. (If you don't have an American or Canadian passport, you may need to obtain your visa prior to your arrival in Turkey—contact your nation's consulate for information.) Once the visa has been affixed to your passport, you can go through passport control, where the visa will be stamped. You can also get your visa in advance from a Turkish consulate in the US; this is required for stays of more than three months (visit www.turkishembassy.org for details).

Make sure your passport is good for at least six months after your ticketed date of return to the US; otherwise you could be denied entry. Keep your passport with you. You are required to have proof of identity with you at all times in Istanbul, and may be asked to show it when entering sights or using a credit card. Pack a photocopy of your passport in your luggage in case the original is lost or stolen.

Time: In Istanbul—and in this book—you'll be using the 24-hour clock. After 12:00 noon, keep going—13:00, 14:00, and

Just the FAQs, Please

Whom do I call in case of emergency?
For English-language medical help, call Med-line Ambulance at 0212/282-0000. The following numbers are Turkish-language only (and would require the help of a local person such as your hotelier to communicate for you): 112 for medical emergencies and 155 for police.

What if my credit card is stolen?
Act immediately. See "Damage Control for Lost Cards," page 12, for instructions.

How do I make a phone call to, within, and from Turkey?
For detailed dialing instructions, refer to page 348.

How can I get tourist information about my destination?
Turkey has three national tourist information offices in the US (see page 343). You'll also find several tourist information offices in Istanbul (page 24). Note that Tourist Information is abbreviated "TI" in this book.

What's the best way to pack?
Light. For a recommended packing list, see page 359.

Does Rick have other resources that could help me?
For info on Rick's guidebooks, public television series, free audiotours, public radio show, website, guided tours, travel bags, accessories, and railpasses, see page 344.

Are there any updates to this guidebook?
Check www.ricksteves.com/update for changes to the most recent edition of this book.

Can you recommend any good books and movies for my trip?
For suggestions, see page 346.

Do you have information on train, bus, or air travel?
See the Transportation Connections chapter on page 317.

How much do I tip?
Relatively little. For tips on tipping, see page 13.

Will I get a student or senior discount?
While discounts for sightseeing and transportation are not listed in this book, youths (under 18) and students (with International Student Identity Cards) often get discounts—but only by asking. To get a teacher or student ID card, visit www.statravel.com or www.isic.org.

How can I get a VAT refund on major purchases?
See the details on page 14.

Does Turkey use the metric system?
Yes. A liter is about a quart, four to a gallon. A kilometer is six-tenths of a mile. I figure kilometers to miles by cutting them in half and adding back 10 percent of the original (120 km: 60 + 12 = 72 miles, 300 km: 150 + 30 = 180 miles). For more metric conversions, see page 357.

so on. For anything after 12, subtract 12 and add P.M. (14:00 is 2:00 P.M.).

Istanbul is seven/ten hours ahead of the East/West Coasts of the US (and it's one hour ahead of most of continental Europe). For a handy online time converter, try www.timeanddate.com.

Business Hours: Most shops are open daily 9:00–19:00; on Sundays, they open a little later in the morning. On holidays, most museums and shops in tourist areas are open (and shops may stay open a little later than usual). The Grand Bazaar and the Spice Market are closed on Sundays and usually also on the first day of religious festivals.

Most government offices and banks are open Monday–Friday 9:00–17:00; some are also open Saturday 9:00–12:00 (closed Saturday afternoon and all day Sunday and holidays). On the day before a national or religious holiday, many government offices and banks close in the afternoon.

Watt's Up? Europe's electrical system is different from North America's in two ways: the shape of the plug (two round prongs) and the voltage of the current (220 volts instead of 110 volts). For your North American plug to work in Turkey, you'll need an adapter, sold inexpensively at travel stores in the US. As for the voltage, most newer electronics or travel appliances (such as hair dryers, laptops, and battery chargers) automatically convert the voltage—if you see a range of voltages printed on the item or its plug (such as "110–220"), it'll work in Turkey. Otherwise, you can buy a converter separately in the US (about $20).

News: For news specific to Turkey, see "Resources" on page 343. Americans keep in touch in Europe with the *International Herald Tribune* (published almost daily via satellite throughout Europe). Every Tuesday, the European editions of *Time* and *Newsweek* hit the stands with articles of particular interest to travelers. Sports addicts can get their fix from *USA Today*. News in English will be sold only where there's enough demand: in major tourist areas or at international hotels. Good websites include http://news.bbc.co.uk, www.iht.com, and www.european times.com.

MONEY

Cash from ATMs

Throughout Turkey, cash machines (ATMs) are the standard way for travelers to get local currency. Bring plastic—credit and/or debit cards—along with several hundred dollars in hard cash as an emergency backup. It's smart to bring two cards, in case one gets demagnetized or eaten by a temperamental machine. Avoid travelers checks, which are difficult to cash in Turkey. If you do want to

Exchange Rate

In this book, we list most prices in New Turkish Liras (Yeni Türk Lirası, or YTL).

1.50 New Turkish Liras (YTL) = about $1

Just like the dollar, one YTL is broken down into 100 cents, or *kuruş* (koo-roosh; abbreviated Ykr). You'll find coins of 1, 5, 10, 25, and 50 *kuruş* and 1 lira; and bills of 5, 10, 20, 50, and 100 liras (the 200-lira bill is on the way).

To roughly convert prices from liras to dollars, subtract about one-third. (Pretend everything is on a "30 percent off sale.") So that 10-YTL coffee-and-baklava break is about $6.50, that 50-YTL shawl is about $35, and that 100-YTL taxi ride is...uh-oh.

In 2009, Turkey's Central Bank is dropping the word "New"—that is, the letter "Y"—from "YTL," making the currency's name "TL" (Turkish Lira). You'll see bills and coins—including the new 200-lira bill—with the shorter "TL" designation, as well as ones with the older "YTL."

Prices are also sometimes listed in either dollars or euros, especially in tourist areas. This is partly for convenience, but also to protect vendors against YTL inflation. Hotels almost always list prices in euros, and we've followed suit in the Sleeping chapter.

1 euro (€) = about $1.40

To roughly convert prices in euros to dollars, add about 40 percent to prices in euros: €20 is about $28, €50 is about $70, and so on.

For the latest rates and a handy printable cheat sheet, see www.oanda.com.

30 euros =

change a substantial amount of cash or travelers checks, be warned that the airport exchange booths generally don't offer very good rates. Instead, just change what you need to get into town, then go to one of the many private exchange offices in Istanbul, which have better rates than banks.

You'll find ATMs all over Istanbul, and all have instructions in English. Most Turks call an ATM a *Bankamatik* (bahn-kah-mah-teek), though some banks use different names—"24," "self-service," or *paramatik* (literally "money-matic").

To use an ATM to withdraw money from your account, you'll need a debit card (ideally with a Visa or MasterCard logo for maximum usability), plus a PIN code. Know your PIN code in numbers; there are only numbers—no letters—on Turkish keypads. It's smart to bring two cards, in case one gets demagnetized or eaten by a temperamental machine.

Before you go, verify with your bank that your cards will work overseas, and alert them that you'll be making withdrawals in Turkey; otherwise, the bank may not approve transactions if it perceives unusual spending patterns. Also ask about international fees; see "Credit and Debit Cards," below.

Try to take out large sums of money to reduce your per-transaction bank fees. If the machine refuses your request, don't take it personally. Just try again and select a smaller amount. If that doesn't work, try a different machine. Once you've got Turkish cash, it can be difficult to change big bills into smaller denominations. The easiest solution is to break big bills at a bank.

Keep your cash safe. Thieves target tourists. Use a money belt—a pouch with a strap that you buckle around your waist like a belt—and wear under your clothes. A money belt provides peace of mind, allowing you to carry lots of cash safely. Don't waste time every few days tracking down a cash machine—withdraw a week's worth of money, stuff it in your money belt, and travel!

Credit and Debit Cards

For purchases, Visa and MasterCard are more commonly accepted than American Express. Just like at home, credit and debit cards work easily at larger hotels, restaurants, and shops, but smaller businesses prefer payment in local currency (in small bills—break large bills at a bank or larger store). If your receipts show your credit-card number, don't toss them thoughtlessly.

Fees: Most credit and debit cards—whether used for purchases or ATM withdrawals—now charge additional "international transaction" fees of up to 3 percent; some also tack on an extra $5 per transaction. To avoid unpleasant surprises, call your bank or credit-card company before your trip to ask about these fees. If the fees are too high, consider getting a card just for your trip: Capital One (www.capitalone.com) and most credit unions have low-to-no international transaction fees.

Damage Control for Lost Cards

If you lose your credit, debit, or ATM card, you can stop people from using it by reporting the loss immediately to the respective global customer-assistance centers. Call these 24-hour US numbers collect: Visa (410/581-9994), MasterCard (636/722-7111), and American Express (623/492-8427).

At a minimum, you'll need to know the name of the financial institution that issued you the card, along with the type of card (classic, platinum, or whatever). Providing the following information will allow for a quicker cancellation of your missing card: full card number, whether you are the primary or secondary cardholder, the cardholder's name exactly as printed on the card, billing address, home phone number, circumstances of the loss or theft, and identification verification (your birth date, your mother's maiden name, or your Social Security number—memorize this, don't carry a copy). If you are the secondary cardholder, you'll also need to provide the primary cardholder's identification-verification details. You can generally receive a temporary card within two or three business days in Turkey.

If you promptly report your card lost or stolen, you typically won't be responsible for any unauthorized transactions on your account, although many banks charge a liability fee of $50.

Tipping

Tipping in Turkey isn't as automatic and generous as it is in the US—but for special service, tips are appreciated, if not expected. As in the US, the proper amount depends on your resources, tipping philosophy, and the circumstances, but some general guidelines apply.

Restaurants: If you order your food at a counter, don't tip (though it's nice to leave a lira or two on the table for the busser).

At cafés and restaurants that have a waitstaff, tip 10 percent for good service. If you're not satisfied, tip less—or not at all. Occasionally, some upscale restaurants include a service charge in the bill; but this fee goes to the restaurant, not the servers, so it's still appropriate to round up your bill about 10 percent. If you're not sure whether your bill includes the tip, just ask.

Taxis: To tip the cabbie, round up to the next YTL on the fare (for a 14-YTL fare, pay 15 YTL); for a long ride, round to the nearest 5 YTL (for a 47-YTL fare, pay 50 YTL). If the cabbie hauls your bags and zips you to the airport to help you catch your flight, you might want to toss in a little more. But if you feel like you're being driven in circles or otherwise ripped off, skip the tip.

Special Services: It's thoughtful to tip a few liras to someone who shows you a special sight and who is paid in no other way. Tour guides at public sights sometimes hold out their hands for tips after they give their spiels. If we've already paid for the tour, we don't tip extra. We don't tip at hotels, but if you do, give the porter a lira or two for carrying bags, and, at the end of your stay, leave a few liras for the maid if the room was kept clean. In general, if someone in the service industry does a super job for you, a tip of a few liras is appropriate, but not required.

When in doubt, ask: If you're not sure whether (or how much) to tip for a service, ask your hotelier or the tourist information office; they'll fill you in on how it's done on their turf.

Getting a VAT Refund

Wrapped into the purchase price of your Turkish souvenirs is a Value Added Tax (VAT) of 18 percent. If you spend a minimum amount (118 YTL, or about $80) at a store that participates in the VAT refund scheme, you're entitled to get most of that tax back.

Getting your refund is usually straightforward and, if you buy a substantial amount of souvenirs, well worth the hassle. If you're lucky, the merchant will subtract the tax when you make your purchase. (This is more likely to occur if the store ships the goods to your home.) Otherwise, you'll need to:

Get the paperwork. Have the merchant completely fill out the necessary refund document, called a "cheque."

Get your stamp at the border or airport. Process your cheque(s) at your last stop in Turkey with the customs agent who deals with VAT refunds. It's best to keep your purchases in your carry-on for viewing, but if they're too large or dangerous (such as knives) to carry on, track down the proper customs agent to inspect them before you check your bag. To qualify, your purchased goods should be unused. If you show up at customs wearing your new outfit from the Grand Bazaar, officials might look the other way—or deny you a refund.

Collect your refund. You'll need to return your stamped document to the retailer or its representative. Many merchants work with a service that has offices at major airports, ports, and border crossings, such as Global Refund (www.globalrefund.com) or Premier Tax Free (www.premiertaxfree.com). These services, which extract a 4 percent fee, usually can refund your money immediately in your currency of choice or credit your card (within two billing cycles). If the retailer handles VAT refunds directly, it's up to you to contact the merchant for your refund. You can mail the documents from home, or quicker, from your point of departure (using a stamped, addressed envelope you've prepared or one that's been provided by the merchant)—and then wait. It could take months.

Customs for American Shoppers

You are allowed to take home $800 worth of items per person duty-free, once every 30 days. The next $1,000 is taxed at a flat 3 percent. After that, you pay the individual item's duty rate. You can also bring in duty-free a liter of alcohol (slightly more than a standard-size bottle of wine; you must be at least 21), 200 cigarettes, and up to 100 non-Cuban cigars. You may take home vacuum-packed cheeses; dried herbs, spices, or mushrooms; and canned fruits or vegetables, including jams and vegetable spreads. Meats (even vacuum-packed or canned) and fresh fruits or vegetables are not permitted. Note that you'll need to carefully pack any bottles of wine and other liquid-containing items in your checked luggage, due to limits on liquids in carry-ons. To check customs rules and duty rates before you go, visit www.cbp.gov, and click on "Travel," then "Know Before You Go."

INTRODUCTION

SIGHTSEEING

Sightseeing can be hard work. Use these tips to make your visits to Istanbul's finest sights meaningful, fun, fast, and painless.

Plan Ahead: Set up an itinerary that allows you to fit in all your must-see sights. For a one-stop look at opening hours, see "Istanbul at a Glance" (page 42; also see "Daily Reminder" on page 22). If you have your heart set on a particular sight, it's always smart to confirm the latest hours at the local TI.

Don't put off visiting a must-see sight—you never know when a place will close unexpectedly for a holiday or restoration. If you'll be visiting during a holiday, find out if a particular sight will be open by phoning ahead or visiting its website. Keep in mind, too, that opening times can change without warning.

When possible, visit key sights and museums first thing (when your energy is best) and save other activities for the afternoon. Hit the highlights first, then go back to other things if you have the stamina and time. However, note that the major sights, Hagia Sophia and Topkapı Palace, attract crowds during high season, particularly in the morning (mid-April–June and Sept–Oct). In peak season, consider visiting these sights in the afternoon or evening.

To get the most out of the self-guided tours and sight descriptions in this book, read them the night before your visit. When you arrive at the sight, use the overview map to get the lay of the land and the basic tour route.

At Sights: All sights have rules, and if you know about these in advance, they're no big deal.

Some important sights have metal detectors or conduct bag searches that will slow your entry.

At mosques, respect the dress code (covered knees and shoulders, and head scarves for women). For more information, see "Visiting a Mosque" on page 61.

Museums often require you to check daypacks and coats, usually for free. The cloakrooms are generally safe, but if you have something you can't bear to part with, stash it in a pocket or purse. If you don't want to check a small backpack, carry it under your arm like a purse as you enter. From a guard's point of view, a backpack is generally a problem, while a purse is not.

Photography is sometimes banned at major sights. Look for signs or ask. If cameras are allowed, flashes or tripods are usually not. Flashes damage oil paintings and distract others in the room. Even without a flash, a handheld camera will take a decent picture (or buy postcards or posters at the museum bookstore). It's also common for a museum to generally allow photography but prohibit it for special exhibits—look for signs.

If sights have special exhibits in addition to their permanent collection, the exhibits may be included in the normal entry price or may require a separate ticket. Be aware that some museums bump up the normal entry fee when there's a special exhibit (in that case you have to pay even if you don't want to see the exhibit).

A few sights in Istanbul rent audioguides (usually for about $8); unfortunately, the commentary is likely to be dry. While most readers will find this book's tours more interesting, eager students take advantage of both types of tours and learn even more. If you bring along your own pair of headphones and a Y-jack, two people can sometimes share one audioguide and save. Guided tours (widely ranging in quality) are most likely to occur during peak season.

Expect changes—artifacts can be on tour, on loan, out sick, or shifted at the whim of the curator. To adapt, pick up any available free floor plans as you enter, and ask museum staff if you can't find a particular item. Point to the photograph in this book and ask, *"Nerede?"* (neh-reh-deh; "Where is?").

Some sights have an on-site café or cafeteria (usually a good place to rest and have a snack or light meal). Museum WCs are generally free and clean.

If the museum has a bookshop, stop in before leaving and scan the postcards or thumb through the biggest guidebook (or skim its index) to be sure you haven't overlooked something that you'd like to see.

Most sights stop admitting people 30–60 minutes before closing time, and some rooms may close early (generally about 45 minutes before the official closing time). Guards usher people out, so don't save the best for last.

Every sight or museum offers more than what is covered in this book. Use the information in this book as an introduction—not as the final word.

TRANSPORTATION

Transportation options within Istanbul include trams, ferries, taxis, buses, and the Metro (subway)—all explained in depth in the Orientation chapter (see page 19). Because the public

How Was Your Trip?

Were your travels fun, smooth, and meaningful? If you'd like to share your tips, concerns, and discoveries, please fill out the survey at www.ricksteves.com/feedback. We value your feedback. Thanks in advance—it helps a lot.

transportation network is so user-friendly, and traffic is a headache, we strongly advise against renting a car to get around Istanbul. For information on international arrivals and departures, and travel within Turkey, see the Transportation Connections chapter (page 317).

TRAVELING AS A TEMPORARY LOCAL

Americans travel all the way to Turkey to enjoy differences—to become temporary locals. You'll experience frustrations. Certain truths that you've found "God-given" or "self-evident"—like cold beer, ice in drinks, bottomless cups of coffee, hot showers, cigarette smoke being irritating, and bigger being better—are suddenly not so true. One of the benefits of travel is the eye-opening realization that there are logical, civil, and even better alternatives.

If there is a negative aspect to the Turkish image of Americans, it is that we are big, loud, aggressive, impolite, rich, superficially friendly, and a bit naive.

While the Turks look bemusedly at some of our Yankee excesses—and worriedly at others—they nearly always afford us individual travelers all the warmth we deserve. Thank you in advance for traveling as temporary locals who are sensitive to the culture. It's fun to follow you in my travels.

Judging from all the happy feedback we receive from travelers who have used this book, it's safe to assume you'll enjoy a great, affordable vacation—with the finesse of an independent, experienced traveler.

Thanks, and happy travels!

BACK DOOR TRAVEL PHILOSOPHY
From *Rick Steves' Europe Through the Back Door*

Travel is intensified living—maximum thrills per minute and one of the last great sources of legal adventure. Travel is freedom. It's recess, and we need it.

Experiencing the real Europe requires catching it by surprise, going casual..."Through the Back Door."

Affording travel is a matter of priorities. (Make do with the old car.) You can travel—simply, safely, and comfortably—nearly anywhere in Europe for $120 a day plus transportation costs. In many ways, spending more money only builds a thicker wall between you and what you came to see. Europe is a cultural carnival, and, time after time, you'll find that its best acts are free and the best seats are the cheap ones.

A tight budget forces you to travel close to the ground, meeting and communicating with the people, not relying on service with a purchased smile. Never sacrifice sleep, nutrition, safety, or cleanliness in the name of budget. Simply enjoy the local-style alternatives to expensive hotels and restaurants.

Extroverts have more fun. If your trip is low on magic moments, kick yourself and make things happen. If you don't enjoy a place, maybe you don't know enough about it. Seek the truth. Recognize tourist traps. Give a culture the benefit of your open mind. See things as different but not better or worse. Any culture has much to share.

Of course, travel, like the world, is a series of hills and valleys. Be fanatically positive and militantly optimistic. If something's not to your liking, change your liking. Travel is addictive. It can make you a happier American as well as a citizen of the world. Our Earth is home to six and a half billion equally important people. It's humbling to travel and find that people don't envy Americans. Europeans—and Turks—like us, but, with all due respect, they wouldn't trade passports.

Globe-trotting destroys ethnocentricity. It helps you understand and appreciate different cultures. Regrettably, there are forces in our society that want you dumbed down for their convenience. Don't let it happen. Thoughtful travel engages you with the world—more important than ever these days. Travel changes people. It broadens perspectives and teaches new ways to measure quality of life. Rather than fear the diversity on this planet, travelers celebrate it. Many travelers toss aside their hometown blinders. Their prized souvenirs are the strands of different cultures they decide to knit into their own character. The world is a cultural yarn shop, and Back Door travelers are weaving the ultimate tapestry. Join in!

ORIENTATION

Istanbul is the crossroads of civilizations, where Europe meets Asia, and where West meets East. Truly one of the world's great historic cities, Istanbul was once called Constantinople, named for the fourth-century Roman Emperor Constantine the Great. Over the centuries, the city has been the capital of two grand empires. The Byzantine Empire was born here in the fourth century A.D. and lasted until the 15th century, when the Ottoman Empire took over, ruling through the end of World War I. Even though Turkey isn't actually governed from Istanbul (Ankara, in the east, is the official capital), the city remains the historical, cultural, and financial center of the country.

Istanbul: A Verbal Map

Istanbul, with over 15 million people, sprawls over an enormous area on both banks of the **Bosphorus Strait** (Boğaziçi). The Bosphorus runs north to south (from the Black Sea to the Sea of Marmara) through the middle of Istanbul, splitting the city in half and causing it to straddle two continents: Asia and Europe. Asian Istanbul (east of the Bosphorus) is mostly residential, while European Istanbul (west of the Bosphorus) is densely populated,

containing virtually all of the city's main attractions. Two suspension bridges—the Bosphorus Bridge and the Fatih Sultan Mehmet Bridge—span the Bosphorus Strait, connecting the two halves. Public ferries

Istanbul Essentials

English	Turkish	Pronounced
Blue Mosque	*Sultanahmet Camii*	sool-tah-nah-meht jah-mee
Bosphorus Strait	*Boğaziçi*	boh-ahz-ee-chee
Burned Column (and major tram stop)	*Çemberlitaş*	chehm-behr-lee-tahsh
Chora Church Museum	*Kariye Müzesi*	kah-ree-yeh mew-zeh-see
Divan Yolu (main street in Old Town)	*Divan Yolu*	dee-vahn yoh-loo
Galata Bridge	*Galata Köprüsü*	gah-lah-tah kohp-rew-sew
Galata Dervish Monastery	*Galata Mevlevihanesi*	gah-lah-tah mehv-leh-vee-hah-neh-see
Galata Tower	*Galata Kulesi*	gah-lah-tah koo-leh-see
Golden Horn (inlet between Old Town and New District)	*Haliç*	hah-leech
Grand Bazaar	*Kapalı Çarşı*	kah-pah-luh chahr-shuh
Gülhane Park	*Gülhane Parkı*	gewl-hah-neh pahr-kuh
Hagia Sophia (church-and-mosque museum)	*Aya Sofya*	eye-ah soh-fee-yah

also link both banks, carrying millions of people each day to and from work.

A tapering inlet of the Bosphorus, called the **Golden Horn** (Haliç), runs roughly east to west, slicing through the middle of European Istanbul.

South of the Golden Horn is a peninsula known as the **Old Town**—the 3,000-year-old historical core of the city surrounded by fragments of the original Byzantine wall. Near the tip of the Old Town peninsula is a compact and welcoming district called Sultanahmet, home to many of the city's most famous sights (Hagia Sophia, Blue Mosque, Topkapı Palace) and its highest concentration of hotels.

North of the Golden Horn is the modern, westward-looking,

Hippodrome (ancient chariot racetrack)	*Hipodrom*	hee-poh-drohm
Historic Core of the Old Town	*Sultanahmet*	sool-tah-nah-meht
İstiklal Street (main street in New District)	*İstiklal Caddesi*	ees-teek-lahl jahd-deh-see
Mosque of Süleyman the Magnificent	*Süleymaniye Camii*	sew-lay-mah-nee-yeh jah-mee
New District	*Pera*	peh-rah
Rüstem Paşa Mosque	*Rüstem Paşa Camii*	rew-stehm pah-shah jah-mee
Sirkeci Train Station	*Sirkeci Tren Garı*	seer-keh-jee trehn gah-ruh
Spice Market	*Mısır Çarşışı*	muh-suhr chahr-shuh-shuh
Süleymaniye neighborhood	*Süleymaniye*	sew-lay-mah-nee-yeh
Taksim Square (heart of New District)	*Taksim Meydanı*	tahk-seem may-dah-nuh
Topkapı Palace	*Topkapı Sarayı*	tohp-kah-puh sah-rah-yuh
Tünel (old-fashioned funicular in New District)	*Tünel*	tew-nehl
Underground Cistern	*Yerebatan Sarayı*	yeh-reh-bah-tahn sah-rah-yuh

European-feeling **New District** (called "Pera" by locals), centered on Taksim Square and bisected by the main pedestrian drag called İstiklal Caddesi (which we'll refer to as İstiklal street). The New District offers some interesting sights, good hotels and restaurants, and a 21st-century contrast to the Old Town.

Unlike many other European cities, Istanbul doesn't branch out from a main Town Hall or central square. In many parts of town, you may get lost if you're searching for a predictable, European-style square. (The Turkish word for "square"—*meydanı*—actually means something more like "area.") Instead, Istanbul is a cobbled-together collection of various landmarks and patches of land, all interconnected by twisty alleys. Sightseeing this decentralized, seemingly disorganized city can be intimidating for first-time

ORIENTATION

Daily Reminder

Every Day: The Underground Cistern, Bosphorus cruise boats, Galata Tower, and most Turkish baths welcome tourists daily. Mosques are open daily, but close to tourists five times each day, when worshippers come to pray. The closure lasts from about 30 minutes before the service begins until after it ends (services last 15–30 minutes). Specific prayer times change daily and are listed in local newspapers, or you can ask your hotel. For details on visiting a mosque, see page 61.

Monday: Most of Istanbul's museums are closed today, including those operated by the Ministry of Culture—such as Hagia Sophia, the Istanbul Archaeological Museum, and the Turkish and Islamic Arts Museum. The Dolmabahçe Palace, Military Museum, Istanbul Modern Arts Museum, Pera Museum, and Rahmi Koç Industrial Museum are also closed. Topkapı Palace is open (and crowded).

Tuesday: Topkapı Palace, Galata Dervish Monastery, and Military Museum are closed. Hagia Sophia is busy today.

Wednesday: Sights closed today are Chora Church, Rumeli Fortress, and Sadberk Hanım Museum. Because Topkapı Palace is closed on Tuesday, it may be especially crowded first thing this morning.

Thursday: All sights are open except for Dolmabahçe Palace. The Istanbul Modern Arts Museum is free and open late (until 20:00).

Friday: For Muslims, the Friday noon service is the week's most important. All mosques are closed as usual for the service, and very crowded before and after.

Saturday: Everything is open except the Quincentennial Museum of Turkish Jews. The Rahmi Koç Industrial Museum is open until 19:00.

Sunday: The Grand Bazaar and Spice Market are closed. The Rahmi Koç Industrial Museum is open until 19:00.

Ramadan: During the Muslim holy month (Aug 11–Sept 8 in 2010), a big, convivial, multi-generational festival breaks out each evening at sunset (ask for time locally). The Hippodrome square is most convenient for most visitors. There's hardly a tourist in sight as the fun builds, the sun sets, the call to prayer rings out, people eat, and the party starts. For more information, see page 62.

visitors. But even though the city is an enormous metropolis, the tourist's Istanbul is amazingly compact and walkable, and an impressive public-transportation network efficiently connects the major sightseeing zones (see "Getting Around Istanbul," page 29).

Planning Your Time

Istanbul demands a minimum of two days, but we'd suggest at least four days to do it justice. Even with a week, you'll find yourself running out of time to tackle everything the city has to offer.

Istanbul in Two Days

On the morning of Day One, focus on the Sultanahmet district in the center of the Old Town. Take our self-guided Historic Core of Istanbul Walk to get your bearings, visiting Hagia Sophia, the Underground Cistern, and the Blue Mosque. With additional time, tour the Turkish and Islamic Arts Museum (small collection in the heart of Sultanahmet) or Topkapı Palace (time-consuming sultans' complex a short walk away).

On Day Two, follow the self-guided Old Town Back Streets Walk—including tours of the Grand Bazaar, Mosque of Süleyman the Magnificent, and Spice Market. You'll finish near the Galata Bridge, where you can end your day with the self-guided Golden Horn Walk.

Day Three

If you haven't done so already, tour Topkapı Palace and the nearby Istanbul Archaeological Museum. Or, if you're museumed out, consider Day Four's New District activities, next.

Day Four

Devote this day to the New District, following our self-guided walk (including the Pera Museum and Galata Tower). When you're finished with the walk, consider taking a taxi to Chora Church to see its sumptuous Byzantine mosaics. Or, if you'd rather stay in the New District, choose from a range of other sights: Dolmabahçe Palace, Military Museum, Quincentennial Museum of Turkish Jews, or Istanbul Modern Arts Museum.

Day Five

Go to Asia. Set sail on the Bosphorus Strait, spending a full day going up to the Asian fishing village of Anadolu Kavağı, then returning to the Old Town.

Istanbul in a Week

More time gives you more options, from some of the smaller museums to quintessential Istanbul experiences such as soaking in a Turkish bath, watching Whirling Dervishes spin themselves into a trance, or lazily smoking a water pipe *(nargile)* filled with apple tobacco.

OVERVIEW

Tourist Information

Istanbul's state-run tourist offices, abbreviated as **TI** in this book (and marked with an *i* sign in Istanbul), are often not the best sources of information. They suffer from long lines, offer little or no information, and usually have only colorful promotional booklets, brochures, and maps. The only reason to visit is to pick up the good, free city map. The TI staff, many of whom are not fluent in English, will try to help you with your requests, but most likely with mixed results.

Tourist Offices

If you must visit a tourist office, here are some handy locations. The first two are in the Old Town, the third and fourth are in the New District, and the last is at the airport (all have sporadic hours; generally daily 9:00–17:00):

• In the **Sultanahmet** neighborhood, in the center of the Old Town (Divan Yolu 3, at the bottom of the square called the Hippodrome, next to the tram tracks, tel. 0212/518-8754 or 0212/518-1802).

• At the **Sirkeci Train Station,** near the Golden Horn in the Old Town's Eminönü district (TI located by station entrance, in the left corner next to a ticket booth, tel. 0212/511-5888).

• Near **Taksim Square** in the New District (this TI is usually closed Sun; at the entrance of Hilton Hotel in Elmadağ, a 10-min walk from Taksim Square; tel. 0212/233-0592).

• At **Karaköy,** a port for cruise ships, located where the Golden Horn and Bosphorus meet in the New District (Rıhtım Caddesi 2, inside the passenger terminal, tel. 0212/249-5776).

• At **Atatürk Airport,** Istanbul's main airport, located nine miles outside the city center (at the International Arrivals desk inside the terminal, tel. 0212/465-3151).

More Resources

For current information on cultural activities, entertainment options, shopping ideas, and classy restaurants, pick up *The Guide*, a magazine published every two months and written by Turks and expats (6.50 YTL). You can find it at bigger newspaper stands and major bookshops on İstiklal street in the New District.

The English edition of the monthly *Time Out Istanbul* magazine lists sights, hotels, restaurants, nightclubs, and more (5 YTL, sold at most Istanbul newsstands, www.timeout.com).

The *Turkish Daily News* (1.50 YTL) is a daily Turkish newspaper in English with a good website, www.turkishdailynews.com.tr. Visit this site prior to your trip for a local perspective on headline news.

Hürriyet is one of the most popular daily national papers. It's not printed in English, but an English summary is online at www.hurriyet.com.tr/english.

Arrival in Istanbul

For a rundown of Istanbul's train stations and airports, see the Transportation Connections chapter on page 317.

Helpful Hints

Theft Alert: In Turkey, travelers are rarely mugged, but often pickpocketed. Thieves thrive on fresh-off-the-plane tourists. Try to keep a low profile. You'll be better off without your best clothes, expensive-looking gear, and fancy jewelry or watches. Be careful on all public transportation and in crowds. Watch for distraction tactics such as dropped coins, "accidental" spills, kids who seem to be fighting for no reason, and locals who ask you for directions.

If you're out late, avoid dark back streets or any place with dim lighting and minimal pedestrian activity. Ignore anyone who asks if you need help or a cab ride into the city. Wear a money belt, be smart with your bags, sling your daypack across your front, and keep change in buttoned or front pockets. Carry a photocopy of your passport and plane ticket in your luggage or money belt in case the original is lost or stolen. Especially valuable items are more secure left in your hotel room (and in a hotel safe, if available) rather than with you on the streets.

Street Safety: Be extremely cautious crossing streets that lack traffic lights. Look both ways, since many streets are one-way, and be careful of seemingly quiet bus or taxi lanes. Don't assume you have the right-of-way, even in a crosswalk. When crossing a street, keep your pace constant and don't stop suddenly. Drivers calculate your speed and won't hit you, provided you

Turkish Do's and Don'ts

Turkey gives Western visitors a refreshing dose of culture shock. Here are a few of the finer points to consider when interacting with your Turkish hosts:

- Don't signal to someone with your hands or your fingers, except when you're hailing a cab or trying to get your waiter's attention. In any other situation, it's considered rude.

- Don't get too close to people as you talk. Allow for plenty of personal space (an arm's length is fine). Especially when talking to someone of the opposite sex, keep your distance and don't touch them as you talk.

- Be careful with gestures: A "thumbs up" is—and means— OK. But putting your thumb between your index and middle finger and making a fist is equivalent to showing your middle finger in the US. (And I always thought my grandma was "stealing my nose.") Making a circle with your thumb and index finger while twisting your hand is a homophobic insult.

- Be aware of Turkish body language for "yes" and "no." A Turk nods her head down to say yes. She shakes it back and forth to say no, like we do. But she might also say no by tilting her head back. Learn the Turkish words for "yes" (*evet;* eh-veht) and "no" (*hayır;* hah-yur) to confirm.

- If you're offered food or a gift, either keep it for yourself or politely decline. People of Turkey love to share what they have, but what they offer to you is for you alone. If you invite others to share the food, you may put your Turkish friend in a difficult position (they may not have more to share). If you don't want the food or gift, don't wave it away. Do as the locals do: Either put your right hand on your heart and say "thank you" (*teşekkür ederim;* teh-shehk-koor eh-deh-reem), or if it's food, pat your abdomen to indicate that you're full.

- Don't blow your nose at the dining table—either leave the table, or turn to face the other way. And afterwards, don't shake hands right away. (Come to think of it, that's a rule we could use back home, too.)

don't alter your route and pace. (Don't expect them to stop for you; they probably won't.)

Although it's technically illegal, cars park on sidewalks, especially in the Old Town. These parked cars, as well as free-standing merchandise kiosks or makeshift stands, can make sidewalks difficult to navigate. Try to stay by the side of the road, but pay attention to passing cars.

Finding Addresses: When you're trying to locate a particular place, you may notice several different elements in the address. Sometimes it's as straightforward as a street name (usually with *Caddesi*—"street," or *Sokak*—"alley"), followed by a number, such as: Yeni Akbıyık Caddesi 21. This is sometimes preceded by the name of a larger street that's nearby, to help you (or your cabbie) find the general area before searching for a tiny alley: İstiklal Caddesi, Meşelik Sokak 10. And sometimes the address is followed by the name of the specific neighborhood it's in: Şifahane Sokak 6, Süleymaniye. So "İstiklal Caddesi, Meşelik Sokak 10, Taksim" is near İstiklal street, house number 10 on Meşelik alley, in the Taksim district.

US Consulate: In case of an emergency, call for 24-hour assistance (tel. 0212/335-9000, recorded info tel. 0212/335-9200). American citizen services are available in person on a walk-in basis (Mon–Thu 8:00–11:30 & 13:30–15:00, closed Fri–Sun and Turkish and American holidays, Kaplıcalar Mevkii Sokak 2, Istinye, roughly a 30-min cab ride from downtown Istanbul via the Bosphorus coastal road).

Medical Problems: Local hospitals *(hastane)* usually have 24-hour emergency care centers *(acil servis;* "emergency service"), but are short on English-speaking personnel. Unless you need to be rushed to the nearest hospital, go to a private facility that has English-speaking staff. The **American Hospital** in the New District is a good option (Güzelbahçe Sokak 20, Nişantaşı, tel. 0212/444-3777—dial ext. 9 for English, then 1 for ambulance services). **Med-line** has medical assistance and ambulance service (tel. 0212/444-1212). The **International Hospital** is close to the airport (Istanbul Caddesi 82, Yeşilköy, tel. 0212/663-3000, for an ambulance call 0212/444-4505).

Pharmacies: Pharmacies *(eczane;* edge-zah-neh) are generally open daily except Sunday (Mon–Sat 9:00–19:00). In every neighborhood, one pharmacy stays open late and on holidays for emergencies. These *nöbetçi eczane* (noh-bet-chee edge-zah-neh; "pharmacy on duty") are generally within walking distance or a 5- to 10-minute cab ride from wherever you are. Just ask your hotel for help. Or, if you're on your own, the location of the nearest *nöbetçi eczane* is posted by the entrance to any pharmacy. When interpreting signs, note these translations: *bu gece* (tonight), *Pazar* (Sunday), and *gün/günü* (day). Remember that dates are listed day first, then month (e.g., 06/04 is April 6).

Local Help: SRM Travel—a travel company owned and operated by the authors of this book, Lale and Tankut Aran—offers city walking tours and local guides, as well as custom-tailored travel services for individuals visiting Istanbul, Turkey, and neighboring countries (tel. 0216/386-7623, www.srmtravel .com, tour@srmtravel.com).

ORIENTATION

Aggressive Sales Pitches: Anywhere in the Old Town, you'll constantly be approached by locals who greet you enthusiastically, ask if you need any help, and tell you about their cousin who just happens to live where you came from. Before long, what began as a friendly conversation devolves into a greedy sales pitch. These salesmen—who prey on Americans' gregariousness and desire to respond politely to a friendly greeting—are irritating and can waste a lot of your valuable sightseeing time. While not dangerous, the salesmen can be particularly aggressive, or even intimidating, to single women. Just smile and say "No, thank you!" without breaking stride...then ignore the escalating attempts to grab your attention (or elbow) as you walk past. For more on dealing with salesmen, see page 209.

English-Language Church: Christian services are held in English each Sunday at the Dutch Chapel (Union Church of Istanbul—just off İstiklal street by the Dutch Consulate at #393, contemporary service at 9:30, traditional worship at 11:00, tel. 0212/244-5212, www.unionchurchofistanbul.org).

Baggage Storage: Both the domestic and international terminals at Atatürk Airport have left-luggage counters available 24 hours daily (depending on size, 10–12 YTL per bag per day, tel. 0212/465-3442). Train stations and bus terminals don't have left-luggage storage. If you're leaving Istanbul and returning later, ask your hotel staff if they can store the items you don't need to take with you.

Public WCs: You'll generally pay 0.50 YTL or less to use a public WC. Carry toilet paper or tissues with you, since some WCs are poorly supplied. Use the WCs in museums (likely free and better than public WCs), or walk into any sidewalk café or American fast-food joint like you own the place and find the WC in the back.

In the heart of the Old Town, plumbing isn't always up to modern standards. Rather than flush away soiled toilet paper, locals dispose of it in a trash can next to the toilet. It's culturally sensitive for visitors to do the same (especially if there's a sign requesting this).

Western-style toilets are the norm nowadays, but don't

be surprised if you see an "Oriental toilet," also known as a "Turkish toilet." This squat-and-aim system is basically a porcelain hole in the ground flanked by platforms for your feet. If this seems outrageous to you, spend your squatting time pondering the fact that those of us who need a throne to sit on are in the minority; most humans sit on their haunches and nothing more.

Getting Around Istanbul

Even though Istanbul is a huge city, most of the tourist areas are easily walkable. You'll likely need public transportation only to connect sightseeing zones (for example, going from the Old Town to the New District across the Golden Horn). Fortunately, Istanbul has an impressively slick, modern, affordable, and user-friendly network of trams, funiculars, and Metro lines. Once you learn the system, it seems custom-made for tourists—stops are conveniently located within a short walking distance of major attractions. Taxis, buses, and public ferries round out your transportation options.

By Taxi

Taxis are an efficient and relatively cheap way to get around town (2 YTL drop fee, then roughly 1.30 YTL/kilometer; nighttime tariff 50 percent higher 24:00–6:00). Figure about 10–20 YTL for a long trip within the Old Town or New District (such as from Sultanahmet to Chora Church), or about 35–55 YTL between Atatürk Airport and a hotel in European Istanbul.

All taxis are painted yellow, with the license plate number, name, and phone number of its home station written on the front doors. All have electronic meters, and the only ways you can be cheated are if the driver takes a needlessly long route or charges you the nighttime tariff. Since most taxi meters periodically blink to show you the selected tariff, you can check to be sure your driver is charging you the right one: *Gündüz* (or *gunduz*) is for daytime, and *gece* is for nighttime. Never go for an "off-meter" deal, because you'll always pay more than if you'd used the meter.

If a taxi's top light is on, it's available—just wave it down. Drivers usually flash their lights when they see you waiting by the side of the road to indicate that they will pick you up. Taxis can take up to four passengers. If you aren't able to hail a cab off the street, ask a local where you can find a taxi stand. You can also call a taxi company, usually for no extra charge. Hotels, restaurants, museums, and even shopkeepers almost always have the phone number of a nearby taxi company—just ask.

To tip, simply round up the bill (generally 1–2 YTL; for exceptional service, you could add a few liras more). If you need a receipt, ask: *"Fiş, lütfen"* (fish lewt-fehn; receipt, please).

ORIENTATION

ORIENTATION

Public Transportation Tokens and Passes

Istanbul's tram, light rail, Metro, ferries, "nostalgic tram" (on İstiklal street in the New District), and historic Tünel funicular (connecting İstiklal street to Galata Bridge) are covered by a system of tokens and passes. Buses accept passes only (no tokens).

A basic **single-ride token** (*jeton;* zheh-tohn)—the simplest way to go—costs 1.50 YTL per ride, not including transfers. (You'll have to buy a second token to transfer from one train to another.) Tokens cost 0.90 YTL for the Tünel funicular and nostalgic tram. Buy the tokens at ticket booths, and stock up to avoid lines if you'll be making frequent trips. Simply insert a token in the turnstile as you enter the public-transportation network. The two exceptions are the buses (which only take passes) and the Taksim-Kabataş funicular (which requires a different-size token, sold at the funicular).

The **Beşibiryerde** (beh-shee-beer-yehr-deh) pass costs 7 YTL and covers five single rides. It does not allow you to transfer between services (e.g., tram to light rail). Beşibiryerde passes are sold at major tram, light rail, and Metro stops.

Skip the rechargeable transit passes, called **Akbil,** geared for local commuters rather than tourists. The savings are minimal, they're sold at only a few places (such as the Taksim Metro station), and they require a passport photo.

The tokens and passes described here don't cover seabuses *(deniz otobüsü)*, hydrofoils, Bosphorus cruise boats (see page 249), ferries to the islands, or the double-decker buses that cross the Bosphorus.

By Tram, Light Rail, Funicular, and Metro

Istanbul's rail network is convenient and efficient. Tram, light rail, funicular, and Metro lines intersect at central locations, and all except the Taksim-Kabataş funicular use the same tokens and passes. See the sidebar (above) and refer to the color map of the transit system at the beginning of this book (timetables and maps also at www.istanbul-ulasim.com.tr/en).

By Tram: The seemingly made-for-tourists *tramvay* (trahm-vay) cuts a boomerang-shaped swath through the core of Istanbul's Old Town, then crosses the Golden Horn to the New District, where it continues along the Bosphorus. Destinations are posted on the outside of the tram—just hop on the one heading in the direction you want to go. Key tram stops include the following (from south to north):

ORIENTATION

• **Beyazıt** and **Çemberlitaş:** Flanking the Grand Bazaar in the Old Town.

• **Sultanahmet:** Dead-center in the Old Town, near Hagia Sophia, the Blue Mosque, the Hippodrome, and most recommended hotels and restaurants.

• **Gülhane:** At the side entrance to the Topkapı Palace grounds, near the Istanbul Archaeological Museum.

• **Sirkeci:** Sirkeci Train Station, near the Golden Horn and several Bosphorus ferry terminals.

• **Eminönü:** On the Golden Horn in the Old Town, near the Spice Market, Galata Bridge, and additional Bosphorus ferry terminals.

• **Karaköy:** In the New District (directly across Galata Bridge from the Old Town), near the Galata Tower and Tünel train up to İstiklal street.

• **Tophane:** Near Istanbul Modern Arts Museum.

• **Kabataş:** End of the line in the New District, next to the funicular up to Taksim Square (described later) and a few blocks from Dolmabahçe Palace.

There's also a **"nostalgic tram"** that runs up and down İstiklal street, through the middle of the New District. For details, see the New District Walk on page 108.

By Light Rail: West of the Grand Bazaar in the Old Town (at the Yusufpaşa stop), the tram connects to the *hafif raylı sistem* (hah-feef rahy-luh sees-tehm; light-rail system), which stretches west and south. While few sights are on this light-rail line, it's handy for reaching the city's main bus terminal (Otogar) and Atatürk Airport (the stop called Havalimanı, at the end of the line). This tram-and-light rail connection to the bus terminal or airport—while a hassle with a lot of luggage—is cheap (4.20 YTL), costing much less than a cab ride or airport shuttle. For more information on the bus terminal and airport, see the Transportation Connections chapter.

By Funicular: An easy one-stop, two-minute underground *finiküler* connects Taksim Square (and İstiklal street) in the New District with the Kabataş tram stop along the Bosphorus below.

At Kabataş, the tram and funicular stations are side by side; to find the funicular station from Taksim Square, look for the combined funicular/Metro entrance at the center of the square, right across from the Marmara Hotel, and follow *Kabataş-Finiküler* signs. Note that the Taksim-Kabataş funicular uses a different-size token, sold next to the turnstiles at either station.

A second underground funicular, called **Tünel,** connects the Galata Bridge on the Golden Horn with İstiklal street on the hill above. This late-19th-century funicular is as historic as it is convenient. For details, see page 124.

By Metro: The underground Metro—generally not useful for tourists—begins at Taksim Square and heads north into the business and residential Levent district. To find a Metro entrance, look for the big *M* signs.

By Bus

The bus system was designed for commuters, but it can work as a last resort for tourists. It's often crowded during rush hour, and it can be difficult to tell where you're going and where to transfer or get off. Bus numbers on a particular route are clearly marked on signs at the stops. Avoid the buses altogether during morning and evening rush hours (bus info at www.iett.gov.tr/en).

Complicating matters, you'll need a pass (Beşibiryerde or Akbil) to use the bus—tokens aren't accepted (see "Public Transportation Tokens and Passes," on page 30). Bus drivers occasionally take cash (carry the exact amount: 1.50 YTL) and use their own pass to pay your fare, but this is rare.

We'd take the bus only to get to the Chora Church (bus #32 or #91O from Eminönü; see tour on page 227), but other potentially useful routes include the following:

• **Bus #40** (Taksim–Sarıyer–Taksim) is a scenic route along the Bosphorus (every 10–25 min, runs 6:00–24:00, less frequent after 21:30), connecting places of interest along the European side of the strait.

• **Bus #25E** (Kabataş–Sarıyer–Kabataş) follows the same route as #40, along the Bosphorus, but departs from Kabataş in the New District (runs 6:15–22:30). It connects easily with the Old Town *tramvay*.

By Ferry and Seabus

In this city where millions of people sail across the Bosphorus to work each day, the ferry system had better work well...and it does. In fact, locals much prefer ferries to avoid heavy traffic on the bridges over the Bosphorus, especially during rush hour. Ferries are convenient and inexpensive—just 1.40 YTL one-way. (The Bosphorus cruise boats and ferries to the Princes' Islands cost more—see page 249.)

Seabuses (*deniz otobüsü;* deh-neez ow-toh-bew-sew) are a new, faster alternative to Istanbul's increasingly congested roads. They're speedy and comfortable, but not as popular or as frequent as public ferries. The cost of a ticket varies depending on the destination.

The main ports for ferries and seabuses in European Istanbul are in the **Eminönü district** in the Old Town (by the Spice Market and Galata Bridge, near the mouth of the Golden Horn), **Karaköy** (across the Golden Horn from Eminönü, in the New District; there's a TI here—see page 24), and **Beşiktaş** on the Bosphorus. The main ports in Asian Istanbul are **Üsküdar** and **Kadıköy.** For more on these commuter ferry ports, see page 105.

TOURS

In Istanbul

Hop-On, Hop-Off Bus Tours—City Sightseeing's narrated double-decker bus tours enable you to hop off at any stop, tour a sight, and then catch a later bus to your next destination—but departures are so infrequent that this isn't really practical. The tour amounts to a pricey 90-minute ride in heavy traffic with useless multilingual commentary (a recorded voice occasionally interrupts the obnoxious loop of music to identify sights and to cross-promote other tours they run). The Old Town's single tram line will take you to any of these sights without the hassle, for a lot less money. The bus does, however, take you along the entire old city wall (quite impressive and hard to see otherwise, unless you catch a glimpse on your way from the airport), and offers views from the top deck—making it a convenient and scenic place to munch a kebab or picnic. (Thanks to a convertible roof, this still works in rainy or cold weather.) Pick up their brochure at most hotel lobbies or from their booth across from Hagia Sophia. The loop starts on the main street across from Hagia Sophia, but you can hop on at nearly any of the major sights along the route. Buses run year-round, with hourly departures in peak season (roughly mid-April–mid-Oct) and departures every two hours off-season (35 YTL, 10 percent discount with this book, tel. 0212/234-7777, www.plantours.com).

Big Bus and Boat Tours—**Istanbul Vision,** owned by the same company that offers the hop-on, hop-off bus tours just described, runs bus tours of Istanbul and boat trips on the Bosphorus. These tours are mass-produced, commercial, and multilingual. They'll pick you up at your hotel, stopping at several other hotels before the tour starts. While a good choice for easy transportation to the sights, the narration is generally even less worthwhile than the hop-on, hop-off bus tours. They run nine different city tours, with prices ranging from 35–115 YTL (10 percent discount with this book, see their pamphlets at hotels, tel. 0212/234-7777, www.plan tours.com).

Basic Boat Tours—**Turyol** offers cruises on the Bosphorus for 7.50 YTL per person. There's no narration, but you can follow the route using this book's Bosphorus Cruise Tour chapter. You don't need a reservation. Boats leave from the Golden Horn, right behind Eminönü bus stop, across from the Spice Market (hourly mid-June–mid-Sept Mon–Fri 12:00–18:00, Sat 12:00–19:00, Sun 11:00–19:30, fewer boats off-season, tel. 0212/527-9952, ask for Mr. İhsan or Mr. Şenol).

Walking Tours—**SRM Travel** offers walking tours of Istanbul (see page 28).

Beyond Istanbul

Fezbus—Geared for backpackers with a flexible itinerary, Fezbus is a hop-on, hop-off bus for sightseeing in Turkey (mention this book for a 10 percent discount, tel. 0212/516-9024, www.fez travel.com).

SIGHTS

The sights listed in this chapter are arranged by neighborhood for handy sightseeing. When you see a ✪ in a listing, it means the sight is covered in much more depth in one of our walks or self-guided tours. This is why Istanbul's most important attractions get the least coverage in this chapter—we'll explore them later in the book.

In the Old Town

Istanbul's highest concentration of sights (and hotels) is in its Old Town, mostly in the Sultanahmet neighborhood.

In the Sultanahmet Area

Most of the following sights are covered in the Historic Core of Istanbul Walk on page 72.

▲▲▲Hagia Sophia (Aya Sofya)—It's been called the greatest house of worship in the Christian and Muslim worlds: Hagia

Sophia (eye-ah soh-fee-yah), the Great Church of Constantinople. Built by the Byzantine Emperor Justinian in A.D. 537 on the grandest scale possible, it was later converted into a mosque by the conquering Ottomans, and now serves as Istanbul's most impressive museum. Hagia Sophia remains the high point of Byzantine architecture. Inside, restoration work attempts to do justice to the Christian and Islamic elements that meld peacefully under Hagia Sophia's soaring arches.

Cost, Hours, Location: 20 YTL, covers entire museum; Tue–Sun 9:00–18:30 (until 16:30 off-season), temporary exhibits and upper galleries close 30 minutes earlier, last entry one hour before closing, closed Mon. In the heart of the Old Town at Sultanahmet Meydanı, tel. 0212/528-4500.

○ See Hagia Sophia Tour on page 125.

▲▲▲**Blue Mosque (Sultanahmet Camii)**—Officially named for its patron, but nicknamed for the cool hues of the tiles that

decorate its interior, the Blue Mosque was Sultan Ahmet I's 17th-century answer to Hagia Sophia. Its six minarets rivaled the mosque in Mecca, and beautiful tiles from the İznik school fill the interior with exquisite floral motifs. The tombs of Ahmet I and his wife Kösem Sultan are nearby.

Cost, Hours, Location: Free, generally open daily one hour after sunrise until one hour before sunset, closed to visitors five times a day for prayer, Sultanahmet Meydanı.

For more on the Blue Mosque, ○ see the Historic Core of Istanbul Walk on page 77.

▲▲**Underground Cistern (Yerebatan Sarayı)**—Stroll through an underground rain forest of pillars in this vast, subter-

ranean water reservoir. Built in the sixth century A.D. to store water for a thirsty and fast-growing capital city, the 27-million-gallon–capacity cistern covers an area about the size of two football fields. Your visit to the dimly lit, cavernous chamber includes two stone Medusa heads recycled from earlier Roman structures. The cistern also hosts occasional concerts of traditional Turkish and classical Western music.

Cost, Hours, Location: 10 YTL, daily 9:00–17:30, until 18:30 in summer, Yerebatan Caddesi 13, Sultanahmet, tel. 0212/512-1570.

For more on the Underground Cistern, ○ see the Historic Core of Istanbul Walk on page 76.

▲**Hippodrome**—This long, narrow park-like square in the center of Istanbul's Old Town was once a fourth-century Roman chariot racetrack. Today it's the front yard for many of Istanbul's most famous sights, including Hagia Sophia, the Blue Mosque, and the İbrahim Paşa Palace (home to the Turkish and Islamic Arts Museum). Strolling the Hippodrome's length, you'll admire monuments that span the ages, including the Egyptian Obelisk, Column of Constantine, and German Fountain.

For more on the Hippodrome, ○ see the Historic Core of Istanbul Walk on page 82.

▲▲Turkish and Islamic Arts Museum (Türk-İslam Eserleri Müzesi)—Housed in the former İbrahim Paşa Palace on the Hippodrome, this museum's 40,000-piece collection covers the breadth of Islamic art over the centuries. The compact exhibit displays carefully selected, easy-to-appreciate works from the Selçuks to the Ottomans, including carpets, calligraphy, ceramics, glass, and art represented in wood, stone, and metal.

Cost, Hours, Location: 10 YTL, Tue–Sun 9:00–17:00, last entry at 16:30, closed Mon, Sultanahmet Meydanı, tel. 0212/518-1805, in the Sultanahmet district, next to the Hippodrome's Egyptian Obelisk.

○ See the Turkish and Islamic Arts Museum Tour on page 187.

Sokullu Mosque (Kardirga Sokullu Camii)—This 16th-century mosque, a few hundred yards from the Hippodrome, is more down-to-earth than the big showpiece mosques around Sultanahmet, but contains some notable decorations. The famous royal architect Sinan (see page 225) built the Sokullu Mosque for Grand Vizier Sokullu. The mosque, a fine example of Sinan's mature work, is decorated with İznik tiles even older than those used in the Blue Mosque. But what makes the Sokullu Mosque unique are several gold-framed fragments of the Black Stone of Kaaba—priceless relics for Muslims, who believe that this stone descended from the heavens to show the Prophet Abraham where to build a temple. One piece is displayed above the mosque's main door, another is directly above the *mihrab* (prayer niche in the apse), and another is on the entrance to the *mimber* (pulpit-like staircase).

Cost, Hours, Location: Free, generally open daily one hour after sunrise until one hour before sunset, closed to visitors five times a day for prayer. The imam may lock the door if there are no visitors, but he's usually nearby, so try waiting a few minutes. It's at Şehit Mehmet Paşa Yokuşu 20–24, Sultanahmet.

Getting There: Leave the Hippodrome at its south end (past the Column of Constantine) and take the street called Şehit Mehmet Paşa Yokuşu to the right of the big building at the bottom of the square. Follow this road downhill, and after it makes a sharp right turn, continue on it another block. You'll see the mosque on the left, at the corner of the intersecting Su Terazisi Sokak. Walk a little farther and take the steps to the north to enter the courtyard.

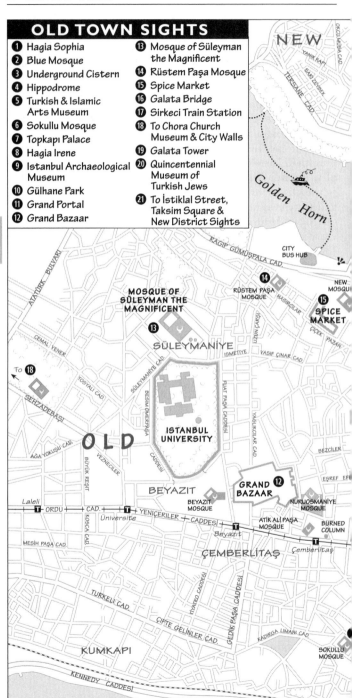

OLD TOWN SIGHTS

1 Hagia Sophia
2 Blue Mosque
3 Underground Cistern
4 Hippodrome
5 Turkish & Islamic Arts Museum
6 Sokullu Mosque
7 Topkapı Palace
8 Hagia Irene
9 Istanbul Archaeological Museum
10 Gülhane Park
11 Grand Portal
12 Grand Bazaar
13 Mosque of Süleyman the Magnificent
14 Rüstem Paşa Mosque
15 Spice Market
16 Galata Bridge
17 Sirkeci Train Station
18 To Chora Church Museum & City Walls
19 Galata Tower
20 Quincentennial Museum of Turkish Jews
21 To İstiklal Street, Taksim Square & New District Sights

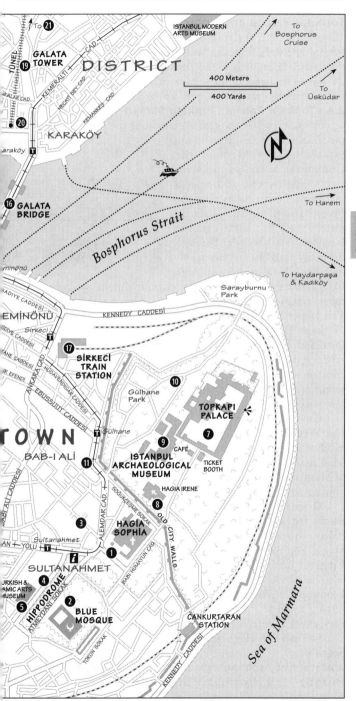

To 21

**GALATA
TOWER** 19

DISTRICT

ISTANBUL MODERN
ARTS MUSEUM

To
Bosphorus
Cruise

400 Meters

400 Yards

To
Üsküdar

KARAKÖY

20

N

araköy

**GALATA
BRIDGE** 16

To Harem

Bosphorus Strait

minönü

To Haydarpaşa
& Kadıköy

Sarayburnu
Park

EMİNÖNÜ

KENNEDY CADDESİ

Sirkeci

**SİRKECİ
TRAIN
STATION** 17

10

Gülhane
Park

**TOPKAPI
PALACE** 7

TOWN

Gülhane

9

BAB-I ALİ

CAFÉ

11

**İSTANBUL
ARCHAEOLOGICAL
MUSEUM**

TICKET
BOOTH

HAGIA IRENE

3

8

**HAGİA
SOPHİA**

OLD CITY WALLS

Sultanahmet

i

1

SULTANAHMET

JRKISH &
AMIC ARTS
MUSEUM 4

HIPPODROME

5

BLUE
MOSQUE 2

CANKURTARAN
STATION

Sea of Marmara

KENNEDY CADDESİ

Topkapı Palace and Nearby

This walled zone, at the tip of the Old Town Peninsula, is a short five-minute walk from the heart of the Sultanahmet district. On the sprawling grounds of the Topkapı Palace complex, you'll find the former residence of the sultans, one of Istanbul's top museums, and all the historical trappings of a once-thriving empire.

▲▲▲**Topkapı Palace (Topkapı Sarayı)**—For centuries, this was the palace where the great sultans hung their turbans. Built on

the remains of ancient Byzantium, established by Mehmet the Conqueror as an administrative headquarters, and turned into a home by Süleyman the Magnificent, Topkapı Palace's history reads like a who's who of Istanbul. Your wander through the many pavilions and courtyards includes a 16th-century kitchen, 10,000 pieces of fine Chinese porcelain, traditional weapons, royal robes, ceremonial thrones, and Sultan Ahmet III's tulip garden. The Imperial Treasury is home to the famous jewel-encrusted Topkapı Dagger and the stunning 86-carat Spoonmaker's Diamond. Its Holy Relics exhibit—with some of the most important fragments of Islamic history anywhere—sends chills down even non-Muslims' spines. A separate ticket covers the cloistered rooms of the famous Harem, where the sultan's wives and concubines lived.

Cost, Hours, Location: Palace—20 YTL, late March–late Oct Wed–Mon 9:00–19:00, closed Tue, until 16:45 off-season, exhibits begin to close one hour earlier; Harem—15 YTL, Wed–Mon 10:00–16:00, closed Tue; between the Golden Horn and Sea of Marmara in the Sultanahmet district, tel. 0212/512-0480, www.topkapisarayi.gov.tr.

○ See the Topkapı Palace Tour on page 140.

Hagia Irene (Aya İrini)—Tucked within the walls of Topkapı Palace, this was the patriarchal church of Constantinople before Hagia Sophia. While the current structure was built by the Emperor Justinian in the sixth century, the original may have been built by Constantine. In the early days of the Eastern Roman Empire, this was the site of the Second Ecumenical Council—setting a course for the future of the Orthodox Church (hours vary; check at entrance for exhibition and concert schedule).

For more on Hagia Irene, ○ see the Topkapı Palace Tour on page 145.

▲▲**Istanbul Archaeological Museum (İstanbul Arkeoloji Müzesi)**—In a city as richly layered with the remains of fallen

civilizations as Istanbul, this museum is an essential stop. Although not as extensive as its more-established European counterparts (such as London's British Museum), the variety and quality of the Istanbul Archaeological Museum's collection rivals any. The complex consists of three separate museums (all covered by the same ticket). The Museum of Archaeology houses a vast exhibit on the Greeks, Romans, and other early Istanbul civilizations. The star attraction here is the world-class collection of ancient sarcophagi, including the elaborately decorated and remarkably well-preserved Alexander Sarcophagus. The Museum of the Ancient Orient shows off striking fragments from the even-more-ancient civilizations of Mesopotamia and Anatolia (the Asian portion of modern-day Turkey, east of the Bosphorus Strait), such as the 13th-century B.C. Kadesh Treaty—the first written peace agreement in world history. And the Tiled Kiosk sparkles with a staggering array of sumptuous ceramics and tiles.

Cost, Hours, Location: 10 YTL includes all three sections; Museum of Archaeology and Tiled Kiosk—Tue–Sun 9:00–17:00, closed Mon; Museum of the Ancient Orient—Tue–Sun 9:00–16:45, closed Mon; last entry at 16:00, Osman Hamdi Bey Yokuşu, Gülhane, Eminönü, tel. 0212/520-7740.

✪ See the Istanbul Archaeological Museum Tour on page 168.

▲**Gülhane Park**—Originally Topkapı Palace's imperial garden, today it's Istanbul's oldest park and a welcoming swath of open green space within the bustling city. Located on the hillside below the palace, with terraces stretching to the shore below, Gülhane is a favorite spot for locals on weekends. Come here to commune with Turks as they picnic with their families and enjoy a meander along the park's shady paths. On some summer weekends, the park hosts free concerts.

Grand Portal (Bab-ı Ali)—In the 19th century, this grand gate with its wavy roof and twin fountains was the entrance to the office of the Grand Vizier. The gate was called Bab-ı Ali because, historically, the word *bab* (door) was also used to refer to the authority of the state. Each Wednesday and Friday, commoners could enter here and tell their problems to public officials. It was here that all domestic and foreign affairs were discussed and presented to the sultan for a final decision. In the last century, the surrounding neighborhood (also known as Bab-ı Ali) was the center of the

Istanbul at a Glance

▲▲▲**Hagia Sophia** Constantinople's Great Church, later converted to an Ottoman mosque, and now a museum. **Hours:** Tue-Sun 9:00–18:30, off-season until 16:30, closed Mon. See page 125.

▲▲▲**Blue Mosque** Ahmet I's 17th-century "so there!" response to Hagia Sophia, named for its brightly colored tiles. **Hours:** Generally open daily one hour after sunrise until one hour before sunset, closed to visitors five times a day for prayer. See page 36.

▲▲▲**Topkapı Palace** Storied residence of the sultans, with endless museum exhibits, astonishing artifacts, and the famous Harem. **Hours:** Palace—late March-late Oct Wed-Mon 9:00–19:00, until 16:45 off-season, closed Tue. Harem—Wed-Mon 10:00–16:00, closed Tue. See page 140.

▲▲▲**Grand Bazaar** World's oldest shopping mall, with more than 4,000 playfully pushy merchants. **Hours:** Mon-Sat 9:00–19:00, shops begin to close at 18:30, closed Sun. See page 206.

▲▲▲**Mosque of Süleyman the Magnificent** The architect Sinan's 16th-century masterpiece, known for its serene interior and the tombs of Süleyman and his wife Roxelana. **Hours:** Mosque—generally open daily one hour after sunrise until one hour before sunset, closed to visitors five times a day for prayer; mausoleum—daily 9:00–17:00, until 18:00 in summer. See page 218.

▲▲▲**Bosphorus Cruise** Public ferry ride on the Bosphorus Strait, offering a glimpse of untouristy Istanbul (and an Asian adventure). **Hours:** Mid-June–mid-Sept at 10:35 and 13:35; mid-Sept–mid-June at 10:35 only. See page 249.

▲▲▲**İstiklal Street** Cosmopolitan pedestrian-only street in the New District, teeming with shops, eateries, and people. **Hours:** Always open. See page 48.

▲▲**Underground Cistern** Vast sixth-century subterranean water reservoir built with recycled Roman columns. **Hours:** Daily 9:00–17:30, until 18:30 in summer. See page 76.

▲▲**Turkish and Islamic Arts Museum** Carpets, calligraphy, ceramics, and other traditional art forms on display at the former İbrahim Paşa Palace. **Hours:** Tue-Sun 9:00–17:00, closed Mon. See page 187.

▲▲**Istanbul Archaeological Museum** Three-part museum complex covering Istanbul's ancient civilizations, including sumptuous tiles and highly decorated sarcophagi. **Hours:** Museum of Archaeology and Tiled Kiosk—Tue–Sun 9:00–17:00, closed Mon; Museum of the Ancient Orient—Tue–Sun 9:00–16:45, closed Mon. See page 168.

▲▲**Spice Market** Fragrant and colorful spices, dried fruit, and roasted nuts inside a 350-year-old market hall. **Hours:** Mon–Sat 9:00–19:30, closed Sun. See page 45.

▲▲**Galata Bridge** Restaurant-lined bridge spanning the Golden Horn, bristling with fishermen's poles and offering sweeping views of the Old Town. **Hours:** Always open. See page 99.

▲▲**Chora Church Museum** Modest church on the edge of the Old Town with some of the best Byzantine mosaics in captivity. **Hours:** Late March–late Oct Thu–Tue 9:00–19:00, off-season until 17:00, closed Wed. See page 227.

▲▲**Galata Tower** 14th-century stone Genoese tower with the city's best views. **Hours:** Daily 9:00–20:00. See page 52.

SIGHTS

▲**Hippodrome** Roman chariot racetrack-turned-square, linking Hagia Sophia and the Blue Mosque. **Hours:** Always open. See page 36.

▲**Gülhane Park** Former imperial rose garden, now a grassy park. **Hours:** Always open. See page 41.

▲**Rüstem Paşa Mosque** Small 16th-century mosque of Süleyman's Grand Vizier with extravagant tile decor. **Hours:** Generally open daily one hour after sunrise until one hour before sunset, closed to visitors five times a day for prayer. See page 45.

▲**Taksim Square** Gateway to the pedestrianized İstiklal street, and heart of Istanbul's New District. **Hours:** Always open. See page 109.

▲**Pera Museum** Compact New District collection of world-class Oriental paintings, Anatolian weights and measures, and Kütahya tiles. **Hours:** Tue–Sat 10:00–19:00, Sun 12:00–18:00, closed Mon. See page 49.

▲**Dolmabahçe Palace** Opulent 19th-century European-style home of the sultans, accessible only by guided tour. **Hours:** Tours run late March–late Oct Tue–Wed and Fri–Sun 9:00–16:00, until 15:00 off-season, closed Mon and Thu. See page 54.

Turkish news media for about 50 years (until the 1990s). Now it's a dull administrative district. But you can still find the historic gate just outside the Topkapı Palace wall, near the Gülhane tram stop.

West of Sultanahmet: From the Grand Bazaar to the Golden Horn

Heading west from Sultanahmet, you enter an area that's more residential and less touristy, offering an opportunity to delve into the "real" Istanbul—rubbing elbows with locals at some of its best mosques and markets. While some attractions here—such as the Grand Bazaar—are tourist magnets, the lanes connecting them are filled mostly with residents (and described in the ✪ Old Town Back Streets Walk on page 87).

▲▲▲Grand Bazaar (Kapalı Çarşı)—Shop till you drop at the world's oldest market venue. Although many of its stalls have been

overtaken by souvenir shops, in many ways Istanbul's unique Grand Bazaar remains much as it was centuries ago: enchanting and perplexing visitors with its mazelike network of more than 4,000 colorful shops, fragrant eateries, and insistent shopkeepers. Despite the tourists and the knickknacks, the heart of the Grand Bazaar still beats—giving the observant visitor a glimpse of the living Istanbul.

Cost, Hours, Location: Free, Mon–Sat 9:00–19:00, shops begin closing at 18:30, closed Sun. It's across the parking lot from the Çemberlitaş tram stop, behind the Nuruosmaniye Mosque.

✪ See the Grand Bazaar Tour on page 206.

▲▲▲Mosque of Süleyman the Magnificent (Süleymaniye Camii)—This soothing and restrained—but suitably magnificent—house of worship was built by the great 16th-century archi-

tect Sinan for his sultan Süleyman. Although less colorful than the Blue Mosque, this mosque rivals it in size, scope, and beauty. Enjoy the numerous courtyards and tranquil interior, decorated in pastel hues and stained glass. Out back are the elaborate tombs of Süleyman the Magnificent and his wife, Roxelana.

Cost, Hours, Location: Mosque—free, generally open daily one hour after sunrise until one hour before sunset, closed to visitors five times a day for prayer; mausoleum—free, daily 9:00–17:00, until 18:00 in summer. It's on Sıddık Sami Onar Caddesi, in the Süleymaniye district.

○ See the Mosque of Süleyman the Magnificent Tour on page 218.

▲**Rüstem Paşa Mosque (Rüstem Paşa Camii)**—This small 16th-century mosque, designed by the prolific and talented architect Sinan, was built to honor Süleyman the Magnificent's Grand Vizier, Rüstem Paşa. Elevated one story above street level in a bustling market zone, its facade is studded with impressive İznik tiles—but the wall-to-wall decorations inside are even more breathtaking.

Cost, Hours, Location: Free, generally open daily one hour after sunrise until one hour before sunset, closed to visitors five times a day for prayer, on Hasırcılar Caddesi, Eminönü.

○ For more on the Rüstem Paşa Mosque, see the Old Town Back Streets Walk on page 93.

▲▲**Spice Market (Mısır Çarşışı)**—This market was built about 350 years ago to promote the spice trade in Istanbul...and, aside from a few souvenir stands that have wriggled their way in, it still serves essentially the same purpose. Today the halls of the Spice Market are filled with equal numbers of locals and tourists. In addition to mounds of colorful spices (such as green henna and deep-red saffron), you can also get dried fruits (including apricots and figs), fresh roasted nuts, Turkish delight, supposed aphrodisiacs (Sultan's paste, or "Turkish Viagra"), imported caviar, and lots more.

Cost, Hours, Location: Free to enter, Mon–Sat 9:00–19:30, shops begin to close at 19:00, closed Sun. It's right on Cami Meydanı Sokak along the Golden Horn, at the Old Town end of the Galata Bridge, near the Eminönü tram stop.

For more on the Spice Market, ○ see the Old Town Back Streets Walk on page 96.

On the Golden Horn

The following sights are on the inlet called the Golden Horn, near the Spice Market. Known as Eminönü, this district is a major transit hub, where the tram, bus, seabus, and ferry systems link up—so it can be packed at rush hour. This area is covered by the ○ Golden Horn Walk on page 99.

▲▲**Galata Bridge (Galata Köprüsü)**—In 1994, this modern bridge replaced what had been the first and, for many years, only bridge spanning the Golden Horn. Now, lined with hundreds of fishermen dipping their hooks into the water below, the new Galata Bridge is an Istanbul fixture. A stroll across the Galata Bridge offers panoramic views of Istanbul's Old Town. Consider stopping for a drink or a meal at one of the many restaurants built into the bridge's lower level (tram stops: Eminönü on the Old Town end of the bridge, and Karaköy on the New District end).

For more on the Galata Bridge, ✪ see the Golden Horn Walk on page 99.

▲▲▲**Bosphorus Cruise**—Between the Galata Bridge and the Sirkeci Train Station is the dock where you can catch a public ferry for a relaxing day-long cruise on the Bosphorus Strait. The round-trip ferry cruise goes by mansions, fortresses, and two intercontinental bridges before stopping for lunch at an Asian fishing village. As an alternative, take the ferry only to Sarıyer to access sights north of Istanbul.

Cost, Hours, Location: 10 YTL one-way, 17.50 YTL round-trip, mid-June–mid-Sept at 10:35 and 13:35; mid-Sept–mid-June at 10:35 only. The public ferry leaves from the Bosphorus Ferry Port (Boğaz İskelesi) in Istanbul's Eminönü district. Private cruises are also available nearby.

For details, ✪ see the Bosphorus Cruise Tour on page 249.

Sirkeci Train Station (Sirkeci Tren Garı)—This 19th-century example of European-Orientalism architecture was the terminus of the Orient Express. The famous train, which traveled from Paris through exotic Eastern Europe to Istanbul, was immortalized by Agatha Christie in *Murder on the Orient Express*. Though trains still depart to Europe from here, today the station is used mostly by local commuters. The modest Railway Museum inside the station is worth a look.

Cost, Hours, Location: Station—free, always open; Railway Museum—free, Tue–Sat 9:00–12:30 & 13:00–17:00, closed Sun–Mon; near the ferry ports, tram stop: Sirkeci, tel. 0212/520-6575.

For more on the Sirkeci Train Station, ✪ see the Golden Horn Walk on page 106.

▲▲Chora Church Museum (Kariye Müzesi)

This remarkable ancient church—now a museum—is packed full of some of the most impressive Byzantine mosaics anywhere. Although it's tucked just inside the Old Town wall, far from the rest of Istanbul's sights, art-lovers and history buffs find Chora Church worth the trip. Tilt back your head and squint at the thousands of tiny tiles artfully plastered on the ceilings and domes. Mosaics depict the birth, life, and death of Christ, as well as the Holy Family, saints, and other Christian figures. Vivid frescoes show the agony and the ecstasy of Judgment Day.

Cost, Hours, Location: 15 YTL, open late March–late Oct Thu–Tue 9:00–19:00, off-season until 17:00, last entry 30 min before closing, closed Wed, tel. 0212/631-9241. It's in the Edirnekapı district, west of downtown (15-YTL taxi ride from

Sultanahmet, bus #87 from Taksim Square, or bus #32 or #910 from Eminönü).

For a self-guided tour and details on getting there, ✪ see the Chora Church Museum Tour on page 227.

In the New District

The New District, which is across the Golden Horn from the Old Town, offers a modern, urban, and very European-flavored contrast to the historic creaks and quirks of the Old Town. The New District Walk on page 108 covers the best of these sights. These are listed roughly in the order you'll reach them going from Taksim Square toward the Golden Horn.

On or near Taksim Square

▲**Taksim Square (Taksim Meydanı)**—At the center of the New District is the busy, vibrant Taksim Square. Taksim is the gateway to Istanbul's main pedestrian thoroughfare, İstiklal street, with its historic buildings and colorful shops. This enormous square is also the New District's "Grand Central Station," connecting to the rest of the city via bus, Metro, funicular, and "nostalgic tram."

For more on Taksim Square, ✪ see the New District Walk on page 109.

Military Museum (Askeri Müze)—Organized with military precision, this museum is a scaled-up version of the Imperial Treasury's Armory collection at Topkapı Palace (see page 151), focusing on the progress of Turkish military might. The collection itself—including imperial tents of Ottoman sultans and the sword of Süleyman the Magnificent—thrills military historians, but bores everyone else. But the Janissary Band, which puts on a one-hour performance at 15:00 each day the museum is open, can make it worth the trip (and is rated ▲). Also known as the Ottoman Military Band (Mehter Bandosu), the Janissary Band was the first of its kind—eventually prompting other European monarchs to create similar military bands of their own. The band's  primary role was to lead the army into war, but in peacetime, it would also entertain the public with Turkish folk tunes. (Turkish-style rhythms were fashionable in 18th-century Europe, inspiring the likes of Mozart and Beethoven.) Today's costumed concerts—with all the regal pomp of ages past—still evoke the Golden Age of the Ottoman Empire.

Cost, Hours, Location: Museum—3 YTL, Wed–Sun 9:00–17:00, last entry one hour before closing, closed Mon–Tue; Janissary Band concert—included in museum ticket, Wed–Sun

NEW DISTRICT SIGHTS

1. Taksim Square
2. İstiklal Street
3. Pera Museum
4. Galata Dervish Monastery
5. To Galata Tower

at 15:00 at the Atatürk auditorium, no performances Mon–Tue; Harbiye district, tel. 0212/233-2720. You can take photos of the Janissary Band, but you'll have to pay extra to photograph museum exhibits (6 YTL for still cameras, 12 YTL for video cameras).

Getting There: The Military Museum is a huge, walled complex at the end of Cumhuriyet Caddesi (joom-hoo-ree-yeht jah-deh-see), which is the main avenue leading north from Taksim Square into the trendy residential and business districts. You can walk there from Taksim Square in about 15 minutes (you'll see the museum on the right just before the avenue forks, past the multistory military club). Or you can take the Metro from Taksim one stop to Osmanbey, then backtrack a few blocks on Halaskargazi Caddesi to the museum (on your left, just as Halaskargazi runs into Cumhuriyet).

On or near İstiklal Street

▲▲▲**İstiklal Street (İstiklal Caddesi)**—Linking Taksim Square with the Tünel district (and, below that, the Galata district), İstiklal street is urban Istanbul's main pedestrian drag, passing through the most sophisticated part of town. The vibrant

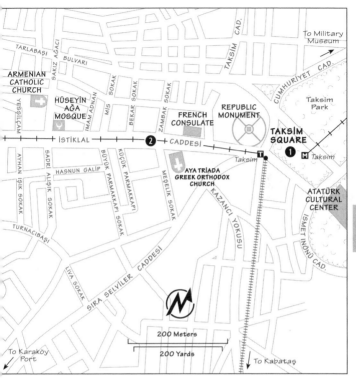

thoroughfare, whose name translates as "Independence Street," is lined with a lively mix of restaurants, cafés, shops, theaters, and art galleries. Visitors are enchanted by İstiklal street's beautiful Art Nouveau facades and intrigued by the multicultural mix of tourists, international businesspeople, and locals who throng its elegant sidewalks.

For more on İstiklal street, ✪ see the New District Walk on page 110.

▲**Pera Museum (Pera Müzesi)**—This museum beautifully displays its modest but interesting collection of historic weights and measures, Kütahya tiles, and Oriental paintings and portraits. It's housed in a renovated late-19th-century building typical of the once high-end Pera neighborhood.

Floor 1 (one floor up from the lobby) displays centuries of **weights and measures** from the Anatolian peninsula. Circling clockwise, you'll watch the weights evolve more or less chronologically—from prehistoric times to the Republic—to suit an ever-more-sophisticated economy. Look for the weights shaped like fine statues.

Also on Floor 1 is a collection of **Kütahya tiles** (named after a city southeast of here). During the 18th and 19th centuries—the scope of this collection—İznik tiles were used by the Ottoman court, Çanakkale tiles were for the common folk, and Kütahya tiles were for both. This exhibit shows off pieces that Turks of that time bought to decorate their homes.

On Floor 2, you'll find the museum's most striking exhibit: one of the world's best collections of **Oriental paintings.** More than 300 canvases capture both royal pomp and everyday life during Ottoman times. Dating from the 17th to the 19th centuries, most of these were actually painted by visiting Europeans, who were mesmerized by the "mysteries of the Orient" they found here. Imagine a painter from buttoned-down Victorian England or Habsburg Austria traveling to this faraway land, with its pointy minarets, exotically scented spices, and seductive harems. Indeed, one of the themes of the exhibit is Ottoman women and harems, and the way they were distorted through a European lens. (The paintings are works of fancy, as the painters never set foot in a harem. For the real story on harems, see page 160.) You'll also see works by the leading Turkish Oriental painter, Osman Hamdi. Find Hamdi's masterpiece, *The Tortoise Trainer*. The patience required to train slow-motion tortoises is a metaphor for the patience required to live life. Rounding out the collection is a who's who of royal portraits, depicting both Ottoman bigwigs (find the sultans you've been learning about) and foreign ambassadors wearing Ottoman clothing (to curry favor with the sultan).

Cost, Hours, Location: 7 YTL, Tue–Sat 10:00–19:00, Sun 12:00–18:00, closed Mon, Meşrutiyet Caddesi 141, Tepebaşı, Beyoğlu, tel. 0212/334-9900. The museum's 2-YTL audioguide, which covers only the paintings, is fast-moving and worthwhile.

Pera Palas Hotel—Agatha Christie fans will want to visit this hotel across the street from the Pera Museum (just past the multistory Hotel Pera Marmara). This historic landmark, recently under renovation, should be open again by early 2010 (www.perapalas.com).

By the late 19th century, the Orient Express train service from Western Europe had become all the rage (see page 106). But Istanbul lacked a European-style hotel elegant enough to impress the posh passengers arriving on those trains. To satisfy upper-crust demand, the company that operated the Orient Express built the top-of-the-top Pera Palas Hotel in 1892. Allied forces used the hotel as a base during the occupation of Istanbul at the end of World War I. In World War II, it was a hotbed of spies and counterspies. The hotel's guest book reads like a history lesson: Atatürk, the Duke of Windsor, Yugoslav president Josip Broz Tito, Jackie Kennedy, Mata Hari, and Agatha Christie (who stayed here several times in the 1920s and '30s while writing *Murder on the Orient Express*).

In the Galata District

The old-feeling neighborhood climbing up a hill from the Golden Horn into the New District is called Galata, and has a seedier, less modern-European ambience than Taksim Square or İstiklal street. Running up and down the hill under Galata is the old-fashioned subterranean funicular called Tünel (the entrance at the top of the hill is at the end of İstiklal street; down below, it's near the Karaköy tram stop and Galata Bridge). You can visit these sights after finishing the New District Walk (see page 108); they're listed in order from the top of the hill down to the waterfront.

SIGHTS

Galata Dervish Monastery (Galata Mevlevihanesi)—In the 13th century, a Muslim mystic named Rumi (better known

to Turks as Mevlana, meaning "master" in Persian) began to incorporate whirling meditation into his teachings. He believed that a Dervish, spinning in a circle, becomes part of the universal harmony. A *mevlevihane* (mehv-leh-vee-hah-neh) is a gathering place or residence for Dervishes—similar to a monastery in Christian Europe. This particular *mevlevihane* is one of the few meeting places for the Dervishes left in Istanbul.

Poke into this modest courtyard, and its surrounding religious buildings, to learn more about the Whirling Dervishes. Although the modest museum is dull (5 YTL, Wed–Mon summer 9:30–17:00, winter 9:00–16:00, closed Tue, Galip Dede Caddesi 15, Tünel), once a week the Dervishes actually perform a service here. Knock-off Whirling Dervish performances are a dime a dozen in Istanbul—this is a rare opportunity to witness one enacted by real worshippers, rather than performers (about 40 YTL, Sun in summer at 17:00, in winter at 15:00, sometimes also on Sat, confirm ahead by visiting or calling 0212/245-4141). Tickets are sold only in person (no online or phone reservations); show up 30–60 minutes before the performance starts to be sure you get a ticket. Once inside, it's open seating, so try to get a seat as close as you can to the center of the hall. As this is a prayer service rather than a show, it's pensive and very slow-paced (about 2 hours total)—not ideal for impatient camcorder-toting tourists who wish those guys would just start spinning already.

While wandering the grounds or watching the Dervishes whirl, consider the theology behind this unusual ceremony (called *Sema*). Rumi believed that the purpose of life was to purify oneself from the material desires of the flesh that entrap the soul, such as greed, rage, and jealousy. Once free from these influences, a person's soul can attain eternal happiness. To accomplish this, one must "die before death"—so the Dervish ritual symbolizes finding enlightenment through the death of one's self (unchaining the soul from worldly desires). Everything in the universe whirls, from the smallest to the largest particle. So by whirling, the Dervish becomes one with the created and the Creator. Even the costume worn by Dervishes evokes death: a tall camel-felt hat, resembling a tombstone, and a black cloak that represents earthly attachments. As the ritual begins, the black cloak is removed, revealing a long, white dress—similar to the shroud that deceased Muslims are wrapped in when they are buried.

▲▲Galata Tower (Galata Kulesi)—The most prominent feature of the New District skyline, the 205-foot-tall stone Galata Tower

was built by the Genoese in the mid-14th century and has been used over the centuries as a fire tower, barracks, dungeon, and even as a launch pad to test the possibility of human-powered flight.

In the Middle Ages, when Byzantines controlled the historic core of the city, this was the territory of Genoa (the Italian city once controlled much of the Mediterranean). This tower—sometimes called the "Genoese Tower"—was part of a mid-14th-century fortification. But, with a key location facing the Byzantine capital across the Golden Horn, the dramatic tower's purpose was likely as much to show off as to defend.

Today, the tower is a tourist attraction—offering visitors perhaps the best view of Istanbul. Climb the little staircase around behind the tower, take the elevator to the seventh-floor restaurant, and go to the observation terrace (tower admission—10 YTL, daily 9:00–20:00, Büyük Hendek Sokak, tel. 0212/293-8180).

As you enjoy the view, ponder the strange-but-true story of the 17th-century aviation pioneer Hezarfen Ahmet Çelebi. According to eyewitnesses, Hezarfen Ahmet was so inspired by the drawings and models of Leonardo da Vinci that he built his own set of artificial wings, which allowed him to hang-glide several miles from the top of this tower, across the Bosphorus, to Üsküdar in Asian Istanbul. What happened to him next is unclear: Some say he was awarded a sack of gold by the sultan, while others claim that the clergy—who didn't believe that humans were supposed to fly—had him exiled to North Africa.

Quincentennial Museum of Turkish Jews (500 Yıl Vakfı Türk Musevileri Müzesi)—In 1492, King Ferdinand and Queen Isabel of Spain ordered their Sephardic Jewish population to accept the Christian faith, or leave and "dare not return." The Ottoman sultan Beyazıt Han was the only monarch of the time who extended an invitation to take in these refugees. Jewish people—many of whom can still trace their roots back to Spain—remain a living, vibrant part of Turkey's cultural mosaic. This museum, founded 500 years after the Spanish expulsion (hence the "quincentennial"), commemorates those first Sephardic Jews who found a new home here. Housed in an inactive early-19th-century synagogue (built on the remains of a much-older synagogue), the small museum displays items donated by the local Jewish community. Particularly interesting are the ethnographic section, showing scenes from daily life, and a chair used in the Jewish circumcision rite.

Cost, Hours, Location: 5 YTL, Mon–Thu 10:00–16:00, Sun and Fri 10:00–14:00, closed Sat and on Jewish holidays, Karaköy Meydanı, Perçemli Sokak, tel. 0212/292-6333, www.muze500.com.

Getting There: The museum is conveniently located in Karaköy, close to the New District end of the Galata Bridge. It's on a dead-end alley, Perçemli Sokak, a few hundred yards from the Karaköy tram stop and a hundred yards from the Tünel funicular exit. If you're coming across the Galata Bridge by tram from the Old Town, get off at Karaköy, then take the pedestrian underpass as if you're heading for Tünel; once you're up the steps, back on the street level, Perçemli Sokak is the alley on your right. Coming from the Tünel exit, keep left as if you are heading for the tram and Galata Bridge; the alley is on the left, by the stairs of the underpass.

Along the Bosphorus, Between Galata and Beşiktaş

This area, stretching north along the Bosphorus from the Galata Bridge, has been enjoying a recent wave of renovation, yet still retains the charm of its genteel past. We've listed these sights in the order you reach them, coming from Galata.

Istanbul Modern Arts Museum (İstanbul Modern Sanat Müzesi)—The first and only museum in Istanbul dedicated to the works of contemporary Turkish artists, "Istanbul Modern" opened in 2004. A huge warehouse in the port area (often dwarfed by the huge cruise ships mooring to the adjacent wharf) offers a look at Istanbul's contemporary art scene and the upper crust of local society it attracts. In a bright and user-friendly space, you'll see the well-described art of a hundred Turkish painters from the 20th century on one floor, with temporary exhibits downstairs.

Cost, Hours, Location: 7 YTL, free on Thu, open Tue–Sun 10:00–18:00, Thu until 20:00, last entry 30 min before closing, closed Mon, Meclis-I Mebusan Caddesi, Liman İşletmeleri Sahası, Antrepo 4, tram stop: Tophane, tel. 0212/334-7300, www.istanbul modern.org. The good but expensive museum cafeteria has an out-door terrace with fine Old Town views (or a claustrophobic peek at the hull of a giant cruise ship, if one happens to be in port).

Getting There: It's in the Tophane neighborhood (close to Karaköy), at the dock behind Nusretiye Mosque, by the mouth of the Golden Horn. From the Old Town, take the tram to the second stop after the Galata Bridge (Tophane), walk a block far-ther past the Nusretiye Mosque, and take the alley to the right (toward the water) into an industrial parking lot. You'll see the big blocky gallery signposted to the right. Between the tram stop and the museum, along the waterfront side of the park that faces the tram tracks, check out the strip of cool lounges where young locals sprawl on big beanbag chairs playing backgammon, sipping tea, and sucking on water pipes.

▲**Dolmabahçe Palace (Dolmabahçe Sarayı)**—This palace was the last hurrah of the Ottoman Empire. By the late 19th century, the empire was called the "Sick Man of Europe," and other European emperors and kings derided its ineffective and back-ward-seeming sultan. In a last-ditch attempt to rejuvenate the declining image of his empire, Sultan Abdülmecit I built the  ostentatious Dolmabahçe (dohl-mah-bah-cheh) Palace—with all the trappings of a European monarch—to replace the unmistak-ably Oriental-feeling Topkapı Palace as the official residence of the sultan. (It didn't work—instead, Dolmabahçe was the final residence of the long line of Ottoman sultans, falling empty when the royal family was sent into exile in 1922.) Dolmabahçe (mean-ing roughly "filled-in garden") sits on what was once a bay, on land long ago reclaimed from the Bosphorus. Built over a decade by an Ottoman-Armenian father-and-son team of architects, and completed in 1853, the palace is a fusion of styles—from Turkish-Ottoman elements to the frilly Rococo that was all the rage in Europe at the time. Its construction drained the already dwindling treasury, and the empire actually had to take a foreign loan to complete Dolmabahçe. Today the building belongs to the Turkish Parliament, which uses it only for important occasions, such as the 2004 NATO summit.

Two parts of the palace can be visited with a tour: the Selamlık (administrative wings, 90 min) and the Harem (45 min more). Visit the Harem only if you have time to spare—it's nothing compared to the Selamlık. After buying your ticket, you'll walk through the palace's well-manicured garden, past a small pool flanked by lion statues, and up the steps to the entrance. Before you line up inside for the tour, take a look at the magnificent ceremonial land gate, on the palace wall to your left. When the palace was the sultan's home and seat of government, this was the door through which royal processions entered the palace grounds.

The decorations in the Selamlık section are alternately breathtaking and tacky. Standouts include huge hand-woven Turkish carpets; the sultan's alabaster bathroom; crystal everywhere (much of it Bohemian), including a Baccarat crystal staircase; and the Imperial Hall, built to accommodate up to 2,500 people. This room's dome is 118 feet high—you can't see it from outside—and the world's largest crystal chandelier hangs down from its center, weighing in at some four tons.

The Selamlık tour ends outside the throne room. Those continuing on to the Harem can stick with the guide; otherwise, take your time to enjoy the garden and the view of the Bosphorus.

Cost, Hours, Location: The palace is accessible only with a guided tour, available in English. Selamlık (administrative section)—12 YTL, tour 45–60 min; Harem—13 YTL, tour 30–45 min; combo-ticket—20 YTL. Both tours run 2–4 times each hour, depending on crowds (open late March–late Oct Tue–Wed and Fri–Sun 9:00–16:00, until 15:00 off-season, closed Mon and Thu). You'll pay an extra 6 YTL for permission to take photos (no flash, tripods, or video cameras). Just as you pass the ticket-taker, WCs are behind the wall to your right, and the baggage check is to your left. A café and a bookstore are on the way to the exit, on the left. The palace is at Dolmabahçe Caddesi, Beşiktaş (tel. 0212/236-9000).

Getting There: Dolmabahçe Palace is a few blocks from the Kabataş tram/funicular stop. From Taksim Square, take the funicular down to Kabataş; from the Old Town, take the tram to Kabataş. Once at Kabataş, walk along the water with the Bosphorus on your right. You'll pass a mosque (its unusual slender minarets have balconies that look like flowery Corinthian capitals), then a parking lot and a clock tower. The ticket office is to the left just before the palace's huge gates (wave at the statuesque honor guard—he's real).

Kadıköy: A Quick Trip to Asia

While virtually all of Istanbul's "sights" are on the European side, the city itself spills over the Bosphorus into Asia. Of Istanbul's 15 million residents, more than a third (including this book's authors) live in Asian Istanbul, a.k.a. Anadolu Yakası (ah-nah-doh-loo yah-kah-suh, "the Anatolian side").

There have long been small towns and villages in this area, but today it consists mostly of modern sprawl. Development boomed here after the first bridge over the Bosphorus was opened in 1974 (though regular ferry service had started in the 1850s). While European Istanbul has its old quarters and traditional living, the residents of Asian Istanbul generally choose to live on the Asian side for its modern infrastructure, bigger houses and condos, and the ability to raise their families amid the efficiency of modern life. The people of Asian Istanbul tend to be more progressive and secular than their counterparts across the strait (for example, you'll see fewer women wearing scarves, and it's a voting stronghold for the modern Social Democrat party). Each day, millions of people commute across the Bosphorus (mostly on ferries) from their homes in Asia to their jobs in Europe.

For the handiest intercontinental trip, ride the ferry from the Old Town to Kadıköy. A historic town known in ancient times as Chalcedon, Kadıköy pre-dates even the Byzantine Empire. Today's Kadıköy, with over a million people, is a modern commercial and residential district that grew up around the ferry stations.

Upon arrival in Kadıköy (see "Getting There," next page), you'll see it's well-designed to deal with hordes of commuters. Buses fan out from the ferry dock. Shops and restaurants fill the grid-planned commercial zone that stretches inland from the dock. Notice the shopping-mall ambience, youthful and Western energy of the crowds, and modern efficiency of the commerce.

As you step off the dock, walk about 100 yards to the right, to the traffic light (past the Atatürk statue at the center of the square). The Town Hall is right across from you, by the traffic light. Cross the street and walk straight (with the Town Hall on your right) by the side of the park, then cross a second street, which puts you in the market area.

Kadıköy Çarşışı (chahr-shuh-suh, market) is the historic core of the area—and it doesn't get more authentic than the surrounding neighborhood. Here in the market area, you can find everything from grocers and fishmongers to popular delis and specialty olive-oil stores. (Watch for a goose, the mascot of shopkeepers, waddling around loose.) The streets are lined with boutiques, bookstores, fast-food kiosks, grocery stores, and cafés, bars, and restaurants (which begin bustling in the late afternoon). Busy as it is with locals throughout the day, it gets even more crowded at rush hour—commuters pause here to enjoy a drink or meal with their friends, or to do some last-minute shopping. Shops start to close around 18:30 or 19:00, and eateries stay open until around 21:00 (places that serve alcohol stay open till midnight). After 21:00, the thriving crowd simply vanishes.

Getting There: From the Old Town side of the Golden Horn, near the Galata Bridge (at Eminönü), catch the boat to the Kadıköy dock (2/hr, 25-min ride, 1.40 YTL). The boat ride itself is enjoyable—the views from the boat alone justify the trip.

Elsewhere in Istanbul

These sights are scattered around the urban sprawl of Istanbul. For locations, see the color "Istanbul Transit" map at the beginning of this book.

Rahmi Koç Industrial Museum (Rahmi Koç Müzesi)

This museum is located on the Golden Horn, in a historic shipyard that once produced anchors and parts for Ottoman navy vessels. Inspired by the Henry Ford Museum in Michigan, Turkey's industry giant Rahmi Koç started this museum in 1994 with his private collection dedicated to the history of industry, transport, and communication. Today the collection has been expanded to include a vast number of metalworking tools, engines of all sizes and applications, scientific instruments, machinery, and vehicles including motorcycles, bicycles, a submarine, and a small train. What makes the Rahmi Koç special is its location—off the beaten path—and its optional but highly recommended Golden Horn cruise (offered only in summer) on an old 65-foot industrial boat powered by a steam engine. Most travelers to Istanbul don't get to see this part of the Golden Horn, let alone in an antique boat. Also of interest is the old olive-oil press. Triggered by a sensor, it starts to run the moment you enter the room. The Rahmi Koç isn't essential if your time in Istanbul is limited, but it's worth considering on a longer visit.

Cost, Hours, Location: Museum—9 YTL, Tue–Fri 10:00–17:00, Sat–Sun 10:00–19:00, closed Mon; 45-min Golden Horn cruise—10 YTL extra, June–Aug Tue–Sun at 13:00, 14:30, 16:00, and 17:30; may also run in May and Sept—confirm by phone at tel. 0212/369-6600. The museum is at Hasköy Caddesi 27, general museum tel. 0212/369-6600, www.rmk-museum.org.tr. The museum's Halat Restaurant serves great food.

Getting There: It's right on the Golden Horn in the Hasköy neighborhood. It's easiest and fastest to take a taxi. You can also reach it by bus, but remember that buses don't take tokens; you'll need a pass (see "Public Transportation Tokens and Passes," page 30). From the Old Town, take bus #47 (Eminönü–Alibeyköy) from Eminönü, next to the Galata Bridge. From Taksim Square, take bus #54HT (Taksim–Hasköy). Tell the driver that you want to get off at Hasköy (hahs-kohy), "Rahmi Koç Müzesi" (rah-mee koch mew-zeh-see).

SIGHTS

Miniatürk

This huge park, by the Golden Horn, has 105 models of Turkish monuments. The display is divided into three groups: monuments of Istanbul, the rest of Turkey, and elsewhere in the former Ottoman Empire. This is a wonderful, kid-friendly sight that gives you a glimpse of the parts of Turkey you're not visiting. It's also just a fun local family scene, especially on sunny weekends. Within Miniatürk are two other, smaller museums: The Victory Museum tells the story of the War of Independence (after World War I, 1919–1922), while the tacky Crystal Museum displays laser carvings of monuments in crystal.

Cost, Hours, Location: 10 YTL, free for children under 8, daily May–Oct 9:00–20:00, Nov–April 9:00–18:00, last entry one hour before closing, children's playground, photography allowed, İmrahor Caddesi, Borsa Durağı Mevkii, Sütlüce, tel. 0212/222-2882, www.miniaturk.com.tr.

Getting There: The park is located near the west end of Golden Horn. It's a 20-minute taxi ride from Taksim Square or Eminönü. By bus, you can take #54HT from Taksim, or #47 or #47E from Eminönü (passes only, no tokens).

Rumeli Fortress (Rumeli Hisarı)

This mighty fortress was built by the Ottoman Sultan Mehmet II in 1452, a year before his conquest of Constantinople. He was

later given the title Fatih (fah-tee; "Conqueror") after he succeeded in capturing the city.

This huge fortress, up the Bosphorus from the Old Town, was completed in a record time of 80 days. It stands across from an earlier, smaller fortress (the Anatolian Fortress of Sultan Beyazıt). Rumeli was built, like its predecessor, to control the Bosphorus and to prevent any aid to Constantinople while the city was under siege. The fortress, with strategic views of both banks of the Bosphorus, was renovated and turned into an open-air museum in the 1950s. Although the mosque that once stood at the castle's center is no longer there, you will see a section of its brick minaret. An outdoor auditorium on the fortress's natural slope is the site for many concerts and other activities during the Istanbul Festival in summer months.

The fortress alone isn't worth the trip. But if you're returning from a Bosphorus cruise (see page 249), consider hopping off the boat at Sarıyer to see the fortress on your way back to town (this option is explained in the sidebar on page 264). If you have plenty of time, join the locals at the fortress for a leisurely morning and a late breakfast at a nearby café, such as the Hisar Café. The fortress can also be combined with a visit to the Sadberk Hanım Museum (described next).

Cost, Hours, Location: 3 YTL, Thu–Tue 9:30–17:00, last entry at 16:30, closed Wed. It's near the second bridge (FSM Bridge) up the Bosphorus, on the European shore at Yahya Kemal Caddesi 42, tel. 212/263-5305.

Getting There: From the Old Town, take the tram to Kabataş, then take northbound bus #25E (Kabataş–Sarıyer). Remember the bus takes passes only, not tokens. From Taksim Square in the New District, take northbound bus #40 (Taksim–Sarıyer); from Sarıyer (where you can disembark from the Bosphorus cruise), take southbound bus #40 (Sarıyer–Taksim) or southbound #25E (Sarıyer–Kabataş). All of these buses stop at Rumelihisarı, near the fortress.

Sadberk Hanım Museum (Sadberk Hanım Müzesi)

Opened in the 1980s, this was one of the first private museums in the country. The museum is named for Sadberk Hanım, wife of industry giant Vehbi Koç (the father of Rahmi Koç, who founded the industrial museum described earlier in this chapter). Two 19th-century mansions overlooking the Bosphorus display separate exhibits dedicated to archaeology and art history. The collection rivals, and sometimes surpasses, that of the Turkish and Islamic Arts Museum, except for the carpets. While not worth the trip on a quick visit, it works well when combined with a visit to Rumeli Fortress (see previous sight) or a Bosphorus cruise (disembark at Sarıyer—see page 265).

Cost, Hours, Location: 7 YTL, Thu–Tue 10:00–17:00, closed Wed, Piyasa Caddesi 25–29, Büyükdere, tel. 0212/242-3813 or 0212/242-3814. Photography is not allowed.

Getting There: Follow the Rumeli Fortress directions (see previous sight), but instead get off the bus at the stop called Sefaret (seh-fah-reht) and walk south a few blocks along the coastal road.

Eyüp Sultan Mosque (Eyüp Sultan Camii)

This mosque attracts a conservative pilgrim crowd, making it one of the most interesting people-watching experiences in the city. You'll be surrounded by Turks in humble mood and attire, each looking for spiritual fulfillment. Ayyub El Ansari, called Eyüp Sultan by the Turks, was the Prophet Muhammad's standard-bearer and companion. He died outside the city walls during the siege of Constantinople by Muslim Arabs, and was buried where he fell. Centuries later, Sultan Mehmet the Conqueror built a mosque and mausoleum at the location of Eyüp's grave. Over the years, the mosque became an important religious center and destination for Muslim pilgrims. Throughout history, this is where new Ottoman sultans received their sword of sovereignty as they took the throne (comparable to being crowned). The complex you see today dates from the 1800s.

The Eyüp Sultan Mosque is crowded with locals at all times of the day. Crowds increase at prayer times—particularly on Fridays for the midday service—and for religious festivals. Year-round, especially from late spring to early fall, you'll see boys in fancy circumcision outfits, and newlyweds in their gowns and tuxedoes, here for a prayer. In the mausoleum, you'll see people praying in front of the tomb of Eyüp Sultan, as well as at the glass screen covering a supposed footprint of the Prophet Muhammad. There are no prayers to the dead in Islam, but it is a tradition to invoke the names of the deceased (such as Eyüp Sultan or Muhammad) to give prayers more weight with Allah.

Because this is a religious shrine, dress modestly, even if you're not going into the mosque—women should cover their hair with a scarf; men and women should cover their shoulders and knees.

Cost, Hours, Location: Free, generally open daily one hour after sunrise until one hour before sunset, closed to visitors five times a day for prayer, Cami-i Kebir Caddesi, Eyüp.

Getting There: From Eminönü in the Old Town, take bus #99 (Eminönü–Akşemseddin Mahiye) to the Eyüp Sultan stop. There are alternative stops, so ask the driver or another passenger where to get off. Other buses that will get you there include #48B, #36CE, #399B, and #399C (passes only, no tokens). By taxi it's a quick 10-YTL ride (consider a detour to see some of the old city wall along the way).

EXPERIENCES

Perhaps more than any city in Europe, Istanbul is a place to experience. Istanbul's best attractions aren't in its museums, but in its streets: coming across a gathering of Muslims washing their hands and feet at a fountain before they enter a mosque; delicately sipping a cup of high-octane Turkish coffee; taking a slow drag of sweet apple-flavored smoke from a traditional water pipe; playing a spirited game of backgammon with a new friend at a teahouse; or having your flesh wrestled by a powerful masseuse in a Turkish bath. This chapter is a how-to guide for these and other unforgettable Istanbul experiences.

▲▲▲Visiting a Mosque

Touring some of Istanbul's many mosques (*camii* in Turkish; pronounced jah-mee) offers Westerners an essential opportunity to better understand the Muslim faith. (For a primer, see the Understanding Islam chapter on page 337.) But, just as touring a church in Christian Europe comes with a certain protocol, the following guidelines should be observed when visiting a mosque.

When to Go

• Most mosques are open to worshippers from the first service in the morning (at sunrise) until the last service in the evening (at sunset). Tourists are generally allowed to enter during these daylight hours, except during the five daily services (explained later). Specific "opening times" can vary greatly, but figure that most mosques are open to visitors from one hour after sunrise until about an hour before sunset.

• Because mosques are active places of worship, visitors are not allowed inside from about a half-hour before the service, until the

Ramadan

Every year, devout Muslims keep the month-long observance of Ramadan—or *Ramazan* in Turkish. During Ramadan (Aug 11–Sept 8 in 2010), Muslim people refrain from eating during daylight hours. This fasting is intended to turn the heart away from the world and toward God. By allowing people of all classes to feel hunger pangs, it also encourages generosity toward the less-fortunate: For many Muslim families, Ramadan concludes with acts of charity and gift-giving.

Ramadan turns Istanbul's Old Town into a particularly colorful place—especially in the evenings, when locals pack the Hippodrome area. The happy, multi-generational partying that follows the breaking of the fast at sunset every night is one of the great travel experiences...definitely not to be missed. After hours of fasting, people are ready for the first meal of the day as the sun goes down. Many rush home, while others stop for a quick bite at one of many temporary food stands. Restaurants that have been empty all day are suddenly marked by long lines stretching up the street.

On and near the Hippodrome, the city presents shadow puppet theaters, public concerts, and traditional folk dances. The Blue Mosque's interior courtyard turns into a huge market with religious books for sale. (If you're here during this time, study this scene in terms of a religion marketing itself, as Christian churches do back home. There are computer programs, trendy teen wear, and plenty of cheap literature.)

end of the service. (Services generally last 15–30 minutes.) If you are already inside, you may be asked to leave so as not to disturb the congregation.

• To avoid showing up at a mosque only to find that it's closed for worship, look up the daily service times in advance. The times generally change a minute or two each day, and are listed in local newspapers: Look for *namaz vakitleri* (service hours) in a frame at the top of the page (usually on the third page). Your hotelier can also find out for you.

• If you're visiting a mosque on Friday, avoid the midday service, which is more heavily attended than others, and longer, because it includes a sermon.

At the Mosque

• Both men and women should have their knees and shoulders covered. At some major mosques (such as the Blue Mosque), you can borrow a sheet the mosque loans out for this purpose.

• Women should also cover their head with a scarf. This is appreciated as a sign of respect. Although scarves are available for loan,

After going to bed late, be ready for traditional drummers to wake you up early. These drummers go from street to street in the Old Town a couple of hours before dawn, reminding people up to get up and have a small bite to eat—or at least a glass of tea—before fasting resumes at sunrise. The drummers start practicing long before Ramadan, and some even sing a bit as they bang out their wake-up call. One musician who trains Ramadan drummers told us that he tries to teach them well so that he can "wake up to an acceptable rhythm."

During Ramadan, the minarets of many mosques are decorated with strings of lights and banners with Muslim sayings...not too different from Christmas lights and wreaths back home.

After Ramadan concludes, Turks celebrate a three-day festival, spend time with their families, and visit the graves of deceased family members. On these days, Istanbul has a particularly festive atmosphere—its streets packed with people who are off work, and its public transportation (often free at this time) jammed with locals enjoying their time off.

EXPERIENCES

you might want to bring your own (easy to buy at a market) for sanitary reasons.

• Shoes must be removed before entering a mosque. If you'll enter and exit the mosque through different doors, borrow a plastic bag at the entrance to carry your shoes with you. Otherwise, leave them on the wooden rack by the entry door.

• Inside the mosque, a large area close to the apse (or mihrab) is often cordoned off and marked as reserved for worshippers. Stay behind this line. Areas in the back of the mosque behind screens, or upper-level galleries, are reserved for female worshippers.

• Amateur photography and videotaping are allowed inside a mosque. Be discreet, and never photograph worshippers without first asking their permission.

▲▲Sipping Turkish Coffee

"Turkish coffee" refers not to a type of coffee, but to the way the coffee is prepared: The coffee grounds float freely in the brew, leaving behind a layer of "mud" at the bottom of the cup. But there's more to it than just coffee grounds and water.

Traditionally, coffee (*kahve;* kah-veh) is added to cold water in a copper pot. (Some use hot or lukewarm water, to speed up the

process, but you can taste the difference—Turks called this hasty version "dishwater.") The coffee-and-water mixture is stirred and slowly heated over medium heat. Just before the water boils, the pot is set aside and its contents are allowed to settle. Then the pot is put back on to boil. This time, half is poured into a cup, while the rest is reheated and then used to top off the drink. Locals joke that the last step is to put a horseshoe in it—if the horseshoe floats, you know it's good coffee.

Locals prefer Turkish coffee without sugar, but first-timers—even coffee-loving ones—often prefer to add sugar to make its powerful flavor a bit more palatable. Since the sugar is added while the coffee is being cooked, you have to ask for it when you place your order: *az şekerli* (ahz sheh-kehr-lee) will get you a little sugar, *orta şekerli* (ohr-tah sheh-kehr-lee) is a medium scoop, and just *şekerli* (sheh-kehr-lee) roughly translates as "tons of sugar—I hate the taste of real coffee."

Because it's unfiltered, the coffee never completely dissolves. When drinking Turkish coffee, the trick is to gently agitate your cup time and time again to re-mix the grounds with the water. Otherwise you'll drink weak coffee, and wind up with a thick layer of grounds at the bottom when you're done.

▲▲Smoking a Water Pipe (Nargile)

Even non-smokers enjoy the Turkish tradition of *nargile* (nahr-ghee-leh)—also known as a "water pipe," "hookah," "hubbly-

bubbly," "shisha," or "really big bong." Sucking on a *nargile* is all about the relaxing social ritual—and it's fun to lounge while you play with the pleasant-smelling smoke.

While similar instruments are happily—and illegally—used by marijuana enthusiasts back home, the water pipes you'll see in Istanbul are filled not with pot or tobacco, but

with dried fruit or herbs (apple is the most common, but you'll also see cappuccino, strawberry, and other flavors). Because the fruit doesn't contain nicotine, it's not addictive and provides no buzz, but it's still fun to let the taste and rich aroma linger in your mouth. Even without the tobacco, you're still inhaling smoke—but it's filtered and cooled by the water before you inhale, allowing you to breathe it deeply. Tobacco enthusiasts can look for the strong, high-nicotine, and relatively rare *tömbeki* (tewm-beh-kee).

One of Turkey's oldest traditions, the water pipe originated in India before migrating to Anatolia (the Asian part of Turkey, east of the Bosphorus Strait). A *nargile* has a glass water jar at the bottom, called a *şişe* (shee-sheh). Attached to the top of the *şişe* is a long metal body with a little metal plate on top, where you place a container called a *lüle* (lew-leh). Fruit or tobacco goes in the *lüle*, with a piece of glowing coal (*mangir*, mahn-gheer) on top. A long, flexible hose (*marpuç*; mahr-pooch) is connected to the metal body. It has a wooden mouthpiece at the end, called an *ağızlık* (ah-uhz-luhk). When you inhale, the smoke fills the little container on top, moves down into the bottle, and makes the water bubble. Impurities are filtered out, and the smoke (as clean and cool as smoke can be) heads up the tube to your mouthpiece.

During the last century, as tobacco-smokers switched to cigarettes, the *nargile* almost vanished. But over the last two decades, nostalgic Turks and curious tourists have revitalized the *nargile* tradition. You can order a water pipe in various coffee shops and trendy *nargile* cafés in the Old Town and New District (figure on paying roughly 7–12 YTL per group). A *nargile* is shareable, and each person will get their own personal plastic mouthpiece to insert into the bigger wooden mouthpiece (sometimes these are free, sometimes you'll pay). After you take a drag, remove your personal mouthpiece and pass the hose to the next person. When you're done, keep your mouthpiece as a souvenir...or use it next time.

▲▲Playing Backgammon (Tavla)

From the ancient Greeks to the Romans, to the teahouses of today, backgammon has been around for thousands of years. Walking the

marble-paved streets of ancient sites in Turkey, such as Ephesus and Aphrodisias, you'll see backgammon boards carved on stones. The game was originally Persian, and Turks still call it by its Persian name, *tavla*.

As with checkers back home, most everyone in Turkey knows how to play backgammon. You'll often see people playing the game in coffee shops. If you're outgoing, challenging a local to a game can be a fun icebreaker.

Note that, while a man can challenge anyone anywhere, it's

considered inappropriate for a solo woman to challenge a man in a traditional coffee shop where most or all of the clientele is male. It's fine for a woman to challenge men if she's traveling with a group that includes men, or even on her own if she's in a mixed-gender coffee shop in modern areas of the city, such as the side alleys of İstiklal street in the New District, the Ortaköy district on the Bosphorus, and the Kadıköy district on the Asian side.

Backgammon is a game of luck and skill, but it's not as drawn-out or cerebral as chess. Turks tend to play the game very quickly, making each move instinctively rather than following a carefully plotted strategy. As you play, onlookers will gather and give you tips on how to win. Money is almost never involved. But to spice things up, players typically challenge one another for baklava, or the loser pays the bill (usually a few glasses of tea). Playing the game online with competitors from around the world is a recent trend in Turkey.

Because the game is of Persian origin, locals like to use the Persian (not Turkish) words for numbers. They'll be tickled and impressed if you do the same:

English	Persian	Pronounced
one	*yek*	yehk
two	*dü*	dew
three	*se*	seh
four	*cahar*	jah-hahr, or jahr for short
five	*beş*	behsh
six	*şeş*	shehsh

The dice are called *zar* (zahr) in Turkish, but their nickname is *kemik* (keh-meek)—literally "bone," since dice were originally made from bone. For luck, kiss the dice in your fist, and as you roll, say, *"Hadi kemik!"* (hah-dee keh-meek)—"Come on, dice!"

How to Play

There are two players, each one with 15 checkers. The board has 24 triangle-shaped spaces, called "doors" (*kapı;* kah-puh), grouped into four sections of six triangles apiece: Each player has a "home board" (the quadrant closest to you on your right, numbered starting with 1 on your right) and an "outer board" (on your left). You begin with all 30 checkers scattered around the board (two on each player's 24 door, five on each player's 13 door, three on each player's 8 door, and five on each player's 6 door). You're the winner if you bring all your checkers "home" and remove them from the board first.

After each player rolls a die to determine who goes first, you take turns rolling the dice and moving your checkers the appropriate number. You always move your checkers counterclockwise, toward your home board. A checker can only be moved to an "open" door (one that is occupied by no more than one opposing checker).

Each die indicates the number of doors for one move. The two moves can be combined into one longer move. For example, if you roll a 3 and a 6, you may move one checker three doors and a different checker six doors; or move a single checker three doors, then six more doors, for a total of nine (but only if the third or sixth door is open). If you roll a double, you can use each number twice—so if you roll double 3's, you have four separate moves of three doors each (which, as always, can be combined). You're required to make any moves that are possible; if you have to choose between two moves, you must make the larger one. If no move is possible (because of closed doors), your checkers stay put.

To make things more competitive, you can "hit" your opponent's checkers. Remember, if a door has only one checker on it, it's still considered open. If the opponent's checker lands on that door, the checker that was there first is "hit" and removed from play. Once your checker is taken off the board, you're required to enter it back into play on your opponent's home board. You can move a hit checker to an open door that corresponds to the number on one of your rolled dice. You can't use your roll to move any of your existing checkers until you bring back the hit one—if the doors corresponding to your roll are closed, you lose that turn. Once your checker re-enters the board, you can resume normal moves.

Ultimately, the goal of the game is collecting all of your checkers. First you need to move all 15 of your checkers to your home board. Then, when you roll the dice, you can collect a checker from a door with a number corresponding to each die. If the rolled number does not have a checker on it, you're still required to perform a move with that roll. If the roll is higher than any of your checkers' doors (for example, you roll a 6 but have no checkers on the six-door), you can remove the highest checker on your board. If one of your checkers is hit and removed from the board, you have to return it to your home board before you can continue collecting your checkers.

If you win the game, you get a point. If you collect all your checkers before your opponent gets all his checkers to his home board, your score doubles to two points (called *mars* in Turkish). Typically you play until one player reaches five points.

Good luck!

▲▲Taking a Turkish Bath

A visit to a *türk hamamı* (tewrk hah-mah-muh; Turkish bath) is perhaps the best way to rejuvenate your tired body while soaking in Turkish culture. It's not for everyone: Several baths— mostly those that cater to tourists—are mixed-sex, and the bathers are at least partially naked. Attendants touch your bare skin. The air inside is hot and humid, and you won't be able to keep any part of your body dry. Still, for most of those who've tried it, one visit isn't enough. For more on the history and practice of this phenomenon, see the sidebar on page 69.

The Bath Procedure

The whole experience generally takes an hour and a half to two hours. It's useful to bring along a hairbrush, shampoo, clean under-wear, flip-flops, *kese* (keh-seh; a raw-silk mitten used to exfoliate dead skin), and a bottle of water.

If being nude in front of strangers makes you uncomfortable, you may wear a bathing suit or your underwear. Flip-flops help you safely navigate the soapy marble floor (though most baths provide slippers).

Unless you bring your own *kese*, bath attendants will use the same *kese* on you that they've used on the last 20 people. *Keses* cost around 5 YTL and make nice souvenirs (see page 307).

All of the sweating will likely dehydrate you; that's why it makes sense to bring a bottle of water. Leave your glasses in your locker, as the steam inside will fog them up. If you eat a huge meal or drink alcohol before going to a Turkish bath, you'll wish you hadn't.

As you enter the bath, you'll find yourself in a waiting cham-ber with sofas and maybe a decorative fountain. You'll be directed to a changing room or cabin and given a large piece of cotton fab-ric, called a *peştemal* (pehsh-teh-mahl), to wrap around your body. Lock your clothes and valuables in the changing room or a separate locker (the key stays around your wrist on an elastic band).

The central section of the bath is the hot, wet caldarium, or *sıcaklık* (suh-jahk-luhk). Marble basins are spaced at regular inter-vals along the walls. Sit next to a basin, adjust the water tempera-ture to your liking (it should be as hot as you can stand), dip the provided metal bowl into the basin, and pour water on yourself. This will soften your skin, and prepare it for exfoliation. Spend

The Turkish Bath

Going to a Turkish *hamam* (bath) on a regular basis is one of the region's oldest traditions. Baths are still popular in today's Turkey, especially in the countryside. Ritual cleansing is an essential part of the Muslim religion, and an important element of Turkish culture.

Turks brought the steam bath from Central Asia, blended it with the Roman bath culture they found here, and created the synthesis we call the Turkish bath. Turkish-style baths use heat and humidity to stimulate perspiration, followed by pouring cool water over the body and vigorous massage.

The Turkish bath was introduced to Europe by the ever-encroaching Ottoman Empire. Europeans loved this exotic experience, especially painters of *turqueries* (fantastical representations of imagined Turkish culture), who used the baths as an excuse to paint frolicking naked girls.

Over time, baths became an integral part of everyday Turkish life. The *hamam* of the past was both health club and beauty parlor—like today's "wellness centers." Rub-downs with a raw-silk mitten, herbal therapy, and oil massage became popular treatments.

Baths were also a place for social interaction. Two centuries ago, a woman could ask for a divorce if her husband failed to finance her twice-weekly bath visits. The baths were a place where Muslim women could socialize outside of their homes. Here they could look for a suitable bride for their sons or celebrate the birth of a new child. Meanwhile, men met at the baths to mark circumcisions, religious festivals...and for bachelor parties.

Turkish baths remain a part of the culture, especially in rural areas and in folk songs and proverbs. A common Turkish maxim about facing the consequences of one's actions goes, "He who enters a bath, sweats."

EXPERIENCES

the next 20–25 minutes lazily pouring hot water over yourself to achieve maximum sweating and relaxation.

At the center of the chamber is a large marble slab. When it's your turn, an attendant will ask you to lie down on this slab. Men keep their *peştemal* on the entire time. Women wear their *peştemal* in co-ed baths, but generally remove it to lie on the slab in segregated facilities. (Again, women who are uncomfortable with nudity can keep on their *peştemal*, or wear a swimsuit.)

If you brought your own *kese*, this is the time to hand it over to the attendant for your scrub-down. Attendants often have a sense of humor, and they may toss you around on the slippery marble. Submit and go along for the ride. You may be amazed by what comes off as the attendant scrubs your skin. If you want the attendant to be gentle, say *"yavaş"* (yah-vahsh; "slow"). If over-enthusiastic scrubbing causes this word to slip your mind, body language and "Ouch!" will suffice.

Then the attendant takes a piece of sponge or knitted wool, dips it into soapy water, bathes you with bubbles, and gives you a short, relaxing massage. (If you're a glutton for punishment, you can get what locals call the "bone-crunching massage.") After your massage, go back next to the basin to wash your hair.

By the time you're finished, you're cleaner than you've ever been, and your skin is softer than a baby's. Take a towel from an attendant when you're ready to return to the waiting chamber. As you cool off for 10–15 minutes in the waiting chamber, you'll usually be offered tea. When you're relaxed and ready to confront the outside temperature, it's time to get dressed.

Choosing a Bath

Baths in the Old Town and New District have become quite touristy (in order to stay in business). On the upside, this means their attendants are usually accustomed to the needs and expectations of international visitors. Don't worry—you're still getting an experience pretty close to an authentic Turkish bath.

If you're not comfortable with mixed-sex bathing, check the bath's policy before heading out. Since most Turks themselves find mixed-sex bathing unacceptable, it's not hard to find single-sex baths. In segregated baths, only attendants of the same sex work on you. In co-ed baths, most attendants are male, serving both men and women.

It's also worth checking the price, and asking what's included. Expect to pay up to 75 YTL for the experience (in fancy tourist-friendly places), plus a tip (of roughly 15 YTL) for the otherwise poorly compensated attendants.

Büyük Hamam—Only recently discovered by travelers, this bath is the most "local" of the bunch. Though the staff is not yet accustomed to serving tourists, they're helpful and make an effort. Enjoy the beautiful surroundings—designed by the famous architect Sinan (see page 225)—for a far more reasonable price than the other baths listed here. Women may want to take along their own bath accessories, as this place provides all necessary supplies for men (towels, *peştemals*, etc.) but not for women—though upon request, they'll borrow these from the men's section (segregated, men's section daily 5:30–22:30, women's section daily 8:30–17:30, Merkez Camii yanı, Potinciler Sokak 22, men's section tel. 0212/253-4229, women's section tel. 0212/256-9835). It's located in the Kasımpaşa (kah-suhm-pah-shah) neighborhood, near the Kasımpaşa Mosque, at the edge of the New District. Even though it's not far from İstiklal street and the Old Town, you'll need to take a cab to get here.

Çemberlitaş Hamamı—This bath, known for its fine architecture, was built by Sinan in the late 16th century for the sultan's mother (segregated, daily 6:00–24:00, credit cards accepted, next to Çemberlitaş tram stop, across from the Burned Column, Vezirhan Caddesi 8, tel. 0212/522-7974, www.cemberlitashamami .com.tr).

Süleymaniye Hamamı—Another of Sinan's creations, these were built to be part of a larger mosque complex. Contact the baths for a complimentary round-trip shuttle (only co-ed, daily 9:00–24:00, right next to the Mosque of Süleyman the Magnificent, Mimar Sinan Caddesi 2, tel. 0212/519-5569 or 0212/520-3410, www .suleymaniyehamami.com).

Cağaloğlu Hamamı—This is one of the more attractive historic baths in Istanbul (segregated, daily 8:00–20:00, men's section open until 22:00, halfway between the Underground Cistern and the Grand Bazaar, Prof. Kazım İsmail Gürkan Caddesi 34, tel. 0212/522-2424, www.cagalogluhamami.com.tr).

Galatasaray Hamamı—Nicely restored, these baths have a more local clientele (segregated, men's section daily 7:00–22:00, women's section daily 8:00–20:00, a block off İstiklal street at Turnacibasi Sokak 24, general info tel. 0212/252-4242, men's section tel. 0212/244-1412, women's section tel. 0212/249-4342).

EXPERIENCES

HISTORIC CORE OF ISTANBUL WALK

Sultanahmet, the Blue Mosque, and the Hippodrome

Just like Rome, Istanbul's Old Town was built on seven hills. The district called Sultanahmet, on top of the first hill, is the historic core of the city. The Greek city of Byzantium was founded nearby, where Topkapı Palace stands today. Early Greek settlers—weary after their long journey—chose this highly strategic location, which could easily be fortified with walls on all sides, gave them control of all three surrounding bodies of water (the Bosphorus Strait, the Golden Horn, and the Sea of Marmara), and was convenient to the Greek colonies on the Black Sea.

Today, Sultanahmet is Istanbul's single best sightseeing zone for visitors, playing host to Istanbul's most important and impressive former church (Hagia Sophia) and mosque (the Blue Mosque), one of its best museums (Turkish and Islamic Arts), and its most significant Byzantine ruins (the Hippodrome and Underground Cistern).

ORIENTATION

Length of This Walk: About three hours.

Hagia Sophia: 20 YTL, Tue–Sun 9:00–18:30, off-season until 16:30, closed Mon, Sultanahmet Meydanı, tel. 0212/528-4500.

Underground Cistern: 10 YTL, daily 9:00–17:30, until 18:30 in summer, Yerebatan Caddesi 13, Sultanahmet, tel. 0212/512-1570.

Blue Mosque: Free, generally open daily from one hour after sunrise until one hour before sunset, closed to visitors five times each day for prayer.

Turkish and Islamic Arts Museum: 10 YTL, Tue–Sun 9:00–17:00, closed Mon, Sultanahmet Meydanı, tel. 0212/518-1805.

Getting There: Start at Hagia Sophia, just down the street from the Sultanahmet tram stop.

THE WALK BEGINS

• *Begin at the pond in Sultanahmet Park, sandwiched between Istanbul's two most famous sights: the Blue Mosque and Hagia Sophia.*

Sultanahmet Spin Tour

With your back to the Blue Mosque, face Hagia Sophia (eye-ah soh-fee-yah), and take a slow spin clockwise to get the lay of the land. Behind Hagia Sophia, not visible from here, are the Topkapı Palace grounds, which also house the Istanbul Archaeological Museum. To reach the main palace entry, you'd walk along the front of Hagia Sophia to the right, then turn left at the first corner and walk along the side of the church until you run into the Imperial Gate.

Now turn 90 degrees to the right. The long terra-cotta-colored building with different-sized domes is the 16th-century **Haseki Sultan Bath,** now a government-owned emporium. Just to the right of that, at the other end of this lively park, is the famous **Blue Mosque.** Farther to the right (out of sight) is the long, narrow Byzantine square called the **Hippodrome** (the green-domed German Fountain you can see through the trees marks the near end of the Hippodrome—where we'll finish this walk). Keep turning until you are again facing Hagia Sophia.

Sultanahmet Park is a fine example (along with the Golden Horn park project) of a city determined to be people-friendly. In spring it's a festival of tulips. If the fountain is on, notice that the spouts are designed to mimic the domes of Hagia Sophia. This is perhaps the best photo op for both Hagia Sophia and the Blue Mosque. The large cobbled street at the end of the park turns into a parking lot during festivals and on some weekends.

• *Across the street, two red Turkish flags mark the entrance to Hagia Sophia. Now, let's go to church.*

Hagia Sophia

Hagia Sophia—the name means "divine wisdom"—served as the patriarchal church of Constantinople for centuries (similar to the Vatican in Rome). When an earlier church on this site was

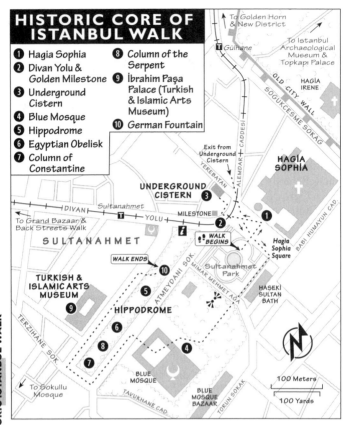

HISTORIC CORE OF ISTANBUL WALK

1. Hagia Sophia
2. Divan Yolu & Golden Milestone
3. Underground Cistern
4. Blue Mosque
5. Hippodrome
6. Egyptian Obelisk
7. Column of Constantine
8. Column of the Serpent
9. İbrahim Paşa Palace (Turkish & Islamic Arts Museum)
10. German Fountain

destroyed during the sixth-century Nika Revolt, the Byzantine Emperor Justinian seized the opportunity—and this prime real estate—to build the most spectacular church the world had ever seen. He hired a mathematician named Anthemius to engineer a building for the ages, with an enormous central dome unlike anything ever constructed. You could fit Paris' Notre-Dame Cathedral under Hagia Sophia's dome—or the Statue of Liberty, minus her torch. Nearly 1,500 years later, Hagia Sophia still dominates Istanbul's skyline.

When the Ottomans conquered Constantinople in 1453, Hagia Sophia (which they called Aya Sofya) was converted to a mosque, and minarets were

added to this otherwise very Byzantine-looking church. Because of its grand scale, grace, and beauty, Hagia Sophia's design influenced Ottoman architects for generations. That's why many mosques built after the Ottoman invasion—and long after the Byzantines became a distant memory—continued to incorporate many Byzantine elements.

Tour Hagia Sophia now (see tour on page 125), or wait until the end of our orientation walk—we'll finish just up the street from here. (If you're visiting in peak season and the line is short, you'd be wise to pop in now—cruise groups can inundate the place at a moment's notice.)

• *Leaving Hagia Sophia, turn right and walk to the busy street corner. (Hop-on, hop-off tour buses leave near here, at the little red tour kiosk.) Head across the tram tracks to the 30-foot-tall stone-and-brick tower that looks like a large chimney, with a fountain built into it.*

Divan Yolu and the Golden Milestone

The busy street with the trams is Divan Yolu (dee-vahn yoh-loo), the main thoroughfare through Sultanahmet. To the left (uphill), it leads to the Grand Bazaar. To the right (downhill), it heads to the Galata Bridge and New District. Notice the dramatic boomerang-shaped swoop made by the tram tracks as they pass Hagia Sophia. Since Istanbul's Old Town tram has only one line, it's remarkably user-friendly. If Istanbul is your jungle, consider this your vine. It swings to nearly all the places of tourist interest and it can't get lost (trams run 6–8 times per hour).

Divan Yolu was also Constantinople's main transportation artery in Byzantine times, when it was named Mese ("Middle Way"). The road started right here, where the Golden Milestone (Miliarium Aureum) still stands (in a pit, to the left of the tower). Some 1,500 years ago, the Byzantines considered this point the center of the world. This ancient and once-gilded milestone showed the distances to key locations within the empire. Today it's a mere stub worn down by the centuries. Nothing remains of its decorative arches, or the statues of Constantine and his mother Helen holding a cross that once adorned it.

• *Go downhill to the first corner and turn left. Across the street from the old yellow police building is the low-profile, red-and-white striped entrance to the...*

Underground Cistern

This vast, underground reservoir dates back to Byzantine Emperor Justinian's reign in the sixth century A.D. Because it was built on the site of an earlier basilica, it's often called the "Basilica Cistern." Turks call it *yerebatan sarayı*, which means "sunken palace."

Buy your ticket and descend into the cistern. The visit is a level 15-minute, 400-yard stroll. (You'll exit through a different gate, about a hundred yards down the street.) While your eyes adjust to the dimness, ponder the history of this spectacular site. The Byzantine Empire enjoyed a Golden Age under Emperor Justinian. Its currency was so strong that merchants in continental Europe and Asia demanded to be paid in Byzantine imperial coins. This enormous wealth can still be seen in the monuments and even the functional buildings (such as other cisterns) of that era. This massive reservoir—larger by far than any other in Constantinople, to provide precious water in case of a shortage—was built to meet the needs of a fast-growing capital city.

A forest of 336 columns supports the brick ceiling. Most of these were recycled from earlier Roman ruins in and around the city. Note the variety of capitals (tops of columns). The cistern covers an area about the size of two football fields—big enough to hold 27 million gallons of fresh water. Clay pipes and aqueducts carried water 12 miles to this cistern. (A half-mile-long chunk of the Valens Aqueduct still stands, spanning Atatürk Bulvarı, or Atatürk Boulevard, roughly a mile west of here.)

Gradually these pipes became clogged, and the cistern fell out of use. As time passed, neglect became ignorance, and people forgot it was even there. An Ottoman historian wrote that residents of this area were luckier than others, as they could easily drop a bucket into any garden well and collect apparently God-given water. They didn't realize they were dipping their buckets into a Byzantine masterpiece.

The platform you're walking on was constructed two decades ago to make the far reaches of the cistern more accessible to visitors. While water once filled this space halfway to the ceiling, today it's just a shallow pond—rainwater that leaks in through cracks and compromised mortar in the ceiling. (Accumulated water is pumped out to prevent damage.) Before the walkway was built, the water was six feet deep, and the only way to see the cistern was to rent a boat and row in the dark—a perfectly evocative setting used for James Bond's adventures in *From Russia with Love*.

Walking towards the far end, notice that part of the cistern (which has suffered structural damage) is separated by a wall.

At the far end of the cistern, find the two Medusa heads lying on the ground, squeezed under pillars. This fearsome mythologi-

cal gorgon—with hair made of snakes and a gaze that could turn people to stone—was often carved by Greeks into tombstones or cemetery walls to scare off grave robbers. In Roman times, she became a protector of temples. When Christianity took hold, Medusa was a reminder of the not-so-distant Roman persecution of Christians—so it may be no coincidence that these pagan fragments were left here in a dark corner of the cistern, never to see daylight again. Another theory suggests that the architect simply needed a proper base to raise the two small columns to ceiling height...and the Medusas were a perfect fit.

On the way out, you'll see huge, blocky concrete columns built more recently to support the structure—quite a contrast to the ancient, graceful Roman columns.

Near the exit, notice the stage in the water. The cistern serves as an exhibition hall for the Istanbul Biennial arts festival, and is a concert venue from time to time—mainly for traditional Turkish or Sufi music. Check the events schedule at the ticket office. You may be able to enjoy a great concert for no more than the regular cistern entrance fee.

• *Leaving the Underground Cistern, turn right and retrace your steps back to the park where this walk began. Cross the park to find the towering Blue Mosque at the far end. You'll note that we've set out some nice wooden benches for you from which to enjoy the view. Read the next page or so while seated here. Notice the schedule (posted by the souvenir kiosk) for the sound-and-light show performed some evenings near the mosque. Back in the 1970s, these were quite impressive.*

Blue Mosque

This famous and gorgeous mosque is one of the world's finest. It was built in just seven years (1609–1616) by the architect Mehmet Aga, who also rebuilt Kaaba (the holiest shrine of Islam—the giant black cube at the center of the mosque in the holy city of Mecca). Locals call it the Sultan Ahmet Mosque for the ruler who

Sultan Ahmet I and Kösem

Sultan Ahmet the First (1590–1617) ascended to the throne at the age of 14. Though young, he was well-educated and talented, spoke several languages, and proved to be an able statesman.

To prevent future conflicts for the throne, it was customary for a new sultan to kill his brothers. Regarded for his compassion, Ahmet I went against two centuries of tradition to spare his brother's life. He allowed his brother Mustafa to live (and Mustafa became sultan after Ahmet I's death). But the tradition was soon revived: When Ahmet I's son Murat IV took the throne, Murat had his young brother, Prince Beyazıt, strangled.

Ahmet I's greatest achievement was the construction of the Blue Mosque, completed in 1616. He died of typhoid one year later at the age of 28. Ahmet I's wife, Kösem (1590–1651), was one of the most influential women in Ottoman history. She became a *haseki* (favorite) of Sultan Ahmet when she was only 15. Notorious for her ambition, Kösem was kept away from the palace by Ahmet I's successors. But when her young son Murat IV became sultan at age 11, Kösem returned to the palace and essentially ran the empire through him. Her control of the state continued through the reign of her second son, the mentally disturbed İbrahim I (a.k.a. İbrahim the Mad).

For nearly a decade, Kösem ruled the empire without intrusion. When İbrahim I was murdered, Kösem introduced her grandson, Mehmet, as the next sultan. But Mehmet's mother, Turhan Sultan, would not tolerate Kösem's domination—and so she sent eunuchs to strangle Kösem in her sleep.

financed it (see above), but travelers know it as the Blue Mosque because of the rich color that dominates the interior.

• *As you face the Blue Mosque, to your right (with the multitude of mini-domes and chimneys) is the madrassa, a school of theology. Facing the mosque, you can see it has…*

Six Minarets

Aside from its impressive scale and opulent interior, the Blue Mosque is unique because of its six minarets. According to Muslim tradition, the imam (the prayer leader) or the muezzin (a man chosen for his talent in correctly voicing the call to prayer) would climb to the top of a minaret five times each day to announce the call to prayer. On hearing this warbling chant, Muslims are to come to the mosque to pray. Today, an imam or muezzin still performs the call to prayer, but now it's amplified by loudspeakers at the top of the minarets.

A single minaret was adequate for its straightforward function, but mosques financed by sultans often wanted to show off with more. According to legend, Sultan Ahmet I asked the architect for a gold *(altın)* minaret—but the man thought he said "six" *(altı)*. In all likelihood, Sultan Ahmet I probably requested the six minarets to flaunt his wealth. But at the time, the central mosque in the holy city of Mecca also had six. The clergy at Mecca feared that Ahmet's new mosque would upstage theirs—so they built a seventh minaret at Mecca.

• *The walkway by the benches leads to the Blue Mosque. Through the gate at the end of the walkway, you enter the mosque's...*

Outer Courtyard

Straight ahead, a staircase leads up to the inner courtyard (described next). To the right of the staircase, notice the line of water taps used for ablution—the ritual cleansing of the body before worshipping, as directed by Islamic law. These are comparatively new, installed to replace the older fountain in the inner courtyard (which we'll see soon). To the left, another set of stairs leads to an entrance into the mosque designated for worshippers (you may exit through this gate when you leave the mosque).

• *Now take the stairs up into the...*

Inner Courtyard

The courtyard is surrounded by a portico, which provides shade and shelter. The shutters along the back wall open in summer for

ventilation. In the center of the courtyard is a fancy fountain, once used for ablutions but no longer functional. When the mosque fills up for special services, worshippers who can't fit inside pray in the large vaulted area in front of the mosque (on your left)—and, if necessary, fill the rest of the courtyard. But today such jam-packed services are rare. Muslims are not required to actually go to the mosque five times each day; they can pray anywhere. The exception is the midday service on Friday, which the Quran dictates should be a time for all worshippers to come together in congregation—making mosques more crowded on Fridays.

• *Now go into the mosque. For instructions and etiquette, see page 61. The main door on this west end is where visitors generally enter. (If this door is closed, you can usually go around the corner on the right.) As you enter, take a plastic bag from the container and use it to carry your shoes, which you should remove before you step on the carpet. Entering the mosque is free, but you can make a donation as you exit. Before you visit, you may want to read the Understanding Islam chapter.*

Interior

Stepping through the heavy leather drape into the interior, you'll understand why this is called the Blue Mosque. Let your eyes

adjust to the dim lighting as you breathe in the vast and intensely decorated interior.

Approach the wood railing to take a closer look at the apse (straight ahead from the main gate). The area beyond this barrier is reserved for worshippers, who fill the space at all times of day. The little shin-high wooden shelves are for storing worshippers' shoes.

On the far wall, look for the highly decorated marble niche with large candles on either side. This is the mihrab (meeh-rahb), which points southeast to Mecca—where all Muslims face when they worship. The surrounding wall is decorated with floral-designed stained-glass windows, many of them original.

On the right side of the apse is a staircase leading up to a platform with a cone on top. This is the *mimber* (meem-behr), similar to a pulpit in a Christian church. A *mimber* is symbolic of the growth of Islam—Muhammad had to stand higher and higher to talk to his growing following. It is used by the imam (prayer leader) to deliver a speech on Fridays, similar to a sermon in Christian services. As a sign of respect for Muhammad, the imam stands only halfway up the staircase.

Farther to the right, next to the main pillar, is a fancy marble platform elevated on columns. This is where the choir sings hymns a cappella (mainstream Islam uses no instruments) on important religious days.

Mosque services are segregated: The main hall is reserved for men, while women use the colonnaded area behind the barriers at the back, on both sides of the main entrance. Women can also use the upper galleries on crowded days. While many visitors think it is demeaning to women to make them stay in back, it's simply a practicality. Just like a co-ed aerobics class at the gym, all those people bending over in front of each other could be very distracting.

The huge dome—reaching a height of 141 feet and a diameter of 110 feet—is modeled after the one in Hagia Sophia, which was the first building to use pillars to support a giant central dome. As

OLD TOWN BACK STREETS WALK

Grand Bazaar, Mosque of Süleyman the Magnificent, and Spice Market

This walk leads you through the back streets of Istanbul's Old Town, giving you a taste of the authentic city (rather than its tourist-filled historic core). You'll share sidewalks with natives going about their daily routines and walk streets that haven't changed in centuries, lined with shops that cater to locals.

The major themes of this walk are markets and mosques. First, the Old Town has been a bustling commercial center for centuries—and you'll enjoy two of its most famous and bustling marketplaces: The Grand Bazaar's aggressive salesmen and tempting souvenirs will threaten to empty your wallet, while the Spice Market's intoxicating aromas and offers of "Turkish Viagra" will titillate your senses. Second, we'll drop into two of the city's most interesting and important mosques: one grand (the Mosque of Süleyman the Magnificent, the finest of all Ottoman mosques in Istanbul), and one cozy (the gorgeously tiled Rüstem Paşa Mosque). In between these main attractions, we'll see a side of Istanbul few tourists experience.

ORIENTATION

Length of This Walk: Allow at least four hours, not counting the Grand Bazaar; if you linger in the shops at the Grand Bazaar and Spice Market, it could fill an entire day.

Grand Bazaar: Mon–Sat 9:00–19:00, shops begin to close at 18:30, closed Sun, across the parking lot from the Çemberlitaş tram stop, behind the Nuruosmaniye Mosque.

Spice Market: Mon–Sat 9:00–19:30, shops start closing at 19:00, closed Sun, at the Old Town end of the Galata Bridge, near the Eminönü tram stop.

Mosque of Süleyman the Magnificent: Mosque—free, generally open daily from one hour after sunrise until one hour before sunset, closed to visitors five times a day for prayer; mausoleum—free, daily 9:00–17:00, until 18:00 in summer; located on Sıddık Sami Onar Caddesi in the Süleymaniye district.

Rüstem Paşa Mosque: Generally open daily from one hour after sunrise until one hour before sunset, closed to visitors five times a day for prayer, on Hasırcılar Caddesi, Eminönü.

Getting There: We'll start at the Sultanahmet tram stop in the heart of the Old Town.

Starring: Some of Istanbul's best markets and mosques...and its people.

THE WALK BEGINS

• *From the Sultanahmet tram stop, we'll walk to the Çemberlitaş tram stop. It's a distance of five gradually uphill blocks along the tram tracks.*

Divan Yolu: from Sultanahmet to Çemberlitaş

The bustling street called Divan Yolu—now reserved mostly for trams and buses, and lined with shops and restaurants—has been the city's transportation thoroughfare since Byzantine times. We'll follow it to an ancient column from Byzantine Constantinople (at the Çemberlitaş tram stop).

Begin at the Sultanahmet tram stop (200 yards uphill from Hagia Sophia and the Underground Cistern). The small mosque near the stop is the 15th-century **Firuz Ağa Camii.** Just beyond the mosque, enter the **park** to your left and climb the stairs to the red-brick platform, which offers grand views of the Blue Mosque (including all six minarets). The Byzantine ruins scattered in and around the circle in front of the platform probably once belonged to the ancient Hippodrome (chariot racecourse), or a related building.

After enjoying the view, continue up Divan Yolu (with Hagia Sophia behind you). The bust you pass as you leave the park depicts the poet **Mehmet Akif,** who wrote Turkey's national anthem.

Walk another block up the street, and cross the tracks at the traffic lights (just past the Starbucks). Ahead, an old **cemetery** filled with Ottoman big shots is behind the wall on your right. Enter near the corner, walk in 15 paces, and look to your right. Amid the traditional pillar- and turban-shaped tombstones, find the unique stone resembling a ship's sail (it belongs to Cudi Paşa, apparently a high-ranking official). The big mausoleum at the far end of the cemetery honors Sultan Mahmut II, who ruled in the first half of the 19th century. His mausoleum represents the eclectic taste of the time (including a beautiful crystal chandelier hanging

OLD TOWN BACK STREETS WALK

1. Çemberlitaş
2. Nuruosmaniye Mosque
3. Grand Bazaar
4. Beyazıt District
5. Istanbul University
6. Mosque of Süleyman the Magnificent
7. Uzun Çarşı
8. Rüstem Paşa Mosque
9. Hasırcılar Alley
10. Food Vendors
11. Eminönü Square
12. New Mosque of Mother Sultan
13. Spice Market

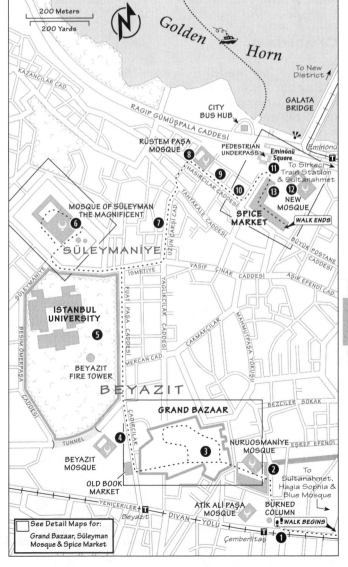

OLD TOWN WALK

down from the center of the dome). To go inside, find the entrance at the far corner of the cemetery (free, donation requested, take off your shoes before entering). Two other sultans, plus some relatives, share this grand space with Mahmut. As was traditional, the "caskets" you see are actually empty—the bodies are buried underground. Caskets with hats were for men; flowers were for women. You may see a visitor saying a prayer for the soul of the deceased (see "An Essential Part of Prayer" sidebar on page 339).

• *Back on Divan Yolu, continue along the tram tracks. After one block, you'll see a towering Byzantine column called...*

Çemberlitaş

Çemberlitaş (chehm-behr-lee-tahsh), also known as the Burned Column, consists of six drums, held together by hoops. ("Çemberlitaş" means "stone with hoops.") Çemberlitaş, dating from the fourth century A.D., once held aloft a larger-than-life statue of Constantine depicted as the god Apollo. When the statue was lost (well before the Ottomans took over the city), it was replaced with a golden cross—which is also now missing. Now the column stands, lonely and forlorn, forgotten behind the tram stop. It's strange to think that in Constantine's day, this column marked the center of the Forum, or main square, ringed with public buildings and churches—none of which remain. Adding insult to injury, frequent fires in this district left the column permanently scorched. After all those years of abuse, it's finally being restored, which is why it'll likely be covered with scaffolding when you visit.

• *At the column, turn right (passing a recommended Turkish bath, Çemberlitaş Hamamı, to your right—see listing on page 71) and head down the hill toward the big, ornate late-Ottoman **Nuruosmaniye Mosque** (noo-roo-os-mah-nee-yeh; "Sacred Light of Osman"). Continue straight past the line of tour buses, and walk along the outer wall of the mosque. The tourist shops you pass on the left were actually built as part of the complex, to provide funds to maintain the mosque.*

After walking one block along the mosque wall, you'll see the entrance into the mosque courtyard on your left (across from a pedestrian street). Go into the courtyard and continue straight past the mosque

(drop in if you like—but be careful not to get mosqued out, as we'll be visiting two more mosques on this walk).

After passing the mosque through the courtyard (WCs at the far end, on the left), you'll enter the Grand Bazaar. Above the gate, between the Arabic inscription and the emblem on top, find the name of this entrance (the same as the mosque)—Nuruosmaniye Kapısı *(kah-puh-suh), or Nuruosmaniye Gate. Before entering the bazaar, consider a straightforward lunch at Tarihi Subaşı Restaurant, one block down the street to your right (on the right-hand corner, marked with red Coca-Cola sign; see listing on page 300). As you enter "How much you pay?" land, button away your valuables and watch your money.*

The Grand Bazaar

This remarkable roofed warren of shops—with Byzantine foundations and an Ottoman floor plan, bustling with merchants and shoppers—is one of Istanbul's top attractions. Of course, this is a colorful and convenient, if predictable, place to do your souvenir shopping. But it also hides nooks and crannies, rarely seen by tourists, that offer rich, vivid insights into the Turkish culture of yesterday and today.

For a self-guided tour of the bazaar, see page 206.

• *If you follow the self-guided tour, you'll wind up at the far end of the Grand Bazaar to continue this walk (see "Beyazıt District," next). To skip the bazaar and get on with this walk, simply walk straight down the main street on which you entered the bazaar (Kalpakçılar Caddesi) and continue out through the exit at the far end.*

This next stretch—through the Beyazıt district, connecting the Grand Bazaar and the Mosque of Süleyman the Magnificent—involves about a half-mile of walking, with relatively little to see in between... but it's worth the trek.

Beyazıt District

Exiting the bazaar, go right and walk a couple hundred yards through the outdoor textile market. At the end of the textile alley, you'll be facing the wall of Istanbul University's main campus (across the street). This area, called Beyazıt, is where the market crowds and the student population mix, giving it a special spice.

• *Continue straight down the busy street (Fuat Paşa Caddesi) with the university wall across the street on your left. Go a block or so along the right side of the road, then cross the street to the left side (along the wall). We'll continue about a quarter-mile straight downhill along this road.*

Notice that many stores along here sell **kitchen utensils.** This district was once Istanbul's coppersmith center. Even up until the early 1980s, many people still used copper utensils. But now that modern materials and methods have taken over, coppersmiths are mainly a thing of the past, and most of the utensils along here are made of steel, aluminum, or pressed copper or brass.

• *At the fenced gate in the wall, the landmark Beyazıt fire tower marks the grounds of...*

Istanbul University

This partly state-subsidized school (closed to tourists) is the city's biggest university, with thousands of students from all over Turkey. This is the larger of Istanbul University's two main campuses.

• *After the shops end, the wall continues. Keep going until the end of the wall. Now's the time to decide if you'll visit the massive Mosque of Süleyman the Magnificent (following the wall 300 yards uphill to your left) or turn right steeply downhill toward the Rüstem Paşa Mosque.*

Mosque of Süleyman the Magnificent

Perched high on a hill overlooking Istanbul, this stately mosque is befitting for the most "Magnificent" sultan of the Ottoman Empire. Designed by the empire's greatest architect (Sinan), and dedicated to one of its greatest sultans, the Mosque of Süleyman the Magnificent gives the Blue Mosque a run for its money. Its pastel interior is a serene counterpoint to the Blue Mosque's vivid colors.

The mosque complex holds the mausoleums of Süleyman and his wife Roxelana, and its "backyard" offers sweeping views of the city below. The surrounding Süleymaniye neighborhood includes a madrassa (former seminary) that now hosts restaurants and tea gardens.

• *For a self-guided **tour** of the mosque, see page 218. If you follow the tour, come back to this intersection afterwards.*

*To **skip the mosque** (or if you're rejoining this walk after touring the mosque), head downhill about 150 yards to the second street on your left (Uzun Çarşı—look for a sycamore tree on the corner, and a fast-food kiosk across the street). As you turn downhill and left onto this street, you'll see the brick minaret of a 15th-century mosque straight ahead, and behind it, the minaret of our next stop—Rüstem Paşa Mosque.*

Uzun Çarşı

As you walk straight ahead along this street—which soon becomes a narrow alley, near the brick minaret—you'll be jostled by shoppers and nudged by delivery trucks trying to sneak their way into the commercial sprawl. Shops on either side cater to locals: hardware stores, stationery shops, toy stores, quilt-makers, sportswear vendors, shoe stores, and so on. If you're looking for a traditional backgammon board—without all that shiny, fake mother-of-pearl and wood inlay that strain your eyes as you play—you'll find it here, and dirt cheap.

• *The alley runs directly into a two-story stone building with an arched entryway. Go through the humble doorway and take the stairs up into the courtyard of the...*

Rüstem Paşa Mosque

Built by Sinan in the 16th century, this mosque stands on an elevated platform, supported by vaults that house shops (which once provided income for the mosque's upkeep). Its namesake, Rüstem Paşa (ruhs-tehm pah-shah), was a Grand Vizier of Süleyman the Magnificent (after the mysterious death of İbrahim Paşa—see page 189). He found great success in this role, not just because he was Süleyman's son-in-law (he married Süleyman and Roxelana's daughter Mihrimah, whose tomb you saw next to Süleyman's), but also because he was clever and efficient.

Like King Midas, Rüstem Paşa could turn anything into revenue, and filled the sultan's treasury. But the public hated him because he taxed everything in sight, and he was frequently accused of embezzling funds.

Admire the giant portico that covers most of the mosque's courtyard, and notice that Rüstem Paşa is missing one feature found at almost every mosque: a fountain for ablution. Because of the limited space in this courtyard, Sinan placed the fountain at street level (down the stairs across the courtyard from where you entered).

The facade is slathered in gorgeous 16th-century İznik tiles, but the interior is even more impressive. To enter, go around the left side to find the visitors' entrance. Inside, virtually every surface is covered with floral-designed tile panels. (Locals say that if the Blue Mosque is Istanbul's Notre-Dame, this tiny gem is its Sainte-Chapelle.)

• *Since the next alley we'll be using is always packed with people—especially on Saturdays—consider reading the following section before you start walking. Leave the mosque complex through the door you entered, passing some enticing tile souvenirs. Turn left and walk down...*

Hasırcılar Alley

Hasırcılar (hah-sur-juh-lahr) Caddesi ("Mat-Weavers' Alley") is a real-life market street—part of the commercial sprawl surrounding our next sight, the Spice Market.

As you walk, notice the porters and the carts squeezing their heavy, wide loads through the alley. You'll pass old *bedestens* (traditional commercial buildings) and stores, many of them family-owned for generations. If you had strolled this street a century ago, only the shoppers' clothes would be different.

At the first corner on your left, notice the store selling hunting knives and rifles. Turkey has strong gun-control laws, but they don't extend to hunting rifles—you just need a hunting license.

One block before the Spice Market entrance, you'll smell the aroma of fresh-roasted coffee and spices. If you're in the market for spices, dried fruits, sweets, and nuts, start checking the prices along here—they're cheaper than in the high-rent Spice Market. Ask for a sample, and don't feel obligated to buy. While bargaining has become common in the Grand Bazaar, around here you'll generally pay what's on the price tag for food and spices—though souvenirs and exotic items (such as saffron and imported caviar) may be haggled over.

• *Half a block before the arched entry to the Spice Market (the big brick-and-stone building at the end of the alley), you'll be immersed in a lively bazaar of...*

Food Vendors

On your left, look for the thriving deli, **Namlı Şarküteri,** with the large containers of olives, pickled peppers, and hanging pastramis out front (get a sample inside). It's been here for over a century, selling a wide range of traditional cold *mezes* (appetizers): dry salted fish, spicy tomato and pepper pastes, pickles, *sucuk* (soo-jook; spicy veal sausage), Turkish pastrami, and a variety of white cheeses made from sheep's and cow's milk. They also make a high-cholesterol sandwich called *kumru* (koom-roo; meaning "dove"), stuffed with spicy sausages, salami, and smoked cow's tongue. Wander through to get a feeling for what locals buy at the grocery store, and say hello to Zeki, the guy who runs the place. Upstairs is an oasis of a cafeteria (air-con, bright, cheery, and fast).

A little farther ahead on the right, just before the Spice Market entrance, is one of the best coffee vendors in town: the venerable **Kurukahveci Mehmet Efendi Mahdumları** (say it three times fast). This is the locals' favorite place to get ground coffee. Remember that only sealed packets can be taken through

US Customs, and pick up the leaflet with preparation instructions when you check out. There's often a long line of loyal customers waiting at the cashier. If you can't find it on the map, just follow your nose.

• *Just after the coffee shop is the Spice Market's Hasırcılar Gate. Rather than entering the market here, let's walk around the side of the L-shaped building to the main entrance, facing the Golden Horn. Turn left and continue along the street (following the Spice Market wall).*

Along this alley, you'll spot several more shops displaying spices, dried fruits, and sweets, alongside butcher, fishmonger, and dairy shops. The Turks have a word for this vibrant scene: *pazar* (pah-zahr), which gave us the English word "bazaar."

The alley opens into the large **Eminönü Square,** with the Golden Horn (not quite visible from here) on the other side of the busy street.

Before or after you tour the Spice Market, consider these options. You could take a break, sitting with locals on the platforms by the side of the square, watching the people pass by. (If you've bought some munchies, here's a good place to picnic. You can get a beverage from a nearby store, or the newspaper stand straight ahead.)

If you'd like a cup of coffee or tea, walk down the alley (bordering the square) to your immediate left as you face the Golden Horn. You'll soon come to **Ender Çikolata,** a chocolate and candy store (on the left). It has tables and chairs across the alley, where you can sit down and relax. Or if you're hungry for a meal, go next door to **Hamdi** (hahm-dee) **Restaurant,** which specializes in meaty kebabs (see listing on page 301).

• *Continue around the corner of the Spice Market to the right to reach the main entrance.*

In Front of the Spice Market

The square in front of the Spice Market is dominated by the **New Mosque of Mother Sultan** (or simply "New Mosque")—one of the latest examples of classical, traditional-style Ottoman mosques.

This square was once a huge outdoor bazaar. You may still see a few makeshift stands with vendors hawking anything from clothes to fake jewelry to giant posters of pop stars. The vendors, who "forget" to pay taxes, are routinely rounded up by local

OLD TOWN WALK

police—so don't be surprised if you see a string of people running up the street with merchandise in their hands, chased by municipal inspectors.

Also notice the **pigeons.** While most Turks believe that it's good luck if a pigeon, ahem, leaves its mark on you, it's smart not to get too close to the buildings (where the birds are likely to be perched overhead, just waiting...).

With the mosque on your left, you're facing the front of the Spice Market. Notice the outdoor plant and pet market to the left.

A WC is just around this corner, in the inner corner of the "L" formed by the Spice Market.

• *Now go through the main entrance into the...*

Spice Market

Built in the mid-17th century, this market hall was gradually taken over by merchants dealing in spices, herbs, medicinal plants, and

pharmaceuticals. While it's quite a touristy scene today, most stalls still sell much of the same products, and the air is heavy with the aroma of exotic spices. Locals call it the Mısır Carşışı (Egyptian Bazaar) because it was once funded by taxes paid by Egypt.

While smaller and less imposing than the Grand Bazaar, the Spice Market is more colorful, with the ambience of a true Oriental market. On either side of the long, vaulted central hall are a wide range of merchant stalls, most of them with sacks and barrels out front showing off their wares. While merchants once sat quietly, cross-legged, next to their shops, today they engage in a never-ending game of one-upmanship, competing for the attention of passersby. If you're offered a sample of something (such as Turkish delight), feel free to accept—but be warned that it can be difficult to pry yourself away from the sales pitch

that's sure to ensue. (To the left as you enter, note the staircase leading to the second floor. Upstairs is the historic **Pandelli Restaurant,** listed on page 301).

Aside from the spice shops, you'll also see stores slinging natural sponges, lentils and beans, dried vegetables, dried fruits (especially figs and apricots),

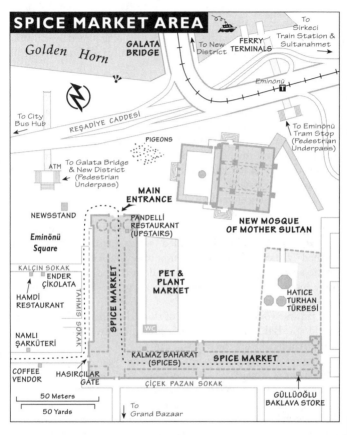

SPICE MARKET AREA

Golden Horn

GALATA BRIDGE

To New District

FERRY TERMINALS

To Sirkeci Train Station & Sultanahmet

Eminönü

To City Bus Hub

REŞADİYE CADDESİ

To Eminönü Tram Stop (Pedestrian Underpass)

PIGEONS

ATM

To Galata Bridge & New District (Pedestrian Underpass)

MAIN ENTRANCE

NEWSSTAND

Eminönü Square

KALÇIN SOKAK

ENDER ÇİKOLATA

HAMDİ RESTAURANT

NAMLI ŞARKÜTERİ

TAHMİS SOKAK

SPICE MARKET

PANDELLİ RESTAURANT (UPSTAIRS)

PET & PLANT MARKET

WC

NEW MOSQUE OF MOTHER SULTAN

HATİCE TURHAN TÜRBESİ

COFFEE VENDOR

HASIRCILAR GATE

KALMAZ BAHARAT (SPICES)

ÇİÇEK PAZAN SOKAK

SPICE MARKET

GÜLLÜOĞLU BAKLAVA STORE

50 Meters
50 Yards

To Grand Bazaar

OLD TOWN WALK

pistachios and hazelnuts, and sweets of several different kinds—including, of course, Turkish delight. While most Westerners' idea of Turkish delight is colored and fruit-flavored, locals prefer more adventurous varieties: with double-roasted pistachios, or the kind with walnuts in grape or mulberry molasses called *sucuk* (soo-jook; also the name of the spicy veal sausage).

Look for the granddaddy of spices, **saffron.** Locals still use saffron (mostly in rice pilaf and dessert), though not as much as they used to. The best saffron is Spanish; the local kind—cheaper and not as dark-red—usually comes mixed with other herbs. The **caviar** you see isn't local; it's mostly from Iran or Russia. More authentic are the Turkish dried **apricots** and **figs.** Dried vegetables, eggplant, and green peppers hang from the walls. Cooks use these to make *dolma* (dohl-mah; "to stuff"), stuffing them with rice and raisins, or rice and meat. You'll also see lots of sacks full of green powder. This is **henna,** traditionally used by women as a hair dye and for skin care. In the countryside, young women stain the palms of their hands with henna the night before they get married. Lately all of these old-fashioned shops are being joined by souvenir shops and jewelry stores, making this a mini–Grand Bazaar of sorts.

• *Walk to the far end of the hall, at the intersection with the side wing of the Spice Market (to the left). Straight ahead is a gate leading to an always-busy street that heads five blocks up to the Grand Bazaar; to the right is the Hasırcılar Gate, leading to the alley we just came down.*

Go left and start walking down the side wing—less crowded and less colorful than the main concourse. After a few steps, look for a tiny shop on the left (second from the corner) called **Kalmaz Baharat.** *Baharat* (bah-hah-raht) means "spice," and this is one of the few remaining shops that still sells the exotic spices of the past. Adnan, the owner, has herbal teas, thick aromatic oils, natural-fiber bath gloves, and olive-oil soap (white is better than green). He also sells the aphrodisiac called "sultan's paste" (more recently dubbed "Turkish Viagra"). This mix of several kinds of herbs and exotic spices supposedly gave the sultan the oomph to enjoy his huge harem, and is still used as an all-purpose energy booster today.

Browse your way to the end of this side wing (notice the great Güllüoğlu Baklava store on the right, the third shop before the exit), then head back the way you came.

• *When you're ready to finish this walk, retrace your steps and leave the Spice Market through the main entrance. You'll be facing the Galata Bridge over the Golden Horn, with the New District beyond it. To visit these sights, look to the left for a pedestrian underpass (with an ATM kiosk nearby) that takes you under the busy street to the Galata Bridge. (Notice the many restaurants on the lower level of the bridge; this area is described in our Golden Horn Walk on page 99.)*

To reach the Eminönü tram stop—where you can catch the tram to the right to get to the Old Town (Sultanahmet stop), or left to cross the Galata Bridge to the New District (Karaköy stop)—walk between the New Mosque and the busy street. Where the mosque ends, you'll see the entrance to a pedestrian underpass. Halfway through the underpass, you'll see steps leading up to separate platforms for either direction.

Alternatively, you can generally wave down a cab along the main street right in front of the Spice Market. Or, to walk all the way up to Sultanahmet, turn right, walk with the New Mosque on your left, go straight ahead five blocks to the Sirkeci Train Station, and follow the tram tracks uphill.

GOLDEN HORN WALK

*From the Galata Bridge to
Sirkeci Train Station*

The famous Golden Horn—a strategic inlet branching off the Bosphorus Strait—defines Istanbul's Old Town peninsula. The city's fate has always been tied to this stretch of sea: The Golden Horn is Istanbul's highway, food source, and historic harbor all rolled into one. While much of the Old Town zone feels dedicated to tourists these days, a visit to the Golden Horn has you rubbing elbows with fishermen and commuters.

This walk offers a handy orientation to the city, since it affords a sweeping panorama of the Old Town peninsula. Because it's near the terminals for the various Bosphorus ferries, this walk also works well either before or after a cruise of the strait (see Bosphorus Cruise Tour chapter on page 249). The walk is short (about a third of a mile), but allow around 45 minutes if you like to linger.

Getting to the Galata Bridge
The walk begins on the New District (north) end of the Galata Bridge, across the bridge from the Old Town.

From the Old Town: Take the tram (direction Kabataş) to the Karaköy neighborhood. Get off at Karaköy, the first stop after you cross the Galata Bridge over the Golden Horn. You want to be on the side of the bridge facing the Bosphorus (to the left, as you face the Golden Horn and Old Town). To get to that point from the tram stop, take the pedestrian underpass—if you get turned around in the poorly marked underground zone, simply do the prairie-dog routine: surface, figure out where you are and where you're going, then burrow your way back down and repeat as necessary until you get to your destination.

From Taksim Square, in the New District: You have two options: Take the funicular down to Kabataş, then take the tram to Karaköy. Or walk (or take the "nostalgic tram," if it's running) down İstiklal street to Tünel, where you can either take the old funicular down to the bottom of the hill, or walk down on Bankalar Caddesi ("Bankers Street"). If you walk along İstiklal street, you can follow our self-guided New District Walk (next chapter).

THE WALK BEGINS

• *Start at the Galata Bridge (at the east side of the north end—see the map in this chapter). If you wind up on the wrong side of the bridge, take the pedestrian underpass (with WC) connecting the two sides. Position yourself on the riverbank, noticing the tulip shapes decorating the railing. With the water at your back, you're facing the neighborhood called...*

Karaköy

The New District covers the area from Karaköy to Taksim Square, a few blocks up the hill. In Byzantine times, this area was inhabited by the commercial colonies of Genoese and Venetian settlers. In the late Ottoman era, it was also a residential area for non-Muslims, including Jews, Catholics, and Eastern Orthodox Christians. Today, this part of the city is dominated by the famous Galata Tower (you can just see its cone-shaped top up the hill).

Karaköy is also Istanbul's main passenger port. As you turn and face the Old Town across the Golden Horn, you'll see public ferry and seabus ports along the embankment to your left. The port is the scene of an extensive rebuilding project, as run-down buildings make way for art galleries and convention centers. A deluxe hotel is also planned. Locals grumble about political connections that made the project possible, but it's too late to go back now.

• *Notice that the bridge has two levels. We'll start by walking across the top level, then duck down to the lower level. Climb the stairs and wander across the bridge—dodging fishing poles as you walk.*

Fishermen

Enjoy the chorus line of fishing rods, dancing their little jig. While some of these intrepid folks are fishing for fun, others are trying to land a little extra income. They mostly catch mackerel or anchovies—better than nothing, especially during the commercial fishing ban (no nets or sonar) from June to September. During the ban, most of what you find in the market is the

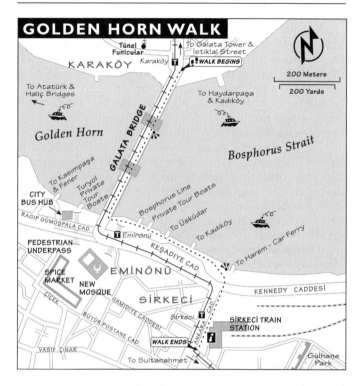

GOLDEN HORN WALK

expensive daily catch, imported frozen fish, or farm-raised fish.

Approach a fisherman and wish him well, saying *"Rastgele"* (pull your lips to your ears and say "rust-geh-leh"; "May you catch some"). Ask to see his catch of the day: *Bakabilir miyim?* (bah-kah-bee-leer mee-yeem; "May I see?"). Each one has a jar, jug, bucket, or Styrofoam cooler full of wriggling fish he'd love to show off. If you're having fun with the language, try this: Point to someone's bucket of tiny fish and ask playfully, *"Yem mi, yemek mi?"* (yehm mee yeh-mehk mee; "Is that bait or dinner?").

Be careful as you walk among the fishermen—occasionally they get careless as they swing back for a cast.

• *The part of the bridge between its two low-profile towers can be raised to let big ships pass. This is a good place to find a spot out of harm's way and ponder the famous...*

Golden Horn (Haliç)

This four-mile-long horn-shaped inlet glitters like precious metal at sunset. But its strategic value is also worth its weight in gold. Protected from the prevailing north winds, the Golden Horn has served as a natural harbor for centuries—it's steeped in the history of Istanbul.

This was once the main commercial port of Constantinople, and a base for the Byzantine fleet. To block enemy fleets sailing into the heart of the city, and to more effectively levy taxes on ships, the Byzantines hung a massive chain across the entrance of the Horn (you can see some of the historic links in the Istanbul Archaeological Museum—see page 168). The chain was breached only a couple times, by the Vikings (10th century), and by the Crusaders during the Fourth Crusade (1204).

In 1453, when the young Ottoman sultan Mehmet set out to capture Constantinople, he knew it was crucial to gain control of the Horn. Rather than breaking the chain, he decided to bypass it altogether. His troops pulled their fleet of ships out of the waters of the Bosphorus, slid them on greased logs over the hills through what later became the New District, and launched them back into the Horn—all in just one night.

During Europe's Industrial Revolution, the Ottoman Empire was slow to adapt to a fast-changing world. It began the industrial race when it was already too late, then rushed to catch up, often without careful planning. The Horn became more and more polluted as industrial plants and shipyards were built along its banks.

In the 1980s, a clever Istanbul mayor used a great gimmick to clean things up: He had light blue eyes, so he got people on board by saying his project would make the Horn as blue as his eyes. Factories were closed down and moved outside the city. Rotting buildings along the water with no historic significance were torn down, and empty space was converted into public parks. The area's entire infrastructure was renewed—a process that's still ongoing.

• *Now look inland over the tram tracks and up the Golden Horn (with your back to the Bosphorus), to see the...*

Bridges over the Horn

Four bridges connect the Old Town to the New District over the Golden Horn. The first one you see is the low-lying Atatürk Bridge, on floating plat-forms. Beyond that is the taller main highway bridge, called Haliç (hah-leech)—which is also the local name for the Golden Horn.

The old Galata Bridge was the first and, for decades, the only bridge spanning the Horn—it's the one you see in historic postcards from Istanbul. But the huge platforms it was built on blocked water circulation, worsening the Horn's pollution woes. So, in 1994, this historic bridge was replaced with the new Galata Bridge—the one you're standing on. A public outcry of nostalgia eventually compelled city leaders to reassemble the original bridge farther down the Horn (between the Atatürk and Haliç bridges—not visible from here).

• *Now take in the...*

Old Town Panorama

Use this sweeping vista of the Old Town to get your bearings. Straight ahead from the end of the bridge, you can see the main entrance to the famous **Spice Market** (stone-and-brick building with three small domes), which sells souvenirs, caviar, dried fruits, Turkish delight, "Turkish Viagra"...and, oh yeah, spices. (For more information, see page 96.)

The handsome mosque just to the left of the Spice Market (partly obscured by the bridge tower) is the New Mosque of Mother Sultan, or simply the **New Mosque.** Dating from the 17th century, it's one of the last examples of classical-style Ottoman mosques. After that time, mosques were built in an eclectic style, heavily influenced by Western architecture.

Behind the Spice Market, twisty streets lined with market stalls wind their way up the hill toward the famous **Grand Bazaar.** While the Spice Market and Grand Bazaar are increasingly deluged with tourists, this in-between zone sells more housewares and everyday textiles than souvenirs—meaning that it's packed tight with locals looking for a bargain, particularly on Saturdays. Thanks to these crowds—and a steady stream of delivery trucks and carts blocking the streets—it can take a half-hour to walk just these four blocks. This is the "real" Istanbul—gritty and authentic. For a longer and more interesting route between these shopping zones, see our Old Town Back Streets Walk on page 87.

Farther to the right, past the open space and near the river, you see the **Rüstem Paşa Mosque.** This tiny mosque, with its single dome and lone minaret, is dwarfed by the larger mosques around it. But a visit there offers a peek into a more intimate and cozy mosque, with some of the finest 16th-century Ottoman tiles around (covered on page 93 in the Old Town Back Streets Walk).

On the hillside just above the Rüstem Paşa Mosque is the 16th-century **Mosque of Süleyman the Magnificent,** with its handsome dome and four tall minarets (see page 218). Elaborate and impressive, yet tastefully restrained, this mosque offers an insightful contrast to the over-the-top and more famous Blue Mosque.

To the left of Süleyman's mosque is the single, tall **Beyazıt Tower.** Sometimes referred to as the "fire tower," it marks the location of bustling Beyazıt Square and Istanbul University's main campus (next door to the Grand Bazaar).

Now look to your left. At the end of the Historical Peninsula, you can see the lush gardens marking the grounds of **Topkapı Palace.** Most of what you see from here is the palace's lower gardens, called Gülhane, now a public park. You can also see the tower marking the entrance to the Harem complex (described on page 160).

To the right of the palace (up the hill, above the modern buildings), notice the gorgeous dome and minarets of **Hagia Sophia**— once the greatest church in Byzantium, then a mosque, and today one of Istanbul's best museums. The famous **Blue Mosque,** which faces Hagia Sophia from across Sultanahmet Park, is not quite visible from here. These sights are covered by the Historic Core of Istanbul Walk on page 72.

If you look far to the left, beyond the Topkapı Palace gardens, you can see the Bosphorus Strait and **Asian Istanbul** (the hilltop that bristles with TV towers, like a sea of giant minarets). The Bosphorus Bridge, an impressive suspension bridge, is visible from here (unless it's really hazy).

• *Continue along the bridge to the second tower. Go inside the tower and take the stairs down...*

Under the Bridge

As you descend the stairs, look up for a fun view of dozens of fishing rods twitching along the railing of the bridge. As you walk down here, watch your head—sometimes an amateur fisherman carelessly lets his weight swing under. And keep an eye out for the flicker of a little silvery fish, thrashing through the air as he's reeled in by a happy predator.

Walk along the bridge (toward the Old Town), enjoying this "restaurant row." Passages lead to the other side of the bridge, which is lined with still more restaurants. As you walk, aggressive waiters will try to lure you into their restaurants. Don't be shy— look around, get into a conversation, and compare prices. You may end up here tonight for a fish dinner (or better yet, on the other side of the bridge, where you can  watch the sun set over the Golden Horn). Even if you don't want a full meal, consider picking up a sandwich or having a drink at a café. The last restaurant, with dozens of simple brown tables, sells barbecued fish sandwiches to go—handy to eat as you walk (you'll smell the outdoor barbecue before you see it). If you cross under, you'll find a line of trendy teahouses and bars facing up the Golden Horn—great for backgammon, drinks, and sunsets. At the end of the bridge on the Old Town side, venerable "fish and bread" boats sell cheap fish sandwiches literally off the boat.

• *At the end of the bridge, turn left and continue along the...*

Commuter Ferry Ports

This embankment bustles with thousands of commuters heading to and from work (during morning and evening rush hours) and shopping chores (especially Saturdays). Peek into the pedestrian underpass beneath the bridge for a taste of the shoulder-to-shoulder commute that many locals endure.

This area is also a hub for intercontinental traffic. Public ferries carry millions of commuters every year between the European and Asian districts of Istanbul. Until the first bridge over the Bosphorus was built in the early 1970s, boats were the only way to cross from Europe to Asia. Locals still prefer the ferries, which are a convenient and cheap (about $1 one-way) way to avoid the gridlock on the bridges.

The first terminal, **Boğaz İskelesi** (boh-ahz ees-keh-leh-see), is for the Bosphorus lines. This is where you can catch a public ferry for a cruise up the Bosphorus (17.50 YTL round-trip, allow 5.5 to 7 hrs with a stop at a small Asian fishing village, seasonal schedule and full route described in the Bosphorus Cruise Tour chapter on page 249).

Just beyond is the dock for **private tour boats** (look for the *Bosphorus Tours* sign). For only 7.50 YTL (hawkers ask more), these boats take you as far as the second bridge on the Bosphorus and back again in 90 minutes. Ignore the posted schedule—boats leave when they fill up, so just hop on board whenever you're ready. While we prefer taking a public ferry for our Bosphorus cruise (see above), these tour boats—which don't go as far up the strait, and don't make any stops—are a faster option if you're pressed for time and just want a taste of the strait.

The next terminal is **Üsküdar İskelesi,** a dock with boats heading to Üsküdar, an important commercial district on the

Asian side (1.40 YTL one-way, 20 min; 2–4/hr in rush hour). It's followed by **Kadıköy İskelesi,** with boats heading to Asian Istanbul's commercial hub, the busy Kadıköy district (1.40 YTL one-way, 25 min; every 30 min, more frequent during rush hour; rush-hour service via the Haydarpaşa Garı train station, near Kadıköy, takes a little longer).

From this vantage point, you can assess how crowded with tourists Istanbul is at the moment. The cruise-ship port is just opposite (at the New District harbor). Big boats routinely unload several thousand tourists apiece. If three ships are in port, more than 6,000 tourists are inundating the city's top three sights: the Blue Mosque, Hagia Sophia, and Topkapı Palace.

The last terminal is for the car ferry to **Harem**—not a place with sultans' wives, but the major commercial harbor in Asian Istanbul (near Üsküdar). Harem is a handy shortcut to the Asian side—and it's definitely the cheapest intercontinental crossing for cars (1.40 YTL one-way for passengers, 30 min; every 30 min).

• *When you spot the Harem ferry, it's time to head inland. For a nice panorama over the Galata Bridge and the New District, you could climb the pedestrian overpass. But for where we're going next, it's better to cross the street at the stoplight so you stay on the proper side of the tram tracks.*

After you cross the street, you're in the Sirkeci neighborhood, and a few steps from the historic train station of the same name.

Sirkeci Train Station

This is a surprisingly low-profile train station for having once been the terminal of the much-vaunted Orient Express. An old loco-

motive decorates the corner of the station, honoring this footnote in history. Pass the locomotive and turn left, finding your way to the station's main entrance (along the modern wall with the white doors, under the sign for *İstanbul Gar*). Once inside the door, a TI and well-signed ticket windows are to your left—and a statue of Atatürk is staring down at you from the head of the tracks.

Wander deeper into the station, past the ticket windows, and go left to find evidence of a more genteel, earlier age. Consider poking into the humble little **Railway Museum,** with its old photos and equipment (free, Tue–Sat 9:00–12:30 & 13:00–17:00, closed Sun–Mon). To the right of the museum is the old passenger waiting room, with wooden benches and stained-glass windows that recall the station's former glory.

The **Orient Express** train line began in the 1880s. You could board a train in Paris, and step off into this very station three days later (after passing through Munich, Vienna, Budapest, and Bucharest). Traversing the mysterious East, and headed for the even more mysterious "Orient," passengers were advised to carry a gun. The train service was re-routed to avoid Germany during the Nazi years, and was temporarily disrupted during both World Wars, but otherwise ran until May of 1977. While this is the most famous route, almost any eastbound train from Western Europe could be called an "Orient Express." The train line was immortalized in literature and film—most famously by Agatha Christie, whose *Murder on the Orient Express* takes place on the Simplon Orient Express (Paris' Gare de Lyon station to Milan, Belgrade, Sofia, and Istanbul).

Though the Orient Express is history, today the Sirkeci station still serves trains bound for Europe, as well as suburban trains (it can get crowded at rush hour). Most of the travelers are urban workers, but you occasionally spot vagabonds or peasants fresh from the countryside, eyes wide as they first set foot in the big city.

• *Your walk is finished. To head back to Sultanahmet, you can take the tram (which departs from directly in front of the station) two stops uphill to the Sultanahmet stop.*

NEW DISTRICT WALK

Taksim Square and İstiklal Street

To fully appreciate the urban Istanbul of today, you must leave the Old Town and plunge into the lively, cosmopolitan, and oh-so-European New District. Start at the vast Taksim Square and stroll the length of teeming İstiklal street (İstiklal Caddesi)—the city's jam-packed main pedestrian drag. Lined with Art Nouveau facades, cafés, restaurants, pubs, bookstores, music shops, art galleries, cinemas, theaters, and a rainbow of shops, İstiklal street is the most cosmopolitan—and most European—part of Istanbul. Pastry shops and restaurants that once served only the upper crust now open their doors to commoners like you and me.

ORIENTATION

Length of This Walk: Allow an hour for the walk...but much longer if you succumb to the many temptations to stop.

Getting There: From the Old Town, ride the tram to Kabataş (the end of the line) and follow the crowds directly into the funicular station (requires a second token). Take the handy little one-stop funicular up to the Taksim Square, and exit following signs for *İstiklal Caddesi*.

Nostalgic Tram: A "nostalgic tram" runs quietly up and down İstiklal street between Taksim Square and Tünel. It's a handy way to quickly skip ahead or backtrack during this walk (covered by a special 0.90 YTL token or use the more expensive tickets or tokens for other Istanbul transit—see page 30).

THE WALK BEGINS

• Begin at Taksim Square, next to the Republic Monument.

Taksim Square

Taksim Square (Taksim Meydanı; tahk-seem may-dah-nuh) is the New District's transportation hub, connected to other parts of

Istanbul by bus, Metro, funicular, and "nostalgic tram." Taksim Square also marks the beginning of modern Istanbul's trendiest business and residential neighborhoods, which stretch in the direction of the big park behind the line of buses.

At the top of Taksim Square is the big, black, blocky **Atatürk Cultural Center,** the setting for classical music concerts, opera, and ballet performances (generally late fall through early spring). Events are usually state-subsidized, so tickets are dirt cheap (drop by to check schedules or to buy tickets—for details, see the Entertainment chapter).

• In the center of the traffic circle opposite, check out the...

Republic Monument (Cumhuriyet Anıtı)

This patriotic monument was unveiled in 1928 and commemorates the fifth anniversary of the founding of the Turkish Republic.

When the government ran out of money to fund the project, the people of Turkey reached into their pockets to finish it.

The monument shows the two sides of Atatürk, the father of modern Turkey (see sidebar on page 112). On one side, he's wearing his military uniform, as the hero of the War of Independence. On the flip side, civilian Atatürk is modern Turkey's first president, surrounded by figures representing the proclamation of the Republic. The other two sides—with soldiers and waving flags—symbolize victory.

• From Taksim Square, the "nostalgic tram" loops around the monument and runs the length of İstiklal street. That's precisely the course we'll walk: from the Republic Monument to the end of İstiklal street (and the top of the Tünel funicular, which leads down to Galata Bridge). Let's start at the top of...

NEW DISTRICT WALK

İstiklal Street

İstiklal Caddesi (ees-teek-lahl jahd-deh-see; "Independence Street") was born after a devastating 1870 fire. The Ottoman government took the opportunity to rebuild the area as a showpiece of Art Nouveau style.

Immersed in the crowds that enliven this boulevard, stand still for a moment just to watch the river of people. İstiklal street is today's Turkey. Where is everyone going? Just "out." Are they Turkish? Yes. Nine out of every ten people you see on this paseo are Turks—modern Turkey is a melting pot of 20-some different ethnic groups. Observe the haircuts and fashions as everyone from teenagers to businesspeople make the scene. Stop and talk with someone in this living celebration of diversity.

From here, this walk goes gradually downhill. Along the way, cafés and eateries offer second-floor refuges from the crowds, and fine vantage points from which to view the scene below. To make the route super-simple to follow, we've posted handy red-metal numbered plates on the buildings, and keyed them to this book's

NEW DISTRICT WALK

1. Taksim Square & Republic Monument
2. İstiklal Street
3. Water Fountain
4. Aya Triada Greek Orthodox Church
5. Ali Muhittin Hacı Bekir Sweet Shop
6. Rumeli Han Shopping Market
7. Alkazar Theater
8. Flower Passage
9. Fish Market & Şampiyon Kokoreç Fast Food
10. Mado Café
11. Former Post Office
12. Galatasaray High School
13. 50th Anniversary Monument
14. Rejans Russian Restaurant
15. St. Anthony's Roman Catholic Church
16. Pera Museum
17. Istanbul Bookstore
18. Dutch Consulate
19. Historic Markiz Café
20. Tünel Square
21. Galata Dervish Monastery

walk (ignore the old blue plaques). Simply follow the tram tracks and match the numbers with this text (odd numbers on left, even on right).

Thronged with people, İstiklal street is no fun for claustrophobes. (The crowds can be so thick that occasionally the tram simply cannot run.) When the street is jammed, it's easier to go with the flow by sticking to the right, as local strollers do.

• *Start out at the...*

Top of İstiklal Street: Food Corner

This first corner has long been a fast-food stop. Fresh-squeezed orange juice and newly sliced *döner kebab* are traditional favorites, but American fast-food joints are just as common these days.

• *A few steps down, take a closer look at a truly local fast-food place...*

Simit Sarayı (at #3)

A *simit* (see-meet) is sort of like a bagel: bread dough dipped in *pekmez* (grape molasses), rolled in sesame seeds, then baked. You'll

NEW DISTRICT WALK

Mustafa Kemal Atatürk
(1881–1938)

Atatürk, the George Washington of the Turks, almost single-handedly created modern-day Turkey. As the map of Europe was being redrawn at the end of World War I, this confident war hero put forth a clear and complete vision that persuaded the Turks, on the brink of crisis, to forge a modern nation.

By the early 20th century, the Turkish people were in dire straits. After centuries of decline, the Ottoman Empire—known as the "Sick Man of Europe"—allied itself with Germany and was pulled into World War I. But even as the Ottoman Empire floundered, a wily officer named Mustafa Kemal proved his military mettle, successfully defending Gallipoli with a handful of poorly equipped soldiers against a huge armada.

As the war came to an end, victorious European armies occupied Istanbul and made plans to dole out pieces of the former Ottoman Empire to their allies. In 1919, the Greeks took the city of İzmir (on the south coast of Turkey) and began pushing toward Istanbul. With lightning speed, the war hero Kemal gathered an army to defend Turkish territory. Over a three-year period (the Turkish War of Independence), he chased out French and Italian troops and repelled the Greek invasion. With the Treaty of Lausanne in 1923, the Ottoman Empire was history, the Turkish Republic was born, and Mustafa Kemal became the most beloved Turkish leader in centuries. The National Assembly

see street vendors with old-fashioned carts selling these sesame-seed bread rings all over town (a filling snack for 0.50 YTL). The popular Simit Sarayı (see-meet sah-rah-yuh) chain has all of Istanbul munching on its sesame-seed-bread-ring sandwiches of cheese, sausages, and olives.

• *Across the street from #3 is a...*

Water Fountain

This water fountain is a physical reminder that "Taksim" means "distribution," and that this square was once part of the town's water system. A new **Museum of the Republic,** telling the stirring story of Atatürk's charismatic leadership and the birth of the modern Turkish nation, is expected to open here in 2010.

elected Mustafa Kemal as the first President of the Republic, and dubbed him Atatürk. Translated literally, Atatürk means "father of the Turks"; in this context, it stands for "great leader," or "grand Turk."

Rescuing his nation from the chopping block would have been enough, but Atatürk was not finished. He envisioned a modern, progressive Turkey that would eschew the outmoded values of the Ottoman Empire in favor of a European-style democracy. Rarely in history has anyone exerted such power with such effect in so short a time. In less than 10 years, Atatürk...

- aligned Turkey with the West;
- separated religion and state (by removing Islam as the state religion and upholding civil law over Islamic law);
- adopted the Western calendar;
- decreed that Turks should have surnames, similar to Western custom;
- changed the alphabet from Arabic script to Roman letters;
- distanced Turkey from the corrupt Ottoman Empire by abolishing the sultanate and caliphate, and outlawing the fez and veil;
- abolished polygamy; and
- emancipated women (by comparison, Swiss women didn't receive the right to vote until 1971).

Atatürk died at 9:05 on November 10, 1938—and every year, all of Turkey still observes a minute of silence at 9:05 on that day to honor the man they regard as the greatest Turk. For a generation, many young Turkish women actually worried that they'd never be able to really love a man because of their love for the father of their country. Because of Atatürk, millions of Turks today have a flag—and reason to wave it.

Coffee Wars: Gloria Jean's (at #17), Starbucks, and Kahve Dünyası

The green mermaid has arrived. Since Turks already love coffee (heck, they claim to have invented it), Turkey is an appealing market. Australia's Gloria Jean's was the first modern coffee shop to hit Istanbul, with Starbucks close behind. The local Kahve Dünyası ("Coffee World") boldly challenges the big chains by selling coffee at a fraction of the price.

Across the street (opposite #13–39) is the **French Consulate.** As this was the most European-friendly district during Ottoman times, many European consulates and churches were located in this district (see sidebar on page 115).

Avea Wireless Shop (at #41)

Mobile phone shops have popped up like mushrooms across Turkey in the last decade. Avea is one of the three wireless operators in Turkey (along with Turkcell and Vodafone). The fast-growing Turkish telecommunications market was worth an estimated $25 billion in 2007. There are now 50 million mobile phone users in Turkey. Two out of three Turks have a cell phone, even though mobile calls are relatively expensive. As elsewhere in Europe, text messaging is popular.

Urban Turks are technophiles—they want the latest and greatest, spending billions of dollars every year for new-generation mobile phones. The average user keeps his phone less than two years before upgrading—making Turkey the world leader in secondhand mobile phone sales.

• *Across from the French Consulate, half a block up the alley (Meşelik Sokak) and on the left, is...*

Aya Triada Greek Orthodox Church

Aya Triada—or, as the locals call it, the Grand Church—is the

largest active Orthodox church in town. While it's often closed, the guard will usually let you in (for a donation to the church-offering box). Built in the Neo-Gothic style in 1880, the church has some interesting flourishes, such as the delicate paintings that line the sanctuary walls. Also enjoy the colorful frescoes and Baroque-style decorations on the ceiling and dome. This is the first of many Christian churches we'll see along the walk today—constant reminders that historically, this was one of the most diverse, cosmopolitan areas of Istanbul.

• *Head back out to İstiklal street and continue our walk.*

Megavision Music Store (at #57)

Pop music is becoming ever more popular among young Turks, with new stars seeming to crop up every day. You'll see their posters decorating music-store showcases and billboards. As in many countries, music and book piracy are problems in Turkey. The rumor is that pirated CDs sell better than the real thing—so music companies are now selling their own versions "under the counter."

As you explore İstiklal street, note the many flagship stores like this one. If something sells here, it is likely to sell in the rest of the country.

NEW DISTRICT WALK

In Istanbul, North Is "West"

The New District was once called Pera (peh-rah; "The Side Across"). Many locals still use this term, which dates from the Middle Ages. When Constantinople's Orthodox Christians clashed with its minority Roman Catholics, the Catholics moved outside the city walls—to "The Side Across," north of the Golden Horn. Ever since, the northern part of Istanbul (the New District) has looked west to Europe, while the southern part (the Old Town) identifies more with the East.

During the Fourth Crusade in 1204, the gap between Constantinople's Orthodox and Catholic populations widened. The Crusaders stayed here for half a century, establishing relations with Venetian and Genoese merchants, who dominated world trade. For political and economic reasons, the emperors reluctantly gave up their claim to "The Side Across," offering it to the Genoese as a self-governing commercial base.

When the Ottomans conquered Constantinople in the 15th century, the Genoese immediately recognized the rule of the young Ottoman sultan. In return, they were granted privileges and commercial rights that would last for centuries.

As the Ottoman Empire became a more powerful player on Europe's political stage, "The Side Across" became a home base for visiting envoys and ambassadors. Genoa, France, Spain, England, Holland, and many of Europe's other great powers built embassies here. Beginning in the 16th century, these embassies became deeply involved in business interests. Foreign merchants wanted to live near their embassies, turning "The Side Across" into a particularly desirable and genteel corner of the city. Schools, churches, and communal buildings were built to meet the needs of the ever-growing expatriate population. Soon İstiklal street became known as the Grand Rue de Pera, and the district became a "little Europe" within the boundaries of greater Istanbul. This cosmopolitan area also began to draw the city's other non-Muslim minorities, such as Greeks, Armenians, and Jews.

The mid-19th century was a time of great change. A new bridge over the Golden Horn connected the still very Eastern-feeling Old Town to newer, European-style neighborhoods in the north. Tired of being viewed as backward by his European contemporaries, the sultan moved out of the historic, Oriental-style Topkapı Palace and into the new, Western-style Dolmabahçe Palace in the New District (on the Bosphorus—see page 54).

The ties between "The Side Across" and Europe are still palpable today. Strolling down the very European-feeling İstiklal street, tourists sometimes forget they're just a short boat trip from Asia. Like the Genoese merchants, ambassadors, and clever sultans before them, today's visitors are figuring out that here in Istanbul, you go north to find the West.

NBA Store (part of the Adidas Store, at #59)

American professional basketball is hugely popular in Istanbul. This is the first NBA store to open anywhere outside the US. In 2000, Hidayet "Hido (hee-doh)" Türkoğlu became the first Turkish-born player in NBA history. Following Türkoğlu's footsteps, Mehmet Okur played for the 2004 NBA champion Detroit Pistons, and became the first Turk to play in an All-Star game (other Turkish NBA stars include Ersan İlyasova and Cenk Akyol). In 2006, the NBA began actively promoting the sport in Europe, including Italy, Spain, Britain...and Turkey. Turks have a hunch that the NBA could expand its league to Europe in the future.

State Lottery Agent (at #71)

Private casinos and gambling were made illegal in Turkey a few years ago after authorities discovered they were used for money laundering. (When the tax office would ask someone shady about a sudden, huge influx of cash, the predictable answer was "I won it gambling.") So the nationwide lottery is hugely popular, with prizes in the millions of dollars. The lottery and all other legal betting opportunities in Turkey are run by the government (except horse races; your bet on a winning horse is handled by a private broker). Also popular are the *kazi kazan* (scratch-to-win) cards and "İddia" (eed-dee-ah; literally "to bet"), a lottery game in which players bet on Turkish and European soccer scores. Conservative Muslims continue to debate the morality of state-organized betting games.

Ali Muhittin Hacı Bekir (at #83)

Turkish delight (*lokum* in Turkish; loh-koom) is a sweet, flavorful cube of gooey gelatin dusted with powdered sugar, sometimes embedded with nuts. Turkish kids cheer when their parents bring home a box of *lokum*—and Hacı Bekir's is the best there is. Browse their selection; the *lokum* comes in boxes of all shapes and sizes, packed with many different flavors and add-ins (pistachios are favorites). Their almond paste, hard candies, and *helva* (a sesame oil and tahini treat) are also good. Prices are by the kilogram—buy a small amount to taste. About 2 YTL will buy you 50 grams, about five pieces of Turkish delight. For an assortment, ask for *karışık* (kah-ruh-shuhk) *lokum*. Or pay 3 YTL to get the same amount of double-roasted pistachio *lokum* (the real stuff).

Rumeli Han (at #48)

Notice the eclectic decorations on the entrance to this old shopping market—Greek Ionic columns, lions' heads, Arabic script, and more. The *han* (a combo marketplace and inn for merchants) was built in the 1870s for the sultan by the same architects who designed Dolmabahçe Palace (see page 54). Later it became a commercial complex with shops, cafés, art studios, and office space on the upper floors. It's hard to tell from here, but this huge complex takes up about a third of the block.

• *Continue down İstiklal street, passing the 16th-century Hüseyin Ağa Mosque (the only mosque on the street) to your right. You'll soon come to the...*

Alkazar Theater (Alkazar Sineması, at #111)

This narrow storefront—with a fancy pseudo-arch supported by little statues on pedestals—hides one of the first movie theaters built in Istanbul, dating from just after World War I. In those first years of the early Republic, it was a gathering place for the aristocracy. Later, when cinema fell out of fashion and other theaters closed down, this one kept its doors open. In the 1970s and 1980s, the only way it could pay the bills was to show erotic films. Today, with the Turkish film industry on the upswing—thanks to bigger-budget attractions, foreign films, and the buzz created by Istanbul's International Film Festival—this theater shows European arthouse films. Movies are generally played in their original language with Turkish subtitles (10–15 YTL).

Garanti Art Gallery (at #115) and the Art Gallery Scene

Several art galleries have recently opened on İstiklal street and nearby. These galleries, primarily sponsored by banks, display permanent and temporary exhibitions of both well-established artists and rising stars in the art world. This is a good opportunity to check out Turkey's often-overlooked contemporary art scene (most galleries are free to enter).

Yeşilçam, the Turkish Hollywood (across from #115)

Look down the first street to the right. This alley, called Yeşilçam (yeh-sheel-chahm; "Green Pine"), was once the heart of the film industry—the "Turkish Hollywood." While the actors, directors, and producers have moved on to other parts of town, "Yeşilçam"

The Turkish Flag

While the modern Turkish Republic was founded only in 1923, its heritage is much older. Today's flag is very similar to the design used by the Ottomans for centuries, often with a red or green background. All were decorated with a crescent moon (and sometimes a verse from the Quran) as a symbol of Islam. Under Ottoman Sultan Selim III (1789–1807), an eight-point star was added to the flag. That star was replaced with today's five-point version some 150 years

later. The design and exact proportions of the Turkish flag were standardized by law in 1937.

The red color of the flag is said to represent the blood that was shed to create the Turkish nation. The crescent and star are the subject of a curious legend. Following the Ottoman victory at the Battle of Kosovo, the Sultan Murat I was killed by a Serbian captive. The legend says that the crescent moon and a star were seen reflected in a pool of Turkish blood at the scene—inspiring the design for the flag. Interestingly, the date of the battle (July 28, 1389) actually was a night when Jupiter and the moon were side by side in the night sky over this part of the world. So it is possible that someone could have seen a reflection that matches the moon and the star on the Turkish flag.

is still the nickname for the local film industry—and in Turkey, filmmaking is all about making a good movie on a small budget.

Traditional Food at Otantik (at #80A)

In the window of this recommended restaurant, a woman prepares and bakes *gözleme* (gohz-leh-meh) in the traditional way. *Gözleme* is thin, flat bread rolled with a rolling pin, folded over the ingredients (such as cheese, potatoes, and spinach), and baked. It's simple, delicious...and a good quick snack midway along this walk. Pick the ingredients (4–8 YTL depending on fillings). To get it wrapped to go, say, "*Paket, lütfen*" (pah-keht lewt-fehn).

Flower Passage (Çiçek Pasajı, at #80)

The original Flower Passage was built in the Neo-Baroque style in the 1870s. Until the 1940s, it was filled only with actual flower shops. Then, over time, lively pubs and taverns began to sprout inside. It became a gathering place for writers, newspaper correspondents, students, and intellectuals sitting around beer-barrel tables.

But in 1978, a century after it was built, the Flower Passage collapsed due to lack of maintenance. It remained in ruins for a decade until the city decided to rebuild it. What you're looking at is a nostalgic reproduction of a place that's long gone. While some people enjoy the new version (and travel writers who pen guidebooks seem to love it), most locals are skeptical. Part of the original Flower Passage's charm was its casual, spontaneous atmo-

sphere—nothing like the white-tablecloth uniformity of today's incarnation.

Fish Market (next to Flower Passage)

A wrought-iron arch with a plaque in the center decorates the alley entrance to the Fish Market (Balık Pazarı; bah-luhk pah-zah-ruh).

True to its name, this is *the* place in the New District to shop for fresh fish. But you'll find other uniquely Turkish taste treats here, too.

A few steps into the alley, notice **Şampiyon Kokoreç** on the left. *Kokoreç* (koh-koh-retch; sounds—but doesn't taste like—"cockroach") is chopped-up sheep intestines, grilled and served with tomatoes, green peppers, and fresh seasonings and herbs.

You can get *kokoreç* by itself on a plate, or in a sandwich. Ask for a stand-alone *porsiyon* (pohr-see-yohn), a half-sandwich (*yarım*; yah-ruhm), or a quarter-sandwich (*çeyrek*; chey-rehk). Try the *çeyrek* first, to be sure you like it, before digging into a *porsiyon*. To enhance the flavor, doll up your sandwich with the hot peppers in the jars.

As you munch, ponder how seriously Turks take their *kokoreç*. Recently a rumor flew through the streets that stringent new EU regulations would outlaw the beloved *kokoreç*. Before the story was proved untrue, many Turks did some soul-searching and decided that if they had to choose, they'd gladly give up EU membership for *kokoreç*.

As you wander along the fish stalls and tiny shops selling herbs, dried fruits, and nuts, you're seeing the reality of workaday Istanbul. About halfway down the alley on the right, a narrow door leads into the courtyard of the Holy Trinity Armenian

Orthodox Church (also known as the Armenian Church of the Three Altars, or Surp Yerrortutyan). Just beyond (also on the right) is the intersection with the street called Nevizade Sokak, lined with lively, down-to-earth restaurants and *meyhanes* (mehy-hah-nehz; taverns). The ambience here is local, and the service is usually attentive. It's busiest near sunset, when locals stop by after work to chat with friends and have a drink or an extended dinner.

Mado Café (at #88)

This is a local favorite for Turkish-style ice cream. Made with goat's milk and wild orchid pollen, it has a thick, stretchy texture. The café also serves good *börek*

(savory pastries) and traditional Turkish desserts such as baklava. Two scoops of their ice cream over a portion of baklava is a real treat. (There's good seating upstairs.)

Next door to Mado is a fine example of Art Nouveau architecture (though it may be covered with scaffolding for renovation). This building was constructed in 1875 for the Sivajian family. Later on, the Post and Telegraph Administration (PTT) converted it into a central post office. Now the post office has moved out, and it's being turned into a sports museum.

• *Across the street from Mado Café is...*

Galatasaray High School

Set in the middle of a huge garden surrounded by a wall marked with a gigantic ornamental gate, this "Royal School" (Mekteb-i Sultani), founded in 1870, was designed to properly raise and educate a new generation of public servants and officials. Its founders hoped to boost the Westernization of the struggling Ottoman Empire. Classes were taught in Turkish and in French (the lingua franca of Europe at the time). The school's first principal was a visionary Frenchman who pursued a secular curriculum years before this was common in Europe. The secular teaching outraged the Catholic Pope, the Greek Orthodox Patriarch, and the leading Muslim clerics.

As the Ottoman Empire declined, so did the quality of education. Many of the school's teachers were sent to fight in World War I and never returned. In 1917, the year before the war ended, only five students graduated. But after the Turkish Republic was founded, Galatasaray High School's fortunes improved. Today it's one of the best schools in the country, with a primary school, a high school, and a university.

Just past the high school wall is a small square decorated with an abstract **monument** celebrating the 50th anniversary of the Turkish Republic (1923–1973). This is the halfway point of İstiklal street.

İpek Silk Shop (at #120)
In this fine shop, prices are fixed, quality is reliable, and the help is friendly and knowledgeable. Isaac and his staff speak English and are happy to demonstrate the latest in scarf fashion. Ask to see the various ways to wear a scarf, depending on your religious leanings. (For more, see page 307 in the Shopping chapter.)

Koska Helva Shop (at #122)
It's time to taste another delicacy: *helva* (hell-vah). The word *helva* is Arabic and means sweet. Today, several countries claim the original recipe. Turkish *helva* is made of crushed sesame seeds, wheat flour, and sugar. Pistachios, vanilla, or cacao is added to create different flavors. *Helva* is also associated with social rituals. For example, when someone dies, loved ones will prepare a certain type of wheat *helva* (without the sesame seeds) and serve it to visitors offering condolences. *Helva* is prepared in large blocks. It costs 10–18 YTL per kilogram. If you go inside this shop and ask for 2 YTL of *karışık* (kah-ruh-shuhk; assorted) *helva*, you'll end up with a mixed bag of about 100 grams (roughly a quarter-pound).
• *A one-block detour off the main drag takes you to a historic little restaurant: Take a right on Emir Nevruz Sokak, and then jog left.*

Rejans Russian Restaurant
After the 1917 Russian Revolution, many of the deposed czar's officers fled to Turkey. For the next 30 years, the New District became an enclave of Russian culture, with Russian restaurants, pubs, music, shows, and dances. Though they had lost the war for their homeland, these Russian transplants spent the rest of their lives pretending they were still living high on the hog in Mother Russia. The locals continued to call them by their former titles: Baron Colonel, Count General, Grand Duke, and so on.

Founded by Russian aristocrats, Rejans (reh-zhahn)—named

for Le Régence Restaurant in Paris—still retains the caviar-and-vodka trappings of that era. Today's owners are proud of the restaurant's heritage, and are eager to share stories of famous patrons (look for Atatürk's photo on the wall). During World War II, German ambassador Franz von Papen dined here frequently. Since Turkey was neutral, Istanbul became a hotbed for under-the-table negotiations and espionage—a Turkish Casablanca. While some Turks think President İsmet İnönü should have entered World War II to regain territory lost in World War I, today most historians agree that his decision to stay neutral helped spare Istanbul (and the rest of the country) from the devastation that swept across Europe.

Oh, yeah—you can eat here, too (see the listing on page 303).

• *Leaving Rejans, the alley named Olivya Geçidi Sokak leads back to İstiklal street. It's lined with people sucking big water pipes* (nargile) *at the Sefa Nargile Café (at #1B, daily 10:00–24:00). (For more on trying out a water pipe, see page 64 in the Experiences chapter.)*

St. Anthony's Roman Catholic Church (between #167 and #173)

Remember that even back in Roman times, today's New District was the place where Western-oriented minorities settled. Franciscan priests built a church here in the 13th century. That church became known as the Hagia Sophia of the Roman Catholic minority in Constantinople (which was then mostly Eastern Orthodox). After that church burned down in the late 17th century, the Franciscans chose to rebuild on this site. The current Neo-Gothic building, with a particularly impressive facade, dates from 1912. St. Anthony's still serves an active Roman Catholic congregation with weekly Mass, and the Christmas service here has become a major social event in Istanbul, attended by Turkey's jet set (even

many Muslims). If the church is open, feel free to take a quick trip west by popping inside.

• *Now's a good time to side-trip to the worthwhile **Pera Museum** with its displays of Kütahya tiles, Oriental paintings, and ancient weights and measures (described on page 49). To reach the museum, go just past the Gloria Jean's Coffee at #140, then take the pedestrian lane under the tall, brown Odakule office building. The museum is on the left corner at the end of the passage. When you're done with the museum, backtrack to İstiklal street to continue our walk.*

Istanbul Bookstore (at #191)

This bookstore, specializing in books on Istanbul (many in English), is owned and operated by the Greater Istanbul Municipality. You're welcome to grab a chair and flip through some of its delightful titles (open daily 9:00–20:00).

Dutch Consulate (#197) and Union Church of Istanbul

Behind this consulate is the Union Church of Istanbul, which holds English services each Sunday (walk a half-block down Postacılar Sokak, entry on left). The Union Church of Istanbul was founded by American missionaries from the Congregational Church in the 1830s. Soon after, the Dutch ambassador invited the congregation to build a permanent home on the embassy grounds. In the years since, the church has attracted many English-speaking, Protestant worshippers. Unfortunately, the chapel's interior is generally closed except for Sunday services: at 9:30 (contemporary worship in English), at 11:00 (traditional worship in English), and at 13:30 (in both English and Turkish; tel. 0212/244-5212, www.union churchofistanbul.org).

Paşabahçe Glass Store (at #150, across from Dutch Consulate)

Browse here for fine handmade Ottoman-style glassware in the Beykoz and Çeşm-i Bülbül styles. Beykoz glassware is made of transparent or opalescent glass with painted and cut designs, often with gold accents. Çeşm-i Bülbül (also known as "eye of the nightingale") bowls and vases have swirling blue-and-white strips twisted within clear crystal. Paşabahçe is famous for producing fine, traditional Turkish-Ottoman glassware, along with more casual daily ware. For locals, a piece from this store is considered a prestigious treasure. Paşabahçe is owned by Turkey's largest bank, Türkiye İş Bankası (whose largest shareholder is the People's Republic Party, founded by Atatürk).

Historic Markiz Café (at #172A)

Today called "Robert's Coffee," this café is a fancy flashback to the architectural style of the late 19th and early 20th centuries. This historical landmark—with gorgeous Art Nouveau tile paintings—is one of Istanbul's oldest and most famous pastry shops. Step inside to be transported to the Golden Age of İstiklal street—a time when places such as the nearby **Pera Palas Hotel** (of Agatha Christie fame) attracted the rich and famous, rather than gawking backpackers. This venerable pastry shop still gathers crowds on their way to the theater. Try the special peach-flavored tea.

• *Just past the Swedish consulate, the tracks for the "nostalgic tram" bend to the right and arrive at the final stop, marking the end of this walk: the end of the funicular called…*

Tünel

To Istanbul natives, "Tünel" (tew-nehl) refers both to this neighborhood (at the bottom point of İstiklal street), and to the underground train that goes from here to the bank of the Golden Horn, below. Look for the entrance to the Tünel funicular at the terminus of the "nostalgic tram."

In the 19th century, as the Golden Horn became Istanbul's bustling commercial hub, it became clear that the narrow alley connecting İstiklal street to the waterway was too narrow to transport the increasing volume of goods and people. When French engineer Henri Gavand visited and saw 50,000 people walking or riding their horses up and down this hill each day, he decided there must be a better way. Funded by the British government, and approved by the sultan, Gavand spent four years building a tunnel for an underground train.

When finished in 1875, Tünel became the second subterranean train in the world (after London's Tube). The cars were lit by gas lamps, and had no roof or seats, so passengers had to stand. At first the public was uncomfortable traveling underground, so most of the train cars carried goods and livestock. But ultimately the efficiency and ease of the Tünel trip won out. Locals still use this old-fashioned underground funicular to get between İstiklal street and Karaköy (a few blocks down the hill, near the Galata Bridge on the Golden Horn).

At Karaköy, you can catch the main tram line, which connects to the Old Town (Sultanahmet stop) and beyond. Riding the Tünel is covered by normal public-transit tokens and passes (0.90 YTL for a single-ride Tünel token; see "Public Transportation Tokens and Passes" on page 30 in the Orientation chapter). Opposite the Tünel terminus, Tünel Pasajı (passage) is a fun place to celebrate the end of your walk with a drink. It has a festive, cozy atmosphere.

• *Our walk is over. From here, you have several options. You can ride the Tünel funicular down to the Galata Bridge (explained above). Or explore the colorful streets downhill to the Galata Bridge—the left fork (Galip Dede Sokak) leads down to the* **Galata Dervish Monastery** *and the* **Galata Tower** *(both described in the Sights chapter), then goes steeply downhill to the Galata Bridge. Or ride the romantic "nostalgic tram" back to Taksim, along the same street you just explored. Or finally, you can catch a taxi to your next destination (a taxi stand is just beyond the tram terminus).*

HAGIA SOPHIA
TOUR

Aya Sofya

For centuries, it was known as Megalo Ekklesia, the "Great Church" of Constantinople. The Greeks called it Hagia Sophia (eye-ah soh-fee-yah), meaning "Divine Wisdom," an attribute of God. The Turkish version is Aya Sofya. But no matter what you call it, this place—first a church, then a mosque, and now a museum—is one of the most important and impressive structures on the planet.

Emperor Justinian built Hagia Sophia between A.D. 532 and 537. For 900 years, it served as the seat of the Orthodox Patriarch of Constantinople—the "eastern Vatican." Replete with shimmering mosaics and fine marble, Hagia Sophia was the single greatest architectural achievement of the Byzantine Empire.

When the Ottomans took Constantinople in 1453, Sultan Mehmet the Conqueror—impressed with the Great Church's beauty—converted it into an imperial mosque. Hagia Sophia remained Istanbul's most important mosque for five centuries. In the early days of the Turkish Republic (1930s), Hagia Sophia was converted again, this time into a museum. It retains unique elements of both the Byzantine and Ottoman empires and their respective religions, Orthodox Christianity and Islam. In short, Hagia Sophia epitomizes the greatest achievements of both East and West, rolled into one.

ORIENTATION

Cost: 20 YTL covers the entire museum, including the Upper Galleries (although in the future, each part may be covered by a different ticket—ask at the ticket office). Avoid the right-hand ticket window, which is reserved for tour guides with groups (unless the other windows are closed, in which case individuals can use the guide window).

Hours: Tue–Sun 9:00–18:30, off-season until 16:30, closed Mon; temporary exhibits and the Upper Galleries close 30 minutes earlier. Last entry one hour before closing.

Getting There: Hagia Sophia is in the Sultanahmet neighborhood in the heart of the Old Town, facing the Blue Mosque. The main entrance is at the southwest corner of the giant building, across the busy street with the tram tracks. If you arrive by tram, get off at the Sultanahmet stop, and walk a couple of hundred yards downhill along the street with the tram tracks. Cross the street at the traffic light.

Getting In: A crowd generally gathers just before 9:00 outside the ticket office and rushes the doors when they open, so arrive at 9:15 to miss the mob. If you are early and also have the Underground Cistern in your plans, go there first (the cistern is across the street with the tram tracks—described in the Historic Core of Istanbul Walk, page 76). Guided tours often bunch up at Hagia Sophia's security checkpoint and ticket-taker. Be patient—the logjam usually clears quickly.

Information: As you approach Hagia Sophia, loitering tour guides may offer to guide you around for a fee (generally 50 YTL). Thanks to this chapter's self-guided tour, you won't need their help. Once inside, most museum descriptions are in English. Tel. 0212/528-4500.

When to Go: Try to avoid Tuesdays in peak season, when Topkapı Palace is closed and Hagia Sophia is busier.

Length of This Tour: Allow at least an hour for the main floor, and 30 minutes or more for the Upper Galleries.

Security and Baggage: After buying your ticket, but before entering, you'll go through an airport-type security checkpoint. There is no bag check, so you will need to carry your bags with you.

Services: The WC is just before the museum exit. The cafeteria is at the end of the long walkway beyond the ticket-taker, across from the main building entrance. There are two bookshops: one at the interior narthex, and the other at the exit, by the Vestibule of Guards.

Photography: Photography is allowed, but don't use your flash when taking pictures of icons, mosaic panels, or frescoes. English-language signs indicate where you should turn off your flash.

Starring: The finest house of worship in the Christian and Muslim worlds.

BACKGROUND

Hagia Sophia was built over the remains of at least two earlier churches (see page 139). After the second of these churches was destroyed in the Nika riots in A.D. 532, Emperor Justinian I (r.

527–565) wasted no time, immediately putting his plan for Hagia Sophia into action. He asked for the near-impossible: a church with unbelievably grand proportions, a monument that would last for centuries and keep his name alive for future generations.

Justinian appointed two geometricians to do the job: Anthemius from the Aegean town of Tralles and his assistant, Isidore of Miletus. Both knew from the start that this would be a risky project. Making Justinian's vision a reality would involve enormous challenges. But they courageously went forward, creating a masterpiece unlike anything seen before.

More than 7,500 architects, stonemasons, bricklayers, plasterers, sculptors, painters, and mosaic artists worked around the clock for five years to complete Hagia Sophia—and drain the treasury—faster than even the emperor had anticipated. In December of 537, the Great Church of Constantinople held its first service in the presence of Emperor Justinian and the Patriarch of Constantinople.

The church was a huge success story for Justinian, who was understandably satisfied with his achievement. As the story goes, when he stepped inside the church, he exclaimed, "Solomon, I have surpassed you!" In the long history of the empire, the Byzantines would never again construct such a grand edifice, but its design would influence architects for centuries.

Hagia Sophia was a legend even before it was completed. People came from all over to watch the great dome slowly rise above the landscape of the city. It was the first thing merchants saw from approaching ships and caravans. Hagia Sophia soon became a landmark, and continues to hold a special place in the mystical skyline of Istanbul.

The structure served as a church for nearly a millennium. It was the largest domed building in Europe until Brunelleschi built Florence's great dome almost a thousand years later during the Renaissance.

The day the Ottomans captured Constantinople in 1453, Hagia Sophia was converted into a mosque. Most of the functional elements that decorated the church were removed, and its figurative mosaics and frescoes were plastered over in accordance with Islamic custom. Today the interior holds mostly elements from the time when Hagia Sophia was used as a mosque (from 1453 until 1934, when it became a museum).

THE TOUR BEGINS

• *After you pass through security and ticket control, you'll see the official walkway leading straight ahead, toward the main entrance. Instead, we'll take a shortcut for a better entrance route: Turn right, cross the big paved path, and slip past the wooden kiosk toward the giant, ornate, Rococo...*

Fountain

The Ottomans added this fountain in the mid-18th century. Across from the fountain, notice the water taps in the portico by the side of the main building. When Hagia Sophia was a mosque, both of these were used for ablution (ritual cleansing before prayer), as part of Islamic tradition.

• *Enter the museum through its exit door at the far end of this courtyard (to the left). On the pillar before the door (to your right as you face the door, at the corner of the small museum bookstore), notice the Arabic translated into Turkish. According to Muslim tradition, in the seventh century, Muhammad himself predicted that Constantinople (which was then Christian and ruled the Western world at that time) would be conquered and he praised the commander and soldiers as "güzel" (elite or distinguished). Eight centuries later, his prediction came to pass. Now step into this historic place of worship...*

Vestibule of Guards

This entry is named for the imperial guards who waited here for the emperor while he was attending church services. Byzantine emperors used this entryway because of its proximity to the royal palace, which stood where the Blue Mosque is today.

Scholars believe that the entrance's imposing **bronze doors** were brought here sometime after Justinian, from an ancient temple in Antioch. At the top of the flat panel (about eye level on the first door), you can see traces of the silver imperial monograms that were once affixed to the bronze sheeting. Notice that these doors can't open or close—they became stuck in place when the marble floor was renovated and raised.

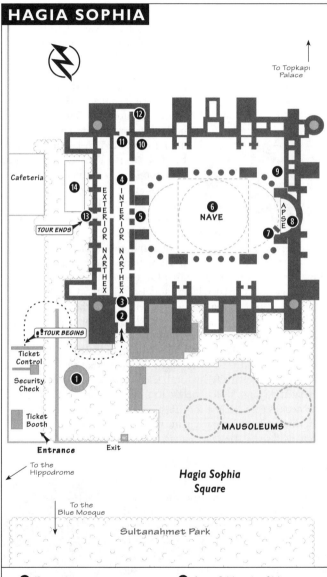

HAGIA SOPHIA

To Topkapı Palace

Cafeteria

14

EXTERIOR NARTHEX

INTERIOR NARTHEX

12
11 **10**

4
5

6
NAVE

9

APSE
8
7

13
TOUR ENDS

3
2
TOUR BEGINS

Ticket Control

Security Check

1

Ticket Booth

MAUSOLEUMS

Entrance   Exit

To the Hippodrome

Hagia Sophia Square

To the Blue Mosque

Sultanahmet Park

1 Fountain
2 Vestibule of Guards
3 Donation Mosaic
4 Interior Narthex
5 Imperial Gate & Mosaic of Christ with Emperor Leo VI
6 Great Dome
7 Mimber

8 Apse & Mosaic of Mary and the Christ Child
9 Sultan's Loge
10 Column of St. Gregory
11 Doorway to Upper Galleries
12 Ramp to Upper Galleries
13 Main Entrance/Exit
14 Ruins of Theodosian Church

Stepping inside the vestibule, look up: The vaulted ceiling is covered with original mosaics, dating back nearly 1,500 years to

Justinian's time. The mosaics in his church—such as these—depicted geometric patterns rather than people, as was the fashion at the time. Later, figurative mosaics were also added. Above the doorway into the church, notice the gorgeous **donation mosaic,** dating from the 11th-century reign of Basil II. Scenes such as this became common in later Orthodox churches, and usually depict the patron who funded the church's construction and to whom the church is dedicated. In

the mosaic, you see Mary and the Christ child enthroned. Jesus holds the Gospels in his left hand, and makes the three-fingered sign of the Trinity with his right hand. Two mighty Roman emperors flank the Holy Family: On the right, Constantine presents Mary and Christ with a model of his city, Constantinople (symbolized by city walls). On the left is Justinian, presenting a model of his greatest achievement, Hagia Sophia. Note the differences between this model and today's Hagia Sophia: Justinian's version had no minarets, and no retaining or garden walls, and its dome was topped with a cross. It's fortunate that this mosaic has survived so beautifully intact, because many such mosaics were destroyed during the Iconoclast Era (see sidebar on next page). If your neck is sore, or just for fun, turn 180 degrees, block the light with this book, and see the same mosaic more comfortably.

• *Now walk under the donation mosaic, and straight into the...*

Interior Narthex

Hagia Sophia's interior narthex is an attractive space, with nine vaulted bays richly decorated with mosaics. The walls on either side are lined with inch-thick **marble panels,** which were glued to the wall with stucco and pinned with iron rods. In some parts of the building, such as the Vestibule of Guards, the iron rusted and over time the marble pieces began to fall off (the Vestibule of Guards' walls are painted to replicate the original marble covering). But here in the interior narthex, which is more protected from the elements, after 15 centuries, the panels hang on.

The Iconoclast Era (A.D. 730-840): The Banning of Icons

Throughout Byzantine history, church and political leaders clashed over the use of icons—depictions of human figures in mosaics, frescoes, and other art forms. In the empire's early stages, Church fathers opposed the images, but the public liked them. So did the emperors, who used icons to bolster their claim to divine power—often depicting themselves as holy figures on coins and church walls.

Opponents (called iconoclasts) argued that icons drove believers away from the very basis of Christianity. If Christ was divine, how could his nature be depicted in mere paint or stone? An icon would show only Jesus' human side, ignoring or incorrectly mingling the separate divine and human parts of his nature.

Fed up with the controversy, Emperor Leo III banned icons in A.D. 730, saying that people had begun worshipping them as idols. His ban did little to end the debate, but instead led to revolts.

Thanks to popular demand and political expediency, icons returned a century later. In the post-Iconoclast Era, craftsmen and mosaic artists were again free to portray religious scenes. Emperors had the artists add events and scenes that had nothing to do with religion but instead furthered political objectives. They saw no harm in portraying themselves with Mary, Christ, and the angels. Icons turned out to be like illustrations from a history book—projected from an imperial point of view—instead of tools to teach religion to the illiterate. Two great examples at Hagia Sophia are the mosaic of Emperor Leo above the Imperial Gate, and the Empress Zoe mosaic in the Upper Galleries.

On the narthex ceiling are original **Justinian mosaics** that survived the Iconoclast Era because they were non-figurative. The church's designer, Anthemius, sought to give the impression of movement. These mosaic pieces—interspersed with randomly placed bits of semi-precious stones—change from muted shades to brilliant reflection depending on the direction of the light. Since services generally took place after sunset, the mosaic artists designed their work to be vivid even in flickering candlelight: simple polychrome crosses and starry shapes on a golden background.

Five doors on the left wall lead into the narrow, unadorned **exterior narthex.** Less splendid than the interior narthex, it holds a few uninteresting relics and the occasional temporary exhibit, along with the main visitors' entrance. We'll skip this for now.

At the far end of the interior narthex, notice the huge doorway leading to the ramp to the Upper Galleries. We'll go up this ramp after visiting the nave.

• *Just ahead of you, the central (and biggest) door to the nave is called the...*

Imperial Gate

This majestic doorway was reserved for the emperor—it was opened only for him. Notice the **metal hooks** attached to the top of the doorway. The Ottomans added these to hold leather curtains—similar to those used in today's mosques—to protect worshippers from dust, and to reduce the interruption of a giant door opening and closing.

Look at the panel glittering above the gate, the **Mosaic of Christ with Emperor Leo VI.** The emperor known as "Leo the Wise" is today remembered more for his multiple marriages than for his intellect. His first three wives died without giving him a child, so he married his mistress—and the mother of his son—Zoe Carbonospina (meaning "Black Eyes"). This sparked a scandal: The emperor was excommunicated by the patriarch, and was barred from attending the Christmas service in A.D. 906. In this scene, Leo seems to be asking for forgiveness—prostrating himself before Jesus, who blesses the emperor. The Greek reads, "May peace be with you. I am the light of the earth." Mary and the Archangel Gabriel are portrayed in the roundels on either side of Jesus. Whitewashed over by the Ottomans, the mosaic was only rediscovered in 1933.

• *Now step through the Imperial Gate and into the main nave of Hagia Sophia.*

The Nave

Overwhelming, unbelievable, fantastic: These are the words that fall from the open mouths of visitors to Hagia Sophia. Take a few steps into the grand space, close this book, shut your ears to the

rumble of excited visitors, and just absorb the experience: You are in Hagia Sophia, the crowning achievement of the Byzantine Empire that once ruled the world.

Blocking your view (and the travelers' buzz) is the looming **scaffolding,** in place for an extensive restoration project. It's been here for over two decades, with at least another decade to go. (Locals grouse that just when they think the restoration is almost finished, it starts all

Math in Practice

Emperor Justinian appointed two great geometry professors to design his Great Church: Anthemius of Tralles and his assistant, Isidore of Miletus. Anthemius' title was "mechanikos," or engineer—not "architect." (Architects of the time worked beneath the engineers, and were considered contractors ranking among the builders and masons.) The mission given to Anthemius was to "apply geometry to solid matter." Hagia Sophia's architectural unity is testament to Anthemius' ability and genius. He knew how to create and integrate spaces within the confines of an architectural style.

In Byzantine architecture, a building's interior was more important than its exterior. The exterior was just a mask, but the interior aimed to impress and overwhelm the visitor with a specific message. Hagia Sophia's message was that the emperor—who created that sacred monument—was backed up by divine power. So in a way, the church was a very expensive propaganda tool.

Byzantines, like the Romans before them, mastered the use of the arch to bear weight. Anthemius wanted to create the feeling that the church's dome was hanging down from the heavens on gold chains. To achieve this, he designed a dome bigger and higher than anything built before, and placed a row of clear glass windows around its base—creating the illusion that the dome is floating on air. (Later engineers in Europe's Gothic Age opened up the space even more, through the use of flying buttresses.)

Anthemius is considered the greatest architect in Byzantine history. But after designing Hagia Sophia, he continued his career as a professor of geometry, living a modest life in a small residence in Constantinople.

over again.) The project has taken so long because of lack of funds, and because of structural problems—mainly leaks through the dome's exterior lead cover.

At least the scaffolding—which is about the size of a 20-story building—gives you some sense of the dome's mammoth dimensions, height, and size. Paris' Notre-Dame would fit within Hagia Sophia's great dome, and New York City's Statue of Liberty could do jumping jacks here.

• *Take a few minutes to appreciate the feat of engineering that is Hagia Sophia. First, tune into the...*

Architecture

Hagia Sophia was designed as a classical basilica covered by a vast central dome. By definition, a "basilica" is characterized by a large, central open space, called a nave, flanked by rows of columns and narrow side aisles. It sounds simple, but even the two geometricians Justinian chose to build Hagia Sophia had doubts about whether the plan would work (see sidebar). Every so often, Anthemius would go to the emperor to tell him about potential risks. And every time, he got the same response: "Have faith in God." Anthemius was right to have worried. Despite his mastery of geometry, he made some miscalculations; a few decades after Hagia Sophia was completed, part of the gigantic dome collapsed. The dome was repaired using steeper angles than the original; even so, it would collapse and be rebuilt again in the sixth and 10th centuries.

The main dome—185 feet high and roughly 105 feet in diameter—appears to float on four great arches. The secret is the clear glass windows at the base of the dome. The triangular pendentives in the corners gracefully connect the round dome to the rectangular building below, and the arches pass the dome's weight to the massive piers at the corners. Semi-domes at the ends extend the open space. Over 100 columns provide further support to the upper parts of the building. Many of these columns were brought here from other, even more ancient monuments and temples.

Hagia Sophia was a worthy attempt to create a vast indoor space, independent from the walls. But in practice, quite a bit of the dome's great weight is held up by the walls, which is why there aren't very many windows. The Byzantines built additional arches inside the walls to further help distribute the weight. These "hidden arches" are visible here and there, where the stucco layers have worn away.

As you look around, note the basic principle of Byzantine architecture: symmetry. All the architectural elements, including decorative pieces, are placed in a symmetrical fashion. If a window or door would weaken a wall, then a false, painted-on one would be created in its place.

Artful use of light creates the interior's stunning effect. The windows at the base of the dome used clear glass, while other windows throughout the building used thin alabaster to further diffuse the light and create a more dramatic effect.

• *With the Imperial Gate directly behind you, face the apse and look up into the massive dome.*

Dome Decorations

Many of Hagia Sophia's original decorations—especially mosaics or frescos depicting people—were covered over with whitewash and plaster during the centuries that Hagia Sophia was used as a mosque. Ironically, in some cases, the plaster actually helped to preserve the artwork. For others, damage was inevitable, as the stucco absorbed the whitewash. In the 19th century, the sultan invited the Swiss-born Fossati brothers to complete an extensive restoration of Hagia Sophia. They cleaned and catalogued many of the Byzantine figural mosaics before covering them up again.

At the base of the dome, between intersecting arches, are winged **seraphim.** These angels' faces are covered with gold-leaf masks or medallions. The two nearest the apse are from the 14th century; the other two are replicas by the Fossati brothers.

The Ottoman additions that immediately draw your attention are Arabic calligraphy, especially the eight 24-foot-wide **medal-**

lions suspended at the bases of the arches supporting the central and side domes. These huge leather-wrapped wooden medallions were added in the 19th century and decorated by master Islamic calligraphers. In a church, you'd see paintings of Biblical figures and saints—however, in a mosque (which allows no depictions of people), you'll see ornately written names of leading Muslim figures. The two medallions on the arches flanking the apse are painted with the names of Allah (on the right) and Muhammad (on the left). The four at the center name the four caliphs—Muslim religious and social leaders who succeeded the Prophet Muhammad: Abu Bakr, Umar, Uthman, and Ali. The two medallions on the arches above the Imperial Gate bear the names of Muhammad's grandchildren and Ali's sons, who were assassinated.

• *Walk toward the front of the church. The heavy chandeliers hanging from the dome are additions from Ottoman times, and held candlesticks, or glass oil lamps with floating wicks.*

The Apse

As you approach the apse, you'll immediately notice the highly decorated staircase set diagonally away from the wall. This is the *mimber* (meem-behr)—the pulpit used in a mosque by the imam (cleric, like a priest or rabbi) to deliver his sermon on Fridays, or to talk to the public on special occasions. The imam stands halfway up the stairs as a sign of respect, reserving the uppermost step for the Prophet Muhammad.

Go beyond the *mimber* and face the apse. When Hagia Sophia (the original church, facing Jerusalem)

was converted into a mosque, a small off-center niche was added in the apse's circular wall. Called the mihrab, this niche shows the precise direction to face during prayers (toward the holy city of Mecca, which is south of Jerusalem). The stately columns flanking the mihrab are actually huge candles—standard fixtures in royal mosques.

High above the mihrab, on the underside of the semi-dome, is a colorful **Mosaic of Mary and the Christ Child** on a gold background (to see better, raise this book to block the light). Christ is also dressed in gold. Part of the background is missing, but most of the scene is intact. This mosaic, the oldest one in Hagia Sophia, dates from the ninth century. It may have been the first figurative mosaic added after the Iconoclast Era, and replaced a cross-design mosaic from the earlier period. The gold "clubs" on Mary's forehead and both shoulders stand for the Trinity. Notice also the red "spades" among the "clubs" on the pillows.

On the right end of the arch, just before the semi-dome (behind the large medallion), find the **Mosaic of Archangel Gabriel** with his wings sweeping down to the ground. On the opposite end of the arch, there was once a similar mosaic of the Archangel Michael.

To your left, by the side of the apse (the frilly gilded room under the big medallion), is the elevated prayer section for the sultans, or the **sultan's loge** (behind the gold-glazed metalwork). This area was added in the 19th century.

• *With your back to the apse, wander to the far right-hand corner of the nave.*

As you walk, notice the golden mosaics on the ceiling from Justinian's age. Past the large buttresses, rows of **green marble columns** separate the aisles from the central nave. These columns carry the Upper Galleries, and also provide support to the domes, easing the burden on the buttresses and the exterior walls. Notice the richly decorated white-marble capitals of these columns (with the joint monograms of Justinian and Theodora). In the far corner is what looks like a five-foot-tall alabaster egg.

Alabaster Urns

This is one of two Hellenistic-era **urns** (second century B.C., one on each side of the nave) that the sultan brought to Istanbul from Pergamon—the formidable ancient acropolis of north Aegean Turkey. Find the tap mounted in the side. Traditionally, Ottoman mosques had functional fountains inside, to provide drinking water for worshippers.

The two purple **porphyry columns** behind each urn are older even than Hagia Sophia. Two columns stand at each corner—eight in all. Long ago, iron girdles were placed around the columns to prevent further damage (they already had cracks in them).

• *In the rear right-hand corner, about 10 yards beyond the alabaster urn, is a quirky column…*

Miracle Column of St. Gregory

This is the legendary "perspiring column," or the Column of St. Gregory, the miracle worker. For centuries, people believed this column "wept" holy water that could cure afflictions such as eye diseases and infertility.

How does it work? Put your thumb in the hole, and if it comes out feeling damp, your prayer will be answered. No? Try this. Put your thumb in the hole again, and this time, make a complete 360-degree circle with your hand, with your thumb still in the hole. The metal surrounding the hole has been polished by millions of hands over the years.

• *Walk through the door to the left of this column, leaving the main nave and re-entering the interior narthex. The huge door to your right leads to the Upper Galleries, which hold Hagia Sophia's best-known mosaics.*

Continue through this door and follow the long, stone-paved ramp up to the galleries (watch your step, as the stones are smooth and uneven). Why a ramp, and not stairs? Because those with exalted rank were carried by their servants, or rode up on horseback.

The Upper Galleries

• *As you step off the ramp, turn to the right and enter the well-lit West Gallery.*

West Gallery

This gallery provides a direct view of the apse. Walk to the center of the gallery and look for a **green marble circle** in the floor right before the balustrade, with an ensemble of matching green columns on either side. This was the spot reserved for the empress' throne, directly across from the apse.

• *Turning left at the end of this gallery, you'll pass through the marble half wall—known as the Gate of Heaven and Hell—into the...*

South Gallery

The south gallery was originally used for church council meetings. The frescoes on the ceiling are copies of ancient designs, redone by the Fossati brothers during their 19th-century restoration.

Go to the first window on your right. To the right of the window is the ***Deesis* Mosaic,** one of the finest of Hagia Sophia's Byzantine mosaics—though certainly not its best-preserved. Dating from the 13th or 14th century, its theme—depicting the Virgin Mary and John the Baptist asking Jesus for the sal-

vation of souls—is common in Eastern Orthodox churches. Notice how Mary's and John's heads tilt slightly toward Christ. The workmanship is fascinating, especially the expression and detail in the faces. Get up close to examine how miniscule and finely cut the pieces are.

• *Walk to the far end of this gallery, for two more Byzantine mosaic panels, placed side by side.*

As you approach the end of the gallery, look for the 12th-century **Mosaic of the Virgin and Child with Emperor John Comnenus and Empress Irene.** Mary stands in the center, holding the Christ Child in her arms. Christ's right hand extends in blessing, and he holds a scroll in his left hand. As in many such mosaics, the emperor offers Christ a bag of money (representing his patronage), and the empress presents a scroll. Their son Prince Alexius is portrayed to his mom's left on the adjoining pier—added to the scene only after he became co-emperor at age 17.

To the left is the 11th-century **Mosaic of Christ with Emperor Constantine IX Monomachus and Empress Zoe.** Constantine and Zoe are portrayed in ceremonial garments, flanking Christ on his throne. The inscription above the emperor's head reads, "Sovereign of Romans, Constantine Monomachus," while the empress is identified as "Zoe, the most pious Augusta."

Standard fare so far, but if we dig deeper, this mosaic gets quite interesting. If you look carefully, you can see that critical sections of text were erased and then restored (in what looks like a different font). Here's the story: Empress Zoe—the daughter of an emperor who had no male heirs—married Romanus Argyrus, but he was killed in his bath a few years later. Zoe then married her young lover, Michael IV—and, within a few years, he was dead, too. His nephew, Michael V, was named co-emperor and sent Zoe into exile. But the well-connected Zoe found a way back, had Michael V deposed, and married a third time, to Constantine Monomachus, at the age of 65.

That's three husbands in all—and a lot of extra work for the mosaic artists. So, instead of changing the image of Zoe's husband each time, they simply changed the title over his head. And Zoe's face, which was erased by Michael V, was restored to her youth-like appearance after she resumed her reign and married Constantine Monomachus.

By the way, if you've enjoyed these mosaics, don't miss the Chora Church Museum, out on the edge of the Old Town (see the tour on page 227).

• *Retrace your steps back down the ramp to the interior narthex, then turn right and exit the way others are entering. Just outside in a hole on your right are the remains of the earlier Theodosian Church.*

Previous Early Churches

Hagia Sophia was built over the remains of at least two earlier churches. No trace remains of the first church, where construction probably began in the fourth century A.D. as Constantine moved to strengthen his hold on the fledgling Byzantine Empire.

The next church, believed to have been built by Theodosius II, was grander in scale and more elaborate. But as fate would have it, this second church was also destroyed during a religious uprising—the Nika riots of 532 that caused the death of more than 30,000 people. Half of the city was reduced to ashes, including the church.

Some remains of the Theodosian Church are visible in the pit just outside the main entrance to Hagia Sophia. You can see part of the steps that led to the entrance portico, the bases of the columns that supported the entry porch, and fragments of marble blocks with carved designs of sheep. Other Theodosian Church artifacts, columns, and capitals are scattered nearby throughout Hagia Sophia's outdoor garden.

• *Your tour is finished. You're close to several other major sights, including the Blue Mosque, Hippodrome, and the Underground Cistern (all described in the Historic Core of Istanbul Walk on page 72). And directly behind Hagia Sophia is the wall of Topkapı Palace (see Topkapı Palace Tour on the next page).*

TOPKAPI PALACE TOUR

Topkapı Sarayı

Topkapı Palace stands on the ruins of Byzantium, the ancient Greek settlement at the eastern tip of the Old Town peninsula. After capturing Constantinople, Ottoman Sultan Mehmet the Conqueror chose this prime location—overlooking the Sea of Marmara, the Bosphorus, and the Golden Horn—as the administrative center of his empire. In the 1470s, he built a large complex with offices, military barracks, a council chamber, and a reception hall. A century later, Topkapı (tohp-kah-puh) became the sultan's residence when Süleyman the Magnificent turned it into a home. Topkapı efficiently served as the sole administrative palace for Ottoman sultans for more than 400 years, until a new European-style palace was built on the Bosphorus in the mid-19th century (Dolmabahçe Palace, described on page 54).

The word Topkapı means "cannon door"—a reference to one of the gates on the old Byzantine wall along the Sea of Marmara. Originally known as the sultan's "New Palace," Topkapı was gradually enlarged over the centuries. Each reigning sultan contributed his own flourishes, according to the style of the era. So, unlike many European palaces, which were built all at once, Topkapı Palace was constructed gradually and organically over time. The result is a funhouse of architectural styles. Since no two buildings of the complex were built at the same time, they're all on different levels—as you pass through the doorways, you'll almost always step up or down. And yet, this hodgepodge is totally functional—each addition had its purpose, and was suited for its time. Taken together, the visual mess of Topkapı Palace adds to a unique sum that represents the sultan lifestyle.

ORIENTATION

Cost: Palace—20 YTL, Harem—15 YTL.

Hours: Palace—Late March–late Oct Wed–Mon 9:00–19:00, closed Tue, until 16:45 off-season, exhibits begin to close one hour earlier. Harem—Wed–Mon 10:00–16:00, closed Tue.

Buying Tickets: You can enter the outer Topkapı complex for free, but going into the inner part, with the **palace museum,** requires a ticket. As you face the Gate of Salutation (the entrance to the inner part), you'll see ticket windows on your right. (Some windows are reserved for tour guides—be sure you're in the correct line.)

To visit the **Harem,** you'll need to buy a separate ticket from the Harem's ticket booth (up the path to the left as you enter).

Getting There: It's located between the Golden Horn and Sea of Marmara, in the Sultanahmet district. The easiest approach, from the Sultanahmet tram stop, is described on the next page (under "The Tour Begins"). You can also take the tram to the Gülhane stop, go in the gate on the side wall of the Topkapı complex, and bear right up the hill. You'll pass the Istanbul Archaeological Museum on your left, then emerge into the First Courtyard (with the Gate of Salutation and inner Topkapı complex ahead and on your left).

Crowd-Beating Tips: If you arrive right at (or before) 9:00, when the palace opens, you'll have to wait outside the Imperial Gate. It's less chaotic to arrive later (10:00 or after). Because the museum is closed on Tuesday, it can be more crowded on Monday and Wednesday.

Expect Changes: Sections may be closed for renovation without prior notice. Popular items are occasionally sent to temporary exhibitions around the world.

Information: Most important items are well-labeled in English. You can also rent an English audioguide; while the information is scant, it's delightfully narrated and makes it easy to meaningfully navigate the sight (10 YTL for the whole palace complex including the Harem; Harem-only audioguide available for 5 YTL at Harem entry). Tel. 0212/512-0480, www.topkapisarayi.gov.tr.

Length of This Tour: Two hours, plus another hour if you visit the Harem.

Services: Just outside the gate by the ticket office, you'll find WCs, a post office, souvenir shop, and exchange office. Once inside the palace, you'll find WCs in various places: right outside the kitchen complex; as you exit the Harem (at the corner of the Third Courtyard); and at the restaurant in Mecidiye Pavilion (all are marked on the map on next page). There's a museum shop just past the security checkpoint, near the exit. There is no cloakroom.

Photography: Indoor photography is not allowed in the sights surrounding the Third Courtyard (Imperial Treasury, Sultans' Clothing Collection, and Muslim Relics). Otherwise, photography is permitted.

Cuisine Art: At the far end of the palace (at Mecidiye Pavilion in the Fourth Courtyard), you'll find a restaurant called **Konyalı,** serving Turkish fare in two sections: sit-down (slow service) or self-service (can be crowded). It's expensive (10-YTL sandwiches at self-service section, 20-YTL entrées in table-service section) but convenient and beautifully located, with sweeping views across the Bosphorus. You can also buy drinks and snacks at the little store next to the Harem entrance.

Starring: The jewel-encrusted Topkapı Dagger, an 86-carat diamond, some remarkable Muslim relics from Mecca, the famous Harem of the sultan (minus the dancing girls), and several centuries of Ottoman history.

Overview

From the palace complex's main entry, you'll pass through the outer wall and the First Courtyard, stopping to admire ceremonial gates and traditional fountains. After buying a ticket, you'll enter the inner complex of the palace itself (the "Museum") and visit several increasingly intimate courtyards, housing the palace kitchens, council chamber, armory, treasury, and tulip garden. With a separate ticket, you can then tour the ornately decorated Harem (see page 160). After exploring the palace and Harem, it's a short walk to the Istanbul Archaeological Museum (see next chapter).

THE TOUR BEGINS

• *From the Sultanahmet tram stop, walk across the street and face Hagia Sophia (with the Blue Mosque at your back). From here, walk around the right (eastern) side of Hagia Sophia, following the brown arrow for* Topkapı Sarayı. *(Notice Hagia Sophia's inclined retaining walls and two stone minarets, which the Ottomans added in the 16th century to reinforce the structure as they converted it into a mosque.) Straight ahead is the Topkapı Palace complex's main Imperial Gate. Just before it, on the right, is the...*

Ahmet III Fountain

In Istanbul, street fountains like this one are an important example of civic architecture (see sidebar). This early-18th-century structure has a fountain on each facade, and each fountain is decorated

TOPKAPI PALACE

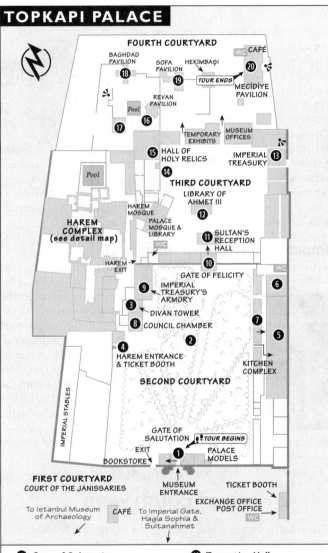

FOURTH COURTYARD

BAGHDAD PAVILION

SOFA PAVILION

HEKİMBAŞI

CAFÉ

WC

20

TOUR ENDS

MECİDİYE PAVILION

18

19

REVAN PAVILION

Pool

16

17

TEMPORARY EXHIBITS

MUSEUM OFFICES

15 HALL OF HOLY RELICS

IMPERIAL TREASURY **13**

14

Pool

THIRD COURTYARD

LIBRARY OF AHMET III

HAREM MOSQUE

12

HAREM COMPLEX *(see detail map)*

PALACE MOSQUE & LIBRARY

SULTAN'S RECEPTION HALL

11

WC

HAREM EXIT

10

WC

GATE OF FELICITY

9 IMPERIAL TREASURY'S ARMORY

6

3 DIVAN TOWER

8 COUNCIL CHAMBER

7

2

5

4 HAREM ENTRANCE & TICKET BOOTH

KITCHEN COMPLEX

IMPERIAL STABLES

SECOND COURTYARD

GATE OF SALUTATION

TOUR BEGINS

1

PALACE MODELS

EXIT

BOOKSTORE

FIRST COURTYARD
COURT OF THE JANISSARIES

MUSEUM ENTRANCE

TICKET BOOTH

To Istanbul Museum of Archaeology

CAFÉ

To Imperial Gate, Hagia Sophia & Sultanahmet

EXCHANGE OFFICE POST OFFICE

WC

1 Gate of Salutation
2 Old Byzantine Cistern
3 Divan Tower
4 Harem Ticket & Audioguide Kiosks
5 Chinese Porcelain Collection
6 Dessert Kitchen
7 Kitchen Dormitory
8 Divan (Council Chamber)
9 Imperial Treasury's Armory
10 Gate of Felicity

11 Reception Hall
12 Library of Ahmet III
13 Imperial Treasury
14 Sultan's Funeral Platform
15 Hall of Holy Relics
16 Revan Pavilion
17 Circumcision Room
18 Baghdad Pavilion
19 Sofa Pavilion
20 Mecidiye Pavilion

with triangular niches on either side (similar to a prayer niche in a mosque, called a mihrab). The walls are decorated with tiles, gilded designs, and calligraphy—including the phrase, "Turn the tap with the name of Allah, the Protector, and the Merciful. Drink the water, and say a prayer for Sultan Ahmet."

• *Before going through the gate, side-trip about 100 yards to your left into a cobblestone lane called **Soğukçeşme**. This quaint street running between the church and the palace is lined with 19th-century townhouses. Recently restored, they are now part of a sterile-but-luxurious boutique hotel. Then return to the entry to the palace.*

Imperial Gate (Bab-ı Hümayun)

This was the main entrance to the Topkapı Palace grounds. Mehmet the Conqueror built the gate when he chose this site as his

administrative center in the 15th century—just above the entryway, notice his imperial signature, or *tuğra* (too-rah). For centuries, the Imperial Gate stayed open from the first prayer of the morning at sunrise, until the last in the evening at sunset. Originally, there was a wooden pavilion

above the gate, from which the women of the Harem could watch the colorful processions into and out of the palace.

• *Going through the Imperial Gate, you find yourself in Topkapı's...*

FIRST COURTYARD

This wide-open space was reserved for public officials, civil servants, and service personnel. It was also called the "Courtyard of Janissaries," for the royal soldiers who assembled here (see sidebar on page 152). Until a destructive mid-19th-century fire, the courtyard was more built-up with court buildings. Close to the Imperial Gate you just entered were the offices of treasury officials. Across from that was the bakery, supplying bread to the staff and palace residents. All of this, plus guard barracks, dormitories, and more, are gone without a trace.

• *As you walk from the Imperial Gate toward the palace through the First Courtyard, notice the terra-cotta church on your left.*

Ottoman Fountains

Throughout old neighborhoods in Istanbul, you'll find elegant fountains, souvenirs of a genteel age. The most famous one is the Ahmet III Fountain, just outside the Imperial Gate of Topkapı Palace.

In the 17th century, there were more than 10,000 fountains in Istanbul, easily accessible everywhere—near streets and street corners, mosques, parks, and gardens. Most private homes did not have plumbing, and people used public fountains as their water source. The fountains were generally simple structures, built for function. The tap was mounted on a marble panel and a basin was placed underneath.

Most of the fountains were connected to the water system, which had been constructed by the architect Sinan a hundred years earlier. Some fountains were built by the royal family and/or local administrators, but most were donated by the wealthy. It was considered prestigious to build a handsome fountain—and those commissioned by the rich were quite fancy and decorative.

The charming fountains (often drowned out by the noise of 21st-century traffic) come with decor typical of the Muslim Ottomans: no images, flamboyant Arabic script of a verse from the Koran, perhaps a local poem or proverb, the name of the benefactor, and a line thanking them for the donation.

Although fading away, the custom of building fountains continues today. People in the countryside sometimes build fountains by the side of the roads for travelers.

Hagia Irene

This important early-Christian church hides inside the Topkapı wall. Often mistakenly interpreted as "St. Irene," the church's name

actually means "Divine Peace," an attribute of God. Many believe that Constantine himself had this church built. Soon after Constantine split the Roman Empire between West and East—with the Eastern capital here, in Byzantium (renamed Constantinople)— Hagia Irene hosted the Second Ecumenical Council to set the course for the new church (in A.D. 381). Decisions made in this building shaped Eastern Orthodox traditions for centuries to come. In the short term, the council— which discussed theological questions such as whether Jesus was human, divine, or both—sparked social struggles and riots in the early history of the capital city.

The present structure dates back to the reign of Justinian (sixth century). Hagia Irene served as the patriarchal (main) church of Constantinople until Hagia Sophia was built. Under Ottoman rule, Hagia Irene was used as an arsenal by the imperial guards, and later to store artifacts from the Istanbul Archaeological Museum.

The stark and beautiful interior of Hagia Irene is not generally open to the public. Check the signs by the entrance to see if there's an exhibition or concert here during your visit.

• *Continue the rest of the way up through the First Courtyard. On the right, along the wall, you'll see a gift shop, post office, WC, exchange office, and ticket window. Buy your palace ticket here. Just beyond the ticket window, in the wall, notice the little fountain. This is called Cellat (jel-lot), or the Executioner's Fountain—where the executioner washed his hands...and blade. With that cheerful thought, turn your attention to the...*

Gate of Salutation (Bab-üs Selam)

Also known as the Middle Gate, the Gate of Salutation dates from the mid-16th century, when the towers were used for defense as

much as for decoration. It's reminiscent of European castles from the Middle Ages, and was likely modeled after those fortresses. Guards who defended the towers (notice the slits for archers) lived on either side of the gate. Right above the doorway is the gilded *tuğra* (imperial signature) of Sultan Mahmut II. Above that, in Arabic calligraphy, is the phrase, "There is no other God but Allah, and Muhammad is his Prophet." Beyond this point, everyone except the sultan had to leave their horse outside and walk in.

• *Unless you're a sultan, tie up your horse and go through the gate, noticing the original hand-beaten iron doors. As you pass through security and ticket control, look up to see the ornate decorations on the underside of the large eave. Once through the gate, you're in the...*

SECOND COURTYARD

This was not a private garden, but a ceremonial courtyard—host to centuries of coronations, successions, and other major benchmarks. Imagine the courtyard filled with hundreds of residents, royal family members, viziers, soldiers, and staff, all dressed in their finest attire, standing patiently in line for their turn to kiss the skirt of the sultan's caftan (gown) to show their respect and obedience.

To get your historical orientation, head around to the right side of the security checkpoint (with the gate at your back) to find two glass showcases with elaborate models of Topkapı Palace. Behind these, find the map showing the growing Ottoman Empire.

Now get your palace orientation. Stand with the Gate of Salutation behind you. Straight ahead, at the end of the long, central walkway, is the Gate of Felicity, which leads to the Third Courtyard of the palace.

Along the right side of the courtyard, marked by the domes and tall chimneys, are the palace workshops and imperial kitchens, which now house a porcelain and silver collection.

Now look to the left, to see the tall Divan Tower. In front of the tower, with a large eave, is the Divan—the council chamber where the viziers (ministers) of the imperial council met. To the right of the Divan Tower, at the far-left corner of the courtyard, is the Armory section of the Imperial Treasury. To the left of the Divan, just around the corner, is the ticket booth and entrance to the Harem.

• *If there is no line at the Harem entrance, you'd be wise to visit it now (for details, see page 160), then return here and continue on to the kitchen complex. Take the walkway leading diagonally to the portico running along the right side of the courtyard. Before going through the passage in the middle of this portico...*

Notice the stone panels with Arabic calligraphy lined up along the wall behind the columns. A builder or architect would adorn his new building with an inscription like this, explaining the donor, construction date, architect, and so on—not unlike the bronze plaques on many public buildings back home.

• *Now go through the passage into the...*

Kitchen Complex

Much of Topkapı Palace burned down in the 16th century—thanks to a fire started in these kitchens (overheated oil in a pan, plus soot-clogged chimneys). Süleyman the Magnificent's royal architect, Sinan, rebuilt the grand-scale complex you see today, featuring 10 separate kitchen chambers, each with an elevated dome and a tall chimney for better ventilation (it worked—no more fires). Today this complex houses three different exhibits.

• *Entering the long, narrow courtyard, take a few steps to the right, and go through the first door on the left into the actual kitchens. This section exhibits Topkapı's impressive...*

Chinese Porcelain Collection

Feast your eyes on a few hundred of the more than 10,000 pieces of Chinese porcelain that survive (about half of the sultan's original supply). Work your way counterclockwise around the collection, through 800 years of Chinese porcelain, covering four dynasties: Sung, Yuan, Ming, and Ch'ing.

First you'll come to plates, pitchers, vases, and cups fired with the green glaze called celadon, which supposedly changed color if touched by poisoned food. Most of these have traditional dragon and fish designs on them, but you'll also see a few with plant and geometric patterns.

Next, the blue-and-white porcelain items are in particularly exquisite condition, as most went into storage and never saw the light of day after being purchased. Some earlier examples carry abstract designs, Arabic script, and excerpts from the Quran; later ones have more traditional Chinese designs. The priceless blue-and-white china dating from the Yuan dynasty (1280–1368) are some of the most valuable pieces in the entire collection. A flask from the mid-1300s was recently sold for over $5 million.

The rest of the collection—featuring Chinese polychrome and Japanese Imari porcelain—will likely be closed for renovation during your visit.

• *Leave the porcelain collection the same way you entered, then turn right and walk down the courtyard to the dead-end. Go through the last door on the right, into the...*

Dessert Kitchen (Kitchen Exhibit)

This area was used to prepare traditional desserts, including *helva* (made with sesame oil and tahini)—so it's called the Helvahane (hehl-vah-hah-neh; Dessert Kitchen). This is also where the royal doctor concocted medicinal pastes—such as the famous "sultan's paste," an herbal mix famous for its strength-boosting (and aphrodisiac) qualities. Look for the round stone block across from the entrance, used to mix these ingredients.

Today, this section has been restored to its original form, and shows off kitchen utensils, massive cauldrons, meat trays, coffee sets, and other copper objects (from the collection of about 2,000 pieces).

The narrow door on the left wall leads into the kitchen staff's mosque. Today it houses an exhibit of Turkish porcelain, which

What's for Dinner?

The palace's imperial kitchens didn't feed just the sultan. They routinely dished up enough chow to feed thousands of people—up to 10,000 for religious festivals and when the hungry janissaries (soldiers) had their payday. In the 18th century, the imperial kitchens employed up to 20 chefs, 200 cooks and their assistants, 100 specialized cooks, another 100 dessert experts...and more than 300 busboys to clean up the mess. And this doesn't even count the bakers. As the head of such an immense staff, the master of the kitchens was as important as a vizier.

Sultans spent fortunes on buffet-style receptions for foreign envoys, weddings, circumcisions, and open-invitation public feasts on important religious days (such as the end of Ramadan). The circumcision gathering for one crown prince lasted for days. Each evening, the menu included rice pilaf for a thousand people, and 20 entire roasted cows.

The catering complex had separate kitchens, each run by a specialized chef. For example, the Has (royal) Kitchen cooked only for viziers, Harem residents, and staff. There were two meals a day: mid-morning and before sunset. Food was distributed by boys carrying large trays. The most commonly used ingredients in the kitchens were butter, saffron, and sugar.

The sultan's food was prepared in a special kitchen. Those cooking for the sultan were carefully chosen from among the best—the master chef and his crew of 12 cooks. The master chef was also the caretaker of the fine porcelain used by the sultan and viziers of the Divan, and for the banquets for visiting envoys and ambassadors. When the sultan went on a military campaign, his cooks went with him—and, occasionally, they'd have to grab a sword and join the battle.

Dining habits changed through time, but until the 19th century, there were still no dining tables at the palace. The sultan sat cross-legged in front of a large tray, and usually ate alone. Food and beverages were served in celadon porcelain ware and metal cups. The sultan's dinner menu would be something like this: Mutton (steamed or kebab), a variety of grilled meats (mutton, quail, etc.), and baklava or rice pudding. The sultan would not drink water during the meal, but instead sipped from a large bowl of chilled, stewed fruit juice (*şerbet*), as well as Turkish coffee. To set the proper mood, the room was filled with aloe-wood incense, and the sultan was entertained by mute little people.

was in vogue here in the 19th century. You'll also see some traditional Ottoman glass filigree work: Colored glass rods (usually blue and white) are melted into crystal, creating a spiral design.

• *Exit back into the courtyard. Ahead on the right, just past the passage into the main courtyard, is the entrance to the...*

Kitchen Dormitory (Silverware and European Porcelain)

This collection is displayed in the former dormitory for kitchen staff. First you'll see several pieces of silverware that were gifts from European monarchs to the sultan. Then comes the Ottoman silverware, including a stunning silver model of the Ahmet III Fountain we saw outside the palace wall. Upstairs is an exhibit of European porcelain, which came into fashion after Chinese porcelain became passé in the 18th century. Most of the pieces are from Germany, France, or Russia.

• *Exit the kitchen complex the way you entered, back into the Second Courtyard. Directly across the courtyard is the Divan Tower. Go to the building just below it, to the intricately decorated door under the eave. This is the...*

Divan

The Divan (dee-vahn) was the council chamber where the viziers (ministers) got together to discuss state affairs. In other words, this was where the Ottoman Empire was governed for almost 400 years.

Like much of the rest of Topkapı Palace, the Divan was built by Mehmet the Conqueror in the 15th century, then burned

down; it was rebuilt a century later by the royal architect Sinan. Then, during the "Tulip Era" in the early 18th century (see sidebar on page 156), Sultan Ahmet III redecorated the rooms in Rococo style, which was the European trend of the time.

Stepping inside, notice how the Divan's frilly Rococo flourishes clash with the rest of the Topkapı ensemble. The first room you enter is the office of the Record-Keeper, who kept track of every word spoken in the Divan. The larger, second room was the actual Divan, or Council Chamber, decorated with original 16th-century tiles. The viziers would sit on the sofa according to their rank in the hierarchy. (This is why some people call sofas "divans.") The Grand Vizier (prime minister) took the seat directly across from the door (see the red cloth with dark tulip designs). In the early years of the Divan, the sultan actually attended these meetings; later, the sultan would simply relax in the next room and eavesdrop as he liked through the window with the metal grill right above the Grand Vizier's seat. This window was known as "the Eye."

• *Exiting the Divan, turn left and walk to the brick-and-stone building next door, the...*

Imperial Treasury's Armory

This treasury was responsible for collecting taxes from the provinces—and was also where the janissaries and palace staff went to collect their paychecks. Today the building exhibits a small but interesting armory collection. Keep an eye out for several unique items: Two pistols that have little bayonets attached to them. A *yatağan*, which is a lightweight, curved sword carried by janissaries. The enormous two-hand sword dates from the Crusades. The Samurai outfit was a gift from Japan to the sultan. Some of the other displayed swords once belonged to sultans—including one that was Mehmet the Conqueror's, with Quran verses inscribed on the blade.

• *Now continue to the top of the Second Courtyard—past some centuries-old sycamore trees—to the...*

Gate of Felicity (Bab-üs Saade)

This striking gate consists of a domed roof delicately carried by four slender columns. On either side of the gate, notice the antique designs, decorative columns, and landscape paintings (which were the trend during the last two centuries of the Ottoman Empire). Walking under the dome, notice the hole in the raised marble paving stone. This was used to hold the royal banner, which flew here when new sultans were

The Janissaries

When the Ottomans first rose to power, their military was made up of Turkish Muslim soldiers and cavalry from neighboring clans, who gathered only during times of war. The sultans would sometimes levy a "tax" of soldiers on large landowners, depending on the size of their holdings. Eventually captured prisoners of war were also forced to serve in the Ottoman military.

But as the Ottoman Empire spread into Europe, the army—now made up of a hodgepodge of allies and POWs—became more diverse and difficult to control. So Mehmet the Conqueror re-envisioned his military as a reliable and controllable standing army. He created a new division of Christian converts to Islam, known as the janissaries. Young boys were taken from Christian families, converted to Islam, and raised to be soldiers for the sultan. Janissaries were professional soldiers—paid a salary even in peacetime—and eventually became the backbone of Ottoman military might.

Mehmet the Conqueror also founded the palace school at Topkapı Palace, where the brightest young janissaries were educated to prepare them to serve the sultan and the state. Graduates of the palace school could work for the sultan's treasury, administration, and military—and the best of the best might even become viziers.

Often janissaries never saw their families again after they left their homes. But, while this system tore families apart, it was also beneficial for those who were left behind—a janissary's parents became exempt from taxes. And many janissaries went on to achieve a much greater degree of power and influence than they ever could have had as non-Muslim farm boys.

While this system began as a simple and efficient way to "draft" a powerful army, eventually the janissaries caused problems for the sultan. The janissaries—who generally preferred the status quo—often stood in the way of a sultan's reforms, and if angered, were known to dethrone or literally strangle a sultan to death. In fact, many historians fault the janissaries' influence for contributing to the empire's eventual decline.

coronated on this very spot.

The gate is also known as the "Gate of the White Eunuchs." White eunuchs were instructors, guards, and caretakers for the palace school, which occupied much of the Third Courtyard beyond this gate. Here the empire's top officials were educated, including ranking janissary leaders (see sidebar).

• *Walk through the Gate of Felicity, into the...*

THIRD COURTYARD

As you emerge from the gate, you're in front of the sultans' **Reception Hall,** a throne room designed to impress visitors. Recycled marble columns support the overhanging roof, creating an attractive portico around the hall. On the wall to the right of the entrance, notice the illustration showing a sultan receiving a foreign envoy. Flanking the door are imperial signatures.

Go right into the throne room—admiring the gorgeous 16th-century throne—and out the other side. The gray-white marble building straight ahead is the 18th-century **Library of Ahmet III.** The interior is decorated with mother-of-pearl and tortoiseshell inlayed cupboard doors, and comfortable sofas next to the windows. If you're interested, the entrance is around the far side of the building, via a marble staircase.

• *For now, go down the stairs on your right, and walk straight to the edge of the courtyard to reach the impressive...*

Imperial Treasury

The sultans used this building—with fireplaces and charming stained-glass windows—as a private chamber and occasional reception hall. Today it displays a sumptuous collection of the sultans' riches.

• *The Imperial Treasury is made up of four chambers linked together on a handy one-way route—just follow the signs. The first room is actually separate from the other three (you'll go in and out through the same door); the rest are all connected. Be warned that this area can be especially crowded—consider reading these descriptions before you enter.*

The **first room** shows off imperial thrones. As you enter, turn right to find the 17th-century ceremonial throne of Ahmet I. Along the opposite wall are three more, each one distinct in style: From right to left, you'll see an 18th-century Persian throne (a gift from an Iranian shah); the ebony throne of Süleyman the Magnificent (decorated with ivory and mother-of-pearl); and a gold-sheeted ceremonial throne from the 18th century. Notice the huge emeralds on the pendant hanging over the Persian throne (more emeralds are in the showcase to the right of the thrones).

• *As you exit (the same way you entered), keep right to reach the second room.*

The **second room** is the least interesting, displaying jade objects and jewels—either designed by palace craftsmen or sent to the sultan as gifts.

• *Follow the crowds into the third room.*

In the **third room,** in a small showcase to the right of the fireplace, find the expertly crafted 16th-century gold helmet and mace, decorated with rubies and turquoise. In the left wall as you

face the fireplace, notice the two massive candlesticks, designed in the 19th century to adorn the tomb of the Prophet Muhammad. These solid-gold candlesticks—weighing more than 100 pounds each—were brought here by Ottomans retreating from Mecca and Medina during World War I.

• *This room is connected to the next via a balcony with a pretty marble fountain. Stop for a minute to enjoy the sweeping views: the Bosphorus, Bosphorus Bridge, Asian Istanbul, and Sea of Marmara.*

The **fourth room** is more spectacular than the last three combined. As you enter, go to the far right corner—past a bowl of emeralds and rock crystals—to see the famous Topkapı Dagger, lying on a burgundy pillow. This was created here in the palace workshop as a gift for the shah of Iran—but, since the shah was killed in an uprising, it never reached its intended destination. The octagonal emerald on top of the handle hides a watch underneath.

Now proceed counterclockwise around the room. A few steps to the left, on the right side of the fireplace, is the 86-carat pearl-shaped Spoonmaker's Diamond (surrounded by a double-row of 49 diamonds)—one of the biggest diamonds in the world. They say a poor man found this diamond in the dirt in the 17th century, and bartered it to a spoonmaker for wooden spoons; the spoonmaker then sold it to a jeweler for 10 silver coins. How it ended up in the royal treasury is still a mystery...but might have something to do with its enormous size.

Across from the balcony entrance is the 18th-century ceremonial body armor of Sultan Mustafa III, embroidered with solid gold and brilliant gems. Just to the right of the exit, look for the gold-sheeted wood cradle in which the sultan's newborn baby was presented to his daddy.

• *Exiting back into the Third Courtyard, you'll proceed counterclockwise (to the right) around the courtyard to the next exhibit, the Hall of Holy Relics. As you walk along the portico, notice the stairs (to your immediate right) leading down into the Fourth Courtyard and the Mecidiye Pavilion, with its restaurant, cafeteria, and WC. After these stairs, you'll pass the so-called "Pantry," where servants prepared and served the sultans' meals (now used for museum offices). Notice the river pebbles paving the floor of the domed portico in front. You'll pass a second staircase leading into the Fourth Courtyard, then the former Treasury Hall that today houses free, good temporary exhibits (if the current offering seems interesting, drop in). After passing a third passage to the Fourth Courtyard (with turnstiles), you come to the Hall of Holy Relics. Before entering, look for the marble platform to the left of the door, next to the columns. This is the...*

Sultan's Funeral Platform

According to Muslim tradition, after a dead body is washed and wrapped in a white shroud, it's laid on a slab like this one for a final religious service—to honor and pray for the deceased. You'll see platforms like this one in virtually every mosque. But this platform is special, since it was used to celebrate the last service of a deceased sultan. It was located here because it's near the important relics you'll see in the next section.

• *Now turn and face the highly ornamented door of the...*

Hall of Holy Relics

This collection shows off some of the most significant holy items of the Muslim faith. These relics were brought to Istanbul in the early 16th century, when their original locations—Egypt, Mecca, and Medina—were conquered by the Ottomans. In the past, the relics were only available to members of the Ottoman dynasty and handpicked guests, and presented to the public only on religious days. But today they're viewable at any time, offering an impressive glimpse into the world of Islam.

The **door** is a sight in itself, with gilded decorations and Arabic calligraphy reading, "There is no other God but Allah, and

Muhammad is his Prophet." On either side of the entrance, you see the imperial signatures *(tuğra)*. As this is a very holy site for Muslims, you'll see many people praying with their hands open. Read the rules on the sign next to the entrance, and be respectful as you visit this exhibit.

Going through the door, you find yourself in the so-called **Fountain Room,** beautifully decorated with 16th- to 18th-century tiles and wall paintings. Listen for the chanting: In the next room, an imam (cleric) reads verses from the Quran 24 hours a day—as they have nonstop since the 16th century. (We'll see him soon.) The pool in the center is not just decorative: It was a tradition to wash your hands when you entered and left the chamber. As you approach the back wall, you'll see on both sides of the room a collection of keys and locks for the Kabaa—the holiest of Muslim shrines, the big black cube in the center of the mosque at Mecca. Straight

The Tulip Era
(1718–1730)

During the early 18th century, the Ottoman Empire enjoyed an unprecedented era of peace and prosperity: For a half-century, there were no wars, no border disputes, and no uprisings. The Ottomans signed treaties with longstanding rivals such as Russia, Austria, and Venice...and found themselves out of enemies. Thus began the so-called Tulip Era.

Sultan Ahmet III (1673–1736), who took the throne in 1703, reigned over this era. But historians give more credit to his Grand Vizier (prime minister), İbrahim Paşa—who is known as Damat (dah-maht; "Groom") since he married the sultan's daughter. (Don't confuse Damat İbrahim Paşa with plain old İbrahim Paşa, who was Süleyman the Magnificent's Grand Vizier and brother-in-law.) Aside from his fame as an able statesman, Damat İbrahim Paşa was an intellectual with a great interest in science and history, and a healthy appreciation for art and literature. He set the tone for the unusually cultured upper-class lifestyle of the Tulip Era.

Many scholars consider the Tulip Era an "Ottoman Renaissance"—a time of political, social, and cultural advancement. Free from the worries of a war-torn empire, people could explore and celebrate the finer things in life. The city's first print shop was established (more than two centuries after the printing press became commonplace in Europe). Literature, especially poetry, came into fashion—even the sultan was a poet. There was also a newfound appreciation for fine arts, particularly tile production—Turkish tiles from this period decorate monuments and museums all over the world. Gardening caught on among the wealthy, as "Tulipmania" swept the country. A single sought-after bulb could be sold for more than 30 ounces of gold. Hedonism took hold, as lavish waterfront parties sprawled along the Golden Horn at night—lit by candles placed on the backs of hundreds of roaming tortoises.

But as with any time of prosperity and decadence, the Tulip Era couldn't last. Because it was peacetime, the sultan's frivolity wasn't funded by war spoils—but instead by outrageous tax increases on the common people. Before long, revolution was in the air, led by a janissary named Patrona Halil, who was working as a bath attendant. Halil gathered a mob, recruited the royal guards, stormed Topkapı Palace, and beheaded Damat İbrahim Paşa. The uprisers also executed several scholars, poets, and philosophers, and burned down tulip gardens all over the city. Ahmet III had to leave the throne to ease the anger of the rebels. When the dust cleared, Halil and several other rebels were executed as Sultan Mahmut I took the throne. Since Halil was Albanian, one of Mahmut I's first acts was to ban Albanian attendants in the city's baths.

ahead is the Repentance Door of Kabaa. Glass showcases on either side of this door display swords of the caliphs—the religious and social leaders of the Muslim community after Muhammad's death (like the apostles in Christian history).

The room to the left (as you face the Repentance Door) is filled with strangely well-preserved **everyday items** from the lives of religious figures: Muhammad's sandals, Moses' staff, Abraham's granite cooking pot, David's sword, and Joseph's turban.

Backtrack into the Fountain Room and go through the door by the fountain (passing the model of the Dome of the Rock in Jerusalem) into the **Petition Room** (Arz Odası; ahrz oh-dah-suh). Before it was a museum, this room was a waiting lounge for those who wanted to petition the sultan. Look to the right as you enter, to see the little kiosk where the imam reads from the Quran. The showcase in the center of the room holds the footprint of Muhammad, plus hair from his beard, his tooth, letters he wrote, and more relics.

To your left as you enter the Petition Room is the door to the **Sultan's Privy Chamber** (Has Oda; hahs oh-dah), where the sultan received petitioners. The doorway is partitioned off, but you can see the mantle that Muhammad wore (in the gold chest in front of the throne). Right behind the glass screen is Muhammad's bow and its silver cover. To the right is the gold cover of the revered "Black Stone," which Muslims believe descended from Heaven. Prophet Abraham placed this stone at the eastern corner of the Kabaa—the temple he built in Mecca.

• *Exit this chamber through the door at the end of the Petition Room. If the door isn't open, you'll have to go around: Backtrack into the Third Courtyard, and walk along the portico on the left to the passageway into the Fourth Courtyard. After the turnstiles, go down the steps into the tulip garden of Ahmet III, and keep left along the wall until you get to the marble staircase. Climb the stairs to the marble terrace.*

You are now in the...

FOURTH COURTYARD

The most intimate and cozy of Topkapı's zones, the Fourth Courtyard enjoys fine views over the Golden Horn and Bosphorus, and is dotted with several decorative pavilions—most of them built in the mid-17th century by Murat IV and his younger brother, İbrahim the Mad.

• *Proceed straight ahead to the...*

Revan Pavilion

Sultan Murat IV built this pavilion to commemorate a military victory against the Persians on the eastern front. Step inside to take a look at the interior, which is very typical of the style of the time: decorated with mostly blue-and-white 17th-century İznik tiles; window shutters and cupboard doors inlaid with mother-of-pearl and tortoiseshell; and roofed with a central dome, with three bays decorated with sofas and large pillows.

• *Exiting the pavilion, turn right and walk straight past the pool to the highly decorated pavilion at the edge of the terrace, the...*

Circumcision Room

Murat's younger brother, İbrahim the Mad, built this pavilion, which was used over the next two centuries for the ritual circumcision of heirs to the throne. It's slathered inside and out with a contrasting patchwork of fine 17th-century İznik tiles.

Stroll along the pool and pop over to the left to the bronze-gilded **kiosk** with a perfect panorama of the Golden Horn and New District. This was also built by İbrahim the Mad, who enjoyed dining with this view at the end of a long day of fasting for Ramadan.

• *With İbrahim's kiosk and that grand view on your left, continue straight ahead to the...*

Baghdad Pavilion

This one was also built by Sultan Murat IV, this time to celebrate the conquest of Baghdad. One of the more authoritarian sultans, Murat IV was feared by everyone. To intimidate dissenting janissaries, he'd lift a massive iron mace when he spoke to them at gatherings—as if to challenge them to defy him. (They rarely did.) Murat also

banned alcohol use in the city—not because he disapproved of drinking, but because it gave him an excuse to demonstrate his authority by executing violators. But after a long day of throwing his weight around, Murat IV retreated to the Baghdad Pavilion to find peace. In a strong contrast to his tough-guy image, he actually spent much of his time here reading poetry and listening to music.

As for the **pool** on the terrace, no one knows much about it. Tour guides love to spin tall tales of the wild fantasies enacted poolside by İbrahim the Mad and members of his harem, or how he would throw gold coins into the water to watch guards dive in after them.

• *When you're finished here, head down the stairs into the...*

Tulip Garden

Ahmet III, also known as the "Tulip Sultan," had a short but sweet reign—an unusual time of peace, prosperity, and, of course, tulips (see sidebar on page 156). This is the private garden where Ahmet grew rare bulbs. Turks first brought tulips here from central Asia; in the late 16th century, they began shipping them to Holland. Tulip designs were a popular motif in Turkish art (such as on tiles or textiles) long before Ahmet III—but they became an obsession under his reign.

The first building on the left, just beyond the garden, is the late-17th-century **Sofa Pavilion.** Sultan Ahmet III spent a lot of time here, lounging on a sofa and gazing at his tulips after a long night of worldly pleasures.

Behind the Sofa Pavilion is the tower-like **Hekimbaşı** (heh-keem-bah-shuh; "Chief Doctor's Chamber"). Dating all the way back to the 15th-century reign of Mehmet the Conqueror, this building was used by doctors as well as caretakers of the prince.

• *At the far end of the courtyard is the...*

Mecidiye Pavilion

Notice that this pavilion—built in the mid-19th century—looks more "European" than the other buildings at Topkapı. After centuries of living in the old-fashioned, Oriental-flavored opulence of Topkapı, Ottoman sultans began to realize that their European counterparts saw them as backwards. To keep up with these Western-oriented neighbors, the sultans' architects began to adopt an eclectic mix of various European influences. The Mecidiye Pavilion marked a sea change in both the architecture and the culture of the time; just two decades later, Topkapı was abandoned in favor of the more modern, Western-style Dolmabahçe Palace on the Bosphorus (see page 54).

In addition to spectacular views over the Bosphorus Strait, Asian Istanbul, Sea of Marmara, and (in clear weather) the Princes' Islands, the Mecidiye Pavilion hosts a pair of restaurants (one self-service, the other with table service) offering a convenient and scenic resting point after a busy palace visit.

• *Our tour is finished. When you're ready to leave Topkapı Palace, simply backtrack out to the Gate of Salutation (the exit is to the right of the security checkpoint, through the side door by the fountain). If you haven't yet, now's the time to tour...*

Harem 101

"All the goodness and evil comes from the mother sultan."
—Paolo Contarini, Ambassador of Venice

To Westerners, the word "harem" conjures up images of a vast roomful of nubile young sex slaves, eager and willing to satisfy the sultan's every desire. But this dated notion is a romanticized and inaccurate picture painted by Europeans who'd never actually laid eyes on a real harem. The Arabic word "harem" actually means "forbidden." In common use, it usually refers to the part of a Turkish house that's reserved for family members, specifically women. To Turks, "harem" connotes respect and dignity—not sexual fantasy.

At Topkapı Palace, the Harem was more than just a living area. It was an institution—part of the state. Its primary role was to provide future heirs to the Ottoman throne, an essential responsibility that was too important to be left to coincidence. Thanks largely to the Harem, the Ottoman Empire was ruled by a single dynasty from start to finish—avoiding many of the squabbles and battles for succession that tainted other great empires.

The Harem at Topkapı Palace worked like this: The sultan was the head of the household, which he shared with his mother (the "mother sultan"). The sultan could have up to four wives, with the first one being considered the senior, most influential wife. Also living in the Harem was a collection of several hundred concubines—female slaves who kept house, but were not

THE HAREM

The word "harem" refers to two things: the wives, favorites, and concubines of the sultan; and the part of the palace where they lived. Touring the Harem (hah-rehm) is an essential part of a Topkapı Palace visit, allowing curious Westerners to pull back the veil on this mysterious and titillating phenomenon. As you'll learn, the Harem was not a mindless orgy, but a carefully administered social institution that ensured the longevity of the Ottoman Empire.

A separate 15-YTL ticket is required to enter the Harem (purchase at Harem entry ticket booth). Here you can also pick up a 5-YTL audioguide of the Harem (not necessary if you already have the 10-YTL palace audioguide, which also covers the Harem).

The one-way route includes about 20 rooms, including stunning tile work, the mother sultan's private apartments, wives' and concubines' courts, and the grand reception hall. While the sexually active with the sultan. From among the concubines (his "harem"), the sultan—or, more often, his mother or wife—might select up to four "favorites," or *haseki* (hah-seh-kee), with whom he could become more, ahem, familiar. A favorite who bore a child of the sultan became known as a *haseki sultan*, and was often treated as a wife. Again, the sultan could only have sex with chosen women, not with anyone he wanted. Every night he spent with a woman was written down.

Even though they were permitted up to four wives, sultans were often cautious about marriage. Many sultans chose to have just one wife—or no wife at all, but only favorites. One reason not to marry was to protect potential wives from getting caught in the crossfire of history. Legend holds that after Sultan Beyazıt was defeated by Tamerlane the Mongolian in the early 15th century, his wife swept the floors of Tamerlane's mansion as a slave. But sultans were also careful to guard the supreme power of the dynasty, and not to weaken this power through marriages. For example, Süleyman the Magnificent married Roxelana, who went on to wield tremendous influence over the empire, kick-starting a "reign of the ladies" that would last for a century and a half (see sidebar on page 222).

When the sultan died or was replaced, the mother of the new sultan (who was almost always a member of the previous sultan's harem) was the only one who could stay. Wives and favorites alike had to leave the Harem, and were given a house and a healthy pension.

following information should follow the route fairly closely, the route can change as various rooms close for renovation. Before visiting, read the "Harem 101" sidebar, above.

• *You'll begin by passing through the bronze-plated door (the Carriage Gate) into the antechamber known as the...*

Dome

In the 16th century, this was the entryway into the Harem grounds. Draped carriages would pull up to this gate to take the Harem women in and out, for shopping, a picnic, or a private visit. New women would enter the Harem and be introduced to the staff here. The only men who could enter the Dome—other than the sultan and young princes—were the sultan's close relatives, and when necessary, doctors. These guests were escorted by the Black Eunuchs (see next), who were caretakers of the Harem.

• *Follow the attractive stone-paved corridor into a long open courtyard surrounded by functional buildings. This was the...*

THE HAREM

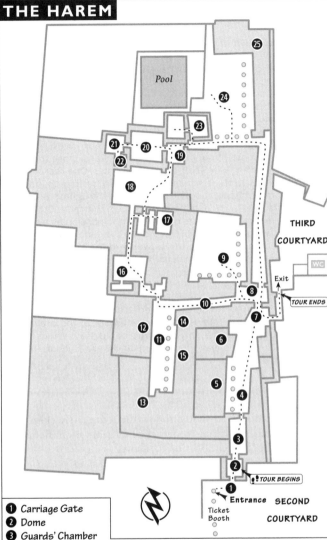

1 Carriage Gate
2 Dome
3 Guards' Chamber
4 Court of the Black Eunuchs
5 Quarters of the Black Eunuchs
6 School of the Princes
7 "Gate for All" (Women's Quarters)
8 Guard Room
9 Courtyard of the Mother Sultan
10 Corridor of Concubines
11 Courtyard of the Wives & Concubines
12 Wives' Apartments
13 Residence of the Concubines
14 Bath & Laundry
15 Kitchen
16 Mother Sultan's Private Apartment
17 Sultan's Private Bath
18 Imperial Hall
19 Tiled Antechamber
20 Fountain Room
21 Library of Ahmet I
22 Fruit Room
23 Twin Pavilions
24 Courtyard of the Favorites
25 Favorites' Apartments

Courtyard of the Black Eunuchs

The Black Eunuchs were slaves from North Africa, Egypt, and Sudan who were trained and educated to serve in the Harem—to protect the women and take care of Harem administration. The sultan knew they wouldn't be tempted by their charges because they had been castrated by slave traders on the road from Africa. When this section was built in the 16th century, there were about 50 eunuchs employed; in later years, that number doubled.

On the left, recessed from the court behind the portico, are the **Quarters of the Black Eunuchs.** Look through the windows to see the dormitories where the Black Eunuchs lived. The room with mannequins near the end of the portico was reserved for the Chief Black Eunuch as a private apartment. You see the Chief seated at his sofa, his assistant waiting for his orders.

Just past the eunuchs' quarters on the left, a porch with one column leads to the **School of the Princes.** This was where heirs to the throne received their primary education. Then, when they hit puberty, they were sent out of the Harem—often for field training in remote provinces of the empire.

• *At the end of the courtyard, you'll enter the women's quarters through the Cümle Kapısı (jewm-leh kah-puh-suh), or* **"Gate for All."** *(You'll wind up back here at the end of the tour.) The gate opens into a guard room with large Venetian mirrors on the walls, surrounded by gold-leaf frames. As you enter, go to the mirror on the left wall; through the vault to the right of this mirror, you can peek into the fancy-looking, stone-paved...*

Courtyard of the Mother Sultan

This courtyard—the centerpiece of the Harem complex—is where the various people living here could most easily mingle. The courtyard is fronted by apartments belonging to (from left to right) the mother sultan, the sultan, his senior wife (wife #1), and heirs to the throne. The tour takes us roughly clockwise around the interiors of these buildings.

• *Now turn left and go down the* **Corridor of Concubines.** *Notice the long marble counter (on the left), used for service trays and cleaning up after meals. At the end of the corridor, you'll walk along the edge of a courtyard surrounded on three sides by a portico, the...*

Courtyard of the Wives and Concubines

This courtyard was reserved for the use of the **non-senior wives** of the sultan. The building complex on the right is divided into three apartments—one each for wife #2, #3, and #4, plus their children and servants. Although they were neighbors, the sultan's wives were hardly friends. Rather, each one vied with the others to promote the interests of her own son. The wives received lavish gifts from the sultan, which they often invested in real estate, bazaars, baths, shops, and so on. The more wealth they had squirreled away, the better they could protect themselves from internal enemies. And their most hated enemy was often the wife next door—or, worse, the elderly woman up the hall: the mother sultan.

The quarters at the far end of the court were the residence of **concubines,** or female servants. (Notice the water taps on the left—used for ablution, or ritual cleansing—marking a bath and laundry room, followed by a small kitchen.) Concubines began as young slave girls, who were brought into the Harem and trained to serve the senior women. Being a concubine could be a major opportunity: Many were granted their freedom after just a few years in the Harem, and others attracted the attention of the sultan (or, more often, his mother) and were granted "favorite" *(haseki)* status. Again, the concubines were not sex slaves at the beck and call of the sultan—rather, the mother sultan and the sultan's wives carefully orchestrated which concubines the sultan could un-veil. (In other words, the man's mother and wives chose his girlfriends.)
• *Now continue into the...*

Mother Sultan's Private Apartment

Notice how the mother sultan's apartment is strategically situated between the sultan's quarters and his wives'—yet another reminder of her strict control over her son's liaisons.

Beyond the antechamber with the fireplace, you enter the mother sultan's main hall and dining room. The 17th-century decor

includes Kütahya tiles and landscape paintings (notice there are no people—since Islam discourages the depiction of humans in art). You can also see later, 19th-century touches that show the influence of European trends: Western-style paintings, and cupboard doors embroidered with tortoiseshell and mother-of-pearl. To the right of the fireplace is the entrance to the mother sultan's bedroom and prayer chamber.

As you explore, ponder the tremendous influence wielded by the mother sultan. Traditionally, she always had a word in state affairs. But the mid-16th to the 17th centuries are known as the "reign of the ladies," when the sultans' mothers and wives (aided by the Chief of the Black Eunuchs) essentially ran the Ottoman Empire. This began with the incompetent, do-nothing heirs of Süleyman the Magnificent in the mid-16th century; by the time

Take My Wives...Please!
A Few Words on Polygamy

Contrary to popular belief, the majority of Turks have always been monogamous. Even though the Quran permits a man to marry up to four times, this is reserved for extraordinary situations. When the rule was instituted, wars had decimated the male population, leaving more women than men. And so, because there was no social-welfare network to care for war widows, men began to take additional wives. The Quran sets strict criteria for polygamy: You must have the financial means to support all your wives, and must treat each one equally. Under Ottoman rule, polygamy was practiced only among minorities, traditional Arab communities...and, of course, the ruling class who could afford it. Polygamy is illegal in Turkey—it exists today only on the fringes of Turkish society (such as in some mostly Arab communities of eastern Turkey). Besides, in most of the country, today's progressive Turkish women would never accept their husbands taking second wives. Legally, Turkish women have had equal rights with men since the days of Atatürk—including the right to vote and run for election.

İbrahim the Mad took the throne a century later, the only thing his mother Kösem didn't do was lead armies into war.

• *Next is the...*

Sultan's Private Apartments

At the end of the corridor, turn right and enter the **sultan's private bath.** This is basically a smaller-scale version of any Turkish bath, with a dressing room and a hot section for bathing, all paved with marble. The large marble tub at the end was added in the 18th century, when this room was renovated in the Western style. Traditional Turkish bathing doesn't use a tub; rather, the water should always be running. Also notice the locked gold-leaf cage separating the sultan's private area from the rest of the bath.

• *Backtrack and turn right. (On the way, watch for an "Oriental toilet" to the left—porcelain footprints on either side of a hole in the ground— with gilded taps on the wall for hot and cold water.)*

The **Imperial Hall,** used as a reception hall for special occasions, is the largest room in the sultan's private apartments. The gallery with windows was reserved for the senior women. On the right, under a canopy carried by four slender columns, is the sultan's throne—actually a long sofa. Dutch Delft tiles with geometric designs decorate the walls; higher up is a line of Turkish İznik tiles. Excerpts from the Quran are written in calligraphy.

• *Next is an antechamber with beautiful 17th-century tilework. Take the door on the left.*

Named for the marble fountains set into the wall, the **Fountain Room** is covered with colorful 16th-century İznik tiles,

many with Quran verses. Through the doorway at the far end of the room (notice the elaborate little carved fountain on the left), you enter the **library of Ahmet I**—better-lit, more tranquil, and more private-feeling than the Fountain Room. Notice the shutters and drawers with more inlaid mother-of-pearl, tortoiseshell, and ivory. To the left is a tiny chamber known as the **Fruit Room.** Built in the early 18th century, it's decorated with wood panels with fruit and flower designs.

• *Pass back through the Fountain Room, go through the doorway, and continue. On the left, just before the big courtyard, is the entrance to the...*

Twin Pavilions

These two connected pavilions, richly decorated with stained-glass windows and floral tiles, were the living quarters for young heirs to the throne.

The rooms used to be mistakenly identified as "the Cage," where brothers (and potential rivals) of the sultans were kept under house arrest. As draconian as that sounds, it was an improvement on the original tradition, when sultans would kill their brothers to avoid conflicts over the throne. Sultan Ahmet I, the patron of the Blue Mosque, chose imprisonment for his brothers rather than death. This caused a new problem: If a sultan died or became unable to rule, his brother would take the throne after having spent his entire life under lock and key—and without any knowledge of how to run an empire. These incompetent brother sultans have often been blamed for hastening the decline of the Ottoman Empire.

• *Now continue into the...*

Courtyard of the Favorites

As the name implies, this is where the sultan's favorites—the *haseki*—resided (in the white two-story building that surrounds

the courtyard). In addition to their interactions with the sultan, these favorites had a great view. Belly up to the marble banister and enjoy it yourself.

The mother sultan selected the favorites from among the concubines. Despite birth-control methods—and the disapproval of the wives—a favorite would often bear the child of a sultan. In this case, she became a *haseki sultan,* joined the ranks of the senior women...and her life would change forever. Now she was powerful, protected, envied...and in danger of attack.

• *From here, continue down a long corridor to eventually reach the Harem exit. Exiting the Harem, you'll find yourself in the Third Courtyard. To go back to where you started, turn right and follow the wall to the Gate of Felicity, which deposits you back in the Second Courtyard (if you have yet to visit the kitchen complex and rest of the palace, see page 147).*

TOPKAPI PALACE TOUR

ISTANBUL ARCHAEOLOGICAL MUSEUM TOUR

İstanbul Arkeoloji Müzesi

The Istanbul Archaeological Museum's collection rivals any on earth, with intricately carved sarcophagi, an army of Greek and Roman sculptures, gorgeous İznik tiles, ancient Babylonian friezes, the world's oldest peace treaty, and an actual chunk of the chain that the Byzantines stretched across the Golden Horn. Divided into three parts (Museum of Archaeology, Tiled Kiosk, and Museum of the Ancient Orient), this underrated but impressive museum is worth consideration even by visitors who think they couldn't care less about archaeology.

ORIENTATION

Cost: 10 YTL includes entry to all three sections.

Hours: Museum of Archaeology and Tiled Kiosk—Tue–Sun 9:00–17:00, closed Mon; Museum of the Ancient Orient—Tue–Sun 9:00–16:45, closed Mon. Last entry at 16:00.

Getting There: It's inside the outer wall of the Topkapı Palace complex, at Osman Hamdi Bey Yokuşu. The easiest way to get there is by tram; get off at the Gülhane stop. From the stop, walk two blocks away from the Golden Horn along the old palace wall. Go through the entryway with three arches into Gülhane Park, and bear right up the cobbled lane. The museum is near the top of this lane, on the left.

You can also approach the museum from the First Courtyard of the Topkapı Palace (see the Topkapı Palace Tour on page 140): After entering the First Courtyard through the Imperial Gate, go diagonally to the left (with Hagia Irene church on your left-hand side), pass through the arched entryway, and follow the alley down the hill to the museum (on your right).

As you face the big entrance gate for the museum complex, the ticket-seller is to the left. Buy your ticket, then go through the gate. As you enter, the Museum of the Ancient Orient is directly to your left; the Tiled Kiosk is ahead on the left; and the main Museum of Archaeology is ahead on the right, across the courtyard.

Information: Exhibits throughout are labeled in English, and a sign at the gate lists exhibits closed for renovation. Tel. 0212/520-7740.

Length of This Tour: Allow at least two hours to tour all three parts. If you're in a hurry, spend an hour at the Museum of Archaeology, sprint through the Tiled Kiosk, and skip the Ancient Orient.

Cloakroom and WCs: Both are in the main building (Museum of Archaeology).

Photography: Photography without a flash is generally allowed.

Cuisine Art: An outdoor café (with only a few food items) hides among trees and columns between the Museum of the Ancient Orient and the Tiled Kiosk. Having a bite or drink here is like living out your own archaeological fantasy.

Starring: A slew of sarcophagi (including the remarkable Alexander Sarcophagus), sumptuous İznik tiles, the ancient Kadesh Treaty, and several millennia of Turkey's past.

Overview

The museum has three separate sections: The main collection—the Museum of Archaeology—features the world-renowned Alexander

Sarcophagus, a selective and engaging collection of ancient sculpture, and archaeological finds from the Trojans and the Byzantines, predominantly from the sixth century B.C. on. The 15th-century Tiled Kiosk is one of the oldest examples of Ottoman civic architecture, and contains an outstanding collection of centuries-old Turkish tiles. And the Museum of the Ancient Orient displays artifacts from early Mesopotamian and Anatolian cultures, mostly dating from before the sixth century B.C. (with some going all the way back to 2700 B.C.).

There's a lot of ground to cover here. If your attention span is limited, spend most of your time at the Museum of Archaeology. The Tiled Kiosk and the Museum of Ancient Orient are small enough to merit at least a quick walk-through.

THE TOUR BEGINS

• *We'll begin at the museum's highlight: the Museum of Archaeology. Enter the long courtyard and walk toward the end (passing the Museum of the Ancient Orient, then a little park with a café, then the Tiled Kiosk on your left). Near the end of the courtyard, on your right, is the...*

MUSEUM OF ARCHAEOLOGY

This ornamental building has two entrances, framed by pediments supported by four tall columns—resembling the designs on some of the museum's sarcophagi. Inside you'll find those sarcophagi, as well as piles of artifacts from the Greeks, Romans, Byzantines, Trojans, and more.

• *Use the left entrance, across from the Tiled Kiosk.*

As you enter, you'll find yourself in the antechamber. The bust near the staircase depicts the museum's founder, Osman Hamdi, and is surrounded by backlit information panels about his life and paintings. Famous in his own time as a painter, Hamdi (1842–1910) is now regarded as the father of Turkish museums.

• *The halls on either side of the antechamber display the museum's...*

Sarcophagi Collection

Hamdi brought these sarcophagi here in the 1880s from the royal necropolis of Sidon (in present-day Lebanon, but part of the Ottoman Empire back then). The Sidon sarcophagi are among the most important classical works ever unearthed. They were discovered accidentally by a villager who was digging for water. Hamdi personally directed the excavations. The marble sarcophagi were found miraculously intact in two separate burial chambers, insulated against humidity and water leakage.

• *Now go through the door to your left to see the...*

Alexander Sarcophagus

The museum's star exhibit is in the center of the hall, inside a large, red-framed glass case. Other than a few dents in the marble caused by careless movers, this fourth-century B.C. sarcophagus is in excellent condition. Although it's known as the Alexander Sarcophagus—that's Alexander the Great portrayed in battle and hunting scenes on the sides—it was actually carved for King Abdalonymos of Sidon.

While faded after two

thousand years, some of the sarcophagus' colors remain, and the bas-reliefs that decorate the casket and its lid are impressive. Some figures are almost freestanding, giving the impression that their next step will take them right out of the scene and into the room with you. Look for a color model of the "Alexander on his horse" scene next to the sarcophagus, offering a better idea of how the relief looked in full sarcophi-color.

The side of the casket facing the entrance shows Alexander's army battling the Persians. This is the Battle of Issus in 333

B.C. Alexander's victory here paved the way for him to conquer the Middle East. The battle also changed the life of Abdalonymos, the sarcophagus' likely "owner": Distantly related to Sidon's royal family, he was appointed as the new king when the Macedonians marched into Sidon. It's easy to tell who's who:

Persian troops wear long pants, several layers of loose shirts, and turbans. The Macedonians are either naked or half-naked, in short tunics. On the far left, Alexander wears a lion pelt as he attacks a Persian soldier from horseback. His arm is raised as he prepares to hurl a (missing) spear.

Move counterclockwise around the sarcophagus. The battle scene continues on the short end of the casket to the right. The relief on the lid, in the triangular pediment, is another battle scene—likely the battle of Gazze (312 B.C.), in which King Abdalonymos was killed. The dominant red color is best preserved on this side.

The next, long side of the sarcophagus depicts two separate hunting scenes. This relief, less crowded than the battle scene, is

dominated by the lion hunt at its center. The lion's body is pierced at several points, and blood flows from his wounds. Still, he manages to bite and claw at the horse's shoulder. The rider of the horse is King Abdalonymos, dressed in a traditional Persian outfit.

Pay attention to the different garb of the soldiers—here, they're all hunting together. This was a scene Alexander fought for: to create a united empire. The Macedonian on the horse behind the lion is Alexander's general, Hephaestion, who appointed Abdalonymos as king. Alexander is on horseback to the left of Abdalonymos.

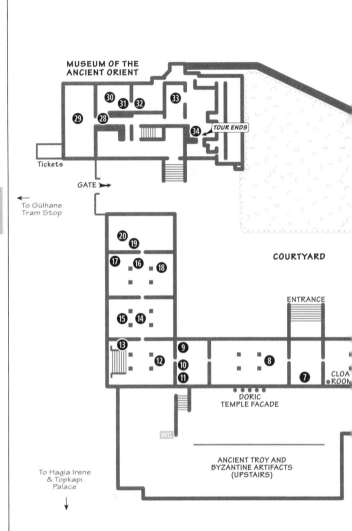

ARCHAEOLOGICAL MUSEUM

MUSEUM OF THE
ANCIENT ORIENT

30 31 32 33

29 28 34 *TOUR ENDS*

Tickets

GATE ➤

To Gülhane
Tram Stop

20
19
17 16 18

15 14

13 9
12 10
11

COURTYARD

ENTRANCE

8 7

CLOAK
ROOM

DORIC
TEMPLE FACADE

WC

ANCIENT TROY AND
BYZANTINE ARTIFACTS
(UPSTAIRS)

To Hagia Irene
& Topkapı
Palace

Museum of Archaeology

1 Antechamber
2 Alexander Sarcophagus
3 Sarcophagus of the
   Mourning Women
4 Satrap Sarcophagus
5 Lycian Sarcophagus
6 Egyptian (and Egyptian-
   Looking) Sarcophagi

7 Bes
8 Kouros
9 Statue and Head of
   Alexander the Great
10 Satyr Marsyas
11 Hermaphrodite
12 Athlete Statue
13 Caryatid

14 Sappho
15 Roman Busts
16 River God
17 Apollo Playing
   the Lyre
18 Aphrodisias
19 Tyche
20 Cupids

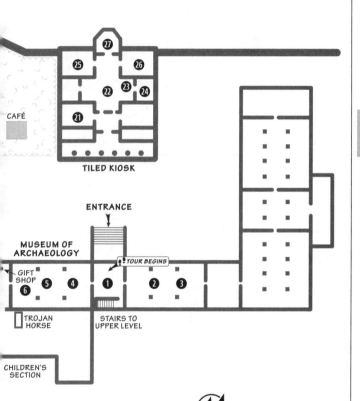

ISTANBUL ARCHAEOLOGICAL MUSEUM

ARCHAEOLOGICAL MUSEUM

27

25   26

22   23
24

21

CAFÉ

TILED KIOSK

ENTRANCE

MUSEUM OF
ARCHAEOLOGY

 TOUR BEGINS

GIFT
SHOP
6   5   4   1   2   3

TROJAN
HORSE

STAIRS TO
UPPER LEVEL

CHILDREN'S
SECTION

Tiled Kiosk
21 Selçuk Tiles
22 Main Hall
23 Prayer Niche
24 Çanakkale Ceramics
25 Room with Hidden Fountain
26 Kütahya Tiles
27 İznik Vessels

Museum of the Ancient Orient
28 Babylonian Friezes
29 The Bronze Age and
   the Assyrians
30 Cuneiform and Steles
31 "Cursed Stele"
32 Assyrian Soldier Friezes
33 The Hittites
34 The Kadesh Treaty

On the final short end is a panther hunt, but this time all the hunters are dressed in the same Persian style. There's more fighting in the pediment, but the figures here are not as refined as the rest. Apparently the first sculptor ran out of time to complete his work, so another took up the hammer.

• *Immediately behind the Alexander Sarcophagus, at the end of the hall, is another perfectly preserved sarcophagus, the...*

Sarcophagus of the Mourning Women

The museum building you are in was modeled after this mid-fourth-century B.C. sarcophagus, arguably the best example of its kind. Although Greek in style, Eastern influences are apparent in the mourning figures' wailing gestures and long robes (called chitons).

The sarcophagus belonged to King Straton of Sidon. Professional mourners—women hired to cry and wail at funerals—were common when he died around 360 B.C., but the women portrayed on this sarcophagus were members of Straton's harem, genuinely affected by his death. Notice that their gestures are very natural, almost lifelike. Scholars believe the sculptor may have used models to create such realistic emotion. The designs along the lid's long sides represent the funerary procession. From right to left, find the young man leading the cortege, two horses to be sacrificed at the service, a Persian quadriga (chariot with four horses), and a funeral cart pulled by four horses, followed by the attendants.

• *Go back to the antechamber and walk straight through, to the facing door. This is the second hall of Sidon sarcophagi. The first sarcophagus is the...*

Satrap Sarcophagus

Satraps were Persian governors, akin to viceroys ruling in the king's

name. This sarcophagus dates back to the fifth century B.C. Its specific occupant is unknown, but the scenes on the sides of the casket trace the life of a powerful satrap. The once-bright colors of the palm and lotus flower borders faded long ago. On the long side (which you face as you enter the hall), the satrap and his men prepare his chariot for a ride. As you walk around the sarcophagus to the right, the short end shows the satrap reclining on a bench in his private chamber, accompanied by his wife (who's resting her back on the border). A servant pours wine, while a second servant stands by with a cloth in one hand and an unseen fan in the other. In the next scene, on the opposite long side, the satrap uses a spear to hunt a panther. The final short end shows the satrap's grooms with their spears, helping him out of a potentially embarrassing situation.

• *Behind the Satrap Sarcophagus, you'll see the...*

Lycian Sarcophagus

Dating from the late fifth century B.C., this sarcophagus is named for Lycia—a small area in Mediterranean Turkey—because its shape resembles the distinctive, monumental Lycian tombs there. But that's where the connection ends: The three-quarter poses of this sarcophagus' figures and their Thracian attire—popular in Athens at the time—instead link it to the Greek mainland, as does the layered portrayal of horses and hunters on the casket's long sides. This experimentation with 3-D perspective winds up as a clutter of horse heads and hooves—like equine Rockettes.

The two long sides feature detailed, lifelike hunting scenes: a lion on one side, a wild boar on the other. The horses show their

Arabic and European ancestry, with large foreheads, deep chests, and lean bellies—similar to the horses in friezes at the Parthenon in Athens.

On the narrow end to the right, two centaurs fight over a deer. One is naked, while the other—wearing a panther skin—is about to spear his opponent in the eye. On the opposite end (to the left), the centaurs beat a man to death. This half-buried man is Kaineus, the mythological centaur-slayer. The centaur on his left is about to hit him with an amphora jug. The simple lid is decorated with seated (and remarkably sexy) sphinxes on one side, and griffons on the other.

• *Beyond the Lycian Sarcophagus and the mummified corpse of a king who would have inhabited one of these sarcophagi are several...*

Egyptian (and Egyptian-Looking) Sarcophagi

Just before the exit is an Egyptian sarcophagus carved from dark diorite (similar to granite). Dating from the sixth century B.C., this is the oldest sarcophagus found in the Sidon excavations.

Hieroglyphs on the lid tell about the owner, an Egyptian commander named Penephtah. He was later moved from his tomb to make room for the local king, Tabnit of Sidon. The inscription at the foot is Tabnit's epitaph.

To the right, two light-colored, Egyptian-style sarcophagi lie side by side. Beginning in the fifth century B.C., Greek sculptors carved Egyptian-looking sarcophagi for their wealthy clients. Although the basic style was Egyptian, the Greeks felt free to play around with the design. The result: archaic Greek statues trapped in an Egyptian sarcophagus. The extensions at the shoulders were used to lift or carry the sarcophagus, and were usually chopped off once they reached their final destination.

• Continue ahead through the exit. The museum store is on your right, followed by the cloakroom (on the left), and the museum's second entrance (on the right). WCs are nearby.

For the next part of our tour, continue straight ahead through the lobby. Facing the museum's second entrance, you'll see a statue of...

Bes

This colossal statue of Bes, a demi-god of ancient Egypt, is from the first century A.D. Often confused with Hercules, Bes was a popular figure in the Cypriot pantheon of gods at the time. Here we see Bes holding a lion by its legs. Scholars' best guess is that the statue served as a fountain.

• Walk through the doorway ahead of you, into the exhibit of...

Greek and Roman Sculpture

• Just past the doorway, you're greeted by the head of a...

Kouros

This kouros (a Greek statue of a boy), dating from 600 B.C., was brought from the Greek island of Sámos. His face is round, with a blunt profile, almond eyes, and raised eyebrows. His lips are closed and straight, but grooves at the corners give the impression that he's smiling. In south Aegean art, kouros statues represented the idealized Greek youth. Similar heads and statues have been found in excavations on Sámos, Rhodes, Cos, and other Greek islands. Two other kouros statues stand stiffly at either side of the bay.

• *Continue about 30 yards into the next hall, dedicated to...*

Hellenistic Sculpture (330 B.C.–First Century B.C.)

Entering this hall, on your immediate right is a fine statue of a **young woman** from ancient Kyme, a beautiful example of the Hellenistic period. Rather than noble, idealized gods, the Hellenistic artists gave us real people with real emotions.

ARCHAEOLOGICAL MUSEUM

Look to the opposite side of the hall. Just to the right of the exit door are the exhibit highlights: a pair of Alexander the Greats. Both were discovered in Pergamon, the world-famous acropolis in Aegean Turkey.

Alexander the Great is a pivotal figure in art history. Swooping down from Macedonia (in present-day Serbia and the far north of Greece) in the fourth century B.C., he conquered the Greeks politically but embraced their culture, spreading it across the vast empire he went on to establish. By the time he died, in 323 B.C., his empire—and Greek culture—stretched all the way to India. Every city's main square had a Greek temple and Greek was the language of his vast domain. From an art perspective, Alexander's Macedonian conquest marked the end of the Greek Golden Age (when balance was celebrated). The Hellenistic period that followed was characterized not by idealized and composed beauty but by rippling energy and jump-off-the-stage exuberance.

Carved from fine white marble, the powerful **statue of Alexander the Great** dates from the second century B.C. It's likely he once held a bronze spear in his right hand, although his right arm and hand are missing. The hilt of the sword he held in his left hand remains. The statue bears a rare inscription naming its sculptor: "Menas of Pergamon, son of Aias."

To the right, in the corner, is the very natural-looking **head of Alexander the Great,** also dating from the second century B.C. Some believe it was carved to decorate the renowned "Altar of Zeus" in Pergamon (the altar is now in Berlin, Germany). This head is a copy of the fourth century B.C.

original, by the renowned sculptor Lysippus. Alexander has a slightly tilted head, round eyes with heavy eyelids, and an open mouth that doesn't show his teeth. Gentle lines, deep furrows on the forehead, and the overall natural rendering of the face are characteristic of Hellenistic Pergamon sculpture.

To the left of the doorway is a third-century B.C. statue of the **satyr Marsyas.** Marsyas isn't stretching—he's tied to a tree by his arms, his face contorted in terrible pain. According to myth, Marsyas—provoked by peasants—invented a flute and challenged Apollo to a musical contest. Marsyas lost the contest, and Apollo hanged him from a branch and skinned him alive. Usually portrayed alone, this Marsyas statue was found in a group, next to Apollo...with a slave by his side, ominously sharpening his knife.

To the left is a fine, if surprising, statue of a **hermaphrodite,** also found in Pergamon.
• *The next hall is dedicated to statues from two other ancient cities of Aegean Turkey...*

Magnesia and Tralles

These statues were found in the late 19th century in Magnesia and Tralles. As you enter this larger hall, you'll see a statue of a cloaked **athlete** (some say he was a wrestler), which probably decorated the gymnasium at ancient Tralles in the first century A.D. The muscular young man with the playful smile relaxes against a column, having just finished his exercise.

To the right of the staircase is a beautifully shaped **caryatid**—a support column carved as a woman. Dressed in a traditional gown, she looks well-suited for her architectural role.

Through the doorway on the right, you enter a hall with bays on either side, separated by columns. At the center of this hall is the head of the poet **Sappho,** born 2,700 years ago on the island of Lesbos. Her romantic poems to other women, including Aphrodite, gave us the words "lesbian" and "Sapphic." The left bay is dedicated to Roman portrait busts. The statue and bust (second century A.D.) of emperor **Marcus Aurelius** at the far corner are particularly interesting and realistic.
• *The next hall displays findings from renowned...*

Ancient Cities in Turkey

This hall is marked by the reclining **River God** (second century A.D., from Ephesus) at its center, just before the doorway into the last section.

In the left bay are more statues from Miletus and Ephesus.

At the far end, find the statue of **Apollo playing the lyre** (to the left of the door). In this second-century Roman copy of the Hellenistic original, Apollo is portrayed as more graceful than divine. His missing fingers were on the strings, and his right hand holds the plectrum (used to pluck the strings)—ready to play. Here and there are traces of the reddish-brown and blue paint that once decorated the statue.

The right bay is dedicated to the ancient city of **Aphrodisias,** which had its own school of fine arts and distinct artistic style. The room is named for Kenan Erim, the professor who spent a lifetime excavating at Aphrodisias. (Asked why he never married, Erim said he already was married—to Aphrodite.) Erim was buried at the site, next to the monumental entry to the Temple of Aphrodite.

• *Past the River God, you enter the last exhibition hall, with statues from the...*

Roman Imperial Period

Although of lesser importance, a few of these statues stand out for their intricate work—like **Tyche,** the city goddess, to your immediate left as you enter. Also check out the two **cupids**—betting on a rooster fight—in the glass case on the left wing at the center of the hall.

• *You've now seen the best of the Museum of Archaeology. If you're getting museumed out, head for the museum exit and skip down to the Tiled Kiosk.*

Or, if you can't get enough of ancient Turkey, consider detouring upstairs to see ancient Troy and Byzantine artifacts. While less compelling than the rest of the collection, the upstairs exhibits will help flesh out your understanding of this part of the world.

Optional Upstairs Detour: Ancient Troy and Byzantine Artifacts

If you choose to go upstairs, backtrack to the antechamber where you first entered (near the sarcophagi). Head up the stairs—enjoying views over the Tiled Kiosk across the courtyard—and tour the museum's humble exhibit of artifacts from the ancient city of **Troy.** At the

end of this long hall, dip into the hall to the left, with findings from a **tumulus** (ancient burial mound). Then backtrack to the end of the Troy exhibit, and take the stairs down toward the mezzanine level. Halfway down the stairs is an exhibit of **Byzantine artifacts.** Follow the zigzag tour route past a few interesting items, including the impressive chain the Byzantines pulled across the mouth of the Golden Horn to block enemy fleets; fine Byzantine church frescoes; and massive Byzantine water pipes carved out of marble and caked with lime deposits. You'll also have views down into the atrium, where you can see a replica of the facade from the Doric Temple of Athena at Assos (580 B.C.), a fun replica of the Trojan Horse, and a children's museum (Turkish-language only). You'll wind up back where you started, in the gift-shop area, by the cloakroom and exits.

• *As you leave the Museum of Archaeology, the small, older building directly ahead of you—fronted by a gorgeous two-story colonnade, and to the right of the little park and café—is the...*

TILED KIOSK

The word "kiosk" comes from the Turkish word *köşk,* meaning "mansion" or "pavilion." This one contains some of the finest examples of Selçuk, Ottoman, and regional tiles ever assembled. As you tour the sumptuous collection, keep in mind that in Turkey, "tile" (*çini;* chee-nee) refers to a high-quartz material that can be used both to decorate architectural surfaces (with flat tiles) and to create functional vessels (such as bowls, vases, cups, and so on).

While much of what you'll see inside might be called "ceramics" or "pottery" in English, Turks consider them all "tiles."

Stroll through the collection. Displayed on one easy floor, you can treat it like eye candy, lingering only at your favorite pieces to read the fine English descriptions. For extra credit, follow the self-guided commentary here.

The steps leading up to the entrance are in the center of the lower gallery, hiding behind the stone wall with the barred window. The Arabic **inscription** above the doorway explains that the building was constructed in A.D. 1472, during the reign of Mehmet the Conqueror—roughly 20 years after the Ottomans had taken Constantinople from the Byzantines. The Tiled Kiosk, which represents the earliest stages of Ottoman civic architecture, is the only one of its kind in Istanbul dating from this time period.

As you step into the antechamber (its floor covered in glass, to protect the original pavement), head for the large **map** on the opposite wall, which shows the historically important tile-manu-facturing regions in Turkey and throughout the Middle East and Asia.

• *This entrance chamber is flanked by two small rooms. Enter the room on the left, which contains some of the oldest objects in the exhibition.*

Selçuk Tiles

This room is dedicated to the early **tiles** of Selçuk (the Turkish empire before the Ottomans) and Middle Eastern origin. As you enter the room, the case in front of you displays Syrian and Iranian pieces; the one behind it has some fine designs of Selçuk pottery.

At the end of the room, on the right wall, are decorative **tile** pieces with colored glaze from a 13th-century mosque. This turquoise-colored glaze is still in use, although only a few master potters remain who can apply it correctly. Across the room in the opposite wall are **star-shaped wall tiles** with animal and floral designs. Dating from the 13th century, these are from the summer palace of the Selçuk sultans in Konya (central Turkey).

• *Exit back into the antechamber, and take the door to your left into the main hall. Approach the larger case in the center of the hall.*

Main Hall

The objects that look like vases are actu-ally **ceramic lamps** that were used in mosques. These oil-burning lamps were hung from the ceiling using the little handles. The 16th-century pieces from İznik were probably the best available in the market at the time.

Notice the colorful circa-1430 **prayer niche** on the right side of the hall, brought from Konya in central Turkey. Its pieces are fired with colored glaze.

Stand in the middle of the main hall with the entrance behind you. The annex to your right displays curiously designed 18th- and 19th-century **ceramics** from Çanakkale (a city on the Dardannelles).

• *Now walk to the end of the room, across from the entrance.*

Find the two world-renowned **glazed plates,** displayed in the side walls, across

from each other. Dating from A.D. 1500, these are two of the finest surviving pieces of İznik tile—frequently showing up in reference books as textbook Turkish tiles.

• *Walk past the plates, and go through the doorway on your left, which opens into a highly decorated room.*

The walls contain color-glazed tiles and intricate gold designs. Part of this so-called **"gold embroidery"** was redone over the centuries. It may look a little tacky, but it was the height of style in its day. At the end of the room, on the left corner, is a beautiful hidden fountain.

The room to your right displays **Kütahya tiles.** The town of Kütahya (south of the Sea of Marmara) began making tiles during the 18th century, using similar techniques to the master potters at İznik, but never quite matching the quality of their work.

For the real deal, head into the next room, with outstanding blue-and-white **İznik vessels** from the early 15th century.

• *When you're done in the Tiled Kiosk, exit back into the courtyard and turn right. Head back toward the entrance gate to the complex. Just inside the gate, on the right-hand side, are stairs leading up to the third and final part of the museum, the...*

MUSEUM OF THE ANCIENT ORIENT

Well worth a look, this small collection offers an exquisite peek at the ancient cultures of the Near and Middle East. Most of what you'll see here comes from Mesopotamia, an area between the Tigris and Euphrates Rivers (parts of present-day Iraq and Syria). On this tour, you'll meet Sumerians, Akkadians, Babylonians, and Assyrians (all of whom were sovereign in the Middle East), as well as the Hittites (who ruled today's Turkey)—peoples that paved the road to modern civilization.

• *The entry area offers some maps and other posted information worth skimming for a background understanding of the "Ancient Orient." Since the collection is arranged in a one-way loop, you'll also end your tour here. As you head for the collection, notice the cuneiform script in the floor, which says that flash photography is prohibited.*

Walk through the first room of the museum—stopping to see the **Babylonian sundial** *(on the left)—and head for the doorway on the right (next to the adorable little sphinx). Turn left into a corridor, and take a moment to enjoy the tile friezes lining the corridor's walls.*

Babylonian Friezes

These tile friezes once decorated the gate of the ancient city of Babylon (in today's Iraq). The colorful designs of lions, bulls (which, thanks to stylized perspective, look more like unicorns), and dragons (up top, looking like snakes with

lions' paws in front and eagles' feet in back) represented Babylon's mighty gods.

• *Beyond the friezes, at the end of the corridor, you'll emerge into a room with artifacts from...*

ARCHAEOLOGICAL MUSEUM

The Bronze Age and the Assyrians

The marble head of Lamassu—a half-human, half-bull Assyrian creature—guards the doorway. Turn left and tour the collection clockwise. First you'll see early Bronze Age objects from the Sumerian and Akkadian civilizations. If you know your prehistory, you'll notice that Anatolia and Mesopotamia were technologically advanced—progressing through the metal ages (such

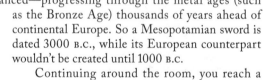

as the Bronze Age) thousands of years ahead of continental Europe. So a Mesopotamian sword is dated 3000 B.C., while its European counterpart wouldn't be created until 1000 B.C.

Continuing around the room, you reach a small showcase with **weight and measurement units** used in Mesopotamia (including the talent, the shekel, and the mina).

Now keep going, into the collection of **Assyrian objects.** The two tall, freestanding statues of kings (ninth century B.C.) were carved out of basalt; although the shorter statue is unfinished, the big one shows fine detail, with cuneiform script pressed into his uniform.

• *For more cuneiform, head back toward the corridor, then take the first left into the collection of...*

Cuneiform and Steles

On the back wall is a group of five steles—small pillars used to commemorate major events. The cases on either side of the steles display **cuneiform tablets.** The wedge-shaped script is the world's first writing system, invented 5,000 years ago by the Sumerians (of southern Iraq) and developed into a syllabic alphabet by their descendants, the Assyrians.

The case on the left traces the progress of cuneiform script.

Who's Who in the Ancient Orient

Who were the peoples of the "Ancient Orient," and how did they relate to each other—and to today's Middle East? While ethnic lines are rarely clear-cut, here's an admittedly oversimplified family tree to help you get your bearings.

One of the clearest ways to track an ethnic group's lineage is to examine its language. Today's Arabs and Jews share a common Semitic language, meaning that they probably also share common ancestors. Today's Turks, Persians (most Iranians), and Kurds speak non-Semitic languages, which indicates they aren't related to the Arabs.

The earliest of the peoples you'll meet in this museum are the **Sumerians** (c. 3000–2000 B.C.). While their origins are unclear, they weren't Semitic. The Sumerians invented a writing system called cuneiform, which marks the beginning of humankind's recorded history.

The **Akkadians** (c. 2300–2100 B.C.) and the **Babylonians** (c. 1900–1600 B.C.) were of Semitic origin—meaning they're the ancestors of today's Arabs. Since the city of Babylon is located in today's Iraq, you could say the Babylonians were "ancient Iraqis."

The **Assyrians** (c. 1900–600 B.C.) were descendants of the Akkadians, and also Semitic (Arab). They created a very efficient trade system throughout the lands they conquered. To secure their borders and prevent uprisings, the Assyrians forced the people they conquered to migrate to other areas of the empire, contributing to the Middle East's ethnic complexity. The Assyrians' descendants today speak Syriac, a form of Aramaic.

The **Hittites** (c. 1700–1200 B.C.) spoke an Indo-European language—meaning their language, and probably their ethnicity, were closer to Europe than to Asia. The Hittites came from the north, and ruled today's Turkey and the Middle East for centuries.

At the bottom left is one of the oldest tablets in the museum (2700 B.C.). The nail-shaped object nearby is actually an inscribed piece. To its right, the item shaped like a roll of paper towels chronicles the acts of the Babylonian king Nebuchadnezzar, describing the temples he built and the reconstruction of Babylon's city walls.

The case to the right of the steles holds interesting tablets, such as the Ur-Nammu law, dating from 2050 B.C. Another tablet records the

Assyrian kings' genealogy, while others list sacred marriage rites, poison remedies, and the court verdict for a man who put off an engagement. There's also a resume and job application, a book of proverbs, and love poems.

Before you continue into the next room, notice the **"cursed stele"** on the wall to the left of the doorway. This eighth-century B.C. stele records the will of an Assyrian palace administrator, Bel-Harran. He tells about a city that he founded, and a temple he constructed and dedicated to the gods. He declares that his citizens will be protected and exempt from tax. And at the end, he tacks on a curse to scare away vandals: "I pray that the great gods of Assyria destroy the future of whomever might destroy my words and my name, and the gods shall have no mercy on them." Maybe that explains how this stele has survived intact for 2,700 years.

• *Now continue into the next room. On the right, notice the long army of knee-high Munchkins marching along the wall...*

Assyrian Soldier Friezes

The first few of these Assyrian troops carry taxpayers' money on the trays balanced on their heads. At the front of the line (at the

opening in the wall) is a highly decorated basalt altar from Cappadocia, in central Turkey. The altar dates from the fifth century B.C. Both the reliefs and the altar have Aramaic text—a "newer" style of writing that replaced cuneiform. Aramaic is also the language spoken by Jesus Christ, most other biblical figures, and Mel Gibson (whose controversial movie *The Passion of the Christ* was filmed entirely in the ancient tongue).

• *After a quick look around in this room, backtrack through the previous room (with the cuneiform tablets and steles). From there, turn left into the main corridor and follow it to its end, into a room with artifacts from...*

The Hittites

The Hittites once controlled a big chunk of Anatolia, reaching their peak in the 13th century B.C. The huge **relief** on the wall depicts a king praying to Tarhunza, the Hittite storm god. Although the king stands on a tall mountain, he still can't reach the height of the gigantic god. Tarhunza was also the god of plants—he carries

grapes in one hand, and wheat in the other. His curly beard and hair, as well as the flares on his skirt, reflect Assyrian influence, while the helmet is Hittite-style. The horns on the helmet are a barometer of his divine importance: the more horns, the more important the god.

• *Go through the doorway on the right, and look to your right. A small case displays the exhibit's highlight...*

The Kadesh Treaty

These few clay fragments are a record in cuneiform script of the world's oldest surviving peace accord: the Kadesh Treaty. This document, created in 1283 B.C., ended the decades-long war between the Hittites and the Egyptians. The United Nations recognizes the importance of this early peace agreement: a large copy of the treaty is displayed at the UN headquarters in New York City.

The text was initially engraved on silver tablets that have been lost to time. Three ancient copies exist. The version you see here was found in the archives of the Hittites' capital city of Hattusha (100 miles north of present-day Ankara). It's written in Akkadian cuneiform, the language of diplomacy at the time.

Egyptian King Ramses II and Hittite King Hattusili III each had his own copy of the treaty—and each version claims victory for that copy's owner. But otherwise, the copies are similar, and include many elements still common in modern-day peace agreements—such as provisions for the return of prisoners and refugees, and a mutual-aid clause. The treaty ends with a curse: "To whomever acts against these words, may the thousand gods of the Land of Hatti and the thousand gods of Egypt destroy his home, his land, and his servants." These final words dictate that the treaty's conditions would be honored by the kings' successors forever. After the Kadesh Treaty, the Middle East enjoyed uninterrupted peace for seven years—which, back then, was a pretty impressive run.

• *Your tour is finished. You're just a short walk from Topkapı Palace: Leave through the main gate to the museum complex, turn left, and head up the hill into the palace's First Courtyard; once there, the entrance to the palace is on your left, and the gate to the Sultanahmet district (and the back of Hagia Sophia) is on your right.*

TURKISH AND ISLAMIC ARTS MUSEUM TOUR

Türk-İslam Eserleri Müzesi

With a thoughtful and manageable collection of artifacts spanning the course of Turkish and Islamic civilizations, this museum is a convenient place to get a glimpse into the rich cultural fabric of this region. You'll see carpets, calligraphy, ceramics, Quran holders, and lots more. The downstairs Ethnographic Department uses fascinating full-size reconstructions and models to show the development of the traditional Turkish home. Almost as interesting as the collection is its setting: the İbrahim Paşa Palace, one of Istanbul's great surviving Ottoman palaces.

ORIENTATION

Cost and Hours: 10 YTL, Tue–Sun 9:00–17:00, last entry at 16:30, closed Mon.

Getting There: It's centrally located in the Old Town's Sultanahmet area, across the Hippodrome (with its Egyptian Obelisk) from the Blue Mosque. From the Sultanahmet tram stop, simply cross through the park toward the Blue Mosque, then jog a few steps to the right when you hit the Hippodrome.

Information: Temporary exhibitions are located on the entrance level. Tel. 0212/518-1805.

Length of This Tour: Allow one hour.

Baggage Check and WCs: A cloakroom is at the entrance, and you're required to check large bags. WCs are located under the staircase that leads up to the central courtyard.

Photography: Not allowed.

Cuisine Art: The cafeteria is just to the right as you enter the central courtyard. On the left side of the courtyard, the terrace has a great view of the Hippodrome and the Blue Mosque.

Starring: The "richest carpet collection in the world," ceramic tiles and containers, rare calligraphy, and a peek inside a Turkish yurt, mountain village house, and 19th-century city home.

Overview

Originally, the İbrahim Paşa Palace was much bigger, rivaling that of the sultan's. But today, its smaller size makes the museum's U-shaped layout easy to figure out. The palace's original reception hall is today's south wing, with a small wooden balcony on its facade facing the Hippodrome, and its north and west wings were once palatial guest rooms.

Today the museum's upstairs north, west, and south wings focus on historical artifacts, while the downstairs south wing focuses on lifestyles, with replicas of traditional Turkish homes. In this tour, we'll start in the north wing, dip into several rooms along the west wing, then enter the large south wing. We'll finish downstairs in the Ethnographic Department.

THE TOUR BEGINS

As you enter the large central courtyard, take the steps to your immediate right, and then go through the first door (to the right of the cafeteria) to enter the north wing. A 13th-century Selçuk lion greets you as you enter the building.

NORTH WING

• *At the top of the entry staircase, turn around 180 degrees. On the back wall of the corridor, behind the staircase, notice the...*

Stones and Steles

The stones you see here, dating from the seventh century A.D., are the oldest pieces in the museum's collection. The slab on the left is a **milestone,** with an inscription in Arabic that states you are only at the beginning of your journey.

• *Turn around again, start down the corridor, and go through the first door on the right (across from the column capitals by the stairs).*

Abbasid Palace Art

These two connecting rooms are filled with Islamic art from the Abbasid palaces. The Abbasid dynasty—which ruled the Muslim world for about 550 years (A.D. 700–1250)—started in Baghdad, and later moved its capital to the nearby city of Samarra. The Abbasid caliph (Islamic leader—see sidebar on page 192) employed slave-soldiers known as the Mamluk. Most of the Mamluk were originally non-Muslims from the north who had been abducted by slave traders or sold into slavery by impoverished parents. In

İbrahim Paşa

The museum building is the former palace of İbrahim Paşa, the Grand Vizier (prime minister) of Süleyman the Magnificent. İbrahim was appointed to serve young prince Süleyman, and when Süleyman succeeded to the throne, İbrahim advanced quickly. He became the sultan's right arm, and also married the sultan's sister, Hatice.

İbrahim appreciated art, and after Budapest was conquered by the Ottomans, he brought back bronze statues of Apollo, Artemis, and Hercules, and placed them in front of his palace. However, these pagan symbols offended the public. One poet even said: "Two İbrahims came to this world. One destroyed idols (Prophet Abraham), and the other re-erected them." İbrahim could not stand this criticism—he had the poet crawl the streets of Istanbul and then hanged him.

The Grand Vizier's arrogant and self-centered attitude gained him strong enemies, among them Süleyman's wife, Roxelana. İbrahim was very powerful, so Roxelana had to get rid of him to guarantee her sons' succession. One day, the Grand Vizier was invited to Topkapı Palace for dinner, and the next morning, his dead body was found outside the palace walls (apparently Roxelana was...a bad cook). Süleyman had İbrahim buried in an unmarked grave, and his enormous wealth was confiscated.

time, they became a powerful military caste, establishing their sovereignty in Egypt. (We'll see some Mamluk sarcophagi later in this tour.)

The presence of the Mamluk soldiers caused friction with the public. In 836, pressured by the communal leaders of Baghdad, the caliph decided to move the center of the caliphate from Baghdad to the new city of Samarra, which was then a simple military garrison town. Thousands of masons were brought in from all over the Middle East to work at what was then the largest construction site in the world. There was limitless room to build, so structures were planned in immense proportions. (Even the homes of officials and administrators were huge palaces.) The masons created single-story buildings of stone, fired brick, and mud-brick, with summer and winter sections that incorporated baths, canals, and pools.

In the first bay, you can see artifacts from the Cevzak (jehv-zahk) Palace of Samarra. The case on the left displays wall frescoes from the harem; the larger fresco of the two dancers is particularly attractive. On the opposite side are ninth-century wooden fragments used for wall decoration.

In the connecting bay, you'll see ivory items and a fragment from a marble floor (all from Cevzak). The case to the immediate

TURKISH & ISLAMIC ARTS MUSEUM

1. Stone Milestone
2. Palace Floor Mosaics
3. Objects from the Grand Mosque of Cizre
4. Metal & Wood Door
5. Tiled Inscription Panel
6. Selçuk Stone Carvings
7. Selçuk Steles
8. Mamluk Sarcophagi
9. Kitchen Door Panels
10. Bronze Drum Set
11. Bronze/Brass Candlesticks
12. Brass Bowl
13. Tile Pieces
14. Glass Oil Lamps
15. Candle/Oil Lamp
16. Gilded Copper Lantern
17. Rüstem Paşa Quran Holder
18. Hagia Sophia Quran Holder
19. Minaret Tops
20. Tuğra
21. Ottoman Title Deeds
22. Tile Frames
23. Holbein Carpets
24. Selçuk Carpets
25. Selçuk Woodwork & Tile Art
26. Ceremonial Wood Sarcophagus
27. Metal Objects
28. Mosque Mimber
29. Uşak Carpets
30. Ottoman Calligraphy
31. Rahle Quran Holder
32. Candlesticks & Quran Holders

left as you enter displays ceramic pieces from Rakka, a city in modern-day Syria.

• *Head back into the corridor. On your right, there's a case built into the wall with marble and stone fragments, and* **mosaics** *used in the floor pavement of Samarra palaces. Enter the next room on the right.*

Objects from the Grand Mosque of Cizre

This room contains the monumental gate of the mid-12th-century Grand Mosque of Cizre (jeez-reh), today a small town in eastern Turkey west of the Tigris River. During the Middle Ages, this mosque was one of the most important monuments in Anatolia (Asian part of present-day Turkey). Note the engraved metal decorations of the gate in the case ahead of you. These adornments are actually patches. Made from recycled metal items such as bowls, they were used to replace missing sheets on the doors' panels,

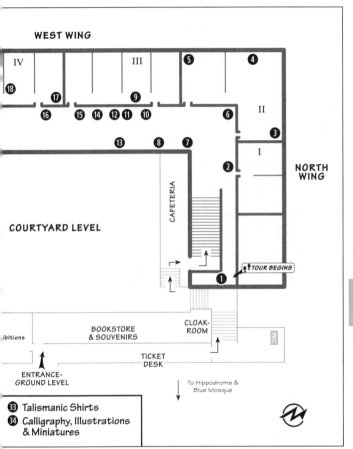

showing hunting scenes and other designs. They also contain inscriptions done in the Kufic style, an earlier form of Arabic script written with straighter lines.

On your right, you'll see plans and pictures of the mosque. At the other end of the room, you'll see a magnificent **door** made of wood, sheeted with copper, held together with iron nails, and reinforced with brass rods. Look at the dragon-shaped handles. The one on the left was stolen in 1969, and somehow showed up in a Copenhagen museum. The lion-shaped middle piece is still on the door wing. Lions and dragons were common designs in

The Great Caliphates

After the death of the Prophet Muhammad in A.D. 632, Islamic leaders created the position of caliph to serve as the religious and social leader of the Muslim community (similar to the apostles or popes in Christian history). But as the first four caliphs (who served consecutively) began to die off, people wondered how to choose their replacements: Some Muslims thought caliphs should be elected, while others felt the position should be hereditary, and pass only to direct descendants of Muhammad.

First the title of "caliph" was handed down through family dynasties, and took on more of a political significance. The **Umayyads** (661–750) became the first significant caliphate dynasty, who ruled from Damascus, in present-day Syria.

Then the **Abbasids**—the descendants of Muttalib, the uncle of Muhammad—used the lineage argument to seize the caliphate, moving its base from Damascus to Baghdad, and eventually to Samarra. Beginning in the early eighth century, the Abbasids ruled the Middle East and the Islamic world for over 500 years. After that, although their power waned, they kept the title until the early 1500s, when the Ottomans took over.

Because the **Ottomans** were Turks rather than Arabs, their claim to the caliphate was less convincing to the Arab communities within their empire. But once the Ottoman sultan's name was officially recorded as the caliph, his authority was accepted.

In the beginning of the 20th century, as Turkey was poised to become a modern republic, the caliphate came into question again. Because Atatürk's vision for the new republic included a separation of mosque and state, Turkey's parliament abolished the caliphate in 1924, once and for all.

Anatolia, and were considered talismans.

• *As you face this monumental gate, the doorway on the left leads into a display of...*

Selçuk Tiles

This small collection boasts rare and unusual pieces from the 11th to the 13th centuries, the zenith of Selçuk tile art. The intact **inscription panel,** hanging on the wall straight ahead of you as you enter the room, is particularly impressive.

The Selçuks used tiles to decorate both the interiors and

The Selçuk Turks

The Selçuk Empire was the first powerful Turkish-Muslim state in Anatolia. The Selçuks governed from 1000 to the early 1300s in the Near East (mainly present-day Iran) and the Middle East. In 1071, a branch of the Selçuks entered the eastern provinces of present-day Turkey and defeated the Byzantine army. The decline of the Selçuks in the early 14th century cleared the way for the autonomy of future Turkish dynasties—just over a century later, the Ottomans would unify the Turks once again.

the exteriors of their monuments. The secret to their artistry was the fine clay they used, which contained a large amount of quartz. The quartz made the tiles durable enough to survive even the harsh weather of the steppes of central Asia. To create the tiles, Selçuk artisans spread a layer of clay several inches thick on a tray, and cut it into smaller shapes such as triangles, quadrangles, and stars. Then they painted the pieces with colored glazes, and fired the tiles. Unlike thin surface tiles used elsewhere, the Selçuks' thick, glazed tiles were actually integrated into the walls, ceilings, and minarets of buildings. The Selçuks—who favored geometric patterns and a blue, turquoise, and purple color scheme—also created everyday objects that were both decorative and functional, such as vases, cups, and pitchers.

Just as you exit the room into the corridor, note the rare pieces of **Selçuk stone carvings** on your left, including a relief with two Selçuk warriors on the corner. More-stylized reliefs on the wall display bird and dragon motifs embedded in intricate, floral designs. The Selçuk Turks used these motifs extensively on wood and stoneworks to decorate facades and entrances on civil as well as religious architecture.

WEST WING

• *Now take a few steps down the long corridor. On your left are a few 11th- to 13th-century* **Selçuk steles.** *Next to them are two nicely detailed...*

Mamluk Sarcophagi

These ceremonial marble sarcophagi date back to the 15th century.

The Mamluk, which means "owned" in Arabic, were slave-soldiers (who were converted to Islam) and served the caliphs during the Middle Ages. (For more on the Mamluk, see page 188.)

• *Walk through the doorway across from the sarcophagi.*

Selçuk Art

This room features more items from the Selçuk Empire. The first bay shows off 12th- and 13th-century Selçuk objects, including belts, bowls, animal figures, and oil lamps. As you enter the second bay, you'll see a great example of Selçuk woodwork on the wall to your left. These 12th-century **door panels,** decorated with bronze sheets, are from a public kitchen. Some of the bronze sheets are missing—notice the traces of nails that once held them. To the left of the fireplace is the wooden door of a *mimber* (pulpit in a mosque).

• *Skip the last two bays, which contain Mamluk and transitional items from the Tamerlane period (named for a 14th-century Mongolian warlord). Instead, return to the corridor through the same doorway that you entered. Stop here for a second. Looking toward the far end of the corridor, the left side is lined all the way to the entrance of the south wing with...*

Carpets

These are 13th- to 18th-century prayer rugs—or what's left of them after centuries of constant use. (You can actually see how after countless calls to prayer, the older carpets have gotten bare spots from the foreheads, knees, and toes of worshippers.) The oldest two, next to the Mamluk sarcophagi, have a dominant red color and prayer-niche designs that reflect their purpose.

Looking at the descriptions, you'll see names such as "Bellini" and "Holbein." These rug designs are named for the European artists who popularized them by painting the designs in the backgrounds of their works. (We'll see more "Holbein carpets" later on this tour.) The European love affair with Turkish or

"Oriental" carpets began in the 13th century. For centuries, upper-class Europeans considered a Turkish rug the ultimate status symbol. If you couldn't afford to buy an actual rug, you'd pay an artist to paint one to hang on the wall—or to paint a rug hanging in the background of a portrait.

• *Walk along the right wall down the corridor, taking some time to peruse the...*

Corridor Showcases

Notice the fun 13th-century bronze **drum set,** then the bronze and brass **candlesticks** from the early 13th century. The adjacent case

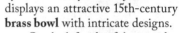

displays an attractive 15th-century **brass bowl** with intricate designs.

On the left side of the corridor are fragments from very fine 12th- and 13th-century **tile pieces.** The next case, on the right-hand wall, displays **glass oil lamps** gathered from mosques and shrines, and then—in the case beyond that—a large, unusual **lamp** with grooves at the bottom to hold candles or oil lamps. Past the doorway, in another case, is a fine, gilded **copper lantern** from the 15th century.

• *Step through the doorway into the next room.*

Objects from the Ottoman Empire and Persia

The first three bays in this room contain items from the Ottoman Empire, while the last one displays objects of Persian origin.

• *Begin with the...*

First Bay: Milet İşi Ceramics

As you enter the first bay, look next to the fireplace to see a beautiful **Quran holder** from the Rüstem Paşa Mosque (described on page 93). Also enjoy the two beautifully shaped candlesticks: 15th-century silver and 14th-century dragon-shaped bronze.

Dominating this bay are ceramic pieces called **Milet İşi** (mee-leht ee-shee), or Miletus Ware. Scholars initially thought they resembled the ceramics of Miletus, an ancient city along the Aegean Sea, near Ephesus. But they're actually late 14th- and 15th-century ceramics manufactured in İznik (ancient Nicaea), a town to the east of the Sea of Marmara. Milet İşi, which was produced for just a short time, usually features purple and cobalt-blue colors on a white undercoat, with basic geometric shapes and plant and animal motifs.

• *Continue into the...*

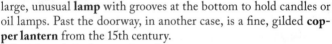

Second Bay: Quran Holder and İznik Tiles

This bay displays classical Ottoman works. As you enter, look for

a separate case on the opposite wall. Full of ornate woodwork and outstanding details, this **Quran holder** was from the mausoleum of Sultan Selim III in Hagia Sophia.

The other case in this bay contains **İznik tiles and ceramics.** In the 16th and 17th centuries, İznik was the center of tile-making in the empire, manufacturing top-quality and extremely expensive pieces. Because İznik tiles were hard to make, they were mostly used to decorate palaces and grand mosques in the capital city. Non-decorative, daily-use pieces are very rare.

• *Continue into the...*

Third Bay: Ottoman Metalwork

In the center of the U-shaped case, you'll see examples of Ottoman metalwork. These large bronze and brass **minaret tops** are called *alem* (ah-lehm). They have a decorative purpose, but they also work as lightning rods. To the right are metal belts, pins, and aigrettes—sprays of gems used on turbans. Most are embellished with precious and semi-precious stones.

• *Finally, head into the...*

Fourth Bay: Persian Items

Dating from the same time period as the Ottoman objects described previously, this collection includes the only Persian carpets in the museum. You'll also find fine examples of book decorations and lacquer covers.

• *Leave this room through the doorway on your left, and go back to the corridor. On your right are displays of...*

Ottoman Calligraphy

Combine Arabic writing with artistic calligraphy, and you've

got *hat* (pronounced "hot"). The calligrapher *(hattat)* ignores the rules of grammar, combining letters in a form that's hard to read but that looks beautiful. At the far end of the corridor, find the 18th-century ***tuğra*** (too-rah), or imperial signature, of Sultan Osman III. (If it's hiding, ask the guard for assistance.)

• *As you near the end of the corridor, the last section on your right is dedicated to...*

Late Ottoman Art

This space, divided into three bays, includes Ottoman **title deeds** on scrolls signed by the sultans (on the right wall as you enter). Go on a scavenger hunt for the following items: examples of *hat* (calligraphy), book decorations, mother-of-pearl writing sets, paper cases, an imperial coat of arms in an extravagant frame, and an interesting compass used for measuring distances.

• *When you're done, exit back into the corridor. On the other side of the corridor is the entrance to the larger and longer south wing of the building. But first, to the left of this doorway are* **tile frames** *decorated with scenes of İznik, Kaaba in Mecca (the holiest place in Islam), and Medina (a Saudi Arabian city, second only to Mecca to Muslims). On the wall behind them is a rug with a Kaaba design.*

Now continue into the...

SOUTH WING

• *As you enter the south wing, you'll see some...*

Holbein Carpets

These are named for the German painter Hans Holbein the Younger (1497–1543). Holbein served as a court painter to Henry VIII, was considered a master portrait artist, and illustrated the first German translation of the Bible. He liked to paint Oriental carpets (and other handicrafts) in the backgrounds of his paintings and court frescoes. Europeans who had seen these designs in the paintings wanted to own a similar carpet in real life...and Turkish carpet-makers happily obliged.

Even though these designs carry his name, Holbein didn't originate the designs. For example, Holbein carpets often have large eight-pointed stars, which was unusual in Ottoman carpets of the time; rather, this motif is more common in earlier Selçuk carpets (shown in the next section). The carpets you see here are mainly based on designs from the Turkish towns of Uşak (oo-shahk) and Bergama (behr-gah-mah; known in ancient times as

Pergamon). Today, Bergama carpets—though limited in quantity—are still being woven there, but none are made in modern Uşak. (For more examples of Uşak carpets, see the upcoming section.) Crafted in a predominantly red color, these carpets have a traditional design and are extremely fine, especially considering the density of their wool. (Pay special attention to the one hanging on the wall across from the entrance.)

• *Walk into the next section, which is reserved for...*

Selçuk Carpets and Other Objects

Only a handful of 13th-century **Selçuk carpets** have survived, and more than half are displayed in this room. They were gathered from mosques and shrines in central Turkey, especially from Konya, the capital city of the Selçuk Empire. The rare carpets on display here show different colors and designs, making each one unique. Their designs are quite stylized, almost to the point of abstraction, as the creators adapted floral and animal motifs into geometric forms. The patterns are often repeated. Designs include stylized eagles, arrowheads, crescents, and eight-pointed stars, as well as Kufic letters (which are also commonly used to decorate borders). These carpets, made of pure wool, are knotted with a double-knot technique, known as the "Turkish knot."

The room also contains Selçuk **woodwork** and **tile art.** To the left of the fireplace, notice the nicely detailed, ceremonial wood **sarcophagus** dating from 1250. (The wooden doors are more recent, and not Selçuk.) The case in the center of the room displays **metal objects**, weights, grinders, and 13th-century Selçuk tile pieces. On the wall opposite the fireplace is the wood siding of a *mimber* (mosque's pulpit), with painted floral designs. The most impressive Selçuk tile fragments—tiled-brick pieces made in the traditional fashion with a high quartz content—are in the wall, in the showcase to your left just before you leave this room.

• *With your back to the fireplace, exit the doorway to the right, which leads to the last and largest hall of the museum, containing...*

Uşak Carpets and Other Objects

These Uşak "palace carpets," from the 16th and 17th centuries, mark the peak of traditional, all-wool carpet weaving in Turkey. In an average Uşak carpet, there are about 103,000 knots in 10 square feet. (Wool carpets don't come any denser.) There are two types: those designed with medallions (the more common type), and those with repetitive star patterns (which are usually smaller).

After admiring the rugs, take a look at the other objects. In the first case (to the right as you enter the hall) are some of the museum's finest examples of **Ottoman calligraphy.** A long scroll, alongside a document from an estate, has a sketch of the city waterway. In the next case are large objects of art, including candleholders. These were decorative as well as functional, used on either side of the apse in a mosque. There is also a huge *rahle* (rah-leh), a holder for a large Quran (or other book), sheeted with silver. A *rahle* supported the fragile binding of the Quran while it was read.

The next case, at the far end of the hall, displays more **candlesticks and Quran holders.** The one made of wood with amazing details dates back to the 16th century. Another, with mother-of-pearl inlay, was made in the 17th century. To the left, in a smaller case, you see **talismanic shirts,** worn to protect the wearer from any kind of danger. The larger case (before the exit on the right) displays great examples of **calligraphy,** book **illustrations**, and Ottoman **miniatures**.

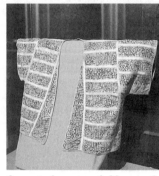

• *Go down the staircase to return to the central courtyard. Next to the base of the stairs is the entrance to the Ethnographic Department.*

ETHNOGRAPHIC DEPARTMENT

This section of the museum describes Turkish lifestyles, from nomadic life in central Asia to 19th-century city living.

• *On the left wall as you enter is a panel about...*

Nomadic Lifestyles

A map traces the lands where the *kara çadir* (kah-rah chah-duhr), the traditional, black goat-hair tent of nomads, has been used—from the shores of the eastern Atlantic Ocean to the Caspian Sea. Nomads in eastern Turkey still follow this traditional lifestyle, occasionally crossing borders while herding their animals.

Considering the nomads' mobile lifestyle, a portable tent that you can fold and pack on an animal is the ideal home. The black tent is made of woven goat hair and connecting wood pins, with a central wood pole for support. Although the tent material looks simple, it is quite difficult to make. The fabric is made of coarse goat hair, which makes the weaver's hands bleed and become calloused.

• *Now, go straight ahead to the display of kilims across from the entrance. On the right wall is a panel about the...*

Where Were the Men?

Except for one man, the fabric merchant, you'll see only female models in this exhibit. There are two main reasons. In the Turkish culture, women traditionally passed down the folk art and traditions to the next generation. Also, particularly in the countryside, men were not usually involved in responsibilities within the house. While women were in charge of what took place beneath the roof of the house—the cooking, cleaning, sewing, and child-rearing—men were responsible for the outside errands. They built the house, tended the flock, sold the produce, chopped the wood, cleaned the stable, cultivated the field, did the jobs that brought in hard cash...and sometimes hung out in the town coffee shop.

TURKISH & ISLAMIC ARTS

Women of Anatolia

Stop here for a look at these photos of Turkish women from different walks of life, to whom this exhibit is dedicated. In Turkish, the term used to describe the ideal woman—generous, hardworking, nurturing, caring, loving, and protective—is "Anadolu Kadını" (ah-nah-doh-loo kah-duh-nuh), meaning "Woman of Anatolia." The word Anatolia (Anadolu in Turkish) has a double meaning. Literally, it means "east" in Greek, and refers to the Asian part of Turkey. Culturally, it is translated as "full of mothers" by breaking the word into its syllables ("ana" meaning mother and "dolu" meaning full). Given the importance Turkish society places on women, translating Anatolia as "full of mothers" makes sense.

• *Look behind the glass wall to see a big weaving hanging on the wall, called a...*

Kilim

Textiles, especially those that can be used as furniture in a Turkish home, are the flagship of Turkish arts and crafts. Once produced for basic needs, textiles eventually turned into a pleasing art form, especially as the Turks prospered under Ottoman rule.

Kilims (kee-leem) are flat woven rugs, consisting of warp (horizontal) and weft (vertical) layers (without the knots added for carpets). These weavings are quite similar to Navajo Indian rugs, and tribal designs are passed down from one generation to the next. The large kilim you see here has two long and narrow parts, like two runners, which were successively woven on the same narrow loom and later connected to form a large rectangle. This was a common way to create large kilims, instead of making a bigger loom. On the left, you'll see a typical wooden kilim loom used by nomads.

ETHNOGRAPHIC DEPARTMENT
TURKISH & ISLAMIC ARTS MUSEUM

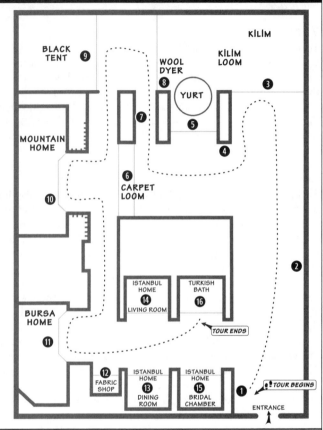

TURKISH & ISLAMIC ARTS

① Nomadic Lifestyles	**⑦** Dye-Making Techniques	**⑫** Fabric Shop
② Women of Anatolia	**⑧** Wool Dyer	**⑬** Dining Room
③ Kilim	**⑨** Black Tent	**⑭** Living Room
④ Wooden Wheel	**⑩** Mountain Home	**⑮** Bridal Chamber
⑤ Yurt	**⑪** Bursa Home	**⑯** Turkish Bath
⑥ Loom & Carpet		

• *Continue to your left, under the arch near a huge* **wooden wheel.** *This wheel is the circular roof of a yurt, a tent shown behind the glass wall on your right...*

Yurt

This is a style of tent that has been commonly used throughout Central Asia by the Turks. The yurt (yoort, which also means "motherland" in Turkish) consists of a cylindrical wooden frame that is covered on the outside with thick felt made of sheep wool, with kilims lining the inside. Behind the same glass wall, outside the yurt, on the right, is a thick felt cloak worn by shepherds, still commonly seen in the countryside.

• *Continue to your left to find the...*

Loom and Carpet

Turkish carpets are usually known by the name of the regions where they are made, and the traditional wool-on-wool carpets from the same region almost always have similar designs and colors. This is not only because traditional designs are passed down across generations, but also because the plants used to dye the wool are grown only in certain areas.

The carpet on this big wooden loom has traditional geometric designs, and is colored with natural dyes. Around the loom are different tools used in weaving: heavy wood combs—called *kirkit* (keer-keet)—used to beat down the pile to tighten the threads, a spinning wheel, and simple drop spindles. To the right of the carpet loom, on either side of the hall, are two panels showing **dye-making techniques** and the plants—and even insects—used in the process. An interesting example is the cochineal, a small insect used to make red dye. The Italian liqueur Campari also gets its color from the same insect.

• *Turn left and walk under the wide arch to find the replica...*

Black Tent

This actual-size black goat-hair tent is filled with models of women going about their daily routines. The tent's interior is multifunctional: During the day, it serves as the living room, kitchen, and dining area, while at night, mattresses, quilts, and pillows are rolled out to transform it into a bedroom. A nomad's multipurpose tent was the prototype of today's rural Turkish home.

The goat hair, with its high oil content, hardly absorbs any rain—the water slides right off. For extra protection in winter, today's nomads stretch nylon covers over their tents.

• *Continue along the hallway to find (on the right) the stone walls of a...*

TURKISH & ISLAMIC ARTS

Mountain Home

Behind the glass wall is a model interior of a typical country home from the Yunt Mountain region in western Turkey. Like the tent,

this village house is multifunctional. The family cooks, cleans, eats, and sleeps in one room. Mattresses piled during the day behind a white embroidered curtain are unfolded at night on the carpeted floor. The house is illuminated by a gas lamp (find it on the central shelf of the wooden cupboard). In Turkish, a gas lamp is a *lüks* (lux), which means "light" in Latin.

The model on the far left wears a red bridal headdress and carries a baby on her back. Red is the color of chastity and is used in traditional wedding clothes.

• *Continue down the hallway to find the...*

Bursa Home

This reconstruction shows the interior of the upper-middle-class home of a family in the 19th-century Turkish city of Bursa. The

walls of the wood-and-brick house are covered with fine plaster and painted a saffron color. This house's several rooms were typically used for multiple purposes. Notice the fine embroidered curtains on the left-hand windows. Between the windows, on the wall, is a gold-

embroidered velvet case that holds the Quran. Below the windows is a wood divan, draped with more finely embroidered cloths. In most homes, the divan doubled as a storage unit with drawers (the material hid the drawers).

The two women sitting on the couch are the ladies of the house; one is embroidering, while the other threads vegetables to be dried on a line. Their garments are made out of fine velvet, embroidered with gold threads. The way they cover their hair and necklines with embroidered scarves signifies their social status.

Sitting on the floor are two more women—the servants, their status made clear by their simple outfits. They cover their hair in the traditional style; while their scarves pull back their hair, it's not completely covered nor are their necklines. One does embroidery while the other makes Turkish coffee on a grill (also a good source of heat during the winter).

• *Turn left to find the...*

Fabric Shop

Here's a scene from a 19th-century city street. A merchant shows his wares to a wealthy woman (her clothing tells her status: a velvet dress embroidered with gold threads). To the right, a commoner passes by a typical Ottoman street fountain.

• *The last few exhibits leading back towards the entrance door show examples of 19th-century Istanbul homes. In these displays, you see early glimpses of Westernization: rooms built for a specific function, furnished with armchairs and chairs instead of divans; and models wearing nontraditional clothes. The first room next to the fabric shop shows a...*

Dining Room

Note the marble table and many chairs, and the dresser heavily inlaid with mother-of-pearl, evidence of the family's wealth. This kind of furniture came from what is today southeastern Turkey and northern Syria. On the floor, the fancy carpet with intricate designs represents the 19th-century style designed to please the ruling class. There are no figurative paintings. The framed decoration instead shows the art of *hat* (calligraphy).

The two women sitting on the armchairs wear jewelry rather than traditional headdresses. When city women of the time would go outside, they would cover themselves from head to toe. The common village women in the countryside never followed this trend—they still use a traditional headdress, a square scarf folded into a triangle, with the ends tied at the back of the head.

• *Directly behind you is the...*

Living Room

The ladies of the house are seated in armchairs, admiring the samples brought by the tailor (she's the woman in blue, with the handmade silver belt). On the table in front of the tailor are drawings of the latest fashions.

• *Down the hall and on the opposite side is the...*

Bridal Chamber

The big brass bed is covered in heavily embroidered bedspreads and pillows, and the furniture is inlaid with mother-of-pearl. The bride's white bridal dress is embellished with gold threads.

TURKISH & ISLAMIC ARTS

The traditional Turkish bridal dress was either completely red or dominated by red, but with Western influence, more brides began wearing white.

• *Turn around to see the last exhibit, which shows a Turkish bath.*

Turkish Bath

The woman on the very left is dressed for the bath, covered in a wrap called a *peştemal* (pehsh-teh-mahl). Commoners wore simple

 wooden non-slip slippers called *takunya* (tah-koon-yah), while the rich would wear the fancier silver or bronze *nalın* (nah-luhn) you see here, inlaid with mother-of-pearl. The bowls in the display are similar to those still used today in Turkish baths. Notice the bowls on the right side with the Arabic words. These are prayers from the

Quran, talismanic bowls that people believed gave them strength and help for certain troubles (so they could wash away the trouble). Bath towels and a *peştemal* hang on the wall, over the metal taps.

• *Our tour is over. As you walk back across the garden, notice the terrace overlooking the Hippodrome, with sweeping views of the Hippodrome monuments and the Blue Mosque.*

GRAND BAZAAR TOUR

Kapalı Çarşı

The world's oldest shopping mall is a labyrinthine warren of shops and pushy merchants—a unique Istanbul experience that shouldn't be missed, even if you're not a shopper. While parts of the bazaar are overrun with international visitors, it also has many virtually tourist-free nooks and crannies that offer an insightful glimpse into the "real" Istanbul.

ORIENTATION

Cost: Free to enter and browse.

Hours: Mon–Sat 9:00–19:00, shops begin to close at 18:30; closed Sun and on the first day of most religious festivals.

Getting There: It's behind the Nuruosmaniye Mosque, across the parking-lot square from the Çemberlitaş tram stop. For detailed instructions on getting here from Sultanahmet (in the center of the Old Town), see the beginning of the Old Town Back Streets Walk on page 87.

Length of This Tour: Allow one to three hours, depending on how much shopping you want to do.

Shopping Tips: This tour goes hand-in-hand with the Shopping chapter, near the end of this book. Consider reading that chapter beforehand, perhaps while nursing a cup of Turkish coffee in the bazaar (focus on the bargaining tips if you plan to buy anything). For advice on dealing with the aggressive merchants here (and elsewhere), see the sidebar on page 209.

Navigating the Bazaar: The Grand Bazaar is a giant commercial complex with named "streets" *(caddesi)* and "alleys" *(sokak)*. But few of these streets and alleys are well-marked, or the signs are covered by merchandise, so relying on these names isn't always successful. Complicating matters is the bazaar's mazelike floor plan. To make things easier, navigate using the map on pages 210–211, and by asking people for help. (But be warned that asking a merchant for help may suck you into a lengthy conversation about the wonders of his wares.) Most of the specific shops we describe in this tour are well-established landmarks that are unlikely to go out of business before your visit.

Pickpocket Alert: The Grand Bazaar may contain the single highest concentration of pickpockets in Istanbul. Watch your valuables.

Rainy Day: This tour is a good bad-weather activity, since almost the entire bazaar is covered.

Background

Sprawling over a huge area in the city center, Kapalı Çarşı (kah-pah-luh chahr-shuh; "Covered Market") was the first shopping mall ever built. During Byzantine times, this was the site of a bus-tling market; when the Ottomans arrived, it grew bigger and more diverse. The prime location attracted guilds, manufacturers, and traders, and it grew quickly—its separate chunks were eventually connected and roofed to form a single market hall. Before long, the Grand Bazaar became the center for trade in the entire Ottoman Empire. At its prime, the market was locked down and guarded by more than a hundred soldiers every night, like a fortified castle.

The Grand Bazaar remained Turkey's commercial hub—for both locals and international traders—through the 1950s, its 4,000 shops bursting with everything you can imagine, from jewelry to silk clothing, and traditional copperware to exotic Oriental imports. But then the Grand Bazaar was discovered by travelers seeking the ultimate "Oriental market" experience. Prodded by shopaholic tourists with fat wallets, prices and rents skyrocketed, and soon modest shopkeepers and manufacturers found themselves unable to compete with the big money circulating through the bazaar's lanes. These humble merchants moved outside the bazaar, displaced by souvenir and carpet shops.

Today's Grand Bazaar sells 10 times more jewelry than it used to. And, while tourists find it plenty atmospheric, locals now con-sider its flavor more Western than Oriental. And yet, even though the bazaar has lost some of its traditional ambience, enough arti-facts remain to make it an irreplaceable Istanbul experience. This tour takes you through the schlocky tourist zones...but it also takes you by the hand to the market's outer fringe, still frequented by more Turks than visitors.

THE TOUR BEGINS

• *Enter the Grand Bazaar through the* ❶ *Nuruosmaniye Gate behind the Nuruosmaniye Mosque. As you walk through the gate, you're at the start of...*

❷ Kalpakçılar Caddesi

Stepping through the door into air heated by thousands of watts of electric bulbs—and by bustling shoppers and merchants—you'll notice the temperature rise by several degrees. This scene is a little overwhelming at first sight. Welcome to the Grand Bizarre...er, Bazaar.

You're standing on the bazaar's main street, which leads straight from the Nuruosmaniye Mosque to the Beyazıt district, where we'll exit, though we'll take a very roundabout route along the way. This street, Kalpakçılar Caddesi (kahl-pahk-chuh-lahr jahd-deh-see), is "Hatmakers' Street." Historically each street, alley, or corner of the bazaar was dedicated to a particular craft or item, and they still bear those names.

• *All those light bulbs are illuminating...*

❸ Jewelry Showcases

Today's high-traffic, high-rent Kalpakçılar Caddesi is dominated by these glittering displays, containing bigger-ticket items than the traditional hats. Turks love gold, not because they're vain or greedy, but because they're practical: Since local currency has a tendency to devalue, people prefer to invest in something more tangible. Traditionally, Turks celebrating special occasions—such as a wedding or a boy's circumcision—receive gold as a gift. In fact, in the most traditional corners of Turkey, the groom's family still must present the bride's family with gold bracelets before the couple can marry.

Because all this gold is used primarily as an investment, and only secondarily as an accessory, it's most commonly sold in the form of simple 22-carat bracelets (24-carat is too soft to wear). If you see a woman whose arm is lined with five or six of these bracelets, she's not making a fashion statement—she's wearing her family's savings on her sleeve...literally. Recently, jewelers are selling more elaborately decorated designer pieces. These are more expensive and less appealing to thrifty locals

Dealing with Aggressive Merchants

Throughout the Grand Bazaar—and just about everywhere in the Old Town—you'll constantly be barraged by people selling everything you can imagine. This can be intimidating, but it's fun if you loosen up and approach it with a sense of humor. The main rule of thumb: Don't feel compelled to look at or buy anything you don't want. These salesmen prey on Americans' gregariousness, and our tendency to respond politely to anyone who offers us a friendly greeting. They often use surprising or attention-grabbing openers:

"Hello, Americans! Where are you from? I have a cousin there!"

"Are you lost? Can I help you find something?"

"Nice shoes! Are those Turkish shoes?"

"Would you like a cup of tea?"

The list is endless—collect your favorites.

If you're not interested, simply say a firm, "No, thanks!" and brush past them, ignoring any additional comments. This seems cold, but it's the only way to cover the market without constantly getting tied up in a conversation. Depending on my mood, sometimes I just look at them with great seriousness and declare, "Pay peanuts, get monkeys" and then walk away.

If, on the other hand, you're looking to chat, merchants are often very talkative—but be warned that a lengthy conversation may give them false hopes that you're looking to buy, and could make it even more difficult to extract yourself gracefully from the interaction.

(since you're paying for the workmanship, not just the gold itself). Instead, locals who want jewelry for fashion buy cheaper 14- or 18-carat bracelets.

• *A few steps into the bazaar from the Nuruosmaniye Gate (after the fifth shop on the right), look for the entrance marked* Old Bazaar—Sandal Bedesteni *over the doorway, a little off the main street. Duck into the courtyard called...*

❹ Sandal Bedesteni

The Grand Bazaar is made up of a series of *bedestens* (beh-dehs-tehn)—commercial complexes of related shops. The Sandal Bedesteni is one of the oldest, dating from the late 15th century. After the Ottomans arrived and took over a Byzantine marketplace here, the bazaar grew organically—new buildings sporadically sprouted up, each one devoted to a particular trade or item. For the convenience of both the shopkeeper and the customer, shops dealing with similar items clustered together. These distinct units, many of which survive today, are called *bedesten* or *han* (hahn). The most traditional *bedestens* (like this one) have a central courtyard

surrounded by shops and workshops on two floors. Later, developers roofed these commercial units and connected them with alleys, creating a unified central market hall. But if you pay attention, you'll notice that each part of the bazaar still has its own unique characteristics (and characters).

The Sandal Bedesteni once housed merchants of valuable fabrics (such as silk and velvet), turban-makers, and jewelers specializing in precious stones. Today it carries ordinary textile products and assorted tourist knock-offs.

• Backtrack out to the main drag (Kalpakçılar Caddesi), turn right, and continue to the first intersection, where you'll turn right on Sandal Bedesteni Sokak. Look high above. As in confusing Venice, signs point to various landmarks. Walk straight downhill on this alley—with a high

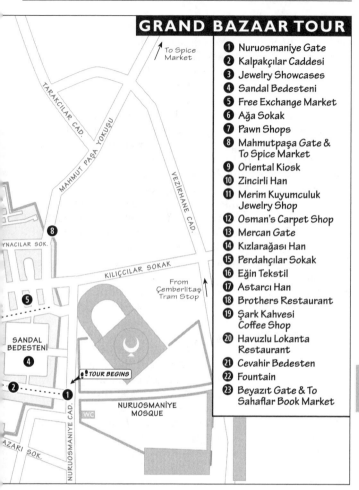

GRAND BAZAAR TOUR

To Spice Market

1. Nuruosmaniye Gate
2. Kalpakçılar Caddesi
3. Jewelry Showcases
4. Sandal Bedesteni
5. Free Exchange Market
6. Ağa Sokak
7. Pawn Shops
8. Mahmutpaşa Gate & To Spice Market
9. Oriental Kiosk
10. Zincirli Han
11. Merim Kuyumculuk Jewelry Shop
12. Osman's Carpet Shop
13. Mercan Gate
14. Kızlarağası Han
15. Perdahçılar Sokak
16. Eğin Tekstil
17. Astarcı Han
18. Brothers Restaurant
19. Şark Kahvesi Coffee Shop
20. Havuzlu Lokanta Restaurant
21. Cevahir Bedesten
22. Fountain
23. Beyazıt Gate & To Sahaflar Book Market

TARAKÇILAR CAD.

MAHMUT PAŞA YOKUŞU

VEZIRHANE CAD.

YNACILAR SOK.

KILIÇCILAR SOKAK

From Çemberlitaş Tram Stop

SANDAL BEDESTENİ

TOUR BEGINS

NURUOSMANIYE CAD.

NURUOSMANIYE MOSQUE

WC

AZARI SOK.

GRAND BAZAAR TOUR

concentration of souvenir shops, carpets, tiles, leather and kilim bags, and chandeliers—toward the intersecting arches. On the right, you'll pass another entrance to the Sandal Bedesteni we just visited. After that, take the next alley on the right. Walk 50 yards to the...

❺ Free Exchange Market

You'll hear it before you see it. From about 10:00 until 17:00, the little alleys branching off this strip are squeezed full of hundreds of boisterous men shouting into their mobile phones and waving their arms. These are currency brokers, and this zone of the bazaar is like a poor man's Wall Street. In this humble setting, people are cutting deals involving hundreds of thousands of dollars and euros every minute.

The Turkish lira is (by European standards) an unstable currency. So, in addition to gold, many Turks still invest in euros or dollars to shore up their savings. Turkey tried to grow with controlled inflation in the 1980s, in order to be more compatible in the international markets. But inflation got out of control—reaching almost 100 percent annually in the 1990s. During this time, people began buying US dollars or German marks. Exchange offices popped up on every corner. On payday, you'd immediately take your paycheck to be converted into dollars, then convert it back to lira when you were ready to buy something with it. Gradually, $100 billion worth of non-Turkish currency was circulating in Turkey—and one-third of this huge amount never showed up in bank accounts. On January 1, 2005, the New Turkish Lira (Yeni Türk Lirası, or YTL) entered into circulation, trimming off six zeroes and sporting a fresh new look. Now $1 is worth about 1.50 YTL...and tourists can leave their calculators at home. As of 2009, the central bank isn't even calling the currency "new" anymore.

• *Backtrack to the alley called Sandal Bedesteni Sokak, turn right, and continue one block to where it intersects with the wider...*

❻ Ağa Sokak

Remember, since the "ğ" is a vowel lengthener, without any sound of its own, this is pronounced "Aaaa-aah." Looking to the left up Ağa Sokak, you'll see the entrance to Cevahir Bedesteni, where they sell antiques, semi-precious stones, and silver items. We'll pass through that *bedesten* later on the walk.

• *Continue up the narrow alley called Sandal Bedesteni Sokak. Notice that the shops become less colorful and the clientele becomes more local. This section of the bazaar is mostly devoted to...*

❼ Pawn Shops

Many of these shops look empty, with signs on the windows and a few gold items and coins on display. This is where locals can exchange those "investment bracelets" and valuables for some hard cash. When these shops buy jewelry, they deduct whatever the seller paid for workmanship, charge a small commission, and pay for the actual value of the gold.

• *Continue to the end of the alley, where it ends at Aynacılar Sokak (ahy-nah-juh-lahr; "Mirror-Makers' Alley"). Looking to your right, you'll see another gate of the bazaar, named after the neighboring district...*

❽ Mahmutpaşa Gate

If you went through this exit and walked five blocks down the hill, you'd reach the Spice Market. The area between here and there is a huge outdoor textile bazaar, with retail shops, wholesalers, and workshops. Vendors sell a range of textile products, from underwear and socks to wool sweaters and jackets, to more conservative clothing, turbans, and raincoats. The week before schools open (the second week of September), the area is packed with bargain-hunters seeking back-to-school deals.

• *For now, instead of going out that exit to Mahmutpaşa, go the opposite direction, turning left onto Aynacılar Sokak. After 30 yards, you'll hit an intersection marked by a charming little...*

❾ Oriental Kiosk

This adorable structure was built as a teahouse in the 17th century, and sells jewelry today. Notice the fountain next to the kiosk. The alley it's on is Acı Çeşme (ah-juh chesh-meh), which means "Bitter Fountain." Avoid the water here...just in case.

• *Turn right at the kiosk onto Acı Çeşme, and walk to the end of the alley. On your right just before the bazaar exit, marked by an arrow hanging from the vaulted ceiling, is the entrance to...*

❿ Zincirli Han

Rough steps take you into Zincirli Han (zeen-jeer-lee hahn; "Chain Han"), which is surrounded by mostly jewelry shops, with some workshops on the upper floor. The shops here are less polished and fancy, and less aggressive, than those in the more touristy zones back in the heart of the bazaar.

At the far end of the courtyard, on the right (unmarked, at #13), is ⓫ **Merim Kuyumculuk** (koo-yoom-joo-look; jewelry). Rather than selling lots of jewelry, this place is focused on production and wholesale—one of the few jewelers in the bazaar with its own workshop nearby. If the owner Ferdi is around, ask him nicely if you can take a look into his tiny workshop upstairs (he may refuse if they're very busy).

To the left of Merim, fronting the courtyard, is ⓬ **Osman's Carpet Shop.** Run by a hard-to-miss "professor of carpets"

nicknamed Şişko (sheesh-koh; "Fatty"), this shop is regarded as *the* place to go to get a high-quality, expensive carpet with expert advice. Şişko—often assisted by son Nurullah or nephew Bilgin—won't hustle you and try to talk you into something, like the cheap carpet hawkers elsewhere in the bazaar. He prefers to equip customers with information to be sure they get the carpet that's right for them. This fifth-generation shop is hardly a secret—notice the celebrity photos, magazine clippings, and guidebook blurbs hanging on the wall.

• *Leave Zincirli Han back onto Acı Çeşme, turn right, and step outside the Grand Bazaar. The jewelry shop to your left just outside the* ⓫ *Mercan Gate—with hundreds of 22-karat gold bracelets—will give an idea what most jewelry around here looked like a decade or two ago, before fancier bracelets came into fashion.*

Continue a few steps beyond the Mercan Gate, and go through the first building entrance to your left. You're now in...

⓮ Kızlarağası Han

The *kızlarağası* was the master of all eunuchs (castrated slaves who looked after the sultan's palace and harem). This humble courtyard is where you'll find middlemen who recycle secondhand gold and silver—or shavings and unwanted fragments from other workshops—and turn them into something usable.

Notice the low-profile teahouse in the center, serving simple glasses of tea to an almost exclusively local crowd. If you've got some time, buy a glass of tea and join the gang playing backgammon at the little table. If any children or teenagers are around—as they usually are in the summer—they might know a few words of English, and can translate for you.

Ayhan Usta (eye-hahn oos-tah; "Ayhan the Master") is one of the goldsmiths who works here. His shop is the third one on the left as you enter, across from the teahouse. Cautious at first, but sweet and easygoing, Ayhan enjoys showing travelers what he does—as long as he's not too busy. Ayhan speaks only Turkish, but if you peek into his shop and he's up for visitors, he'll motion you inside  to watch him at work. You need not pay or tip him in return—he simply likes to share his craft with curious travelers. Stay safely away from the fire (burning at 2,200°F)—especially when he tosses

in some white powder to increase the temperature as he melts the gold.

Ayhan belongs to a dying breed. Not much gold production still takes place near the Grand Bazaar, and the few goldsmiths who remain may soon be moved to a plant outside the city. Craftspeople such as Ayhan like where they are, and loudly oppose this new plan. To locals, the Grand Bazaar needs both shops and workshops to be successful. Traditionally, if a customer wants to buy something, but it's not ideal—such as a garment that doesn't quite fit—the shopkeeper can send it to his workshop (or a neighbor's) for an adjustment to make it just right. But if all of the workshops are forced out by high rents, and replaced with nothing but "Made in Taiwan" gift shops, locals fear the soul of the Grand Bazaar will be lost.

On the way out (a few steps from Ayhan's shop), note the tiny shoeshine hut with Cafer (jah-fehr) happily polishing shoes (2–4 YTL). Let him give you a shine, and he'll get you tea. You'll step out with slick shoes and a shiny memory.

• *Now go back in the Grand Bazaar, and take the first right as you step in. You'll walk down the big lane called...*

❶❺ Perdahçılar Sokak

Perdahçılar Sokak (pehr-dah-chuh-lahr soh-kahk) was once the main clothing section of the bazaar; now it's a combination of carpet stores, souvenir shops, "genuine fake items" stands, and shops selling tourist knock-off versions of traditional clothes—like fake pashminas or a tongue-in-cheek "one size fits all" belly-dancing outfit.

• *Continue to the T-junction, and turn right onto Yağlıkçılar Sokak (yaah-luhk-chuh-lahr soh-kahk), with similar items to what you've just seen. Walk all the way to the bazaar exit. To the right, just inside the exit door, notice the textile store called...*

❶❻ Eğin Tekstil

This unassuming little shop provided many of the costumes for the 2004 blockbuster *Troy*—about the ancient city-state near today's Truva, in northwestern Turkey. Go inside and say hello to owner Süleyman or his assistants, who'd be happy to tell you all about their shop's history...and, of course, what they're selling. Eğin Tekstil (eh-een tehks-teel) has been in the same family for five generations, nearly 150 years. In fact, Süleyman—who continues the family tradition even though he's actually a doctor by trade—still has the Ottoman deed to the store. Their specialty is the *peştemal* (pehsh-teh-mahl), the traditional wrap-around sheet for visits to a Turkish bath. This is one of the Grand Bazaar's stores that actually has an annex behind the main shop built during Byzantine times, which is used for storage (the entrance is on the back wall).

• *Stepping outside the store, turn left and head back the way you came on Yağlıkçılar Sokak. After about 50 yards, on the right—marked with a sign for Brothers Restaurant—you'll see the entrance to...*

⓱ Astarcı Han

Go through the doorway, between shops and stands, into Astarcı Han (ahs-tahr-juh hahn; "Courtyard of the Cloth Lining"). Historically, this courtyard was home to textile workshops. A few still remain here: Notice the one in the right-hand corner as you enter (peek inside with a smile to see the textile-makers in action).

• *On the left as you enter the courtyard is the recommended...*

⓲ Brothers (Kardeşler) Restaurant

This place specializes in southeastern Turkish cuisine (see page 301 in the Eating chapter). WCs are next to the restaurant. And if you'd like a cup of Turkish coffee after (or instead of) a meal, the perfect spot is coming right up.

• *Exit Astarcı Han and turn right onto Yağlıkçılar Sokak, continuing in the same direction as before. After a few blocks, keep an eye out on the right-hand side for the tiny green box-like wooden balcony—used for the call to prayer, like a low-tech minaret—marking one of the bazaar's mosques (attached to the wall above the jewelry store); next to it are steps leading up to the mosque.*

Go 50 yards past the mosque on the right-hand corner to find a venerable tea and coffee house called...

⓳ Şark Kahvesi

Şark Kahvesi (shark kah-veh-see; "Oriental Coffee Shop") is an Istanbul institution, and a good place to sample Turkish coffee if you haven't yet (cup-3 YTL, double-6 YTL, desserts). For more on Turkish coffee, see page 63 in the Experiences chapter.

• *Just past Şark Kahvesi on Yağlıkçılar Sokak, a lane on the right leads to the recommended ⓴ Havuzlu Lokanta restaurant (see page 300 in the Eating chapter). But instead, we'll head left, down Zenneciler Sokak (zehn-neh-jee-lehr soh-kahk). After about 100 yards, you'll emerge into a courtyard we saw earlier from the other side...*

㉑ Cevahir Bedesten

Cevahir Bedesten (jeh-vah-heer beh-dehs-tehn) was built as a freestanding warehouse for merchants in the 15th century. It has been used for many purposes since, but the basic structure—with domed bays supported by eight massive pillars—is still intact. Entering the courtyard, you may notice it's taller than the rest of the bazaar—and, since it's devoted to big-ticket items, it's a bit quieter. Most merchants here are antique dealers, selling icons, metal objects, miniatures, coins, cameras, daggers, and so on; while others sell semiprecious stones, either by the piece or on chains. There are also a few silver shops and places where you can buy worry beads with semiprecious stones.

• *From here, you can explore the bazaar on your own. But first, we'll head back to the main drag and get oriented; we'll also suggest a possible detour to an enjoyable book market nearby.*

From the center of Cevahir Bedesten, turn 90 degrees to the right and leave through the door into the bustling alleys of the bazaar—this zone is packed with souvenir shops, as well as carpets and traditional metal items. Soon you'll run into the main street, Kalpakçılar Caddesi.

To leave the market now and go back the way we came, turn left on this main drag and walk back to the Nuruosmaniye Gate (at the Nuruosmaniye Mosque, near the Çemberlitaş tram stop—you can take the tram from here right back to Sultanahmet).

If you want to see more, instead turn right on Kalpakçılar Caddesi and walk about 200 yards to the gate leading to the Beyazıt (beh-yah-zuht) district, where you can continue following our self-guided Old Town Back Streets Walk. Halfway to the Beyazıt exit, keep an eye on your right, behind the ❷ **fountain,** for a stretch of shops selling leather, denim, and other textiles. At the end of Kalpakçılar Caddesi, you'll exit through the...

❷ Beyazıt Gate and Sahaflar Book Market

You may feel that you've only seen a small part of the very Grand Bazaar. You're right—there are another 4,000 shops we haven't passed on this tour. Entire trips, books, and lifetimes are devoted to the wonders of the Grand Bazaar.

But for now, let's look at one more interesting corner of the Grand Bazaar scene. As you exit through the Beyazıt Gate (with a tram stop 100 yards to your left), turn right and walk toward the crowded market area for textiles, clothes, and shoes—popular with local bargain-hunters. After about 20 yards, look on your left for steps leading to Sahaflar (sah-hahf-lahr), or the old book market. For two centuries, this was a magnet for bibliophiles—even 20 years ago, you could find rare old collector's items with fancy illustrations. But today only a few shops sell those items (or handmade replicas of them), while most others carry textbooks, books that are hard to sell at a mainstream bookstore, and books on religious topics.

• *Our bazaar tour is finished. To head home, you can go to Beyazıt Square and catch a tram back to Sultanahmet and beyond. To continue the Old Town Back Streets Walk from the Beyazıt Gate,* *turn to page 91.*

MOSQUE of SÜLEYMAN the MAGNIFICENT TOUR

Süleymaniye Camii

Built for the sultan by his prolific architect, Sinan, and completed in 1557, the Mosque of Süleyman the Magnificent almost outdoes the Blue Mosque in its sheer size, architecture, and design. Its subtly understated interior, decorated in pastel tones, was restored in the 1950s.

The term "Süleymaniye" applies not just to the mosque, but to the huge network of related buildings that nestle around it on a hilltop overlooking the city. Within this complex are the ornate mausoleums of Süleyman and his wife Roxelana, as well as a madrassa (former theological school).

Imagine the pomp and circumstance on the summer day in 1550 when construction began: Sultan Süleyman the Magnificent arrives on his horse, along with the clergy. He orders his guards to give alms to the poor and to sacrifice rams for a fortunate start. As the crowd recites verses from the Quran, the head of the clergy sets the first stone of the foundation. Within six years, the dome was complete; the following year, the mosque opened for worship. The whole shebang took only a decade to finish.

ORIENTATION

Cost and Hours: Mosque—free, generally open daily one hour after sunrise until one hour before sunset, closed to visitors five times a day for prayer; Mausoleum—free, daily 9:00–17:00, until 18:00 in summer.

Location: It's on a hill near Istanbul University, on Sıddık Sami Onar Caddesi in the Süleymaniye neighborhood.

Getting There: This is an easy stop on the Old Town Back Streets Walk (see page 87).

Length of This Tour: Allow one hour.

Services: WCs are located just outside either end of the mosque wall. Several eateries are located within the former madrassa alongside the mosque.

No-No's: Before going inside, be sure to read "Visiting a Mosque" on page 61.

Starring: One of Sinan's great mosques, the mausoleums of Süleyman and his wife Roxelana, and the Süleymaniye neighborhood.

THE TOUR BEGINS

• *Enter the mosque complex at its southern corner, by the large street fountain.*

Standing in the square with the mosque behind you, you're facing the corner of the **madrassa.** Originally, this school of theology was divided into three sections: the first two were devoted to interpreting the Quran, while the third (at the far end with the flagpole at its entrance) was a medical school—now it's a hospital.

This peaceful space, stretching along the mosque's outer courtyard wall, is lined with good restaurants (see page 299 for recommendations). There's a WC just outside the wall at this end of the mosque, and another at the opposite corner of the mosque's outer courtyard.

• *Now use the gate near the big fountain to enter the...*

Outer Courtyard

As you enter this courtyard, walk straight ahead to the gate leading into the cemetery. Just before you enter the cemetery, look to your left to see two elevated stone slabs—used to support the coffin during a funeral service. According to Muslim tradition, the body of the deceased is washed and wrapped in a white shroud, then placed in a wood coffin and brought to stone slabs such as these. Relatives and friends gather nearby, and the imam (cleric) leads them in one last prayer for the soul of the deceased. The body is then taken into the cemetery and buried, still in the shroud but without the coffin. Just as a Muslim faces Mecca to pray, the body of a Muslim is buried so that it points eternally toward Mecca.

• *Go through the gate into the...*

Cemetery: The Mausoleums of Süleyman the Magnificent and Roxelana

As you walk through the headstones (some dating back to the early 17th century), notice that each tomb has two stones. The larger stone was inscribed with the epitaph, while the smaller one was for decoration.

Follow the stone sidewalk to the first and bigger mausoleum

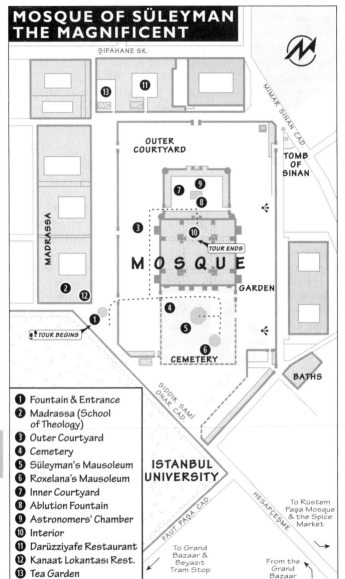

MOSQUE OF SÜLEYMAN THE MAGNIFICENT

ŞİFAHANE SK.

MIMAR SINAN CAD.

OUTER COURTYARD

TOMB OF SINAN

MADRASSA

M O S Q U E

TOUR ENDS

GARDEN

TOUR BEGINS

CEMETERY

BATHS

SİDDİK SAMİ ONAR CAD.

ISTANBUL UNIVERSITY

FAUT PAŞA CAD.

HESAPÇEŞME

To Rüstem Paşa Mosque & the Spice Market

To Grand Bazaar & Beyazit Tram Stop

From the Grand Bazaar

SÜLEYMAN MOSQUE TOUR

1 Fountain & Entrance
2 Madrassa (School of Theology)
3 Outer Courtyard
4 Cemetery
5 Süleyman's Mausoleum
6 Roxelana's Mausoleum
7 Inner Courtyard
8 Ablution Fountain
9 Astronomers' Chamber
10 Interior
11 Darüzziyafe Restaurant
12 Kanaat Lokantası Rest.
13 Tea Garden

(on your right). In 1566, the aging Süleyman the Magnificent went on one last military campaign to Zigetvar, where he died silently in his tent. His clever Grand Vizier knew that the army would disband if they knew the sultan was dead, so he covertly had Süleyman's body mummified. (Meanwhile, the Grand Vizier sent a note to Süleyman's son, Selim, telling him to grab the throne before someone else could.) The magnificent sultan's death was kept secret until after the army returned in victory to Istanbul, when his body was interred next to the mosque that bears his name.

At the entrance porch, remove your shoes and stow them on the wooden shelves, then step inside. A year after Süleyman's death, the best stonemasons and marble-workers in the empire came here to build a *türbe* (tuhr-beh), or mausoleum, that would mirror Süleyman's fame. They were led by Sinan, the master architect who'd also built the mosque. The mausoleum was considered complete when it was decorated with precious tiles from İznik (bordered with Arabic inscriptions—excerpts from the Quran). Candles and oil lamps were lit, Süleyman's robe was laid over the green cover of the ceremonial coffin, and imams began reading from the Quran...and didn't stop for years.

On either side of the entrance are some of the most beautiful tile frames anywhere. Above the door are inscribed the words,

"There is no other God but Allah, and Muhammad is his Prophet." The larger tomb (cenotaph) at the center of the mausoleum is Süleyman's. On either side are Süleyman's two heirs, their relatives, and Süleyman and Roxelana's daughter (to his right). Notice the room's gorgeous details: floral-designed İznik tiles, marble paintwork, beautiful woodwork on the window and door shutters, and decorative ostrich eggs and colored replicas in the frame hanging from the ceiling.

As you exit, the entrance to Roxelana's mausoleum is to your right. While not as impressive as her husband's, it's worth a look. Enjoy the attractive tiles, and notice the "stalactites" decorating the niches between the windows. Roxelana's cenotaph is the first one, surrounded by an attractive inlaid wood panel. Take a close

Süleyman the Magnificent (1494–1566) and Roxelana (c. 1498–1558)

Süleyman the Magnificent, the 10th sultan of the Ottoman Empire, ruled for nearly a half-century (1520–1566). His reign was the Golden Age of Ottoman history, when the Ottoman Empire was the world's greatest power. The treasury was bursting, and the empire's borders stretched from North Africa to Central Europe to the Near East. The Mediterranean Sea—which the Romans had once called Mare Nostrum ("Our Sea")—became a Turkish lake. One-third of the Western world's population lived under the Ottoman flag.

Süleyman ruled during the age of powerful leaders. His contemporaries were Charles V of the Holy Roman Empire, François I of France, and Henry VIII of England. A peace treaty ending a dispute with Austria refers to Süleyman as the "Emperor of the East and the West"—the first time someone laid claim to this title since the Byzantine Emperor Justinian. In signing the treaty, Charles V accepted Süleyman's superiority despite his own title of "Holy Roman Emperor."

While Westerners know him as Süleyman the Magnificent, the Turkish people call him "Süleyman the Legislator" or "Süleyman the Law-Giver." His greatest contribution was to codify Ottoman law. As the ruler of a multinational empire, Süleyman realized that different regions and different peoples needed different laws.

Süleyman's biggest weakness was a woman. His first son, Crown Prince Mustafa, was born to Süleyman's chief consort, Gülbahar. But Süleyman later fell deeply in love with one of his concubines, Roxelana.

Said to be the daughter of an Orthodox priest from Ukraine, Roxelana was bought at a slave market and sent to the palace harem. She wasn't the most beautiful, but Roxelana was ambi-

look at the workmanship—thousands of tiny wood pieces were studded in to create its elegance.

• *Exit the cemetery back into the outer courtyard, turn right, and walk along the mosque. You'll see stairs leading up to a gate reserved for worshippers (no visitors allowed). Continue beyond this gate to the far end of the mosque, and climb a few stairs into the...*

Inner Courtyard

Like the rest of the Süleymaniye complex, this courtyard was designed by the architect Sinan. He was a master of creating spaces that were at once plain and beautiful. Looking around the courtyard, appreciate Sinan's command of architectural grace: It's not ostentatious, but the surrounding porticos and soaring minarets make it feel appropriately majestic. Take a moment to consider the tious and managed to get herself presented to the sultan, drawing his attention by daring to laugh in his presence. Süleyman named her "Hürrem"—his "Laughing One."

Underestimating this simple Ukrainian girl, the jealous Gülbahar snubbed Roxelana, addressed her as "slave," and even physically attacked her. Süleyman had Gülbahar banished, and Roxelana became his chief consort. She persuaded Süleyman to legally marry her—a first for a slave concubine—and bore the sultan five children (four sons and a daughter).

Gülbahar's son, Crown Prince Mustafa, remained an obstacle for Roxelana, who hoped one of her sons would become sultan after Süleyman. She convinced Süleyman that Mustafa was plotting against him, and Süleyman had him strangled.

Of Roxelana's four sons, two died of natural causes, and a third was strangled at his father's orders. The remaining son survived to eventually take the throne...but, never able to quite fill daddy's shoes, became known as Selim the Blonde.

During her lifetime, Roxelana grew in influence as Süleyman turned to her for advice in all his decisions. She was the first of several powerful women who ruled the Ottoman Empire from "behind the curtain"—the so-called "reign of the ladies" that continued for about 150 years. Relentless in her ambition, Roxelana is said to have orchestrated dozens of murders to secure her surviving son's crown. In what may have been a sort of public apology, Roxelana later spent her personal fortune creating charitable institutions.

When Roxelana died in 1558, Süleyman had a separate mausoleum built for her. After Süleyman's death eight years later, he was buried in a mausoleum of his own—forever separated from the strong-headed woman who'd compelled him to do things he may later have regretted.

architectural beauty of what is the finest mosque in Istanbul, and one of the finest in all of Islam.

If you've been to the Blue Mosque already, you'll notice some similar features: The domed porticos around the perimeter look decorative, but they're also functional—providing shade in summer and shelter in winter. The shutters are opened for ventilation in the summer. The portico that runs along the front of the mosque is elevated, giving it a grand appearance. This area is reserved for overflow when services fill up. The old marble **fountain** in the middle of the courtyard was used for ablution—ritual cleansing before worship.

The main gate of the courtyard is across from the entrance to the mosque. (This door is usually kept closed, but we'll see it from the other side later on this tour.) Notice the first shutters on either side of this door, and the windows above them. These appear identical to the other shutters around the courtyard, but they actually hide the entrance to a special **chamber** used by astronomers—who had the important responsibility of calculating the exact time for worship, five times each day, based on the position of the sun.

This mosque has four minarets. Mosques financed by sultans often had more than one minaret, to show off the sultan's wealth. In Süleyman's mosque, the extra minarets are symbols of the initial four caliphs (Muslim religious and social leaders who succeeded the Prophet Muhammad). Notice that there are a total of 10 balconies on the minarets. This is also symbolic: Muhammad

told 10 Muslim saints that they were going straight to heaven. (Or maybe it's because Süleyman was the 10th sultan of the Ottoman dynasty.)

• *Enter the mosque, removing your shoes and placing them on the wooden shelves. Notice the beautiful stalactite designs on the niche over the door, and the woodwork on the door wings. There's no fee to enter the mosque, but you can leave a donation as you exit. Now go through the leather curtain and into the mosque's...*

Interior

Tranquility. Especially compared to the riot of color and design in the Blue Mosque, the sedate interior of Süleyman's mosque puts the worshipper at ease. Appreciate the genius of the architect Sinan: Somehow the plain-seeming pastel decoration and tasteful stained-glass windows merge in a harmonious whole.

The architect behind this building—whom Turks call "Sinan the Great"—struggled his whole life to engineer a single dome that could span an entire building, without bulky support arches and pillars. He considered this mosque an important milestone in his quest. (He later succeeded with the Selimiye Mosque in Edirne, near the Turkish-Bulgarian border.)

Turkey's Greatest Architect: Mimar Sinan
(1489–1588)

Mimar Sinan was one of the greatest architects the world has ever seen. Named Joseph by his parents, he was born to a Christian, Greek-speaking family in a small village in Kayseri (ancient Caesarea, in central Turkey). His father was a mason and carpenter, and young Joseph spent his childhood as his father's apprentice. At the age of 23, Joseph was conscripted into the elite janissaries, converted to Islam, and changed his name to Mimar Sinan. (For more on the system of janissaries, see the sidebar on page 152.)

Sinan received the customary janissary education, living with a Turkish family to learn the Turkish language and culture. Sinan built tile kilns in İznik, developing an appreciation for tiles (and later using them to adorn his most important works). He also worked in the construction of government and military buildings, polishing his skills, and learning techniques that would serve him well as an architect.

Later, Sinan traveled extensively with the army—from Vienna to Baghdad. He was a student of architecture everywhere he went, examining what made structures strong or weak, beautiful or ugly. During military campaigns, Sinan built bridges, forts, siege towers, and canals. His abilities—literally paving the way for the army—impressed the sultan. Sinan became the royal architect in 1539, serving Süleyman the Magnificent and two of his successors as the chief royal architect. Sinan worked until the day he died, at age 99. During his prolific career, Sinan built 477 monuments, including 20 royal mosques in Istanbul alone. Most of his buildings are still standing—including his masterpiece, the Mosque of Süleyman the Magnificent.

Less visually striking, but arguably more important, were Sinan's improvements to Istanbul's water-distribution infrastructure. Süleyman was so happy with the results that he allowed Sinan to pipe running water into the architect's own home, a privilege previously enjoyed only by the sultan.

Sinan was an intellectual, a researcher, and an avid reader who spent extravagant sums on books. One of his greatest joys upon becoming the royal architect was gaining access to the royal library. Though he achieved personal glory and success, Sinan always remained a loyal servant to the Ottoman dynasty, praising those who encouraged him to follow his passion. While largely unfamiliar to Westerners, this contemporary of Leonardo da Vinci and Michelangelo certainly ranks among those greats.

For this mosque, Sinan used four irregularly shaped "elephant's feet" pillars to support the arches and the dome. His simple and elegant design masks the pillars with an arcaded gallery. The bulky buttresses blend in with their surroundings, giving the impression of an uncluttered space. You have to really look hard to see the pillars (unlike the Blue Mosque, where the pillars immediately pop into view).

The impressive dome (flanked by two semi-domes, as at Hagia Sophia) has a diameter of 90 feet. While Renaissance architects in

Europe were struggling to sort out the technical difficulties of domes, Sinan succeeded in creating a masterful dome that even included such niceties as open earthenware jars embedded between the brick layers to enhance acoustics.

Look around to find the typical features of a mosque: The wooden barrier marks an area reserved for worshippers. At the end of the apse, a marble niche—or *mihrab*—shows the direction of the holy city Mecca (which Muslims face to pray). To the right is the decorated staircase called a *mimber*, where the imam stands to deliver his sermon. In front of that is an elevated marble platform for the choir. And in the left corner, behind the giant support leg, is the sultan's lodge (on pillars). The decor is non-figurative: floral designs, stained-glass windows, tiles, and calligraphy *(hat)*.

• *Your tour is over. For a sultan's view of the Bosphorus, Europe, and Asia, visit the garden on the far side of the mosque (see map on page 220). Also, consider the recommended Turkish bath just outside the complex walls (**Süleymaniye Hamamı**—see listing on page 71). To rejoin the Old Town Back Streets Walk (see page 87), retrace your steps to the entrance of the complex.*

CHORA CHURCH MUSEUM TOUR

Kariye Müzesi

Certain art forms are indelibly associated with a specific place, time, or civilization. The trademark art form of the Byzantines is the wall mosaic, and the tiny, underrated Chora Church Museum—hiding out on the edge of town—is home to some of the best examples of late-period Byzantine mosaics anywhere. Mosaic art existed in this region a thousand years before Christ, but originally was used only in floors. It was the Byzantines who refined the technique, used lighter material with better plaster, and mastered the application of mosaics to walls and ceilings.

ORIENTATION

Cost and Hours: 15 YTL, late March–late Oct Thu–Tue 9:00–19:00, off-season until 17:00, last entry 30 minutes before closing, closed Wed.

Location: The Chora Church Museum (which most locals know by its Turkish names, Kariye Müzesi or Kariye Camii) is just inside Istanbul's Old Town walls, about four miles northwest of the historic core, in a district called Edirnekapı (eh-deer-neh-kah-puh). The church is on a little square, facing a big café with outdoor tables and lots of souvenir stands.

Getting There: For maximum efficiency, take a **taxi** (about 15 YTL each way from the Sultanahmet area).

You can also reach the church by **bus** (passes only—no tokens accepted; see "Public Transportation Tokens and Passes" on page 30). From Taksim Square in the New District, bus #87 takes you right there (4–5/hr, bus stop at north end of Taksim Square, across from Marmara Hotel, behind Metro entrance). If you're coming from the Old Town, take the tram to the Eminönü stop, near the Galata Bridge. From where you

Chora vs. Ravenna

Visitors tend to compare the mosaics at the Chora Church with the mosaics in the Basilica of San Vitale in Ravenna, Italy (near Venice). But they were completed in very different historical periods.

Ravenna's sixth-century mosaics were commissioned by Emperor Justinian. The basilica was an imperial project intended to show off the emperor's power and wealth. It was a gigantic self-made shrine, and Justinian spent a great deal of money from the royal treasury to bring it to completion.

The Chora's mosaics are from a much later date (the 14th century), and were commissioned by the wealthy Byzantine bureaucrat Theodore Metochites. Instead of showing emperors and empresses standing proud next to holy figures (as at Ravenna's Basilica), donors are generally portrayed as being more humble and vulnerable at the Chora Church. The mosaics' style, use of light, and perspective are also different. Compared to the classical Byzantine mosaics at Ravenna, the newer Chora mosaics show a better sense of 3-D perspective, with more realism, action, and emotion.

While Justinian's reign marked the heyday of the Byzantine Empire, by the time Metochites was decorating the Chora Church, the empire was approaching its final days. The Black Death had killed hundreds of thousands. The Serbs were a serious threat to the west, while the Turks were at Constantinople's gates to the east. Although the Chora Church is glorious in every respect, its mosaics shine brighter than the troubled age they reflect.

emerge on the embankment, go beyond the bridge to catch a local bus (buses stop beneath yellow signs directly across from the Spice Market). Bus #32 (Eminönü–Cevatpaşa) or #910 (Eminönü–Otogar) will both take you to the stop called Edirnekapı (it's the stop just after the huge, sunken stadium, and right before the big fragment of the town wall).

After disembarking at Edirnekapı, face the town wall: The church is down the hill to your right (follow signs for *Kariye Oteli*, a hotel right next to the church). Look for the old dome with the simple minaret, a reminder of the time when the church was used as a mosque.

Length of This Tour: Allow one hour.

Services: Free WCs are on the left down the stairs just after you buy your ticket, but before you pass through the turnstile. A small bookstore is inside the church building. Museum tel. 0212/631-9241.

Photography: Photography is permitted, but no flash and no tripods.

Cuisine Art: Basic tourist restaurants, cafés, and souvenir stands line the leafy square in front of the church. For better (and more expensive) cuisine, consider **Asitane,** in Kariye Hotel next door to the church (see listing on page 301).

Nearby Attraction: Consider combining your visit to the Chora Church with a walk along the nearby Walls of Constantinople (described in the next chapter).

Starring: Thousands upon thousands of glittering little tiles, plus several walls and ceilings slathered with vivid frescoes, all from about 1300.

Background

The Chora Church can be crowded inside, and you'll be craning your neck to see all of its little details. Read the information in this chapter before you arrive, or at the small café across the square from the church.

Locals call this church Kariye (kah-ree-yeh)—the Arabic interpretation of the Greek word *chora,* which means a suburban or rural area. When a church was first built here in the fourth century, it was outside Constantine the Great's city wall. A century later, the walls were enlarged, and the church was no longer outside the city limits. But the name "Chora" stuck, likely because the word had become infused with other meanings and interpretations. In Byzantine religious literature, Mary herself is often referred to as "Chora," in the same sense as an uncultivated field—in other words, a virgin. When she became pregnant with Jesus, Mary (or the "Chora") became "a container for the uncontainable." Inscriptions in the church refer to this, as in *"He chora ton zon ton"* ("the house of the living") and *"He chora tou achoretou"* ("the house of the uncontainable"—the One that cannot be kept within boundaries, a.k.a. Jesus Christ).

CHORA CHURCH MUSEUM

The current church—built after an earthquake damaged the original—dates back to about 1100. The church was further damaged by Crusaders in the 1200s. In the early 1300s, the Byzantine prime minister Theodore Metochites was selected as Chora's patron and directed to oversee the church's reconstruction. It was the first time that someone other than a royal was honored with the title of patron for an imperial monastery (see sidebar on next page). Metochites was powerful and rich, and invested generously in the project. He commissioned the creation of the sumptuous mosaics that attract tourists today.

In the early 16th century, after the Ottomans took Constantinople, the church was converted into a mosque. A mihrab (prayer niche) was built off-center in the main apse (to face Mecca rather than Jerusalem), and the bell tower was replaced with the minaret you see today. The frescoes and mosaics were whitewashed over and remained hidden from daylight until the late 1940s, when they were re-discovered and restored.

Artistically, the Chora Church's decorations represent a set of early and very influential models for depicting Christian figures and events. After the Church split between east and west (Eastern Orthodox and Roman Catholic) in the 11th century, western Christians wriggled free of Roman rule. Western churches became provincial, focused on their own local customs and saints—causing church art to splinter into many different, idiosyncratic visions. Meanwhile, the Eastern Orthodox Church remained consolidated under the stable and wealthy Byzantine Empire. Church power was centralized, so artistic decisions made in Constantinople filtered down to other churches throughout the Eastern Orthodox world—bringing a great consistency to medieval Eastern Orthodox church art. For example, an artist's depiction of Mary, Joseph, and the baby Jesus at the Nativity here became the norm for church art throughout the realm. Lacking a similarly coherent western Christian artistic tradition, artists across the generations have embraced these Eastern Orthodox archetypes...so the artistic vision realized here in Chora eventually trickled down to decorations in today's Christian churches in Italy, Indonesia, and Iowa.

Overview

Theodore Metochites said of Chora Church, "The mosaics and frescoes in the church show how God became a mortal on behalf of human beings." On this tour, we'll concentrate on important events in the lives of Mary and Jesus, to whom the church was dedicated.

The layout of the church is fairly straightforward. The main part is a single nave, facing east (like all European Christian churches of the time). Behind the nave are two narthexes: interior and exterior. These narthexes hold most of the mosaics. Running next to the nave is a long corridor called a paracclesion, or burial chamber. This section is decorated with frescoes, not mosaics.

While the church can be confusing, if you use the map smartly, everything is easy to find.

Theodore Metochites

You're here today because of Theodore Metochites, the man who commissioned these mosaics. Metochites was born in Constantinople in 1270, a few years after the city was taken back from the Crusaders. His father supported the unification of the Eastern Orthodox and Roman Catholic churches—a view that earned the family exile in Nicaea (more than a hundred miles south of Constantinople—the present-day Turkish city of İznik). His parents tried to steer their son away from politics, encouraging him to devote his life to science. But politics was in his blood. By the time he reached his twenties, Metochites was writing essays and critiques.

His work came to the attention of Emperor Andronicus II, who invited Metochites to serve in the palace in Constantinople. Metochites got his start arranging political marriages for royal family members—including a wedding between the emperor's five-year-old daughter and a middle-aged Serbian king. In the early 1300s, Metochites became treasurer, and then prime minister. Anyone who wanted access to the emperor had to see Metochites first. He acquired land and wealth, but wasn't the most effective bureaucrat. Decorating the Chora Church distracted him from the Italian merchants who were becoming superior in naval trade.

As the Ottoman Turks became a clear threat to the empire, panic and chaos led to civil war between Andronicus II and his grandson Andronicus III. The grandson won, and in 1328 Metochites lost his protector. A mob burned his palace, his wealth was confiscated, and Metochites was exiled. Metochites was eventually allowed to return to Constantinople, where he entered Chora's monastery, took the name Theoleptos, and died in 1332.

Give your neck a good stretch before you begin—most of what there is to see is a few feet above eye level. You'll be whirling like a Dervish trying to see all the details. To make things easier, we'll focus on the most interesting or important scenes—skipping lesser figures and events, such as Church fathers, no-name angels, and so on. And to avoid too much needless backtracking, some of the Bible stories will be slightly out of order.

THE TOUR BEGINS

• *The "front" door of the church you see from the square is used as the tourist exit today. The ticket booth is around the left side of the church: Go through the gate, buy your ticket, pass through the turnstile, and circle the church until you reach the entry. As you walk, notice the giant buttress at the back of the church. This originally held up the church...but now, due to settling over time, the church supports the buttress.*

Orientation Walk

The interior visit has four parts—exterior narthex, interior narthex, central nave, and paracclesion (see map). The art tells a story that unfolds as the worshipper enters the building, so we'll view it as a Christian would during Byzantine times (and with the same mindset). Begin by going to the rear of the church (by the current exit door) in the exterior narthex, facing the altar, which is through two doors at the east end of the church.

Take a quick walk around to understand the general structure of the church before studying its many mosaics: The **exterior narthex** tells the story of Jesus—from his conception and childhood through his baptism as an adult. Behind you (above the current exit door) is a mosaic with Jesus in the womb of Mary. A mosaic showing Jesus, finished with childhood—and now an adult creator—ready to work, is above the door leading toward the nave and altar.

Walking into the next chamber, the **interior narthex,** you encounter art that teaches the delicate balance between Jesus (on the right, curing the sick and working miracles) and Mary (on the left, with scenes from her life).

Stepping into the **nave,** you enter a place of worship that functioned as a mosque for 500 years. The centuries-old Christian altar was replaced by the Islamic prayer niche, or mihrab. Notice that the mihrab is made with marble cut from the same quarry to match the exquisite original walls of the much older interior. Rather than destroy the Christian frescoes and mosaics, the Muslim Ottomans covered them over with whitewash.

The last part of your visit is the **paracclesion** (to the right of the nave), which was a chapel for important tombs and is decorated with some more fine art (frescoes rather than mosaics).

Now, return to the exterior narthex and study some of the Bible scenes depicted in the fine mosaic art. (Use the map with keyed numbers to locate each scene.)

Exterior Narthex

❶ **Incarnation of Jesus Christ:** Here the Virgin Mary holds the divine baby Jesus in her womb. She is the Chora, the dwelling place of the uncontainable. The placement of this scene—just above the door to the outside—is interesting. It's likely that when the panel was made, you could see the walls of Constantinople through this door. When the city was in danger, the people would bring icons of Mary to the walls to protect the city. Perhaps this panel was part of that tradition.

❷ **Joseph Dreaming:** In Joseph's dream, the angel explains Mary's pregnancy to him. Behind him are the Virgin and a companion.

❸ **Journey to Bethlehem:** Mary is seated on a donkey; in front of her is Joseph's son (not Jesus—explained later). Joseph walks at the back, trying to catch up. The city behind the hill is Nazareth.

❹ **Enrollment for Taxation:** The governor of Syria is seated upon a throne, wearing the outfit and hat of Byzantine's high government officials. He likely represents Theodore Metochites, who served as a tax collector (and made his fortune as the empire's treasurer) before becoming prime minister. At the center, another official holds an unrolled scroll. On the right is pregnant Mary, her belly straining her tunic. Joseph is behind her.

❺ **Nativity:** This representation of the birth of Jesus Christ is typically Byzantine, in that all the events related to Jesus' birth are shown next to one another. Notice the stable, animals, Joseph in deep thought, Mary resting, and maids bathing the newborn Christ.

❻ **John the Baptist Bears Witness of Christ:** John talks with a group of priests and Levites and gestures toward Christ. The fiery-eyed Baptist is dressed in his usual animal-skin outfit and sports the long beard of a wilderness man.

❼ **Temptation of Christ:** The story of the temptation of Christ is told in four scenes arranged in a semi-circle in the vault, with the Devil represented as a dark, ugly winged creature appearing four times. In the first section, the Devil appears above a box full of stones, asking Jesus to turn them into bread. Next, the Devil offers Jesus the world's many kingdoms (the tiny kings with crowns make the place look like Legoland). In the third scene, we see Jesus on a hill, overlooking the kingdoms. In the last scene, Jesus stands on a tower, as the Devil asks him to prove his divinity by jumping down without hurting himself.

❽ **Miracle of Cana:** Here we see Jesus turning water into wine at a wedding party. Jesus is holding a small scroll with the Virgin Mary behind him. A servant is pouring water into one of five huge jars. Notice that the jar mosaics are made of terra-cotta—the same material the original jars would have been made of.

❾ **Multiplication of the Loaves:** By blessing five loaves of bread, Christ feeds a multitude. Jesus is seen behind three big baskets of bread, giving pieces of bread to his disciples, who pass them to the crowd. If you follow the vault to the right, you'll see the happy conclusion: After everyone was fed, the remaining bread filled 12 large baskets.

❿ **Journey of the Magi:** Three wise men—Melkior, Balthazar, and Gaspar—ride their horses and follow the star to find the

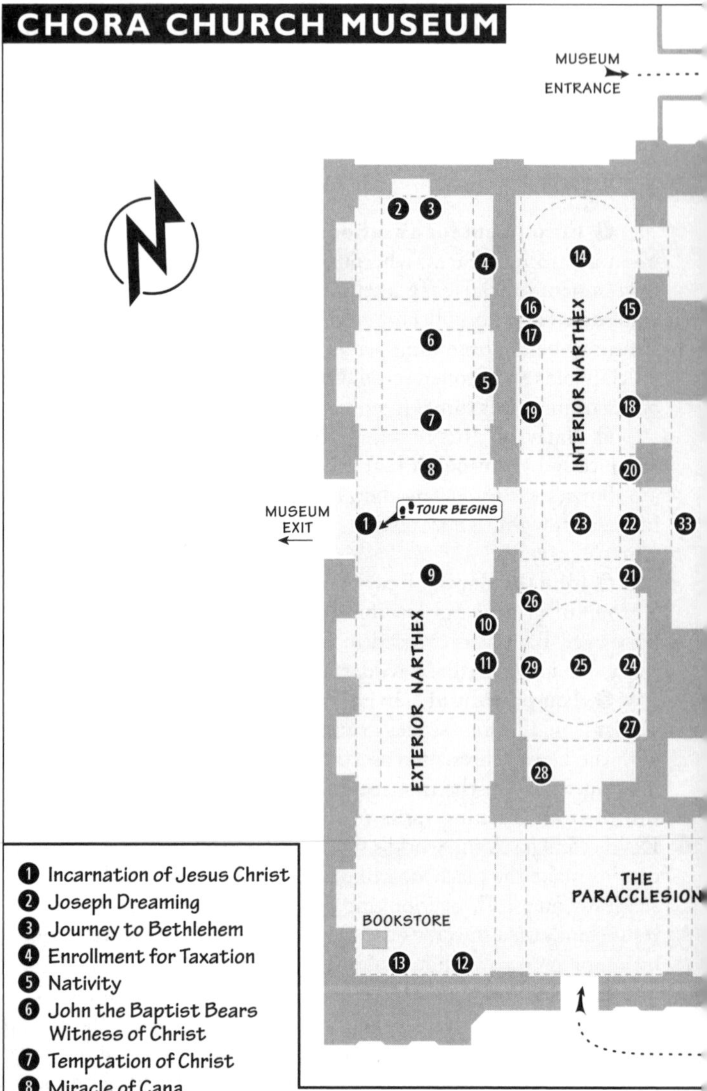

CHORA CHURCH MUSEUM

MUSEUM ENTRANCE

MUSEUM EXIT

TOUR BEGINS

INTERIOR NARTHEX

EXTERIOR NARTHEX

THE PARACCLESION

BOOKSTORE

1. Incarnation of Jesus Christ
2. Joseph Dreaming
3. Journey to Bethlehem
4. Enrollment for Taxation
5. Nativity
6. John the Baptist Bears Witness of Christ
7. Temptation of Christ
8. Miracle of Cana
9. Multiplication of the Loaves
10. Journey of the Magi
11. Magi Before Herod
12. Massacre of the Innocents
13. Mothers Mourn for Their Children
14. Ancestors of Mary
15. Annunciation to St. Anne
16. Annunciation to Mary at the Well
17. Joseph Takes Mary to His Home
18. Birth of Mary
19. Mary Entrusted to Joseph
20. St. Peter
21. St. Paul
22. Dedication Panel
23. Presentation of Mary to the Temple
24. Deesis Mosaic
25. Biblical Genealogy of Christ

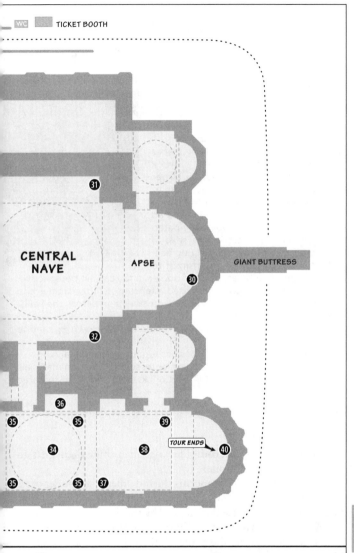

26 Christ Heals the Two Blind Men
27 Christ Heals the Woman With Blood Disease
28 Christ Heals the Leper
29 Christ Heals the Multitude
30 Mihrab
31 The Living Jesus Christ
32 Mother Mary with the Child Jesus
33 Dormition of the Virgin

34 The Virgin and Child and Attendant Angels
35 Four Hymnographers
36 Burial Niche of Theodore Metochites
37 The Ark of the Covenant
38 Last Judgment
39 Entry of the Elect into Paradise
40 Anastasis

CHORA CHURCH MUSEUM

Mosaics 101

Mosaic art was expensive and time-consuming, which is why it's generally seen only in royal residences or churches decorated by wealthy patrons. Mosaicists generally worked in groups, like a small union or lodge. The most experienced—the master—was usually the leader. A metropolis like Constantinople supported several competing mosaicist groups.

Mosaics are made of tiny pieces of glass or other materials stuck to moist plaster to create a larger image. It took about three years to complete the mosaics in the Chora Church. The Chora's art was ahead of its time, and in a way anticipated the Renaissance: art for the sake of religion, but without neglecting aesthetics. You'll notice an attempt to create emotive faces, moving bodies, and realistic perspective. The Chora Church was often used after sunset, lit by candles and oil lamps. Imagine the flickering light sweeping across the walls, each tile glittering in turn.

Feeling inspired? Here's a recipe for your own Byzantine mosaic:

1. Prepare a blueprint. Mosaics require detailed planning.

2. Gather the mosaic pieces, or tesserae. Common materials include glass, stone, marble, and brick. Gold and silver tesserae

---

newborn Christ Child.

⓫ Magi Before Herod: The wise men offer their gifts to Herod, who sits on a throne.

⓬ Massacre of the Innocents: Herod orders the murder of all young male children, in an effort to find and kill the baby Jesus. Notice the motion and action implied by the flying cloaks.

⓭ Mothers Mourn for Their Children: The mothers are grief-stricken, cradling the bodies of their brutally slain children. Above the next window to the right you see Elizabeth and her baby, John the Baptist, hiding safely in a cave.

Interior Narthex

⓮ Ancestors of Mary: At the center of the dome, in the medallion, is Mary with the baby Jesus. Notice the two figures in each section between the ribs. The upper figures are the genealogical ancestors of Mary and Jesus, starting with King David; the lower figures are ancestors outside the official lineage.

are not solid metal—but instead a thin layer of metal sandwiched between two glass pieces. A very thin pink marble can represent the color of human flesh.

3. Stud the walls at random with nails, leaving about one inch of the nail exposed. This helps the plaster adhere to the wall. (Make sure you don't use iron nails—in the past, rusting iron nails ruined many mosaics when they expanded and forced chunks of plaster to crack and fall from the wall.)

4. Apply three layers of plaster, up to two inches thick. The first layer—made of crushed lime and large pieces of straw—should cover the entire work surface, and then be scored so the next layer will adhere better. When the first layer is completely dry, it's time to apply a second layer, consisting of more finely crushed lime and straw pieces. While the second layer is still damp, apply the third and finest layer of plaster: crushed lime and marble dust.

5. Transfer your blueprint to the plaster in the form of a rough painting. This will serve as your guide. (Often, these colored, rough figures can be seen in older mosaics where pieces have fallen out.)

6. Begin by applying smaller pieces to define the contours of your mosaic design, then fill in the rest with the bigger pieces. The frame, hands, feet, face, and hair of any figures require the most skill and are traditionally completed first by the master mosaicist. Then the other mosaicists fill in the spaces. Place your pieces at different angles to capture the light.

7. Stand back and enjoy.

⓯ Annunciation to St. Anne: The mother of Mary, St. Anne, wears a long, red scarf over a blue garment and a red shawl that falls down to her knees. Above the fancy fountain before her is a flying angel giving the good news that she will bear a daughter.

⓰ Annunciation to Mary at the Well: Now it's Mary's turn. Mary is dressed in a blue tunic and holds a golden pitcher. She's surprised by the angel approaching her, who tells her she will bear the Christ child.

⓱ Joseph Takes Mary to His Home: A young and helpless-looking Mary follows her new husband. In front of them is Joseph's son. While this figure may be surprising to Roman Catholics, Eastern Orthodox tradition—based on the apocryphal Gospel of St. James—holds that Joseph was a widower with several children when he wed Mary. Joseph seems a little confused, too—which way is he walking?

⓲ Birth of Mary: The newborn, naked baby Mary is held by a midwife as a maid prepares a bath. Another maid fans St. Anne, while attending women present gifts.

⑲ Mary Entrusted to Joseph: On the left side, the local priest Zachariah is behind young Mary, his hand protectively on her head as he presents her to Joseph. Other suitors stand to the side.

⑳ St. Peter and **㉑ St. Paul:** St. Peter is on the left side of the door, holding the keys to Heaven. On the right side is bald and wrinkled St. Paul, holding the codex of Epistles in his left hand. The wrinkles on Paul's broad brow are said to represent his intellect. The Byzantines often decorate either side of a church's nave door with the twin figures of St. Peter and St. Paul—fathers of the early Christian Church.

㉒ Dedication Panel: The enthroned Jesus Christ is at the center, holding the Bible and making the sign of the Trinity. On his right side, squeezed in the corner, is church patron Theodore Metochites, offering Jesus a model of the church (a common Byzantine way to represent a donation). Metochites wears a fancy garment and a big hat reminiscent of a Turkish turban—both are symbolic of his status.

㉓ Presentation of Mary to the Temple: Mary's parents enthusiastically urge their daughter to go to the priest—Zachariah, father of John the Baptist—who welcomes the Virgin. Behind them, in a separate scene, we see Mary receiving holy bread from an angel.

㉔ Deesis Mosaic: This monumental scene, known as a *deesis* in the Greek Orthodox Church, is a representation of Christ flanked by both Mary and John the Baptist, interceding on behalf of sinners. But John must have been late for his Chora Church sitting, because he's not depicted here. Instead, behind Jesus and Mary are two small figures representing church donors. Mary is asking Jesus to forgive their sins. The woman kneeling before Christ is Melanie, the illegitimate daughter of a Byzantine emperor (the head below Mary) who married a Mongolian king. After the king died, she came back to Constantinople and lived as a nun.

㉕ Biblical Genealogy of Christ: In the center, Jesus Christ—in the usual pose—holds the Bible in one hand and makes the sign of the Trinity with the other. In the sections of the dome are Christ's Old Testament ancestors. If you can't read the Greek names, most of the figures come with attributes that help to identify them. The cycle starts in the upper level with Adam, standing on a snake (he's the one with a long white beard under Jesus' left hand).

If your neck isn't killing you, spend some time here, and try to identify other familiar figures—such as Noah carrying an ark. Hmm...a vessel for holding precious life...yet another metaphor for the Virgin. Nearby, many other miracles of Christ are depicted: ㉖ **Christ Heals the Two Blind Men;** ㉗ **Christ Heals the Woman with Blood Disease;** ㉘ **Christ Heals the Leper;** ㉙ **Christ Heals the Multitude.**

Nave

This square, domed room is the oldest section of the building, probably dating from around 1100. Straight ahead is the main apse—the holiest section of the church, where the altar once stood.

• *The marble niche a little to the right of center is the...*

㉚ **Mihrab:** This was added by the Muslim Ottomans when this church became a mosque. Representing a symbolic doorway leading to the holy city of Mecca, the mihrab's purpose was to show Muslims the correct direction in which to pray.

• *Two mosaics in the central nave use the word "Chora" to describe Jesus and Mary. On the left side of the wall, before the apse, is a framed mosaic depiction of...*

㉛ **The Living Jesus Christ:** The inscription originally was "Dwelling-place (Chora) of the Living."

• *On the right wall before the apse is...*

㉜ **Mother Mary with the Child Jesus:** The inscription originally was "Dwelling-place (Chora) of the Uncontainable." (The mosaic lettering HXOPA spells Chora.)

• *Turn around and look above the door you entered through. This is one of the church's most impressive panels, the...*

㉝ **Dormition of the Virgin:** This Christian mosaic masterpiece was revealed when the whitewash was removed. Byzantine Christians struggled with the theological issue of who Mary was—in the early fifth century, the Church declared her the "Mother of God." This was actually good marketing, as Anatolians were already comfortable with goddesses (see sidebar on next page).

Mary Rules the Orthodox World

Christianity has always proved remarkably adaptable to local traditions. From the Christmas tree to the Easter egg, many "Christian" traditions actually have pagan roots. It was no different in Anatolia (Turkey), where the long tradition of a female "mother goddess" figure provided a convenient foundation for Mary.

Turkey has a long history of reverence for female deities. The idea of a mother goddess originated in Anatolia (likely in the early sixth millennium B.C.), and her popularity spread to encompass virtually all of Mediterranean Europe, western Asia, and North Africa. No matter what she was called or how she looked, the mother goddess always displayed the maternal qualities of fertility and nurturing, and also possessed miraculous gifts. For example, the Phrygian goddess Cybele was a figure of power and protection. Often, a mother goddess figure would give birth to a deity. Leto was impregnated by the Greek god Zeus and gave birth to the twins Apollo and Artemis—who were both highly revered as gods. The mother goddess Aphrodite (Venus) was born pregnant with her child, Eros, the god of love.

By the time Christianity arrived, the stage was set for a powerful mother goddess figure—and Mary easily took her place in the pantheon. Like so many mother goddesses before her, Mary is looked to for comfort and healing in times of trial. As the "container of the uncontainable," she gave birth to God's child, Jesus Christ. And according to Christian tradition, when she completed the course of her earthly life, she was transported ("assumed") body and soul directly to heaven, as no other mere mortal has been.

Whether Mary died at the end of her life, or fell asleep (which "dormition" seems to imply) is debated among theologians but, either way, she passed from this life (or was "assumed") into heaven. August 15 is celebrated as the feast of the Assumption of Mary by both the Eastern Orthodox and Roman Catholic world.

Mary is shown here on her last earthly bed. The scene is made of very small mosaic pieces, allowing the artists to show palpable emotion in the faces of the apostles and other mourners around her deathbed. Behind the bed, in a large heavenly halo, is Jesus Christ. He holds the innocent soul of Mary, in the form of a baby. Angels

CHORA CHURCH MUSEUM

appear in the outer ring of the halo. To the left of the bed, St. Peter swings an incense burner, while on the right, St. Paul bends toward the bed in sorrow.

A gray bubble is taking her soul to heaven. Follow this: In heaven Mary has morphed into a baby (as a child of God). Since God and Jesus are one, baby Mary is the mother of Jesus...or God. It's beyond me. But the point is that she got to heaven, where she's a busy part of God's administration in both the Eastern Orthodox and Roman Catholic Church to this day.

Take a few moments in the nave to study the marble, and notice the slender recycled pieces in the panels placed higher on the walls—these were columns before being cut into panels.

Paracclesion

This funerary chamber is entirely decorated with frescoes. A fresco is painting applied to wet plaster, which provides a smooth surface

for the artist. The plaster absorbs and preserves the pigment, making frescoes more durable than regular wall paintings.

Most of the frescoes on the paracclesion walls deal with the afterlife and salvation—appropriate themes for a burial chamber. Unlike most other Byzantine churches, here the dead were not interred in the ground, but instead were laid to rest in the now-empty niches in the chamber walls.

• *Again, referring to the map, you'll see the following scenes:*

❸❹ **The Virgin and Child and Attendant Angels:** Mary is depicted here as the Queen of Heaven, dressed in her usual blue tunic, now decorated with gold. This is another rib dome, made more impressive by the light from windows at its base. Within the dome's sections are winged angels worshipping Mary and Christ. The angels wear clothing typical of Byzantine officials.

❸❺ **Four Hymnographers:** These four serious-looking Byzantines are poets who were renowned for their verses in Mary's honor: John of Damascus, in the northeast corner wearing a turban; Kosmas the Poet, in the southeast corner with a blank book in his lap; Joseph the Poet, in the southwest corner holding a scroll; and Theophanes Graptos, in the northwest corner, where he's writing verses.

❸❻ **Burial Niche of Theodore Metochites:** The largest of all the chamber's burial niches, this probably belonged to Theodore Metochites. Most of its decorations were lost over the ages,

The Marble of Marmara

Most of the marble used in the Chora Church came from Marmara Island, which is in Turkey's Sea of Marmara. (In fact, *marmara* means "marble" in Greek.) But some of the marble was recycled from buildings in Italy, Greece, and North Africa. These pieces were re-cut before being reused.

Most of the marble panels in the building are slices of stone, cut in half and placed next to one another. The workmanship involved in cutting marble was as painstaking as the workmanship of the mosaics. Only a couple of inches of marble could be cut each day, using a smooth piece of metal that—combined with sand—operated like a saw.

Notice the marble slabs of the nave's upper level. These tall, slender, recycled pieces were formed from columns cut into slices.

The marble lintels above the church's doors and door frames, and most of the column capitals, were recycled as well. The marble arches decorating the paracclesion are the best examples of stone carving from the late Byzantine period.

Whether recycled or genuine, Chora's marble decorations fit harmoniously with the rest of the structure. Originally, many of the marble works were painted or glazed with gold. The small holes and niches in the marble (which you'll see throughout the church) once held icons, crosses, lamps, and holy relics.

although the inscriptions and decorations in some of Chora's other burial niches are among the best sources of information about the lives of 14th-century Byzantine aristocrats.

❸ The Ark of the Covenant: Men are carrying something that looks like a coffin. This is the Ark of the Covenant being taken to Solomon's Temple. This ark, like Noah's ark, is a metaphor for the Virgin Mary: All three contain the treasures of God.

• *Look above the vault to see the most impressive fresco in the church, the...*

❸ Last Judgment: This colorful fresco depicts scenes from the Book of Revelations: Christ's victory over death and the salvation of the righteous. Jesus sits on a glorious throne in the center, flanked by the Virgin Mary and John the Baptist. The 12 apostles, holding books, are seated at either

side. Behind them are groups of angels. The white shell-like object held aloft by an angel represents the sky at the end of time. All around the vault are choirs of the chosen, floating in clouds.

Below this triumphant scene is the dramatic Weighing of the Souls. Christ's right palm is turned up, showing the lucky bunch who will go to heaven. His left hand is turned down and points toward the condemned (the ultimate "thumbs up" or "thumbs down"), as does the river of fire flowing from his left foot.

Notice the stigmata (nail holes) on Jesus' hands. Try to imagine his gold-colored robe and the halo behind his head as they once appeared, covered in sheets of gold (some of the gold still remains in his halo).

Under Jesus are two figures on their knees. These are Adam and Eve. Farther down, you can see a scale. Naked bodies on the right are the souls awaiting judgment. At the center, another naked soul trembles while he is judged. Barely visible is a little demon, craftily trying to pull down the scale. Look closely at the river of fire to see ugly little demons giving the condemned a helpful push.

❸❾ Entry of the Elect into Paradise: A cherub with closed wings protects the entrance into heaven. On the left, St. Peter unlocks the door. The Good Thief—carrying a cross—greets the chosen and points toward the Virgin Mary on her throne.

❹⓿ Anastasis: Also called The Resurrection, this fresco depicts the descent of Jesus Christ into hell to save the righteous people of the Old Testament. You can see Jesus (like a Biblical Rambo) pulling Adam and Eve by their arms out of their coffins. Under Jesus' feet are the broken gates of hell, scattered keys, and Satan bound and powerless.

• *With that promising image, this tour is over. Congratulations. Give yourself a well-deserved rest and neck rub. From here you might explore the city walls (see the City Walls Tour on the next page), the colorful district of Balat, or catch a taxi out to the most conservative religious scene in town at the Eyüp Sultan Mosque (see page 59).*

CITY WALLS TOUR

The Walls of Constantinople rank among the most impressive city walls in the world. Istanbul was born on this peninsula, flanked by the Golden Horn and the Bosphorus, in part because it was so easy to fortify: Simply build a wall across the peninsula. The first wall was built by Greek settlers. Constantine the Great's version was replaced by Theodosius II (ruled A.D. 408–450), who expanded the wall to encompass a greater area, creating the mightiest city wall anywhere in medieval Europe. In total, the land and sea walls stretched 13 miles around the city and remained a virtually impenetrable fortification for more than 1,000 years. These massive walls were breached only twice—by the Fourth Crusade in 1204 and by the Ottoman invasion in 1453. We'll focus on a short section of the walls, between the Chora Church and the Golden Horn.

ORIENTATION

Cost and Hours: Free and always open, although best viewed by day.

Location: The Walls of Constantinople stretch from the Golden Horn to the Sea of Marmara at the western end of the Old Town peninsula, about four miles northwest of the historic core.

Getting There: The best way to see the Walls of Constantinople is to walk there after touring the Chora Church (for a self-guided tour and details on reaching the church by public transportation, see the previous chapter). You can also see the walls by driving alongside; the hop-on, hop-off bus (see page 33) runs the entire length. Or if you're taking a taxi out to Eyüp Sultan Mosque (the only recommended sight located outside the city walls—described on page 59), you can easily detour here.

Length of This Tour: Allow at least one hour.

Starring: Edirnekapı Gate, the Walls of Theodosius, the Byzantine Palace (Tekfur Sarayı—the only surviving Byzantine palace, recently provided shelter for homeless people), and the Dungeons of Anemas.

THE TOUR BEGINS

• *Begin at the Chora Church. With the church behind you, walk uphill and to the left to the busy Fevzi Paşa Caddesi, one of the Old Town's main east–west arteries. To the right is the...*

Edirnekapı Gate

Edirnekapı (eh-deer-neh-kah-puh) was the grand gate of ancient Constantinople (as well as the modern-day name for this district of Istanbul). The physical gate is long gone, with Fevzi Paşa street passing unchallenged through a large opening in the wall. But the two massive towers that once protected the gate still stand like sentinels on either side.

In Byzantine times, the principal thoroughfare, the Mese, led from the gate (the highest point in the city) to Hagia Sophia and the Hippodrome. Outside the gate, the great boulevard wound away from Constantinople toward the city of Edirne (ancient Adrianapolis)—the gate's namesake.

Sultan Mehmet II rode triumphantly through the gate into Constantinople in 1453, ending the Byzantine era and ushering in the Ottoman age. In Ottoman times, Edirnekapı continued as the "official gate" leading into the city—and it was a busy one. Sultans used this gate to leave the city when visiting the Eyüp Sultan Mosque for Friday prayers. Common folk, caravans of merchants, and soldiers on the way to their posts also passed through Edirnekapı. The gate was guarded by a squad of janissaries, and was locked at the end of the day.

• *As you pass the Edirnekapı public bus stop, just before the tower on the right (with a large Turkish flag on top), look for a narrow set of stairs to your right. These will lead you to a cobblestone street (Hoca Çakır Caddesi) that runs along the walls all the way to the Byzantine Palace (Tekfur Sarayı, about 300 yards away). You'll walk downhill from this point.*

Walls of Theodosius

Constantinople was surrounded by both land walls and sea walls. Because the sea itself provided natural fortification (like a giant moat), the land walls were stouter and more impressive. Built by

Emperor Theodosius II, these early fifth-century walls stretch for three and a half miles north to south, from the shores of the Golden Horn up the hill to Edirnekapı, and then downhill to the shoreline of the Sea of Marmara. (If you arrived at Istanbul's Atatürk Airport and drove into the city along the coastal road, you passed a portion of the land walls and bits of the sea walls.)

Fortified with 185 towers, each about 65 feet high, the Walls of Theodosius were actually two separate walls—an outer wall and a stronger inner ring, separated by a defensible no-man's land about 55 feet wide. And just outside the outer wall, a huge moat (about 25 feet deep and 60 feet wide) made access to the wall almost impossible.

After the Ottoman conquest, the walls fell into disrepair, as they were no longer needed for protection. While most of the inner walls are long gone, the outer walls have survived centuries of neglect and are well preserved for their age.

• *Start walking down this street (Hoca Çakır Caddesi). In less than 100 yards, you'll see a staircase set into the wall leading up to a platform at the top of the wall. Take this staircase to access the Fevzi Paşa tower. A metal gate halfway up the first set of stairs is usually open during the day. If it's locked, another staircase slightly farther along the street will take you up to a different section of the wall.* **Warning:** *The steep, narrow staircases have no railings, and neither do the 10-foot-wide platforms on top. Be very careful—or you'll give new meaning to "the fall of Constantinople."*

View from the Wall

The view from the top of the wall is rewarding. Face outside the city wall. Here you can see some of Istanbul's centuries-old cemeteries—they're the patches of green on either side of the busy road (one is Muslim, and the other is Greek Orthodox). This location—outside the city boundaries—was a sanitary, logical place to bury the dead. Off in the distance are the Golden Horn and the Haliç Bridge.

Up top, you have a chance to take a look inside what little survives of the fortified towers. Historically, there was no access between the tower's upper and lower levels—if enemy troops captured the lower section, defenders above could continue to fight.

• *Descend and continue on Hoca Çakır Caddesi 200 yards. Where the wall sharply bends to the left, you'll see a much later structure—with fancy, arched windows and a balcony out front—built into the top of the wall. This is the southern end of the...*

Byzantine Palace

Tekfur Sarayı (tehk-foor sah-rah-yuh; Tekfur Palace), the southern end of the larger Blachernae Palace complex, is Istanbul's only sur-

viving Byzantine palace. Other than this facade, all that remains of the palace is its three-story outer wall. Probably built during the 13th and 14th centuries, the palace grounds are closed to the public while undergoing renovation, and are unlikely to reopen until 2010.

• *Turn left onto Şişhane street, which you'll follow as it twists through a residential neighborhood to the next gate, Eğrikapı. After 100 yards, the street makes a left turn (by the wall of the Alparslan vocational high school). A block later, stick with the street as it bends sharply to the right. Walk down the hill to the intersection with Eğrikapı street. Turn left onto Eğrikapı and walk a few steps to the...*

Eğrikapı Gate and Surdibi Cemetery

Eğrikapı (eh-ree-kah-puh; "Bent Gate") is one of the minor city gates. Step through the gate and outside the city walls to see a small Muslim cemetery, often frequented by tour groups. The cemetery is known as the legendary burial site of several of the *sahabe* (companions of the Prophet Muhammad—the Muslim equivalent of the Christian apostles). The *sahabe* are said to have been buried here in unmarked graves, having fought and died as members of the Arab army that attacked Constantinople in the seventh century.

When Sultan Mahmut II started a major westernization project in the early 19th century, his opponents tried to discredit him by portraying him as an infidel who had turned away from Islam. To prove his faith, the sultan initiated a search to pinpoint and mark the burial sites of the *sahabe* who had fallen during the Arab siege of Constantinople. The historical veracity of these *sahabe* gravesites are—for Muslims—authenticated by faith. Look for the gravestones marked *Sahabe'den*.

• *Take the walkway on the right (through the cemetery), and keep walking along the outside of the wall. Farther down the road, the wall bends again, and gradually splits off from the road. Here you'll see the final section of the wall leading all the way to the Golden Horn.*

Dungeons of Anemas

About midway along the last stretch of wall, you'll notice two towers standing next to one another, sharing a common base. The first tower (on the right) is the Bastion of Isaac II Angelos, a

Byzantine emperor. The tower on the left marks the Dungeons of Anemas, built as a prison in the early seventh century as part of the Blachernae Palace.

The dungeons are named for their first prisoner—a Byzantine soldier of Arab origin called Anemas. He was blinded and imprisoned here after a failed attempt to take an emperor's life in 1107. According to legend, the emperor's daughter later helped Anemas escape.

This prison was also where overthrown emperors were locked up and tortured. In fact, the first emperor to be imprisoned here was Angelos—blinded and held in the dungeons for eight years when his elder brother usurped the throne.

The End of the Wall

Past the Dungeon of Anemas, the rest of the wall forms a rectangular fortress, with three huge hexagonal towers. This is where the land walls connect to the sea walls that face the Golden Horn. A little less than four miles long, but low and largely unfortified, these were the weakest link in Constantinople's defense. The Byzantines stretched a thick chain across the entrance to the Golden Horn, sealing it off from enemy vessels and making thick sea walls unnecessary...or so they thought. This single mistake made the entire network of walls irrelevant. In a remarkable feat of military ingenuity (not to mention engineering prowess), in 1453 Mehmet the Conqueror actually dragged his warships through today's New District under cover of darkness, deposited them into the Golden Horn, and launched a successful surprise attack—ending Byzantine rule and opening a new Ottoman chapter in the city's history. Today, very little of the Golden Horn sea walls survive.

• *Our walk is finished. From here, you can take a cab back to the Eminönü neighborhood (to the right, or east), or continue your walk to Eyüp Sultan Mosque (to the left, or west—see page 59).*

Or, to enjoy a time-passed Istanbul neighborhood scene, walk through the residential area here within the ancient walls. Backtrack to Eğrikapı. Go through the gate, and take the fourth alley to the left (Dervişzade Sokak). It will lead you down through the neighborhood and eventually to the Golden Horn. As you walk, imagine how—as the centuries went by—the walls lost their protective function. No longer needed for fortification, they became a handy quarry for anyone wanting to add on to their home or build a stone fence. Many homes were actually built right up against the wall (to save on building materials)... ensuring that the Walls of Constantinople will always remain integral to the foundation of this grand city.

BOSPHORUS CRUISE TOUR

From Eminönü in Downtown Istanbul to Anadolu Kavağı

In addition to separating two continents, the Bosphorus Strait serves as Istanbul's main highway. A never-ending stream of vessels—from little fishing dinghies to gigantic rusted oil tankers to luxury cruise ships—sails up and down this strategic corridor, day in and day out. Churning ship engines and clanging horns are Istanbul's constant soundtrack. The Bosphorus is one of the busiest waterways in the world, and this constant carnival of commerce is the only outlet for the countries on the Black Sea: Russia, Romania, Bulgaria, Ukraine, and Georgia.

Cruising the Bosphorus—a ▲▲▲ experience—is the best way to appreciate the massive size and scale of 15-million-strong Istanbul, and a convenient way to see many of its outlying landmarks. And since virtually all of Istanbul's key attractions are on the European side, a cruise may be your easiest opportunity to set foot in Asia (the last stop is the fishing village of Anadolu Kavağı, on the Asian side).

In Turkish, the Bosphorus is Boğaziçi (boh-ahz-ee-chee), which means "pass" or "strait." This 19-mile-long waterway curves like a snake as it connects the Black Sea in the north with the Sea of Marmara and—eventually—the Mediterranean to the south. Istanbul's various districts line up along the bays, and the coastline is peppered with cute neighborhoods. Many of these areas, once separate communities, have been incorporated into Istanbul as the town sprawled from north to south over the last several decades. Today Istanbul extends pretty much all the way up to the Black Sea. But a few neighborhoods in the north retain a village-like quality, where the men still fish for a living.

The Turks view the Bosphorus as much more than just a body of water—to them, it's a privilege. For locals, sitting on a bench by the Bosphorus and watching the beautiful scenery as a United Nations of boats drifts past makes for a good day.

ORIENTATION

The best way to cruise the Bosphorus is by taking a day-long cruise on the public ferry, which leaves from the Old Town side of the Golden Horn (details below). For a shorter cruise, consider a private tour operator (see "Private Tours" on page 253).

Cost: 10 YTL one-way, 17.50 YTL round-trip. Get the round-trip ticket. There's little sense in taking the cruise one-way; options for coming back overland from Anadolu Kavağı are limited and expensive. The round-trip ticket gives you the option of coming all the way back to Eminönü, or hopping off early to see other outlying sights on your way back to town (see "Sarıyer Shortcut" on page 253).

Sailing Schedule: The ferry runs mid-June–mid-Sept at 10:35 and 13:35; mid-Sept–mid-June at 10:35 only. Schedules can change, so confirm these times before you plan your day. You could ask your hotelier for help, drop by the dock ahead of your trip, or visit the website for the seasonal schedule (look for "Scenic Bosphorus Tour" in the "Conventional Ferry" timetable at www.ido.com.tr/en).

When to Go: The 10:35 departure puts you in Anadolu Kavağı just in time for lunch, and gets you back to Istanbul early enough for a little evening sightseeing. If you're in Istanbul for several days, check the forecast and plan your cruise during good weather.

Getting There: The public ferry leaves from the Bosphorus ferry port (Boğaz İskelesi; boh-ahz ees-keh-leh-see) in the Old Town's Eminönü district. This is near the mouth of the Golden Horn, along the embankment next to the Galata Bridge. For details, see the Golden Horn Walk (see page 99), and consider combining that walk with this cruise.

To reach the ferry landing from the Old Town, take the tram toward Kabataş and get off at Eminönü. When you emerge from the pedestrian underpass, look for the ferry terminal building marked *Boğaz İskelesi*.

To reach the ferry from Taksim Square in the New District, you can either walk or take the "nostalgic tram" down İstiklal street to Tünel, then take the Tünel funicular down to Karaköy at the Galata Bridge. Walk across the bridge and turn left along the embankment to find the ferry terminal marked *Boğaz İskelesi*. Alternatively, you can ride the funicular down the hill from Taksim Square to Kabataş, and take the tram from there to Eminönü.

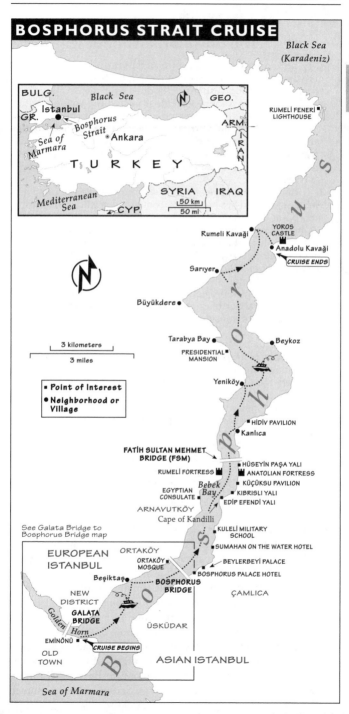

BOSPHORUS STRAIT CRUISE

The Bosphorus Tunnel

City administrators have long discussed ways to solve crowded Istanbul's never-ending traffic problem. In addition to the two existing suspension bridges over the Bosphorus, a third (and even a fourth) bridge is still on the agenda, but officials see the future in the long-neglected rail system.

Istanbul's Asian districts are mostly residential. That means millions of people commute to work across the strait using the bridges and ferries (which don't run in bad weather—making the commute a nightmare over the jammed-up bridges).

The Marmaray (or Marmara Rail) project is likely to bring a viable solution to this heavy intercontinental traffic. It involves incorporating a commuter light-rail system extending roughly 50 miles across both continents into the existing public transit system. It's estimated to cost $2.5 billion; is projected to be completed in 2011 or 2012; and will carry about 150,000 passengers per hour.

The mile-long, rail-only Bosphorus Tunnel (just one-third of this huge transit project) will connect the Old Town to the commercial harbor district straight across the Bosphorus. City officials are considering a second tunnel for motorized vehicles.

Tunnel construction began in 2006 with the arrival of the construction platform. Its huge crane excavates 6,000 tons of sand a day from the bottom of the Bosphorus, to make room for where the massive concrete portions of the tunnel will be placed.

As the tunnel construction continues, boat traffic through the Bosphorus is hard hit. A large section of the strait around the platform, where the Bosphorus opens up into the Sea of Marmara, is largely sealed off for security reasons, leaving just a narrow strip of the strait for commercial traffic. Combine this constriction with the strong surface current, and the Bosphorus traffic is more dangerous than ever.

Cruise Route: The ferry goes from Eminönü in downtown Istanbul to the Black Sea end of the Bosphorus, where it takes a break in the Asian fishing village of Anadolu Kavağı before returning to Eminönü. It makes several other stops along the way, but only long enough to pick up or drop off passengers.

Length of This Cruise: A round-trip Bosphorus cruise by ferry takes about 5.5–7 hours, depending on how long your boat lingers in Anadolu Kavağı (expect about 3–4 hours of actual sailing time, plus a 1.5- to 3-hour break in Anadolu Kavağı).

Here are the approximate durations of the various legs of the trip. Heading north: Eminönü to Beşiktaş (15 min), Kanlıca (40 min), Yeniköy (55 min), Sarıyer (70 min), Rumeli

Kavağı (80 min), Anadolu Kavağı (90 min). Heading south: Anadolu Kavağı to Rumeli Kavağı (10 min), Sarıyer (20 min), Yeniköy (35 min), Kanlıca (50 min), Beşiktaş (75 min), Eminönü (90 min).

Sarıyer Shortcut: If you'd rather not go all the way to the end, consider getting off about 1.25 hours into the trip at the Sarıyer stop and taking the bus back (see sidebar on page 264). This gives you the option of visiting Rumeli Fortress, Sadberk Hanım Museum, and Dolmabahçe Palace, all described in the Sights chapter. You can also get off at Sarıyer on the return trip to see some of these sights on your way home.

Services: WCs and snack bar onboard.

Crowd-Beating Tips: Weekdays are best—the ferry can be miserably crowded on weekends, especially from late spring through early fall. Arrive at least 30 minutes before your scheduled departure time, as the best seats fill fast (on a busy day—such as a sunny weekend—show up even earlier). As you board, you'll have to choose: Have your own seat, which means you're stuck in one place the entire trip (and therefore can't see the other side of the Bosphorus very well); or stand up, giving you maximum flexibility for moving around and taking photos, but without a guaranteed seat for the entire trip (seats may free up as people disembark at later stops on the route).

Private Tours: For a shorter Bosphorus cruise, consider a private excursion. Various companies sell 7.50-YTL cruise tickets on either side of the Galata Bridge (behind bus stops to the west side, and next to Bosphorus ferry port on the east—look for *Bosphorus Tours* sign). These boats will take you as far as the second bridge (Fatih Sultan Mehmet Bridge) and back in 90 minutes, with no stops. **Turyol**—on the west side of the bridge, next to fish sandwich boats and behind the bus stops—is one of many options (cruises generally run hourly Mon–Fri 12:00–18:00, Sat 12:00–19:00, Sun 11:00–19:30, less frequently mid-Sept–mid-June, tel. 0212/527-9952, ask for Mr. Ihsan or Mr. Şenol).

There's no set schedule for these private boats (at least, not one that's strictly adhered to). Boats depart as soon as they have enough people. Just buy your ticket and hop on. These cruises are a good option if you're short on time or not interested in visiting Asia. But keep in mind that they only go up to the second bridge, so you'll see less of the Bosphorus, and won't get a glimpse of the Black Sea. In general, the cruises stick closer to the European side on the way north, and the Asian side on the way back south. Most of the information in this chapter (except for the places the ferry docks) will still be relevant on these smaller cruises.

The Bosphorus Strait: A Critical Location

The Bosphorus Strait connects the Black Sea with the Sea of Marmara (which is then connected on the west by the Dardanelles to the Aegean Sea, and then out to the Mediterranean Sea). Private boats and passenger ferries make more than 2,000 runs a day, carrying 2.5 million people between the two continents. Add in the hundreds of commercial vessels each day—you'll see many at anchor just offshore in the Sea of Marmara—plus fishing boats out there for the daily catch, and you've got a lot of traffic. The Bosphorus has always been of great commercial and strategic importance, and was a factor in the establishment of the city of Constantinople here in A.D. 330.

Navigation through the strait can be extremely difficult due to its narrow width, sharp turns, tricky currents, and the immense size of some of the tankers and cruise ships that ply its waters. Powerful currents funnel through this narrow north–south strait. Less saline water flowing south out of the Black Sea creates a strong surface current, generally strengthened by prevailing winds out of the north. Note the fishing boats off the Old Town peninsula straining to stay in place and pointed toward the Bosphorus—evidence of the strong surface current flowing south through the strait.

Making things even more complicated, because of the difference in salinity between the Black Sea and the saltier Sea of Marmara, another current flows beneath the surface current in the opposite direction (toward the Black Sea). Clever ancient mariners figured this out, and lowered baskets on lines down into the water to catch the lower current and be pulled northward.

Starring: Bridges between the continents, fancy waterfront mansions, fortresses, castles, and the fishing village of Anadolu Kavağı.

Getting Started

Buy your ticket at the windows facing the busy street, then go through the turnstile to reach the ferry. Hang onto your ticket— the ticket-taker will need to check it again on your return journey.

If you arrive at least 30 minutes early, there will usually be some seats left (but show up even earlier if you want to snag a seat on a sunny weekend). On the way up the Bosphorus, most of the attractions are on the left (European) side of the boat, so pick your spot accordingly. Ideally you'd like a clear look at both sides, though because of the width of the boat and crowds on board, this often isn't possible. If you like to take photos, the open upper decks in the front and back of the boat are ideal. If all the good seats are taken, consider staking out a standing spot on the left near the

In 1936, Turkey signed the Montreux Convention, which regulates boat traffic through the Bosphorus and the Dardanelles. In case of war, Turkey has the right to close these critically located straits to any vessel; even during times of peace, military vessels must inform authorities long in advance of their passage.

When the Montreux Convention was signed, ships were smaller and weren't required to use a local pilot to negotiate the dangerous Bosphorus. This oversight proved disastrous. The Bosphorus is flanked by the heavily populated city of Istanbul, magnifying the consequences of any shipboard accidents. Plus, over 10 times the number of boats travel the strait today compared to when the Montreux Convention was signed. As shipping traffic increased in size and volume, boats collided in fiery explosions, tankers leaked thousands of gallons of crude oil into the fragile waters, and more than one disabled ship ran aground—smacking right into waterfront houses. In the words of an Istanbul resident: "I heard an unusual sound getting louder and louder, and all of a sudden, I saw the stern of the ship going right into the room!"

Now local pilots are required, and there are stricter controls on boat traffic, managed by a new radar network (watch for the radar towers along the Bosphorus). In addition, oil pipelines from the eastern Black Sea, the Caucasus region, and the Caspian Sea are providing an alternative way of transporting oil, which is helping to alleviate the bottleneck of tanker traffic through the strait.

back of the boat. Also notice the unobstructed view seats along the water on the lower deck. If you don't mind seeing only one side, grab one of these seats on the left (European side). Realize that people will be constantly jostling for position for the prettiest photos—so no matter where you sit or stand, you may not have the place to yourself.

Coming back, the sunlight is better for photos of the Asian side (during the afternoon, the sun is in your eyes looking at the European side). So a smart plan is to always sit on the left side (views of the European side on the way there, and the Asian side on the way back).

On the upper deck is a snack bar where you can get a *simit* (see-meet—a sesame bread ring, like a Turkish bagel), candy bar, sandwich, or beverage. Attendants also walk around the ferry selling tea, coffee, fresh-squeezed orange juice, and water. The WCs are on the lower deck, on the sides, past the stairs to the second deck toward the front.

For the first half-hour or so, the boat moves fast and there's lots to see. Consider reading ahead so you're ready for the attractions as you pass them.

THE TOUR BEGINS

• *Anchors aweigh!*

Eminönü to Beşiktaş

• *The first few sights are on the right side of the boat.*

As the boat pulls away, you're treated to a fine panorama of the Old Town peninsula—made even more dramatic by the boats scurrying around the harbor, and the embankments and streets teeming with people. You see **Hagia Sophia** first, with its dome and minarets. Sirkeci Train Station is right behind the car ferry dock. As you move along the peninsula, the gardens of **Topkapı Palace** come into view—including Divan Tower, with the buildings of the Harem complex to its left.

On the waterfront, past the car ferry port, is the **Sepetçiler Pavilion** (seh-peht-chee-lehr; "Basketweavers"), today a fine restaurant used mostly for banquets.

Within a few minutes, you reach Seraglio Point, the tip of the Old Town peninsula. This is where the Golden Horn ends and the Bosphorus begins. As you get farther away from the Old Town, behind Hagia Sophia you'll notice the minarets, and later the dome, of the **Blue Mosque.** Soon the skyline of old Istanbul will be dominated by domes,  minarets, and towers. Add a layer of haze, and you have a magical, mystical-looking silhouette.

Just off Seraglio Point, you can see the end of the Bosphorus—where it joins the **Sea of Marmara.** Around the base of the Old Town peninsula are intact portions of the Byzantine wall, which fortified the city until the Ottomans conquered it in the 15th century. As the boat turns left, you'll begin to get some good views of Asian Istanbul, across the Bosphorus. The cranes mark the main commercial port of the city. From this angle, the Princes' Islands appear to the south in the Sea of Marmara, usually as a silhouette a few miles off Asian Istanbul. On a clear day, you can even see the southern shores of Marmara.

• *Look toward Asia.*

You may notice a floating platform in the Bosphorus between Asian Istanbul and the Old Town. This is the construction site of a

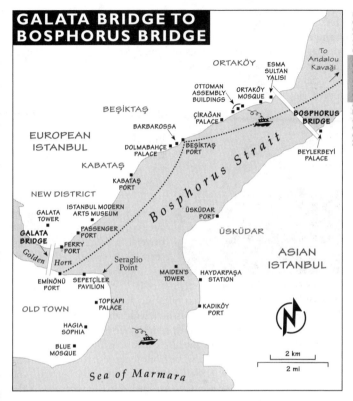

GALATA BRIDGE TO BOSPHORUS BRIDGE

new eight-mile Metro tunnel, the **Marmaray,** that will cross under the Bosphorus—giving locals one more way to make the crossing. (Today the only options are by two bridges—both of which we'll see—or by boat.) For more on the new tunnel, see the sidebar on page 252.

Offshore from Asian Istanbul is one of the city's symbols, the

old Byzantine tower often referred to as the **Maiden's Tower** (just left of the harbor, but before the radar tower). Today this landmark is used as a lighthouse and a restaurant.

• *That's all for Asia for a while. The boat picks up speed—yes, it'll go this fast the whole time—and moves closer to Europe. Get settled and start reading ahead. Now focus your attention on the left, on European Istanbul.*

Just after the harbor building ends, you see the clearly marked

Istanbul Modern Arts Museum (the gray, blocky, modern harbor-front building, sometimes hidden behind parked vessels; described on page 53), then the Academy of Fine Arts. After that you begin to pass residential neighborhoods.

Soon you go by the Kabataş district, and its seabus and ferry ports. Beyond that is the **Dolmabahçe Palace** complex, the 19th-

century palace of the Ottoman sultan (see page 54). The first building is the Dolmabahçe Mosque, built exclusively for the sultans, and sharing the same eclectic style as the palace itself. Next door is the clock tower, built as an extravagant accessory. Right behind the tower is a soccer stadium that seats 30,000 people—but, since it's ingeniously designed to fit into its surroundings, you barely notice it. Unfortunately, the same cannot be said of the tall glass building above, the Ritz-Carlton. The other sore thumb is the Swissotel, right above the palace.

Centuries-old trees partially block your vision of the monumental gate, to the right of the clock tower, leading to the palace. This also marks the start of a waterfront fence, guarded by soldiers. At the back side of the garden, just before the palace starts, you can see a second massive entryway, built for the sole use of the sultan and his guests.

The first wing of the building, including the tall middle part, was the palace's administrative section, called Selamlık (seh-

lahm-luhk). The side gate was for officials and envoys, whom the sultan received in the front-corner rooms, with sweeping Bosphorus views. The next wing was the

Harem, or residential section, extending behind the visible section. The building to the right, set apart from the palace, was for guests and palace employees.

Impressive as Dolmabahçe is from here, a century and a half of humidity and saltwater have taken their toll on the palace's facade. Though the palace walls facing the Bosphorus are ornate, the back is plain and dull—left undecorated when the sultan ran out of money.

Where the palace fence ends is an abandoned ferry port,

named for **Barbarossa**—the famous pirate-turned-Ottoman admiral. When Barbarossa sailed the seas, the Ottoman armada controlled the entire Mediterranean. The park just beyond the dock, and the mosque behind the park, are also both named for the beloved Barbarossa. There's a larger-than-life Barbarossa statue in the park, and his tomb is in the mosque complex. The fenced park belongs to the Naval Museum.

While you were ogling the palace, you may have noticed the ferry starting to slow down for its first stop, at **Beşiktaş** (beh-sheek-tahsh). Enjoy your last views back on the Old Town, which is now little more than an outline. While the boat docks, look down into the water, swirling with garbage and jellyfish—two good reasons why you'll rarely see swimmers in the Bosphorus.

Beşiktaş to Kanlıca

• *Keep watching the left (European) side.*

As you leave Beşiktaş, the next building is one of the private universities of Istanbul *(universitesi)*. In front of the building, you'll see people fishing—either for sport or to catch dinner. Many local fisherfolk have favorite spots along the Bosphorus. These embankments are even more crowded on weekends, with people walking, fishing, enjoying the day with their families—sometimes even (gulp!) swimming. Keep an eye out for barbecue grills, used to cook up the fish as they're pulled from the water.

Past the university, the building under construction—formerly a state guest house—is the new Four Seasons hotel. Next to it is the **Çırağan Palace** (chuh-rah-ahn), another late-Ottoman residence. This was built two decades after Dolmabahçe Palace in the same eclectic style by the same architect. In 1910, it mysteriously burned to the ground—some say because of faulty wiring, others say arson. Only a chunk of the facade remained standing, and a local soccer team used the empty space for practice. More recently, an international hotel chain restored the palace in exchange for the right to build a hotel complex next door, the Çırağan Palace Kempinski Hotel (with the big swimming pool in front). Presidents Clinton and Bush (the Elder) have both stayed here (though not at the same time). It has theme restaurants and a ballroom, as well as a popular—and expensive—jazz bar in the basement, which moves up to the waterfront in summer.

The next building is a maritime high school (easy to recognize, thanks to the ship's mast in front). Past that are three long buildings standing side by side, painted various shades of yellow. These were the 19th-century **Ottoman Assembly** buildings. In the late days of the Ottoman Empire, when it was becoming the "Sick Man of Europe," pressure from elsewhere in Europe—and from forces within the empire, especially the military—compelled the Sultan to agree to the creation of an advisory committee. The parliament lasted only a few decades, and vanished with World War I.

Past the assembly buildings, we enter the lively **Ortaköy** (or-tah-koy) district (with the towers of Istanbul's business zone in the background). Just before

the Bosphorus Bridge is the striking 19th-century **Ortaköy Mosque**—with a Western style similar to the Dolmabahçe Mosque we passed earlier. Right next to the mosque is a 19th-century mansion, **Esma Sultan Yalısı,** that once

belonged to a sultan's daughter. After the birth of the Republic, it was used as a depot to store tobacco. It burned down in the 1970s and was left in ruins for years. Eventually the tenants took matters into their own hands, redecorated with stylish glass and metal elements, and converted the mansion into a banquet hall for dinners, cultural activities, and mini-concerts. For more on the happening Ortaköy scene, see page 315 in the Entertainment chapter.

Now you are under the first bridge ever to connect two conti-

nents—the **Bosphorus Bridge.** It is the first of two suspension bridges over the Bosphorus. Built by a Turkish-British corporation, it was completed in 1973, on the 50th anniversary of the Turkish Republic. It is almost two-thirds of a mile long (a little more than a kilometer), and carries six lanes of traffic between the continents.

• *Now look to the right (Asian) side.*

Just to the left of the bridge is **Beylerbeyi,** the late-19th-century sum-mer palace of the sultan. The hill rising behind the palace is Çamlıca (chahm-luh-jah). Half of the city's TV and radio transmitters are on that hill, the highest point in greater Istanbul at roughly 1,200 feet.

• *Back to the left (European) side.*

Just past the bridge, on the European side, is a string of night-clubs—some of the most popular places in the city for the jet set. There's even a small island that belongs to a private sports club.

We've been cruising along the European coastline since leav-ing Beşiktaş. Now the boat will adjust its course and head for the other side of the strait. As the boat passes the center of the strait, watch for groups of dolphins heading north on their way to the

Black Sea. (To trace our route, turn back to the overview map on page 251.)

• *As the boat heads for Asia, so should your gaze. Look right.*

Coming up on the Asian side is a very wide two-story white building. Named **Kuleli** (koo-leh-lee; "With Towers") for the towers on either end, it was built in the early 1800s as an army barracks. Today it's a military high school.

Beyond Kuleli, the population starts to thin out. There used to be many small fishing villages along the shoreline, but today those simple fishing boats have been replaced by luxury yachts. Especially along the Asian side, from Kuleli all the way to the second bridge, you will see lots of impressive private waterfront **mansions** belonging to wealthy families. The generic name for these mansions is *yalı* (yah-luh). Pay attention to those made of wood—quite a few are over a century old, although many have been renovated. Laws once prohibited the use of non-original materials in renovating historic buildings. But many historic, wooden buildings mysteriously burned down, and were quickly replaced with new, modern constructions. This led to a recent compromise: The core of the structure can be rebuilt according to modern specifications, but a replica of the original wooden facade must adorn the front. Regardless of their historical value, these multi-million-dollar homes on the Bosphorus are among the most expensive in the city.

Next you'll pass the **Cape of Kandilli** (kahn-dee-lee; "With Candles"), named for the lamps lit to warn ships of the strong current here. The cape is marked with a huge electric pole on top of the hill, transferring high voltage wires across to Europe. At the tip of the cape is another radar tower. Next to it is the *yalı* of Edip Efendi, a two-story white-and-gray wood mansion on the water.

• *Now look left (European side).*

Across from the cape is the trendy Arnavutköy district (named for early Albanian settlers), and following that, **Bebek Bay** (beh-behk; "Baby"). This town on the bay is known for its almond paste, sometimes flavored with pistachios. The apartments and condos here cost a small fortune to buy or rent. Notice the many private boats anchored in the bay. To the left of the bay, the unusual-looking gray building with a French-style roof and large flag is the Egyptian consulate.

• *Back to Asia (right).*

Beyond the cape, the Bosphorus makes a sharp turn into a bay. Watch for more impressive homes, especially the terra-cotta-painted one with three antique columns in its garden (it belongs to one of the wealthiest families in Turkey), and the very wide single-story 18th-century *yalı* with the fancy second-floor balcony.

Deeper into the bay, you will notice the Western-looking 19th-century hunting pavilion of the sultans, named after the nearby fresh-water creek, **Küçüksu** (kew-chewk-soo). It was a remote getaway for the royals, who were hunting peace and quiet more than anything.

Less than half a mile from the pavilion, past the pink building (a teachers' social club), notice the round and square towers of an old fortress rising among the houses. This is the **Anatolian Fortress**

(Anadolu Hisarı; ah-nah-doh-loo hee-sah-ruh), built by the Ottoman Sultan Beyazıt at the end of the 14th century. Known as "Thunderbolt" for his speed on the battlefield, Beyazıt built this fortress at one of the narrowest points of the Bosphorus to cut off aid to Constantinople during a siege. Fifty years later, Beyazıt's grandson, Mehmet II, conquered Constantinople by following his grandpa's example across the strait...

• *Now look across to the European side (left).*

Here you see the much bigger **Rumeli Fortress** (Rumeli Hisarı; roo-meh-lee hee-sah-ruh)—built by Sultan Mehmet II a year before the conquest of Constantinople in 1453. Construction was completed in a record time of 80 days. Once the Ottomans had fortresses on both banks of the Bos-phorus, it was virtually impossible for a ship to

pass through without permission. This one-two punch of mighty fortresses was a key component of Mehmet's ultimately successful siege of Constantinople. (Read more about Rumeli Fortress on page 58 in the Sights chapter.)

• *Back to Asia (right).*

As you near the second bridge, look for the oldest surviving *yalı* on the banks of Bosphorus: the mansion of **Hüseyin Paşa.** Run-down but currently under renovation, this terra-cotta-painted *yalı* was built by the Ottoman Grand Vizier around the year 1700. It's taller than you'd expect for a single-story building, because it rises up on wood supports above a stone retaining wall.

Next up is the **Fatih Sultan Mehmet Bridge** (locals call it FSM for short). Newer than the Bosphorus Bridge, it was built in 1988 by a Turkish-Japanese corporation and is longer (almost a mile) and wider (eight lanes) than the Bosphorus Bridge. While the first bridge is used mostly for local city traffic, the FSM sees more intercity and international travel. Trucks are required to use the FSM.

As we approach **Kanlıca,** enjoy the view of impressive *yalıs*, many with drive-in "garages" for private boats. Kanlıca is a popular weekend spot, with many cafeterias and eateries along the water where locals enjoy a cup of tea while soaking up the beautiful scenery. Kanlıca is also famous for its yogurt, served in small plastic containers and sprinkled with powdered sugar. As you leave the port, servers will scamper around the boat selling fresh yogurt just picked up at the port (2 YTL).

Kanlıca to Yeniköy

• *Keep watching Asia.*

In less than a mile, up the hill in the woods, note the fancy tower of the renowned **Hidiv Pavilion.** The pavilion was built in the Art Nouveau style at the end of the 19th century for the Ottoman governor of Egypt. Hidiv (hee-deev) means just that in Turkish— "Governor of Egypt." You'll get a better view of the building as the boat slides away from the Asian shore.

• *The next stop is on the European side (left).*

Now the boat heads back across the Bosphorus to dock at **Yeniköy** (yeh-nee-koy; "New Village"). This is a trendy, high-end

district with some of the most elaborate houses on the Bosphorus. Some are traditional wood constructions, but quite a few of the newer ones have a distinctly

Returning Overland from Sarıyer

If you have a transit pass, you can use the bus to visit some inter-esting sights on the way home (or to cut your Bosphorus cruise short) by getting off the ferry at Sarıyer, and taking a southbound bus (#40, #25E, or #25T) back to central Istanbul. Depending on the time of day and traffic, the bus ride can take between 45–60 minutes. The bus stop is one block from the Sarıyer port: With the port behind you, walk right along the park and look for the bus stop across the street, where the street makes a sudden curve. Bus numbers are marked on a sign at the stop. Once on board, tell your driver (or fellow passengers) where you'd like to get off, so they can help you find the right stop. Remember that buses don't take tokens; you need a pass (see "Public Transportation Tokens and Passes," page 30).

Here are your options:

Bus #40: For a pleasant ride back to **Taksim Square in the New District,** take southbound bus #40 (Sarıyer–Taksim). This bus takes a scenic route along the Bosphorus and runs every 10–25 minutes 6:00–24:00 (less frequently after 21:30). Bus #40 also provides a convenient connection to the Sadberk Hanım Museum and Rumeli Fortress (see page 58 in the Sights chapter), and the ever-popular Ortaköy district by the Bosphorus Bridge.

For the **Sadberk Hanım Museum,** you can easily walk (south) here from the Sarıyer ferry stop in about 10 minutes. Or take bus #40 and get off at the Sefaret (seh-fah-reht) stop and walk a few blocks south along the coastal road (with the Bosphorus on your left). After you visit the museum, walk back to the same stop to catch bus #40 to Taksim or #25E to Eminönü. Or, if you enjoy walking near the water, keep walking south until you get tired, then catch a bus.

modern style. American travelers often compare these to the man-sions along the Mississippi River.

Yeniköy to Sarıyer

• *Keep watching the European side (left).*

About five minutes after you leave Yeniköy, you'll see the **Presidential Mansion.** Built in the 19th century, this has been the summer mansion for the president of Turkey since 1985. A long, tall stone wall runs along the coastal road, with the mansion's two three-story pavilions set behind the wall. The closest pavilion has a steep tile roof, and a decoration that looks like a little onion dome at the front-left corner.

Past that is the small **Tarabya Bay,** marked by the multistory hotel complex at its right end. Here is where you'll start to feel a cool breeze from the north. It's the prevailing wind all year long,

For **Rumeli Fortress,** get off bus #40 at the Rumeli Hisarı (roo-meh-lee hee-sah-ruh) stop. To return to Istanbul, catch another bus where you got off, or walk to the next stop, Aşiyan, on the hillside just past the cemetery (next to the fortress).

For the **Ortaköy district,** get off bus #40 at the Ortaköy (ohr-tah-koy) stop and enjoy one of Istanbul's most picturesque pedestrian areas. Popular among the younger generation, Ortaköy is crowded on weekends, sunny days, and all summer long. It's also full of eateries: seafood restaurants, fast-food joints, cafés, and tea shops. Students and artists display their handicrafts for sale—usually souvenirs and simple jewelry.

Bus #25E: Southbound bus #25E to **Kabataş in the New District** (Sarıyer–Kabataş) follows the same route as the previously described #40 as far as the Beşiktaş district, then continues along the Bosphorus to Kabataş, where you can transfer to the tram for the Old Town. Buses run 6:15–22:30 (every 30 minutes until 20:30, then every hour). This is the only bus that goes to **Dolmabahçe Palace** without a transfer.

Bus #25T: This is the quickest way to get from Sarıyer to **Taksim Square in the New District,** but what you make up in time you lose in scenery, since it takes the inland freeway. Bus #25T runs every 15–30 minutes 6:00–23:00 (6:20–22:00 on Sun). Take this only if you want to make a beeline back to Taksim Square.

At Sarıyer: If you have time to spare before catching a bus, detour to the Sarıyer fish market. With the port behind you, follow the road to the right, and take the first right, soon after the street curves left. The fish market is a couple of blocks down on the right, behind the little square. Try the specialty: deep-fried mussels.

and cools Bosphorus temperatures quite a bit in the summer.

• *Back to Asia (right).*

Half a mile past Tarabya Bay, from the right side of the boat, you'll get your first glimpse of the **Black Sea.**

• *And back to Europe again (left).*

Our next stop, **Sarıyer** (sah-ruh-yehr), is at the far end of the large bay. Transit-pass holders can consider getting off at Sarıyer— either now, or on the way home—to return to downtown Istanbul overland by bus, stopping to see some sights en route (see sidebar).

Sarıyer to Rumeli Kavağı

• *Watch the European side (left).*

As you leave Sarıyer, you'll cruise very close to the bank for one more stop on the European side before the boat heads to its last stop on the Asian side. Beyond this point, the wind gets stronger.

Locals call this wind Poyraz (poy-rahz), after Boreas, the Greek god of wind.

Cruising along fishing communities and narrow marinas where fishing boats are tied up, you'll soon come to the village of **Rumeli Kavağı** (roo-meh-lee kah-vah-uh). Then the ferry heads for its last stop: the fishing village of Anadolu Kavağı on the Asian side, right across from Rumeli Kavağı.

Rumeli Kavağı to Anadolu Kavağı

· *Keep watching the European side (left).*

As the boat turns toward Asia, from the left side you can enjoy a great view of the Bosphorus opening into the **Black Sea.** Even the casual tourist senses the dark, foreboding aura of this zone, where wind and rainstorms can gather within minutes, even in the middle of summer.

Up the shore on the European side are some extremely dangerous hidden rocks that have long plagued navigators. If you know the tale of Jason and the Argonauts, you may remember the  "**Clashing Rocks**" (or Symplegades) the crew encountered as they sailed into the Black Sea. These rocks of legend are believed by some to be based on this stretch of the Bosphorus. In Jason's time, the rocks would dangerously lunge toward each other, demolishing any boats that tried to pass. To make it through, the Argonauts let loose a dove, which was guided by the goddess Athena, and led them to safety. After this, the rocks stopped clashing, but remained a potentially destructive obstacle. Byzantine emperors erected a huge column here to warn passing ships. It worked...except when thick fog made this part of the Bosphorus nearly impossible to navigate. It's still difficult today, even with electronic gear.

· *Turn toward Asia (right) as we near our final stop...*

ANADOLU KAVAĞI

Welcome to Asia: the small fishing village of Anadolu Kavağı (ah-nah-doh-loo kah-vah-uh). *Anadolu* comes from the Greek word *anatoli,* meaning "the land to the East," while *kavak* means "controlled pass." From Byzantine times to the present, this has been a strategic checkpoint for vessels going through the Bosphorus. As you approach the Asian side, watch for the Byzantine **Yoros Castle** that dominates the hilltop above the village. Below that, notice the modern military installations: The area between here and the Black Sea is a restricted-access zone.

The ferry takes a break here in Anadolu Kavağı, usually for an hour and a half (sometimes longer, up to three hours). Look for the scheduled departure time posted near the dock, or ask the attendant what time to be back. Make a point of arriving back at the boat at least 10 minutes before the departure time—or earlier, if you want to secure a prime seat for the return trip.

Planning Your Time: Anadolu Kavağı has two main activities: eating lunch or hiking up to Yoros Castle. If you're speedy or have a longer break (2–3 hours), you'll probably be able to squeeze in both; if you'd like a more leisurely experience, choose one. (Both options are described.)

Overland Return to Istanbul: Don't miss the boat. But if you do, you can either take a taxi back to Istanbul (figure 80 YTL), or use the bus (passes only, no tokens accepted). You can catch the bus at the town center, a block straight ahead from the ferry port. Begin by taking bus #15A (Anadolu Kavağı–Kavacık) to the Körfez (Beykoz) stop. From there you have two options: You can either take bus #E-2 to Taksim Square, or bus #15 to Üsküdar (on the Asian side), where you can catch a ferry back to Eminönü in the Old Town.

Eating in Anadolu Kavağı

Anadolu Kavağı is made-to-order for enjoying a leisurely lunch. The town is packed with down-to-earth restaurants that cater to Bosphorus cruise passengers—both international tourists and Istanbul residents who come up here for a nice meal on the weekends. As you step off the boat, the streets just ahead of you and for two blocks to the left are filled with nothing but restaurants. (The path leading up to the castle is also lined with eateries, but the quality up there isn't as reliable.)

The specialty is seafood, of course. You can find a wide range of fish straight out of the strait (see sidebar on next page). Most eateries advertise *midye tava* (meed-yeh tah-vah)—deep-fried mussels. Popular all over Istanbul, these are mussels dipped in batter and deep-fried, and served with *tarator* (tah-rah-tohr) sauce—made from bread, crushed fresh garlic, lemon juice, yogurt, olive oil, salt, and vinegar. Upscale restaurants sometimes add crushed walnuts to the mix. Fried calamari is also common, but beware: It's not native to Istanbul, and is usually frozen, not fresh.

Before settling in, ignore the hawkers and stroll around to

The Fish of the Bosphorus Strait and the Sea of Marmara

Fish is an essential part of Istanbul cuisine, and offers a flavorful alternative to kebabs. Many locals can tell at a glance just how many hours a fish has been out of the water. But with Istanbul's population now over 15 million, the once-abundant native fish are becoming scarcer, and prospects for the future are uncertain. Fishing stocks have been depleted by the use of large fishing boats, which are consequently now banned from June to September. However, fishing for sport is still allowed, and many people fish along the Bosphorus. Fishermen yell at passing boats that get too close and scare away the fish.

While perusing Istanbul's menus, keep an eye out for the following fish. In some cases, we've listed the months when they're most abundant, but you may also find them outside this time.

Barbun (bahr-boon): This little red mullet, which lives along the muddy seabed, can be caught year-round. A local delicacy, it's delicious when deep-fried, and is often served as a side dish or as a hot appetizer. No need to remove the bones—just crunch them down.

Çinekop (chee-neh-kohp): This young bluefish is popular when grilled, and is available from early October through the end of November.

Hamsi (hahm-see): This anchovy, in season from November to March, is a delicacy from the Black Sea. Natives cook this small

find the place that looks best. Most of the cheaper eateries sell a fixed-price meal for about 20–25 YTL that includes grilled fish, fried mussels, French fries, salad, bread, and a drink. Fancier restaurants have a wider (and more expensive) menu. If you opt to go à la carte, one portion of *midye tava* can be a light meal. For about 30–35 YTL, two people can get two portions of *midye tava*, two drinks, and split a fresh fish fillet.

Other options include sandwiches, salads, *pide* (pee-deh; Turkish pizza), kebabs, and even waffles, although your options may be limited in the off-season (late Oct–late April). For dessert, try the *lokma* (lohk-mah) advertised by stalls and restaurants. This is a crispier version of a donut hole, made by dipping wheat dumplings into hot syrup. Locals love it, and have been known to travel to Anadolu Kavağı just for fresh-cooked *lokma*. **Yosun Restaurant,** to your immediate left as you stand with the ferry dock at your back, has a *lokma* stand at the corner.

The grocery store and the bakery are good options to pick up supplies for a people-watching picnic on a bench in the square, or to munch up at the castle. To find them, follow the narrow street straight ahead from the port. The bakery is on the other side of fish in dozens of ways—including fried, steamed, grilled, cooked in casseroles, and even added to cornbread. Hamsi are especially good when steamed in large trays with onions, tomatoes, green peppers, and lemons—creating a traditional dish called *hamsi buğulama* (hahm-see boo-oo-lah-mah).

Istavrit (ees-tahv-reet): This mackerel, generally served fried, is available throughout the year.

Kalkan (kahl-kahn): This delicious turbot lives in the Sea of Marmara, is best pan-fried, and is usually in the markets from December to April. As it's becoming rarer, you may find it only in upscale restaurants. It has round bones that locals call "buttons"; those with fewer bones are female.

Levrek (lehv-rehk): While its tastier wild cousins are expensive and hard to find, this farm-raised sea bass is cheap and available year-round. Although it's not wild, it's still worth a try—especially grilled.

Lüfer (lew-fehr): Its lack of a "fishy" taste makes this type of bluefish extremely popular in Istanbul. It's becoming rare—and expensive—and is usually available from late September to January.

Mezgit (mehz-geet): Fish-sellers hawk this whiting throughout the year. It's best either pan-fried or steamed with vegetables, though natives of Istanbul have never developed a real taste for its chicken-like flavor.

the intersecting street, just before the parking lot, and the grocery store is past the parking lot. The bakery's specialty is anchovy bread (*hamsili ekmek;* hahm-see-lee ehk-mehk)—a Black Sea delicacy made with corn flour, leeks, tomatoes, fresh peppers, and fresh anchovies.

Yoros Castle (Yoros Kalesi)

Aside from having a meal and wandering the town, the only other activity in Anadolu Kavağı is to hike up to Yoros Castle, on the hilltop above town. While this run-down castle ruin hardly reflects

the glory of its past, it does afford fine views over the Bosphorus and to the Black Sea. You can combine a castle hike with your lunch (bring a picnic from the grocery store in town rather than eat at one of the restaurants on the hillside below the castle). Public WCs are en route. You'll notice lots of litter, as well as friendly but hungry stray dogs eyeing you, hoping for your leftovers.

The moderately strenuous hike takes about 20 minutes each way. Most of the way up, you'll be passing through a military-controlled zone, so put your camera away. Once at the castle, feel free to take photos. Our hike goes up the south side of the hill where there are fewer breezes, so it may feel a little warmer than you'd expect.

○ Castle Hike: Standing with your back to the ferry port, walk straight ahead toward the large, square street fountain (with the gold Arabic script). After the fountain, take the street to your left, and walk about 100 yards (bearing left at the fork) until you reach the corner of the yellow 16th-century Ali Reis Mosque (you'll see a sign to *Yoros Kalesi*—that's Yoros Castle—across the street). Turn right and walk with the mosque on your right-hand side. Soon you'll see the Navy station fence on your left. After about 100 yards, you'll come to a fork—keep to the left.

The road gets steeper and bears right as you continue up and up. After passing a stand of cypress trees, the road makes a sharp curve to the left, offering glances of the Bosphorus beyond the parking lot. Up ahead, you also see part of the lower wall of Yoros Castle. Keep walking.

Past the wall fragments, there's another fork—keep right (the left fork goes to a military checkpoint). Less than 100 yards later, after the road curves left, you'll see a large aerial photo of the castle on the wall to your left (with a sign reading *To Castle/Ceneviz Kalesi*). Follow the steps next to the sign, up past the café tables. Keep to the right as the path, punctuated with simple steps, leads you through more humble eateries on its way to the castle entrance. You'll soon see the castle wall to your left, as well as public WCs, picnic tables, and hammocks.

Reaching the end of the path, take the stairs to your left, through Yoros Café (ignore the plaster lion statues and menus—the steps are public, not part of the restaurant). These steps lead all the way up, straight to the gate of Yoros Castle. As you come through the gate (free, always open), you're in an open courtyard with several rough paths and the graffiti-marred remains of the former military fortress. Head up to the top of the courtyard for your reward: spectacular views of the Bosphorus and the Black Sea—and the cool northerly breeze. Yoros Castle is quite popular on weekends in good weather, when it's packed with locals.

• *Enjoy the view and the town below, then head back to the ferry for the cruise back to Europe, and Istanbul.*

SLEEPING

Istanbul has an abundance of comfortable, well-located hotels. We've focused our recommendations on two safe, handy, and colorful neighborhoods: the Sultanahmet district (in the heart of the historic Old Town); and İstiklal street (a.k.a. İstiklal Caddesi, the main pedestrian drag running through the heart of the New District). Prices aren't cheap, but there are a few good deals to be found.

In each neighborhood, we list good hotels, helpful hints, and a selection of restaurants (see the Eating chapter). Before choosing a hotel, read the descriptions of the two neighborhoods carefully. Your neighborhood is as important as your hotel for the success of your trip (see sidebar, next page).

Reserve ahead for Istanbul. Hotels are crowded in May, June, September, and October. Also see the "Major Holidays and Weekends" sidebar on page 6. Surprisingly, the major Christian holidays can cause prices and demand to spike in Muslim Turkey, since Europeans flock here when they have time off. And conversely, Muslim holidays (listed on page 356 in the appendix) do not generally affect Istanbul hotel prices, as many Turks travel away from the cities during those times. Most hotel rates go down from mid-November through mid-March (except around New Year's, when they charge peak rates). Some also offer small discounts in July and August, when the city is hotter and quieter. Many hotels list special promotional rates on their websites, and some offer free airport transfers (often one-way, either to or from the airport) to those staying three or more nights.

Some hotels offer discounted rates or other bonuses (such as free airport transfers) for readers of this book. We've generally noted these discounts in their listings. To get this special treatment, always reserve direct and tell them that you're using the

SLEEPING

Old Town Versus New District: Where to Sleep?

The character of your stay in Istanbul can be determined to a great extent by where your hotel is located.

If you prefer romantic and classic old Istanbul—calls to prayer, graceful minarets outside your hotel, rough cobbled lanes, and three-star sights (mosques, bazaars, and palaces) within an easy walk—go for the Old Town's Sultanahmet district. Most of the Sultanahmet hotels listed here are in a kind of tourist-friendly "green zone," where "invading" foreigners feel comfortable amid the traditional surroundings.

But if you'd prefer to experience the tempo of today's Istanbul, with modern secular people, big noisy streets, and a high-energy shopping and strolling energy that fills the main pedestrian boulevard until late each night, make the New District your home base in Istanbul. Your New District hotel will be filled with more visiting businesspeople than tourists, with a diverse selection of restaurants and nightlife nearby.

Rick Steves book.

Like most European hotels, Istanbul hotel rooms are smaller than comparable hotel rooms in the US. We look for places that are friendly; clean; a good value; located in a central, safe, quiet neighborhood; English-speaking; and not mentioned in other guidebooks. Obviously, a place meeting every criterion is rare, and all of these recommendations fall short of perfection. But we've listed the best values for each price category, given the above criteria.

In this book, the price for a double room ranges from $30 (very simple—toilet and shower down the hall) to $450 (grand lobbies, maximum plumbing, and the works), with most clustering around $125–150.

TYPES OF ACCOMMODATIONS

Hotels

Turkey has a simple hotel rating system that's based on amenities (one through five stars, indicated in this book by * through *****). Hotels with one star (or no stars) are simple and can be bargains—or depressing dumps. Two stars offer basic facilities but little charm. Three stars have most of the comforts, and four is generally just a three-star with a fancier lobby and more elaborately designed rooms. Five stars offer more luxury than you have time to appreciate.

Generally, the number of stars does not reflect room size or guarantee quality. Some two-star hotels are better than many

Sleep Code

(€1 = about $1.40, 1.50 YTL = about $1, country code: 90)
To help you sort easily through these listings, we've divided the rooms into three categories based on the price for a standard double room with bath:

$$$ **Higher Priced**—Most rooms €200 or more.
  $$ **Moderately Priced**—Most rooms between €90–200.
    $ **Lower Priced**—Most rooms €90 or less.

Prices are listed in euros in this chapter and at most Istanbul hotels, because the euro is a more stable currency than New Turkish Lira (YTL). Hotels will take cash payment in YTL or euros, and all of the recommended accommodations accept credit cards. Remember that, as of 2009, the New Turkish Lira (YTL) is being renamed simply Turkish Lira (TL).

To give maximum information in a minimum of space, we use the following code to describe the accommodations. Prices listed are per room, not per person. Unless otherwise noted, prices include room tax and breakfast (if not included, it's usually optional). All of our recommended hotels have English-speaking staff.

  S = Single room (or price for one person in a double).
  D = Double or twin room.
  T = Triple (a double bed with a single, or three twin beds).
  b = Private bathroom with toilet and shower or tub.
  s = Private shower or tub only (the toilet is down the hall).
  ***** = Turkey's star system for rating hotels.
  SC = "Special Class" (renovated historic building).

According to this code, a couple staying at a "Db-€140" hotel would pay a total of €140 (about $200) for a double room with a private bathroom.

three-star hotels. One- and two-star hotels are inexpensive, but some three-star (and even a few four-star hotels) offer good value, justifying the extra cost.

There's also a separate designation called "Special Class" (which we've marked with this symbol: **SC**). This means the hotel is a historic Turkish-style building converted to lodging—in other words, it has a uniquely Turkish character. There are no sub-categories among Special Class hotels. Some are upscale; others are run-down. While the rooms can be quite comfortable, most don't have Western-style amenities such as saunas, pools, multiple restaurants, or parking. Many of the Old Town's Special Class hotels are equivalent to a two- or three-star hotel.

Types of Rooms and Beds

Study the price list on the hotel's website or posted at the desk, so you know your options. Receptionists often don't mention the cheaper rooms (they assume you want a private bathroom or a bigger room). Here are the types of rooms and beds:

"French bed"
    Double bed (queen size or smaller)
"King bed"
    King-size bed
İki ayrı yatak (ee-kee eye-ruh yah-tahk)
    Twin beds
Çift kişilik oda (cheeft kee-shee-leek oh-dah)
    Double room; indicate whether you want a French bed, king-size bed, or twin beds
Geniş yataklı oda (geh-neesh yah-tahk-luh oh-dah)
    Single or double room with one large bed (usually queen size or smaller)
Tek kişilik oda (tehk kee-shee-leek oh-dah)
    Room for two used by a single person; bed(s) may be French or two twins
Üç kişilik oda (ewch kee-shee-leek oh-dah)
    Triple room (double bed and a twin, or three twin beds)
"Promotion room"
    Smaller room, often with toilet and shower down the hall

Most hotels have lots of doubles and a few singles and triples. Quads are rare. Traveling alone can be expensive, as singles are mostly doubles used by one person—at about two-thirds the price of a double room. Room prices vary within each hotel depending on size, views, whether the room has a bath or shower, and the size of the beds (tubs and twins cost more than showers and double beds—called "French beds" in Turkey). Rooms with king-size beds may be pricier than rooms with double beds. A triple is generally a double bed with a cot. Hotels cannot legally allow more people to stay in a room than what's shown on their price list. Some hotels may have family-friendly connecting rooms. Most hotel rooms have a sink, toilet, and bath or shower en suite, while hostels offer the option of rooms without showers and toilets.

All of the hotels listed in this book have English-speaking staff. Still, it can be helpful to use the correct hotel jargon to get the right size room and bed (see sidebar above). A "double room" isn't necessarily a room with one big bed for two. It can also mean a twin room, with two separate beds. Ask for what you want. You can save money by asking for a smaller room, often called a "promotion room." At some hotels, these rooms may share a bathroom down the hall.

Most hotels include VAT in their posted rates; others add it to your bill. Unless we've noted otherwise, you can assume tax is included in these rates.

Rooms are safe. Still, keep cameras and money out of sight or take them with you when you leave for the day. Better yet, most hotels offer safes at the reception desk, and some have safes in the rooms (you may have to pay a small fee).

If you're planning to visit Istanbul in the summer, it's worthwhile to choose an air-conditioned hotel. When using the air-conditioner in your room, remember that 20°C is a comfortable 68°F (see the temperature conversion chart in the appendix). Extra pillows and blankets are sometimes in the closet or available on request. To get a pillow, ask for *"Yastık, lütfen"* (yahs-tuhk lewt-fehn).

Most hotels provide a public computer terminal with Internet access for guests to use, often for free. Some also offer free wireless Internet access (Wi-Fi) to travelers packing a laptop.

If you need to do laundry, it's best to have your hotel do it—self-service launderettes are rare.

Breakfast: Turkish hotels see a good breakfast as a badge of honor, and are quite competitive—so unless you're sleeping at a dive, you can expect a decent breakfast. (Breakfast is almost always included in the room rate, except at a few international chain hotels.) A Turkish hotel breakfast often consists of cheese, olives, bread, jam or honey, butter, tomatoes, cucumbers, eggs (usually hard-boiled), Turkish tea, and instant coffee. Don't expect the thick "Turkish coffee" for breakfast—Turks drink this not as a side beverage, but as a digestive after meals (see page 290). Fresh-squeezed fruit juice may be available for an additional charge.

Hostels

Istanbul hostels charge about €15 for a dorm bed, more for private rooms. Hostels are concentrated in the Old Town—especially on or near the street called Yeni Akbıyık. Travelers of any age are welcome if they don't mind dorm-style accommodations and meeting other travelers. Hostel membership is not required. Cheap meals may be available, and kitchen facilities are usually provided for do-it-yourselfers.

Apartments

Short-term rental apartments are hard to find. We've listed several apartments (mainly in the New District), worth considering if you're traveling with your family or staying for a week or more.

PRACTICALITIES

Country Code

To phone Turkey, you will need to know its country code: 90. To call Turkey from the US or Canada, dial 011–90, then the area code (without the initial 0), then the local number. If calling Turkey from another European country, dial 00–90, then the area code (without the initial 0), then the local number.

Making Reservations

Given the quality of the accommodations we've found for this book, we recommend that you reserve your rooms in advance, particularly if you'll be traveling during peak season. Book several weeks ahead, or as soon as you've pinned down your travel dates. Note that some holidays merit making reservations far in advance (see "Major Holidays and Weekends" sidebar on page 6).

To make a reservation in advance, email is the best option, a fax is second-best, and a telephone call is the last choice (while most hotels are accustomed to English-only speakers, dueling accents can lead to misunderstandings). In addition, some hotel websites now have online reservation forms. If emailing or faxing, simple English is fine. If phoning from the US, be mindful of time zones (see page 10).

To ensure you have all the information you need for your reservation, use the form in this book's appendix (also at www.ricksteves .com/reservation). If you don't get a response within a few days, call to follow up.

When you request a room in writing for a certain time period, use the European style for writing dates: day/month/year. Hoteliers need to know your arrival and departure dates. For example, for a two-night stay in June, you would request: "2 nights, arrive 10/06/09, depart 12/06/09." Consider in advance how long you'll stay; don't just assume you can extend your reservation for extra days once you arrive.

If you don't get a reply to your email or fax, it usually means the hotel is already fully booked. If the response from the hotel gives its room availability and rates, it's not a confirmation. You must tell them that you want that room at the given rate.

The hotelier will sometimes request your credit-card number for a one-night deposit. While you can email that information (I do), it's safer to share it via phone call, fax, or secure online reservation form (if the hotel has one on its website).

If you must cancel your reservation, it's courteous to do so with as much advance notice as possible (simply send an email or make a quick phone call). Family-run hotels lose money if they turn away customers while holding a room for someone who doesn't show up.

Understandably, most hoteliers bill no-shows for one night. Ask about cancellation policies before you book.

Reconfirm your reservation a few days in advance for safety. If you'll be arriving later than 16:00, let them know. On the small chance that a hotel loses track of your reservation, bring along a hard copy of their emailed or faxed confirmation.

IN THE OLD TOWN'S SULTANAHMET DISTRICT

The Sultanahmet district in the Old Town was the core of the city during the Byzantine and Ottoman periods. Every important building, palace, and government office was here—and many of these places are world-famous museums and sights today. The area is named for the Blue Mosque (officially called the Sultan Ahmet Mosque, after its namesake).

The term "Sultanahmet" is used loosely to refer to the open space near Hagia Sophia, the Blue Mosque, and the Hippodrome. Trams run along the main street, Divan Yolu, and can zip you to most of Istanbul's key sights. The rest of the streets around Sultanahmet are narrow, originally built for horse-drawn carriages.

Sultanahmet's proximity to the sights is a mixed blessing. It was once a strictly residential area, but in recent years more and more of the traditional old Ottoman houses have been converted into hotels and pensions. As property values increase, few locals can afford to live here anymore. So even though the buildings are in the genuine Istanbul style, the people aren't. Many of the Turks you encounter in Sultanahmet are trying to sell you something—an inaccurate and unfortunate first impression of a kind and generous people. For tips on dealing with aggressive salespeople, see page 209.

Daylight hours in Sultanahmet are lively—there's plenty to see and do. Besides the many historical buildings, there are countless cafés and shops. In the evenings, many locals who work nearby go home, leaving the restaurants and cafés to tourists. But a few gems are still frequented by locals, and are listed in the Eating chapter.

Our recommended Sultanahmet hotels are centrally located within a 10-minute walk of Istanbul's biggest sights (Hagia Sophia, Blue Mosque, Grand Bazaar). For a short visit of one or two days, you can sleep in Sultanahmet, walk to all the sights, and never have to take public transportation.

When we've listed seasonal prices, "summer" refers to mid-March through mid-November, and "winter" (or "low season") refers to mid-November through mid-March. Most hotels offer a

10 percent discount if you pay cash.

Tourist Information: The neighborhood TI is at the bottom of the square called the Hippodrome, across from Hagia Sophia (daily 9:00–17:00).

Post Office: The nearest post office is by the ticket office of Topkapı Palace (Mon–Fri 9:00–16:30).

Transportation Connections: The very convenient Sultanahmet tram stop is on Divan Yolu, a few steps from Hagia Sophia. The tram connects you to Eminönü (a hub for public buses and ferries), and can also take you north of the Golden Horn to the New District. For more on getting around Istanbul, see page 29 in the Orientation chapter.

Hotels

$$$ Four Seasons Hotel***,** housed in what was once the city prison, is Istanbul's fanciest splurge hotel. Its 65 luxurious rooms come with all the comforts you'd expect, and then some (superior Sb-€400, superior Db-€430, these prices don't include tax

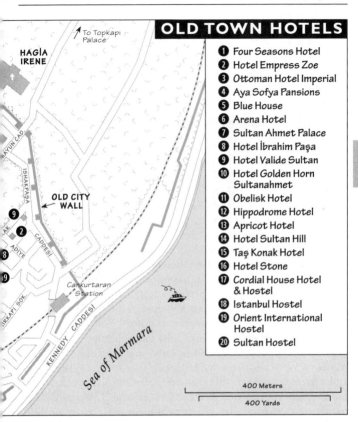

OLD TOWN HOTELS

① Four Seasons Hotel
② Hotel Empress Zoe
③ Ottoman Hotel Imperial
④ Aya Sofya Pansions
⑤ Blue House
⑥ Arena Hotel
⑦ Sultan Ahmet Palace
⑧ Hotel İbrahim Paşa
⑨ Hotel Valide Sultan
⑩ Hotel Golden Horn Sultanahmet
⑪ Obelisk Hotel
⑫ Hippodrome Hotel
⑬ Apricot Hotel
⑭ Hotel Sultan Hill
⑮ Taş Konak Hotel
⑯ Hotel Stone
⑰ Cordial House Hotel & Hostel
⑱ Istanbul Hostel
⑲ Orient International Hostel
⑳ Sultan Hostel

400 Meters

400 Yards

or breakfast, fancier rooms are more expensive, check website for deals, locally famous Sunday brunch-€45, terminal Internet access and Wi-Fi, Tevkifhane Sokak 1, tel. 0212/638-8200, fax 0212/638-8210, www.fourseasons.com).

$$ Hotel Empress Zoe SC, about a hundred yards downhill from the main gate of Topkapı Palace, is well-run and has oodles of character. The 25 rooms are scattered in several fun buildings surrounding a courtyard with chunks of old Ottoman walls. The treehouse floor plan is memorable, and the unique rooms have pizzazz (standard S-€85, standard Db-€125, standard Tb-€135, suite-€150–270, 10 percent discount with cash, prices drop 20–25 percent in low season, air-con, tight spiral staircase with no elevator, Wi-Fi in breakfast room, Cankurtaran Mahallesi, Akbıyık Caddesi 4/1, tel. 0212/518-2504, fax 0212/518-5699, www.emzoe.com, info@emzoe.com).

$$ Ottoman Hotel Imperial SC is a fresh-feeling place across the street from the side of the Hagia Sophia. Its 27 rooms—plus 25 more in a brand-new annex building—are comfortable and plush

(Sb-€79, Db-€99, "premium" rooms with Hagia Sophia view-€21 extra, 5 percent discount with this book, free one-way airport transfer with minimum 3-night stay, air-con, elevator, terminal Internet access and Wi-Fi, Caferiye Sokak 6/1, tel. 0212/513-6151, fax 0212/512-7628, www.ottomanhotelimperial.com, info @ottomanhotelimperial.com).

$$ Aya Sofya Pansions SC is beautifully located on a quiet, traffic-free lane squeezed between Hagia Sophia and the Topkapı Palace wall. The pension consists of a whole street's worth of 19th-century Ottoman row houses, converted into 63 rooms for rent. Higher prices are for rooms with a view of Hagia Sophia (summer: Sb-€120–140, Db-€170–200; winter: Sb-€84–98, Db-€119–140; request room with air-con in summer, lots of stairs and no elevator, all along Soğukçeşme Sokak, tel. 0212/513-3660, fax 0212/513-3669, www.ayasofyapensions.com, info@ayasofyakonaklari.com).

$$ Blue House SC has 26 nicely decorated rooms with a bold color scheme. Some rooms have views of the nearby Blue Mosque (Sb-€70–130, Db-€85–160, higher prices are for summer, 10 percent discount with cash, 10 percent additional discount with this book, air-con, elevator, Albastı Sokak 14, tel. 0212/638-9010, fax 0212/638-9017, www.bluehouse.com.tr, info@bluehouse.com.tr).

$$ Arena Hotel SC is in a quiet neighborhood a few blocks beyond the Hippodrome. This restored stone mansion from 1870 has 27 romantically decorated rooms, helpful staff, a Turkish bath, and a great breakfast buffet (summer: Sb-€100, Db-€125; winter: Sb-€60, Db-€80; upscale "Sultan's Corner" and "Imperial Corner" rooms are more expensive, check website for deals mid-June–mid-Aug, ask for discounts and/or free airport transfer with longer stays, air-con, elevator, Wi-Fi, Şehit Mehmet Paşa Yokuşu, Üçler Hamamı Sokak 13–15, just one block from Sokullu Mosque, tel. 0212/458-0364, fax 0212/458-0366, www.arenahotel.com, info @arenahotel.com).

$$ Sultan Ahmet Palace SC, with 36 clean, classy rooms across the street from the Blue Mosque, will have you feeling like a guest of the sultan. From the deserted-feeling street, you'll pass through a lush garden, then an elegant lobby, to reach the reception desk—and in your bathroom, you'll find faux-Turkish bath fixtures. This place is likely to have space when others are full (standard Sb-€130, standard Db-€145, deluxe Sb/Db-€200, €20 more for 1-night stays, check website for deals, air-con, no elevator, free airport transfer with 2-night stay, Torun Sokak 19, tel. 0212/458-0460, fax 0212/518-6224, www.sultanahmetpalace.com, saray@sultanahmetpalace.com).

$$ Hotel İbrahim Paşa SC, a few steps from the Hippodrome, is a small, comfortable hotel with 12 rooms (Sb/Db-€90–190, price varies with season, 10 percent discount with cash, air-con, terminal

Internet access and Wi-Fi, Terzihane Sokak 5, tel. 0212/518-0394, fax 0212/518-4457, www.ibrahimpasha.com, contact@ibrahim pasha.com).

$$ Hotel Valide Sultan SC ("Sultan's Mother") is a hundred yards down the street from the Topkapı Palace's Imperial Gate. This 19th-century Ottoman mansion has 17 neat rooms, a friendly staff, and an imperial lobby with elegant furnishings, though it's a bit past its prime (Sb-€75–85, Db-€90–100, Tb-€110–120, €20–45 cheaper mid-Nov–mid-March, 10 percent discount with cash, air-con, some rooms have sea views, elevator, terminal Internet access, free one-way airport transfer with 2-night stay, İshak Paşa Caddesi, Kutlugün Sokak 1, tel. 0212/517-6558, fax 0212/638-0705, www.hotelvalidesultan.com, vsultan@hotelvalidesultan.com).

$$ Hotel Golden Horn Sultanahmet****, one block behind the Turkish and Islamic Arts Museum, is very close to the Divan Yolu thoroughfare and the Sultanahmet tram stop. With less character than the "Special Class" listings in this area, this standard four-star hotel in a modern building is a reliable choice. All 71 rooms have air-conditioning, and some have views of the sea and Blue Mosque (S-€110, Db-€140, T-€170, 10 percent discount for guests 65 and older, check website for promotions, additional 10 percent discount if you present this book at check-in, lower prices off-season, terminal Internet access and Wi-Fi, Binbirdirek 1, tel. 0212/518-1717, fax 0212/518-9406, www.goldenhornhotel.com, info@goldenhornhotel.com).

$$ Obelisk Hotel SC, about two blocks from the Blue Mosque, was converted from an old Ottoman house and is now part of the international Best Western chain. Its 41 rooms manage an old-fashioned charm, and the breakfast terrace has sweeping views of the Bosphorus, Sea of Marmara, and the Blue Mosque (standard S-€125, seaview S-€155, standard Db-€135, seaview Db-€165, cheaper in winter, 10 percent discount with cash, show this book at check-in for an additional 5 percent discount, air-con, elevator plus some stairs, free terminal Internet access and Wi-Fi, free airport pick-up with minimum 3-night stay, Mimar Mehmet Ağa 17–19, tel. 0212/517-7173, fax 0212/517-8661, www.obelisk hotel.com, info@obeliskhotel.com, manager Hümeyra).

$ Hippodrome Hotel SC is owned by the nearby Obelisk Hotel (previous listing). Its recently renovated rooms, while small, are comfortably decorated with new furniture. In the building across the street, they also have two three-bedroom apartments with room for six, and a two-bedroom apartment with room for four—ideal for families (standard S-€75, standard Db-€90, apartment-€280, cheaper in winter, show this book at check-in for a 10 percent discount, breakfast at Obelisk Hotel, air-con, elevator, free Wi-Fi, free airport pick-up with minimum 3-night stay, Mimar

Mehmet Ağa 38, tel. 0212/517-6889, fax 0212/516-0268, www .hippodromehotel.com, hippodrome@hippodromehotel.com).

$ Apricot Hotel SC, about a block downhill from the Blue Mosque, is a great budget option. Well-run and well-priced, it has six rooms with whirlpool tubs or Turkish baths, and four rooms with views of the Blue Mosque. Breakfast is served in the Byzantine garden (Sb/Db-€69–119, 30 percent less in winter, no elevator and lots of stairs, free terminal Internet access and Wi-Fi, free airport pick-up with minimum 3-night stay, Amiral Tafdil Sokak 18, tel. 0212/638-1658, fax 0212/458-3574, www.apricot hotel.com).

$ Hotel Sultan Hill SC, immediately behind the Blue Mosque and a few steps off the Hippodrome, has 17 clean, comfortable rooms on three floors of an old Ottoman house. Managers Nilgün and Sedat are straightforward and interested in helping American travelers (Sb-€60, Db-€80, Tb-€120, family room-€140, mention this book when you reserve and present it at check-in for a 15 percent discount, air-con, Wi-Fi, Tavukhane Sokak 17–21, tel. 0212/518-3293, fax 0212/518-3295, www.hotelsultanhill.com, info@hotelsultanhill.com).

$ Taş Konak Hotel SC is a cheap option in a dull residential neighborhood a 10-minute walk below the Blue Mosque. This former Ottoman house has 32 rooms watched over by an indifferent staff. The rooftop breakfast terrace features fine views of the Sea of Marmara (Sb-€75, Db-€85, T-€115, suite-€115, 10 percent discount with cash, check website for promotions and off-season deals, air-con, no elevator, Wi-Fi, free airport transfer with 4-night stay, Küçük Ayasofya Caddesi, Tomurcuk Sokak 5, tel. 0212/518-2882, fax 0212/638-8491, www.hoteltashkonak.com, info@hoteltash konak.com).

$ Hotel Stone SC, two long blocks below the top of the Hippodrome (across from Sokullu Mosque), is a suitable budget option with some of the area's lowest prices. Located in a quiet, mostly residential neighborhood, with a relaxing stone garden out back, it was renovated in 2007 (Sb-€65, Db-€75, T-€95, €10 less off-season, 10 percent discount with cash, discount for longer stays, air-con, elevator, Wi-Fi, free one-way airport transfer with 4-night stay, Binbirdirek Mahallesi, Şehit Mehmet Paşa Yokuşu 34, tel. 0212/517-6331, fax 0212/517-6330, www.stonehotel.net, info@stonehotelistanbul.com).

$ Cordial House Hotel & Hostel, an institutional-feeling place, has 15 no-nonsense rooms with private baths and 30 hostel rooms with shared baths. It's on the alley across from Çemberlitaş, a short walk from the Grand Bazaar and the Hippodrome. Reserve on their website to receive the following discounted Internet rates—walk-in customers pay more (hotel—Sb-€28–35,

Db-€40–50, Tb-€50–60, Qb-€60–80; hostel—dorm bed-€8–10, S-€20–28, D-€26–34, T-€36–45, Q-€44–52, 10 percent discount when you present this book at check-in, no air-con, Wi-Fi, elevator, cheap beer, Peykane Sokak 29 Çemberlitaş, tel. 0212/518-0576, fax 0212/516-4108, www.cordialhouse.com, Tuğrul Gökçe).

Hostels

These three hostels—and several others not listed here—are on or near the bustling-with-backpackers Yeni Akbıyık Caddesi ("White Moustache Street"), a couple of blocks below the Blue Mosque (toward the Sea of Marmara). Each one offers dorm beds and some double rooms, and includes a simple Turkish breakfast. If you're trying to avoid American backpackers and other international travelers, give this street a miss. The **Cordial House** (listed previously, under "Hotels," also offers hostel-type accommodations).

$ Istanbul Hostel, just up the street from the Four Seasons, is nicely located and well-run. Its 62 beds are filled with travelers who enjoy hanging out in the basement bar or rooftop terrace (€13 bunks in 4-, 6-, or 9-bed dorms, D-€35, cheaper off-season, non-smoking, free Internet access, Kutlu Gün Sokak 35, tel. 0212/516-9380, www.istanbulhostel.net, istanbulhostel@hotmail.com).

$ Orient International Hostel is an official HI hostel and a backpacker mecca. The 121 beds in 38 rooms are a bit institutional, but a steady stream of Australian and Kiwi backpackers keeps the place lively (dorm beds-€9–16, S-€30, twin D-€39, Db-€40, free Internet access, check website for promotions and off-season deals, Yeni Akbıyık Caddesi 13, tel. 0212/518-0789, fax 0212/518-3894, www.orienthostel.com, info@orienthostel.com).

$ Sultan Hostel is another HI hostel, but feels less institutional than the Orient (dorm beds-€12–15, Db-€35–40, free Internet access, check website for promotions and off-season discounts, Yeni Akbıyık Caddesi 21, tel. 0212/516-9260, fax 0212/516-9262, www.sultanhostel.com, enquiries@sultanhostel.com).

IN THE NEW DISTRICT: NEAR İSTİKLAL STREET

Sleeping near İstiklal street (İstiklal Caddesi) puts you right at the center of the living city. This hip part of town never sleeps. From restaurants, cafés, theaters, and art galleries to bookstores, fashion boutiques, rock bars, and jazz clubs, there's something here for locals and visitors of all ages. In the New District, you can melt right in and become part of the colorful scene.

Recently, the municipal government has undertaken projects to upgrade Taksim's infrastructure and preserve its Art Nouveau buildings. Due to the New District's popularity, prices here are

SLEEPING

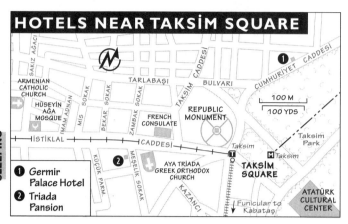

HOTELS NEAR TAKSİM SQUARE

❶ Germir
   Palace Hotel
❷ Triada
   Pansion

higher than the Old Town. Private apartments may be a good budget alternative.

Tourist Information: The neighborhood TI is in Elmadağ, a 10-minute walk from Taksim Square (Mon–Sat 9:00–17:00, closed Sun, at the entrance of Hilton Hotel, tel. 0212/233-0592).

Transportation Connections: Since Taksim Square is one of Istanbul's primary transit hubs, the New District is well-connected to the Old Town (and other parts of the city). Two options are the most convenient for reaching the Old Town sights. From Taksim Square (near the first several hotels listed next), take the funicular down to Kabataş, where you can catch the tram that zips into the historic core (get off at Sultanahmet for Hagia Sophia, the Blue Mosque, and other Old Town attractions). Or, from the opposite end of İstiklal street (near the Galata Tower listings, later), take the old-fashioned funicular from Tünel down to Karaköy, where you can transfer to the same tram mentioned previously (to reach the Old Town, take this tram to Sultanahmet). A convenient "nostalgic tram" runs down the center of İstiklal street, between Taksim Square and Tünel.

Near Taksim Square, at the Top of İstiklal Street

$$ Germir Palace Hotel SC, on a busy street near Taksim Square, comes with an old-fashioned but tastefully plush lobby, and 49 heavily perfumed rooms. Comfortable and classy, in a sophisticated Art Nouveau shell and with a smartly uniformed staff, it's a winner (Sb-€120–130, Db-€140–150, air-con, elevator, terminal Internet access and Wi-Fi, Cumhuriyet Caddesi 17, tel. 0212/361-1110, fax 0212/361-1070, www.germirpalas.com, hotel@germirpalas.com). From Taksim Square, with İstiklal street behind you, walk up the busy street (Cumhuriyet) that runs alongside a big park; the hotel is on the left after two blocks, across from the park.

$ Triada Pansion SC is just below Taksim Square, facing Aya Triada Church a half-block off İstiklal street. This small, friendly place offers 11 good-size, no-nonsense apartments with slightly shabby living rooms and kitchenettes. Its reasonable rates and excellent location make it popular with embassy workers in town for a long stint—book ahead (Sb/Db-€70–80, €20 more for rooftop balcony room #601, air-con, elevator, İstiklal Caddesi, Meşelik Sokak 10, tel. 0212/251-0101, fax 0212/292-6363, www.triada.com .tr, info@triada.com.tr).

Near the Galata Tower, at the Bottom of İstiklal Street

$$ Anemon Galata SC is next door to the Galata Tower. This historic building has been converted into a classy boutique hotel with 21 small, Old World–plush rooms and six suites, some with impressive Bosphorus or Golden Horn views (Sb-€120, Db-€140–160, air-con, elevator, Wi-Fi, spectacular view breakfast terrace, free airport shuttle, Bereketzade Mahallesi Büyükhendek Sokak, tel. 0212/293-2343, fax 0212/292-2340, www.anemonhotels.com, info@anemongalata.com).

$$ Richmond Hotel**,** the only hotel actually on İstiklal street, is all business and no personality—it's all about the location (just a few steps up İstiklal from the Tünel funicular station). The 103 small, uninspired business-class rooms are classified "deluxe" and "executive"—the latter with a slightly bigger desk. Part of the hotel may be under renovation in 2010 (deluxe Sb-€100–120, deluxe Db-€110–135, 5 percent discount with this book, rates can be soft—check website for deals, air-con, elevator, Wi-Fi, İstiklal Caddesi 445, tel. 0212/252-5460, fax 0212/252-9707, www .richmondhotels.com.tr, info@richmondhotels.com.tr).

$$ Eklektik Guest House SC, on a dingy little alley near the Galata Tower, is true to its name—the seven rooms are completely different, each one with its own theme, and all of them brimming with Old World–meets-contemporary style (Sb/Db-€80–110, prices vary by room and season, 10 percent discount with this book, air-con, no elevator but lots of stairs, terminal Internet access and Wi-Fi, gay-friendly, late breakfast available, Serdar Ekrem Mahallesi Şahkulu Sokak 4, tel. 0212/243-7646, fax 0212/243-7445, www.eklektikgalata.com, info@eklektikgalata.com).

$ Galata Residence SC hides down the hill from Galata Tower, a 10-minute uphill walk to the bottom of İstiklal street. They rent 22 apartments in three historical buildings, managed from the main building—an architectural landmark called the Camando Apartments. The apartments are basic and ramshackle, but a good value (2-person apartment: €75/night, €420/week;

HOTELS NEAR THE GALATA TOWER

1 Anemon Galata
2 Richmond Hotel
3 Eklektik Guest House
4 Galata Residence
5 Glorya Apartments
6 Bereket Apartments

4-person apartment: €120/night, €700/week; tax not included, 10 percent discount with this book, optional breakfast-€10/person, air-con, elevator in main building but lots of stairs in the others, free terminal Internet access, Bankalar Caddesi Felek Sokak 2, tel. 0212/292-4841, fax 0212/244-2323, www.galataresidence.com, info@galataresidence.com).

Plush Apartments

Istanbul Holiday Apartments offers seven well-appointed apartment buildings (details for three are listed next—see their website for others). These generously furnished apartments are at-home comfy, with everything from fully equipped kitchens to famous Turkish bathrobes. Owner Ann will send a handy shuttle to pick you up at the airport (up to 12 people—required for night-time arrivals since driver has apartment key, airport pick-up is free for stays of 7 nights or longer), or arrange to meet manager Aynur at the apartment during the day to pick up your key. Rates fluctuate by season so check online for the latest (50 percent deposit required, pay balance upon arrival, 3- to 7-night minimum stay, read rental policy on website before reserving, tel. 0212/251-8530, fax 0212/245-1962, www.istanbulholidayapartments.com, info @istanbulholidayapartments.com).

$$ Glorya Apartments SC and **Bereket Apartments SC** are a short walk from İstiklal street, close to the Galata Tower. The **Glorya** has six apartments ranging from a 375-square-foot garden studio to a 2,500-square-foot duplex big enough for a party (2-person garden studio-€115/night, 2-person penthouse-€170/night, 4-person deluxe view apartment-€165/night, 4-person duplex view apartment-€260/night, extra person-€15, all air-con except the studio, Galata Kulesi Sokak 29, Galata). The **Bereket** has four huge two-bedroom apartments that can comfortably sleep four (€150–180/night, extra person-€15, air-con, terminal Internet access, Camekan Sokak 28, Galata). For locations, see the map on previous page.

$$ Belkıs Apartments SC, a short distance from the top of İstiklal street in Taksim's trendy upper end, range in size from 375 to 500 square feet. The five apartments (all one-bedroom) have air-conditioning and sleep two to four people each (€120–155/night, €15 extra per night for 3rd and 4th person, Wi-Fi, Defterdar Yokusu 106, Cihangir).

EATING

Turkey's cuisine, with its roots in the imperial Ottoman kitchen, reflects the rich cultural interaction of its ethnic ancestry: Turkish, Arab, Persian, and Greek. Indeed, what qualifies as Turkish food—and what doesn't—can be a bit ambiguous. You'll find many similar foods in the countries that neighbor Turkey. Given the immense and diverse territories that once made up the Ottoman Empire, it's no surprise that modern Turkish cuisine is multi-ethnic. The cuisine is further enriched by Turkey's fertile land—the varied geography and climates produce a great array of crops, vegetables, and fruits.

TURKISH CUISINE

Understanding the basics of typical Turkish food will help you better enjoy the cuisine. This chapter focuses on lunch and dinner. For information on a typical Turkish breakfast (almost always provided by your hotel), see page 275 in the Sleeping chapter.

Meze (meh-zeh) is the general term for any appetizer served in small portions, usually eaten before the main course. There are two kinds of *mezes:* cold and hot. **Cold *mezes*** (*soğuk mezes;* soh-ook meh-zeh) are usually cooked in olive oil and can include cheese, stuffed grape leaves, eggplant salad, and *cacık* (jah-juhk; a thick mix of yogurt, cucumbers, and garlic with olive oil—like Greek tzatziki). **Hot *mezes*** (*sıcak mezes;* suh-jahk meh-zeh) are traditionally served after the cold *mezes,* and can include tiny meatballs, grilled or deep-fried calamari or shrimp, or *börek* (boh-rehk; pastry—described later). *Mezes* can be a meal in themselves, so save some room if you're ordering a main course.

In seafood restaurants, you usually choose *mezes* from a tray presented at your table.

The prices we've given here for *mezes* are for one portion. When ordering, keep in mind that waiters are not used to the American custom of sharing appetizers. If you ask for a *meze* you plan to share, your waiter will likely think you want portions for every person at your table. Make sure the waiter understands that you want only a single portion. Or you can avoid any confusion by having each person at the table order one appetizer, then share after the *mezes* arrive.

Soup (*çorba;* chor-bah) is often served at the beginning of the meal. *Mercimek* (mehr-jee-mehk) *çorba* is made with mashed lentils, and *yoğurt çorbası* is made with yogurt and served hot.

Zeytinyağlı (zey-teen-yah-luh; "in olive oil") is a common term for vegetables cooked in olive oil. Vegetables can be a main course or—if they're deep-fried, chilled, and served with yogurt—an appetizer.

Seafood is an essential part of Istanbul cuisine. For details on the local varieties of fish, see the sidebar on page 268.

Kebabs (keh-bahbz) are the primary means of preparing and serving meats—generally marinated, skewered, and grilled.

Kebabs have different names based on how they're cooked. *Şiş* (shish) means "skewer," and *şiş kebab* means any type of meat cut into small pieces and grilled on a skewer. A *döner* (doh-nehr; "to spin") *kebab* is a big chunk of meat that cooks as it rotates in front of a vertical grill; the chef cuts off thin slices that are served either wrapped in pita bread or sandwich bread, or with a side of rice pilaf. *Döner kebabs* were traditionally veal or a mix of lamb and veal, but more recently chicken (*tavuk;* tah-vook) and fish have become popular.

Dolma (dohl-mah) means "stuffed," and typically refers to stuffed vegetables such as bell peppers, tomatoes, eggplants, zucchinis, or grape leaves. When stuffed with rice, raisins, or onions—and cooked in olive oil—dolma is a vegetarian dish served as a cold *meze*. When stuffed with rice and meat, dolma is a main course, often accompanied by yogurt (not to be confused with *dolmuş*—a minibus stuffed with people).

Börek (boh-rehk) is a savory pastry made of sheets of rolled dough with various ingredients nestled between the layers. *Su böreği* (soo boh-reh-ee) is prepared with thick sheets of dough that are briefly dipped in boiling water before they're layered over the stuffing. *Sigara böreği* (see-gah-rah boh-reh-ee), a deep-fried cheese roll served cold, is a popular *meze*.

EATING

Pide (pee-deh) is Turkish-style pita bread (sans pocket) usually topped with vegetables and cheese.

Drinks

Ayran (eye-rahn) is a typical beverage made of yogurt diluted with water and seasoned with a pinch of salt. This refreshing drink pairs well with many local dishes. You'll even see it on the menu at McDonald's and Burger King.

Rakı (rah-kuh) is the quintessentially Turkish firewater you'll see anywhere alcohol is allowed. It's made of distilled grape juice and anise—giving it a strong licorice taste. Turks dilute it with water or ice, which turns the drink a cloudy white color. *Rakı*—like its licorice-flavored Greek equivalent, ouzo—is an acquired taste. It's particularly good with a light meal, meat, fish, or *mezes*. If you drink a lot of *rakı*, watch out—too much *rakı* with too much bread, pasta, or dessert will give you a severe headache the next morning.

Turkish coffee (*kahve;* kah-veh) is unfiltered

coffee, with the grounds mixed right in. It's typically drunk as a digestive after dinner, and sometimes after lunch—but never at breakfast (for more details, see page 63 in the Experiences chapter).

Tea (*çay;* pronounced "chai") is actually a more common drink among Turks than coffee. Tea is grown locally along the Black Sea coastline. Regular Turkish tea tastes like English breakfast tea, but some varieties are closer to Earl Grey. Turks never put milk in their tea. Herbal tea and similar drinks are quite common in Turkey. *Adaçayı* (ah-dah-chah-yuh; sage), *ıhlamur* (uh-lah-moor; linden), and *kuşburnu* (koosh-boor-noo; rosehip) are a few popular flavors. When you ask for herbal tea, unless you're in a specialty café, you'll be given a teabag and a cup of hot water. In the Old Town, you'll likely be offered apple tea made with granulated apple and sugar. The real thing is made from dried and boiled apple skin. You can find dried apple skin in the Spice Market (see page 96). Make it tastier by adding honey or cinnamon.

Practicalities

Turkish eating habits vary by location and lifestyle. Traditionally, the evening dinner is the big meal of the day. As in other

---

May It Please the Sultan

Cooks in royal kitchens concocted quite a few creative dishes to please the sultan. Who else would have thought of cooking stuffed melon, mixing rice with almonds and apricots, or stewing eggplant jam? At restaurants that serve traditional cuisine, you may come across dishes listed as *hünkar beğendi* ("the sultan liked it"), *imam bayıldı* ("the imam loved it"), or *dilber dudağı* ("belle's lips"). These names show the close link between food, people, and the palace.

Mediterranean countries, dinner is eaten late in Turkey (generally between 20:00 and 21:00), and can last for hours. But most restaurants are ready to serve dinner much earlier, and you can make your meal as long or short as you like. Except for high-end, international places, restaurants in Turkey generally have a single menu and price list for both lunch and dinner. For the most part, once a restaurant is open it serves meals non-stop until closing time.

The American custom of asking for separate checks is uncommon in Turkey. Instead, usually one member of the group gets the bill and pays, and the group repays him afterwards.

A 10 percent **tip** is customary at sit-down cafés and restaurants; you can leave it on the table or hand it to your server when you sign the credit-card slip. While a tip isn't expected at self-service, cafeteria-style places, bussers appreciate an extra lira or two.

Some restaurants do not serve **alcohol,** as noted in the listings in this chapter. Alcohol permits are expensive. Also, some restaurants are located too close to a place of worship or a school to qualify for a permit.

Water pipes (a.k.a. hookahs, or *nargile* in Turkish) are available at many restaurants. For more information on this pastime, see page 64 in the Experiences chapter.

During the religious festival of **Ramadan** (Aug 11–Sept 8 in 2010), Muslims fast during the day, then gorge themselves at sunset. This means that restaurants are likely to be empty during the day, and many of them actually close altogether. But as the sun sets, you might see long lines in front of fast-food-type places. For more on Ramadan, see page 62.

Types of Restaurants

A kebab lokantası or **kebabçı** (keh-bahb-chuh) is a restaurant that serves the traditional Turkish meat dish: the kebab (described earlier in this chapter). Kebab restaurants usually start serving around 11:00, and stay open until about 23:00.

Self-Service Survival Guide

Self-service, cafeteria-style restaurants are common in the city, especially along the tram track in the center of the Old Town, and on İstiklal street in the New District. They serve freshly cooked, typical Turkish food at good prices. They also make sense time-wise—you simply choose your food, pay for it, eat, and leave.

Before you get in line for food, survey the counter to see what's available. Bread, water, yogurt, salads, desserts, and beverages may be placed before or after the main courses. Most eateries won't label the dishes in English, so ask a cook, or the person next to you, if you need advice. Keep an eye out for what others are ordering; local eaters know what's good. Make up your mind before getting in line—busy lunchtime eaters aren't too tolerant of dilly-dallying.

Point to what you'd like, and the staff will hand it to you. Prices are firm and for a full portion. If you ask for smaller portions to be served on one plate (like a sampler plate), you'll pay the full price per item. If you're with a companion and want to sample several items, it's easiest if you both order full portions at the counter and split your order when you sit down at your table.

Keep things moving by having your cash ready at the end of the line (most places also accept credit cards). Once you're done, don't bus your dishes, but do leave a lira or two for the staff.

Here are some of the dishes you'll likely find in a self-service restaurant:

Soup (*çorba*): Most places will have at least one kind of soup on hand. Most common are *yayla çorbası* (yay-lah chohr-bah-suh), a light, delicious soup made with yogurt, rice, flour, and egg; *mercimek* (mehr-jee-mehk) *çorbası,* lentil soup; *ezogelin* (eh-zoh-geh-leen) *çorbası,* slightly spicy soup with rice or bulgur, lentils, tomato-and-pepper paste, garlic, and a few spices; and *domates* (doh-mah-tehs) *çorbası,* tomato soup.

Side dishes: Try *pirinç pilavı* (pee-reench pee-lah-vuh; rice pilaf); potatoes (*patates;* pah-tah-tehs), served mashed, steamed, or deep-fried; and *bulgur pilavı* (bool-goor pee-lah-vuh), pilaf made with cracked wheat and fresh tomatoes and/or tomato paste.

Pasta (*makarna*): While not that common, you might see spaghetti with house-specialty dressings, or dishes such as *fırında makarna* (fuh-ruhn-dah mah-kahr-nah): macaroni and cheese.

Vegetables: Seasonal veggies are usually stewed, boiled, fried, or deep-fried. Peas, carrots, zucchini, and out-of-season vegetables may be canned.

Vegetarian dishes: Most common are green string beans (*yeşil fasulye;* yeh-sheel fah-sool-yeh), and different types of *dolma* cooked in olive oil.

Meat dishes: Most main courses have meat, even vegetable dishes. For example, *karnıyarık* (kahr-nuh yah-ruhk; "split tummy") is made by cutting an eggplant open and stuffing it with minced veal, onions, and tomatoes. When cooked in olive oil and made without meat, it's called *imam bayıldı* (ee-mum bah-yuhl-duh; see sidebar on page 291). *Musakka* (moo-sahk-kah) is also similar to *karnıyarık,* but with the eggplant chopped into slices or rings.

Veal (*dana*, dah-nah) is common (usually cooked with tomatoes, onions, green pepper, and/or potatoes), but you'll generally also find **chicken**—steamed, cooked with vegetables, or grilled. **Lamb** *(kuzu),* particularly lamb shanks (*kuzu haşlama;* koo-zoo hush-lah-mah), is a local favorite. Lamb is often cooked and served with carrots, potatoes, and onions. Never hard to find are **meatballs** (*köfte;* kohf-teh), which are usually made of minced veal, and sometimes minced lamb as well. *Köfte,* which come in all kinds of shapes, are grilled or cooked with vegetables, and often accompanied by French fries, fresh tomatoes and peppers, or rice.

Salad: You can count on at least two kinds of salads being available at most restaurants: *Çoban salatası* (choh-bahn sah-lah-tah-suh; "shepherds' salad"), made with small chopped tomatoes, cucumbers, onions, and peppers; and green salad (*yeşil salata;* yeh-sheel sah-lah-tah), which usually has iceberg or green lettuce, tomatoes, onions, and/or shredded carrots.

Yogurt: Turks eat a lot of yogurt. Usually made from cow's milk, it comes in disposable containers or steel bowls. *Cacık* (jah-juhk), a thick yogurt, is popular (see page 288). *Ayran* (eye-rahn), a white, slightly salted yogurt drink, is usually on the beverage list.

Dessert: *Sütlaç* (sewt-lahch; rice pudding) is the most common pudding; others include *fırın* (fuh-ruhn) *sütlaç,* rice pudding with a burned top; and *keşkül* (kash-kuhl), milk pudding with coconuts, vanilla, and eggs. You'll also want to sample Turkish baklava, served with cream or crushed nuts; *kadayıf* (kah-dah-yuhf), shredded wheat served with crushed nuts; and *şekerpare* (sheh-kehr-pah-reh), cookies in honey syrup.

A **meyhane** (mehy-hah-neh) is a tavern-style restaurant. While these places may be open during the day, they do most of their business during dinner and later. People usually go to a *meyhane* to enjoy *rakı* and *mezes*. A *meyhane* is judged not by its main courses, but by the quality and the variety of *mezes* it serves. A *meyhane* usually offers live music for entertainment.

A **balık lokantası** or **balıkçı** (bah-luhk-chuh) is a fish and seafood restaurant, often also offering a variety of *mezes* and salads. Most of the *mezes* are made with seafood, such as calamari, octopus, shrimp, mussels, or seaweed. Waiters usually bring out a tray of cold *mezes* to choose from. *Rakı* is commonly served with seafood, but almost all seafood restaurants also sell wine and soft drinks. When selecting a fish dish, ask how big the portions are: It may be enough for two or three eaters to share. Often fish is priced daily and by weight. (This means you might pay two different prices for the same fish in the same restaurant on two different nights.) Ask your server to explain the pricing if it's not outlined in the menu. Ambiguity here can lead to tourist gouging. Beware.

"Self-servis" restaurants function like cafeterias, but serve restaurant-quality food. These restaurants are some of the best-value and most atmospheric places to eat in town. Don't be put off by the absence of menus—simply survey the scene, and point to what looks good. For tips on navigating self-service restaurants, see the sidebar on the previous page.

Street-Vendor Fare

Cheap and filling, Turkish street food is also easy to find, especially in high-traffic areas such as İstiklal street. Common street-vendor fare includes *döner kebabs,* sandwiches, bagel-like *simit,* mussels, and sheep intestines...which taste better than you might expect.

Döner kebabs, the most popular type of Turkish fast food, are described on page 289.

For **sandwiches,** locals usually use white bread. Ordering *yarım ekmek* (yah-ruhm ehk-mehk; "half bread") will get you half a sandwich. For a smaller snack, request a quarter-sandwich: *çeyrek ekmek* (chehy-rehk).

Simit (see-meet) is made by dipping a ring of dough in grape molasses and sesame seeds before baking. You can buy it from street vendors, or from the growing number of *simit* chains, such as Simit Sarayı (see-meet sah-rah-yuh). Besides plain *simit,* they carry a range of flavors similar to what you'd find in a bagel shop. For a cheap picnic, buy a crunchy, freshly baked *simit,* and

Restaurant Price Code

To help you choose among these listings, we've divided the restaurants into three categories, based on the price for a typical meal without wine (1.50 YTL = about $1).

$$$ **Higher Priced**—Most meals 35 YTL or more.
$$ **Moderately Priced**—Most meals between 20–35 YTL.
$ **Lower Priced**—Most meals under 20 YTL.

top it with tomatoes, cucumbers, and some *beyaz peynir* (beh-yahz pehy-neer; white cheese made from cow's or sheep's milk) from a grocery.

Midye tava (meed-yeh tah-vah), deep-fried mussels, are served either in a sandwich or on a plate, and usually come with *tarator* (tah-rah-tohr), a dip made of breadcrumbs, yogurt, garlic, vinegar, and sometimes walnuts as well. *Midye dolma* (stuffed mussel shells) is a local delicacy. The shell is stuffed with olive-oil-soaked rice, raisins, and herbs.

Standing by the Galata Bridge on the Golden Horn, you'll smell the *balık ekmek* (bah-luhk ehk-mehk; fish sandwich), even from a distance. Usually grilled mackerel sandwiched in bread, it's served with onions and lettuce. Small boats tied by the ferry docks in Eminönü, and a few stands, pubs, and restaurants along the bridge (lower level, pedestrian area), serve *balık ekmek* to go.

A big favorite among Turks is *kokoreç* (koh-koh-retch)—sheep intestines that are chopped up, grilled, seasoned, and served with tomatoes and peppers. (If this sounds inedible, remember that sausages are traditionally packed in sheep intestines.) If you want to give this a try, ask for a small *çeyrek ekmek* (chey-rehk ehk-mehk; "quarter-portion"). A popular place for this local treat is Şampiyon Kokoreç (described on page 119 in the New District Walk).

In the Old Town's Sultanahmet Area

These restaurants—along with most of our recommended hotels and much of Istanbul's best sightseeing—are concentrated in the Sultanahmet area.

$$ Balıkçı Sabahattin is the one Old Town seafood restaurant that locals cross the Bosphorus for. With white-tablecloth outdoor tables on a quiet street about three blocks below the Blue Mosque, it's known for its delicious hot and cold *mezes*—including herbed monkfish, rice pilaf with mussels, and grilled calamari (figure 50 YTL per person for salad, *mezes*, and a glass of wine). If you still have room after the appetizers, try one of the 20–35-YTL fish dishes (daily 11:00–24:00, 5-YTL per person cover

charge, reservations recommended, Seyit Hasan Kuyu Sokak 1, Cankurtaran, tel. 0212/458-1824).

$$ Rami's signature dish is "paper kebab," a vegetable and lamb stew that's wrapped and baked in oiled paper. You'll eat in a small, restored Ottoman house decorated with old furniture and paintings by the owner's father, the Turkish painter Rami Uluer (13–24-YTL starters and salads, 27–30-YTL main courses, daily 12:30–23:00, cash only, 15 percent service charge, behind the Blue Mosque at Utangaç Sokak 6, tel. 0212/517-6593 or 0212/638-5321).

$ On the Backpackers' Strip: Yeni Akbıyık Caddesi ("White Moustache Street") is lined with casual restaurants serving simple Turkish food and beer to a United Nations of gregarious young travelers. Most of these tourist- and budget-friendly eateries open early in the morning to offer breakfast to youth hostelers. You'll find several small grocery stores selling basic food items and fruit on the same street (one block below the Blue Mosque, toward the Sea of Marmara).

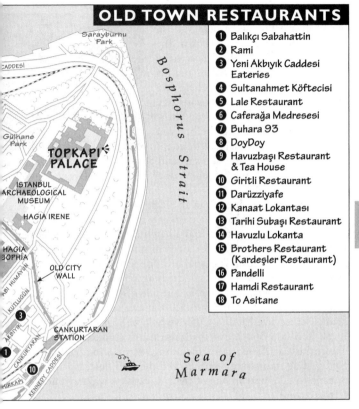

OLD TOWN RESTAURANTS

1. Balıkçı Sabahattin
2. Rami
3. Yeni Akbıyık Caddesi Eateries
4. Sultanahmet Köftecisi
5. Lale Restaurant
6. Caferağa Medresesi
7. Buhara 93
8. DoyDoy
9. Havuzbaşı Restaurant & Tea House
10. Giritli Restaurant
11. Darüzziyafe
12. Kanaat Lokantası
13. Tarihi Subaşı Restaurant
14. Havuzlu Lokanta
15. Brothers Restaurant (Kardeşler Restaurant)
16. Pandelli
17. Hamdi Restaurant
18. To Asitane

EATING

Budget Eateries on Divan Yolu, in the Heart of Sultanahmet

The first two famous and very convenient restaurants stand side-by-side along the busy street called Divan Yolu, across the tram tracks from Hagia Sophia and the Hippodrome (just downhill from the Sultanahmet tram stop).

$ Sultanahmet Köftecisi ("Sultanahmet Meatballs") is so famous for its meatballs that it's inspired an epidemic of imitation joints, rolling out knock-off *köfte* throughout Turkey. The very limited menu includes just two main courses (9-YTL *köfte* and 11-YTL *şiş kebab*), four sides (including tomato-and-onion salad, and the local favorite, *piyaz,* a white-bean salad in olive oil), and two desserts. You can't come to Istanbul without sampling these *köfte* (daily 11:00–23:30, Divan Yolu 12, tel. 0212/520-0566).

$ Lale Restaurant is the famous **"Pudding Shop,"** where a generation of vagabond hippies started their long journey east on the "Freak Road" to Kathmandu in the '60s. (Enjoy the hippie history shared in its wall full of clippings.) Today, the much tamer but still tourist-friendly eatery cranks out a full selection of seasonal Turkish food and chicken and beef kebabs. The misnamed "Pudding Shop" is actually a self-service cafeteria. Adem and his English-speaking staff can help you choose, and will even carry your tray to the upstairs seating area. Show this book to the cashier before you pay and receive a 10 percent discount

(4–5-YTL soups, salads, starters, and desserts; 7-YTL vegetarian dishes, 10–12-YTL main courses, daily 7:00–22:30, Divan Yolu 6, tel. 0212/522-2970).

$ Caferağa Medresesi, in an old madrassa (seminary) next to Hagia Sophia, serves basic food (mostly grilled meat and chicken) to students, amateur artists, and a handful of in-the-know locals. Drop in for a look, or stay for a cup of traditional Turkish coffee or a meal. The setting is casual and friendly, with tables in the atrium—which is filled with hundreds of tulips in the spring (3–5-YTL soups, salads, sandwiches, and side dishes, 7–15-YTL main courses, madrassa open 8:30–19:00, lunch served 11:00–16:00, drinks served until 19:00, Caferiye Sokak, Sogukkuyu Çıkmazı 1, tel. 0212/513-3601). The madrassa trains students in traditional Turkish arts and crafts, including tile painting, calligraphy, gold gilding, miniature painting, and the reed flute. Email ahead of time to take part in one of their workshops (caferagamedrese @ttmail.com).

Budget Eateries near the Blue Mosque and the Top of the Hippodrome

The first two popular budget options—friendly rivals facing each other across the street—are a few steps off the top of the Hippodrome and tucked behind the Blue Mosque. They distinguish themselves by remaining humble, affordable, and local-feeling despite their prime location. To get here from the Hippodrome, face the Column of Constantine with the Blue Mosque on your left, then leave the Hippodrome on the street to the left, and hook downhill to the right...following the sounds of happy al fresco diners.

$ Buhara 93's affordable, down-to-earth food tastes like Grandma just cooked it: simple and tasty. The flat bread (*lavaş*; lah-vahsh) is baked after you order and served right out of the wood-fired oven. When it arrives on your table, it looks like an inflated pillow. This is also a fine place to sample *pide* (6–15-YTL main dishes, daily 8:00–22:30, can be crowded at lunch and early dinner but no reservations needed, no alcohol served, Nakilbend

Caddesi 15, tel. 0212/516-9657).

$ DoyDoy originally catered only to local businesspeople. But with its good food, affordable prices, and terrace view of the Blue Mosque, this popular but unpretentious place soon earned the attention of international travelers...and guidebook writers (8–17-YTL main dishes, daily 8:00–22:30, can be crowded at lunch and early dinner but no reservations needed, no alcohol served, Şifa Hamamı Sokak 13, tel. 0212/517-1588).

$ Havuzbaşı Restaurant and Tea House, situated on a relaxed, idyllic outdoor patio just beyond the tourist crush below the Hippodrome, is a fine place to enjoy a late evening. Stop by for dessert or coffee after dinner with live music, hookahs (10 YTL per group, free extra mouthpieces), backgammon, and non-alcoholic drinks (it's near a mosque). Dervishes whirl nightly at 21:00 (Küçükayasofya Mahiye, Nakilbent Sokak 2, tel. 0212/638-8819).

Seafood Splurge near the Sea of Marmara

$$$ Giritli Restaurant, a short hike from the Blue Mosque action, is a splurge, serving a single 85-YTL multi-course feast with booze. On cold evenings you'll dine in a two-story 19th-century mansion with a dressy white-tablecloth ambience. When it's hot, food is served across the lane in a walled, poolside garden with a Greek-island feel (its owners emigrated from Crete; *giritli* means "Cretan"). Selections range from Aegean- and Mediterranean-style seafood to Cretan-style *mezes* and raw fish. The 100-YTL fixed-price meal includes rice, salad, your choice of 16 varieties of cold *mezes* and three kinds of hot *mezes* (octopus, calamari, or *pide*), a fish main course, and a bottomless local beverage—including *raki,* beer, and wine. While expensive, it's a fine value if you enjoy seafood and wine. Show this book before you pay to get a 10 percent discount (daily 12:00–24:00, reservations smart, several blocks south of the Blue Mosque at Keresteci Hakkı 8, tel. 0212/458-2270).

Elsewhere in the Old Town

We've arranged these eateries by neighborhood, handy to the Old Town's various sights.

Near the Mosque of Süleyman the Magnificent

$$ Darüzziyafe, near the main entrance of the Mosque of Süleyman the Magnificent (by the inner courtyard), was once the mosque's soup kitchen. Today, it's a traditional restaurant, well-regarded for its Ottoman-Turkish cuisine. In summer, sit in the tranquil courtyard; in winter, take shelter in the gorgeously decorated, multi-domed dining hall. The meatballs—prepared with crushed pistachios—are particularly good, and the "Süleymaniye soup" with potatoes, carrots, and tiny meatballs will warm you up on cool days. This is also a good opportunity to sample some unusual Ottoman drinks: *şerbet* (shehr-beht), boiled fruit juice with sugar added (with various fruit flavors, depending on the season); and *ayran* (eye-rahn, see sidebar on page 293). During meals, sultans didn't drink water, but *şerbet* (6–15-YTL starters, 9–26-YTL main dishes, 10 percent discount when you show this book, daily 12:00–23:00, good selection of herbal drinks, no alcohol served, reservations smart, Şifahane Sokak 6, tel. 0212/511-8414). If you plan to eat here after visiting the Süleymaniye Mosque, drop in before your mosque visit to reserve.

$ Kanaat Lokantası, in the mosque's madrassa (a former seminary), has been Istanbul's favorite bean restaurant since 1939. *Kuru fasulye* (koo-roo fah-sool-yeh) is a staple that's eaten at home at least once a week by every Turkish family. The bean soup (5 YTL) is made with dried white beans and pieces of beef or pastrami and served with a side of rice pilaf (3 YTL). After the meal, try the 5-YTL pumpkin dessert. As it's popular with Istanbul University students and neighborhood businesspeople, don't bother calling for a reservation—the staff is so busy they may not pick up the phone. Just drop in (daily 11:00–19:30, cash only, next to fountain and just across from entrance to mosque's outer courtyard at Prof. Sıddık Sami Öner Caddesi 1/3, tel. 0212/520-7655). Other bean joints—not as famous or established, but fine in a pinch—populate the rest of the madrassa.

In or near the Grand Bazaar

$ Tarihi Subaşı Restaurant is a favorite lunch spot for locals who work in the area. The home-cooked Turkish fare here has won awards. The menu of 50 different entrées includes a flavorful spinach puree (*ıspanak püresi;* uh-spah-nahk pew-reh-see) and an eggplant and lamb dish (*hünkar beğendi;* hewn-kahr beh-ehn-dee). There's no menu, so peek into the kitchen and choose by pointing and confirming the price. Squeeze into the small interior, or claim one of the few outdoor tables to enjoy the bazaar bustle (5-YTL salads and starters, 8-YTL vegetarian main courses, 12-YTL meat main courses, Mon–Sat 11:00–17:00, closed Sun; by Nuruosmaniye Mosque, just before Grand Bazaar's main door—as you face bazaar's Nuruosmaniye Gate, it's at the end of cobbled street to your right, on right side with Coke sign; tel. 0212/522-4762).

$ Havuzlu Lokanta, inside the Grand Bazaar, serves a sped-up version of traditional Ottoman cuisine, with a continually changing menu. Look for the *beykoz kebab,* prepared with eggplant, veal, mushrooms, and sweet peas. The vast interior can accommodate an army of tourists (it's in all the guidebooks and quite touristy), but the quaint fountainside seating out front keeps you in the midst of the Grand Bazaar action (4-YTL salads and starters, 7–8-YTL vegetarian dishes, 8–10-YTL main courses, 0.50 YTL extra for water and bread, Mon–Sat 12:00–17:30, closed Sun, look for sign near Şark Kahvesi café, Gani Çelebi Sokak 3, tel. 0212/527-3346).

$ Brothers Restaurant (Kardeşler Restaurant), also inside the Grand Bazaar, sits in a cozy courtyard away from the swirl of shoppers and merchants. Serving up meat and vegetable dishes from southeast Turkey, this place is known for its *kaburga dolma* (kah-buhr-gah dohl-mah, lamb ribs big enough for two), *güveç* (gew-vehch, stewed vegetables and veal or lamb in an earthenware pot), and *bağırsak dolması* (bah-ur-sahk dohl-mah-suh; stuffed intestines—an eastern Turkish specialty). Since the menu changes daily, Muzaffer or one of the other waiters can tell you about their specialty of the day. You're welcome to poke into the kitchen to see what's cooking (8–11-YTL main courses, 11–21-YTL specialty dishes, no alcohol served, Mon–Sat 8:00–17:00, closed Sun, Astarcı Han Yağlıkçılar 23, tel. 0212/519-3006).

In or near the Spice Market

$$ Pandelli, on the Spice Market's second floor, was started by Chef Pandelli in the 1930s and is open for lunch only. The mouth-watering traditional Turkish-Ottoman menu includes an especially good eggplant *börek*. Although the restaurant always appears to be overcrowded with businesspeople, they eat quickly, so you won't wait long for a table (10–30-YTL starters, 15–32-YTL main dishes, Mon–Sat 11:30–19:00, closed Sun, go up tiled staircase just inside Spice Market's main entrance at Eminönü Mısır Çarşısı 1, tel. 0212/527-3909).

$ Hamdi Restaurant is a dressy white-tablecloth place with vested waiters, a bright glassed-in roof terrace, and great views of the city and over the water. They serve a variety of traditional kebabs from southeast Turkey (upper Mesopotamia). Consider the various kebabs: pistachio lamb, grilled eggplant, plum lamb, or grilled garlic lamb. The delicious *beyti* (behy-tee) kebab—a mix of barbecued beef and lamb wrapped in thin filo bread—takes longer to make. The wheat pilaf, called *firik* (fee-reek), is also good. For dessert, try the pistachio *katmer* or the baklava (15–23-YTL kebabs, 6-YTL desserts, slow service, daily 11:30–23:30, next to Spice Market, Kalçın Sokak 17, tel. 0212/528-0390). Take the elevator to the crowded third-floor terrace—the views are best from the narrow balcony (if there's an empty table here, grab it).

Near the Chora Church Museum

$$ Asitane, next door to the Chora Church Museum and attached to Kariye Hotel, is a good choice after a tiring museum visit (the

NEW DISTRICT RESTAURANTS

church is open until 19:00). The classical Ottoman cuisine replicates dishes served at a banquet in honor of Süleyman the Magnificent's sons. Asitane's *mahmudiye* (mah-moo-dee-yeh)—chicken with almonds, dried apricots, and raisins—is a tasty concoction you won't find anywhere else. Sit outside on the leafy patio, or in the white-tablecloth-classy dining room. If you plan to have lunch, stop by the restaurant before you visit the Chora Church Museum, and let them know when you'll be back (10–20-YTL starters, 24–32-YTL mains, daily 12:00–15:00 & 19:00–22:30, dinner reservations a must, Kariye Camii Yanı, Cami Sokak 6, Edirnekapı, tel. 0212/635-7997).

In the New District, on and near İstiklal Street

All of these eateries are on or within a short stroll of İstiklal street.

$$ Changa serves a wide range of "fusion" cuisine to trendy expats and local yuppies. The bar by the entrance is lively on Friday and Saturday evenings, when dinner reservations are smart (Mon–

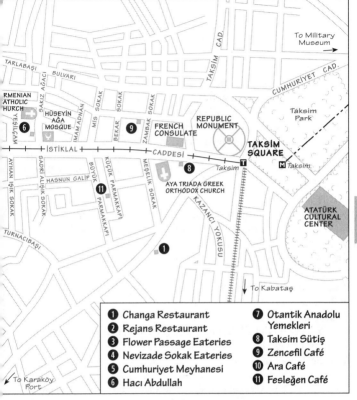

1 Changa Restaurant
2 Rejans Restaurant
3 Flower Passage Eateries
4 Nevizade Sokak Eateries
5 Cumhuriyet Meyhanesi
6 Hacı Abdullah

7 Otantik Anadolu
  Yemekleri
8 Taksim Sütiş
9 Zencefil Café
10 Ara Café
11 Fesleğen Café

Sat 18:00–24:00, closed Sun, short walk from Taksim Square and İstiklal street at Siraselviler Caddesi 47, tel. 0212/249-1348).

$$ Rejans Restaurant has been serving up authentic Russian food—including dishes favored by the czars—for nearly a century. They also make their own vodka—try some for 8 YTL a glass (8–21-YTL salads and soups, 15–45-YTL main courses, 7–22-YTL desserts, daily 12:00–15:00 & 19:00–24:00, Emir Nevruz Sokak 17, tel. 0212/243-3882). For more on the history of this venerable (and smoky) place, see page 121.

$$ In the Flower Passage (Çiçek Pasajı): The Flower Passage is not one restaurant, but a row of seafood places in a historic, beautifully restored passage on İstiklal street. The 10 restaurants are mostly interchangeable, with similar value and quality. In the evening, some have live music, usually traditional Istanbul songs. While the area is grotesquely touristy and overpriced, the Flower Passage eateries boast a genteel late-19th-century atmosphere (most Flower Passage restaurants have 5–15-YTL salads and *mezes*, 10–35-YTL fish dishes, daily 12:00–24:00, İstiklal Caddesi). For more on the history of the passage, see page 118.

$$ On Nevizade Sokak: This lane is home to several reliably good restaurants. Just a block off İstiklal street, past the fish market, it's where trendy locals head for a seafood dinner. Bars and restaurants line up one after the other on either side of the street. In spring and summer, they set tables out front, making the place seem even more crowded, fun, and noisy. Restaurants take pride in their *mezes*, and compete to serve the widest variety. Try the casual pubs if all you want is a glass of beer and simple seafood *meze* (e.g., a platter of calamari or deep-fried mussels). Restaurants here are also casual, but they'll serve you a full meal with all the frills. The prices and variety of food are similar to those in the Flower Passage (described earlier).

$$ Cumhuriyet Meyhanesi ("Republic Tavern") is as old as the Republic—Turkey's founder, Atatürk, was a regular. This place has worked hard to keep its reputation for quality and class. The best ambience is in the upstairs room, or at the few outdoor tables. In the evenings, enjoy the live Turkish music (4–5-YTL *soğuk mezes* and salads, 10–20-YTL grilled fish or meat plates, 55-YTL fixed-price meals, 10 percent service charge added to bill, daily 9:00–2:00 in the morning, in the Fish Market off İstiklal street at Balıkpazarı Sahne Sokak 27, tel. 0212/243-6406).

$$ Hacı Abdullah, just off İstiklal street, is favored by locals and can be very busy. The specialty is Özel Hacı Abdullah Tabağı ("Abdullah's Special Hacı Platter"), loaded down with eggplant kebab, lamb shanks, and two other kebabs—enough food for two (28 YTL). Also good are the quince desserts with honey and bananas topped with water-buffalo cream, and the fresh pomegranate juice from eastern Turkey (6-YTL soups and salads, 6–14-YTL desserts, 6 different fixed-price meals-50–90 YTL, daily 11:00–22:30, closed until sundown during Ramadan, no alcohol served, extra charge for water and bread, 10 percent service charge added to bill, near Ağa Mosque at Atıf Yılmaz Caddesi 9/A, tel. 0212/293-8561).

$ Otantik Anadolu Yemekleri is a recently opened restaurant that quickly turned into a chain. It serves traditional Anatolian food, representing different ethnic groups living within Turkey. This offers a great opportunity to affordably sample several flavors from around the country. Watch as the costumed cooks prepare *gözleme* (gohz-leh-meh), flat bread cooked on a convex steel sheet (5–6 YTL, the filled versions are big enough for a light meal). *Hıngal* (huhn-gahl) is a Caucasian dish with potato-filled steamed dumplings. *İçli köfte* (eech-lee kohf-teh) is a Mesopotamian bulgur pouch filled with meat, onions, and spices. The handy photo menu makes ordering easy, and the four floors of seating ensure that there's plenty of space (9–19-YTL meat dishes, 6–15-YTL traditional dishes, daily 9:00–24:00, next door to entrance to Flower Passage at İstiklal Caddesi 80/A, tel. 0212/293-8451).

$ Taksim Sütiş, while technically a "pudding shop," is a time-warp cafeteria serving everything from puddings to omelets to *döner kebabs*. Among its famous puddings, *tavuk göğüsü* (tah-vook gooh-sew) stands out. It's made with finely shredded chicken breast, but doesn't taste like chicken at all. *Su böreği* (soo boh-reh-ee), a pastry made with sheets of hand-rolled dough, is boiled before being baked. Locals love the baklava and rice pilaf with chicken. On a cold day, try the *sahlep* (sah-lehp), a warm, creamy sweet drink made with the powdered roots of wild Taurus mountain orchids and served with cinnamon. The photo menu is convenient, but you can also step up to the display case and point to what you want (4–5-YTL puddings, 9–16-YTL meat dishes, daily 6:00–24:00, İstiklal Caddesi 13, tel. 0212/251-3270).

$ Zencefil Café, a few minutes off İstiklal street, is a vegetarian restaurant also frequented by carnivores for its appetizing and healthy food. The menu of freshly grown products changes with the season. It also offers pomegranate, blueberry, and cherry fruit wines (8–12-YTL soups and salads, 8–12-YTL main courses, daily 10:30–23:30, at #8–10 on Kurabiye Sokak—a lane that runs parallel to İstiklal street, tel. 0212/243-8234).

$ Ara Café is owned by Ara Güler, a renowned Turkish-Armenian photographic artist. The café is a popular place to see and be seen, and attracts intellectuals, yuppies, and models. Grab a table outdoors in nice weather, or opt for the cozy split-level interior (5–6-YTL soups, meal-size 12–15-YTL salads, 14–20-YTL main courses, daily 7:30–24:00, between post office and İstiklal street at Tosbağa Sokak 8/A, tel. 0212/245-4105).

$ Fesleğen Café, with hip decor, offers a variety that can please nearly any palate, ranging from pasta and falafel to salad and crêpes. Wash it all down with fresh carrot, melon, or apple juice. Enjoy the outdoor seating on the alley out front, or climb the spiral staircase up to the two floors of indoor seating (9–11-YTL salads, 4-YTL soups, 8–15-YTL main courses, daily 11:00–24:00, no alcohol served, just off İstiklal street at Küçükparmakkapı Sokak 40, tel. 0212/251-7942).

EATING

SHOPPING

Shopping can provide a good break from Istanbul's mosques, museums, and monuments. And diving into the city's bustling, colorful marketplaces can be a culturally enlightening experience. In this chapter, you'll find information on shopping for textiles, ceramics and tiles, gold and silver, carpets, souvenirs, and bargains.

İndirim (een-dee-reem) is Turkish for "sale." July, August, January, and February are the big months for sales; in January, sales start right after the shopping frenzy for New Year's Day is over (most Turks don't celebrate Christmas, but they do buy gifts for New Year's).

Istanbul's merchants, especially at the Grand Bazaar and other touristy areas in the Old Town, can be aggressive, and may try to engage you in casual conversation as an entrée to offering products for sale. It's OK to say "No, thanks"—firmly—and walk on by. (For more tips, see the sidebar on page 209.)

For information on VAT refunds and customs, see page 14.

Where to Shop

Shopping in the Grand Bazaar and at other Old Town merchants (such as the craft market tucked behind the Blue Mosque) is lively, memorable, and fun, and prices can be low—but the quality is often questionable. Locals prefer shopping at the more expensive but reliably high-quality stores on and near İstiklal street in the New District. This area is less colorful—it feels like a shopping street in any big European city—but you won't feel preyed upon by vendors. This book includes self-guided tours of each of these areas (Grand Bazaar Tour on page 206, and New District Walk on page 108); you could combine your shopping with one of these tours.

What to Buy
Textiles, Silk, and Leather

Turkish textiles—known around the world—are the country's biggest industry and a source of local pride. While Turkey was once a major manufacturer for Victoria's Secret and other international clothing labels, competition from China has forced local clothing-makers to change tactics: Turkey now focuses on producing its own labels, in the hopes of competing in the world market. These new **clothing** brands, such as Mavi Jeans, are well-made and affordable. Go beyond the Old Town, to the New District and other uptown neighborhoods, to get the best merchandise. İstiklal street and the Taksim Square area are your best bets. The cotton T-shirts you'll see around the Old Town and in the Grand Bazaar make decent souvenirs or gifts, but are usually low-quality—they'll likely fade and shrink after a few washes.

Many people associate Turkey with **pashminas**—high-quality shawls made from a particular kind of goat fleece. And, in fact, the Old Town is a pashmina paradise, with every color of the rainbow. But beware: Turkey doesn't produce pashmina wool, so the ones you see here are fakes. Still, they're practical and fun, and cheaper than the fakes sold in the US.

A *peştemal* (pehsh-teh-mahl) is a large, thin, cotton **bath towel** that Turks wrap around themselves at the baths; nowadays they're also used as curtains or tablecloths. Bathing Turks scrub away dead skin and dirt with *kese* (keh-seh)—simple rectangular mittens made out of raw silk or synthetic fabric. Look for these two authentically Turkish items at the Eğin Tekstil shop on Yağlıkçılar street in the Grand Bazaar (see page 215).

Turkey produces wonderful **silk,** but be careful: In the Grand Bazaar and other Old Town shops, scarves and other items billed as silk are often made of polyester or, at best, low-quality silk. For real silk scarves and shawls, go to the New District. İpek Silk Shop, near St. Anthony's Church on İstiklal street, has knowledgeable employees and reliable quality silk-wear. Isaac and his helpful staff speak English and are happy to demonstrate the latest in scarf fashion (İstiklal Caddesi 120, tel. 0212-249-8207).

Most **leather** goods are a better deal in the US than in Turkey. Shoes are the exception: If you're into Italian-style leather shoes, you're in the right place. Shop for these on İstiklal street in the New District; shoes sold in the Old Town are usually made with cheap glue and synthetic materials. If you're in the market for cheap, knock-off designer handbags, head to the Grand Bazaar and other Old Town vendors.

SHOPPING

Carpets and Kilims

If you want to buy a Turkish carpet, it's worth knowing a bit about what you're looking for—if only to avoid advertising your inexperience. For example, folding a carpet to check the knots will not only give you away as a novice, but can actually ruin the carpet if it's silk. Rubbing a carpet with a piece of wet tissue to test its colorfastness is akin to licking a shirt before you buy it. And beware of shopkeepers who stress "authenticity" over quality. Authenticity is an important consideration when shopping for traditional wool-on-wool carpets. But for wool-on-cotton or silk-on-silk, it can actually be better to get a piece made with newer techniques—for tighter weaves, brighter and more durable colors, and more intricate patterns.

Carpets can range in price from several hundred dollars to several thousand or more, depending on the age, size, quality, and uniqueness. Merchants will ship them home for you, though many tourists find it cheaper and more foolproof to carry them back (the carpets can be folded and tied tightly into a squarish bundle).

Wool-on-wool carpets, which are made of wool pile on a wool skeleton (formed by vertical warp and horizontal weft threads), are the most traditional kind of Turkish carpet. Although becoming less common, these are still woven in countryside villages. Each region has its own distinctive, centuries-old, design and color combination. In general, wool-on-wool carpets cost less than other Turkish rugs. The best way to gauge the authenticity of a wool-on-wool carpet is to look for the natural, less-vibrant colors that come from vegetable dyes obtained from local plants. Density—the number of knots per inch—is less important to the quality of a wool-on-wool carpet. Fewer knots do not signify a lower-quality wool rug, but they do mean that the rug is more likely to stretch over time.

Newer kinds of carpets, made of **wool-on-cotton** (wool pile on a cotton skeleton) and **silk-on-silk,** first appeared in the 19th century. The new materials allowed weavers to create more intricate floral and geometric patterns than traditional designs. (A weaver can fit more knots onto a cotton skeleton than onto a wool one.) Professional designers make these patterns with the exact thickness of the yarn in mind—so irregular hand-spun wool won't work. Wool-on-cotton and silk-on-silk carpets are colored with chemical dyes, which can be as good, or even better, than natural dyes. If someone tries to sell you a new wool-on-cotton carpet by advertising that it's "made with hand-spun wool," "dyed with

How to Get the Best Bargain

Many visitors to Istanbul are surprised to find that bargaining for a lower price is no longer common in much of the city. At modern stores or shopping malls, the posted prices are final. But in the tourist zones—such as the Grand Bazaar, Spice Market, and other shops around the Old Town—merchants know you're expecting to haggle...and they're happy to play along. (Local shoppers have less patience for this game. Notice that even in the Grand Bazaar, locals don't often haggle—if they think something is overpriced, they either ask for a discount or simply walk away.)

In the Old Town market areas where bargaining is common, you'll constantly be bombarded by sales pitches. If you aren't interested in what they're selling, try not to establish eye contact. Although this may feel rude, it's the best way to avoid unnecessary conversations and save your time and energy for the items you do want.

If you are interested in an item, don't make it obvious. Take your time, browse around, and pretend you might just wander off at any moment—feigned disinterest is part of the game. You're better off keeping a low profile—this isn't the time to show off your nicest clothes, jewelry, and wads of cash.

Merchandise often doesn't have price tags, because the shop owner wants you to ask—giving him an opening to launch into a sales pitch. Don't suggest a number; let the shopkeeper be the first to mention a price. When he does, assume it's elevated. Even if you counter with only half their original offer, you may find your price easily accepted—meaning you've already offered too much.

More likely, a spirited haggling war will ensue. If you don't like to bargain, you'll pay more than you should. Play along to get a lower price and a fun cultural interaction. These haggling sessions can drag on for some time, as you sip tea (usually apple-flavored) offered by shopkeepers who want to keep you around. When you start to walk away, that last price he calls out is often the best price you'll get.

There's room for bargaining even on fixed-price commodities, such as gold and silver, where you're being charged not only for the precious metal but also for the workmanship.

If you're haggling over something unique, be prepared to pay a premium. The shopkeeper already knows that you won't be able to find it elsewhere.

vegetable colors," or "features a traditional design, passed from mother to daughter," walk away. Unlike wool-on-wool carpets, density is important in assessing quality for wool-on-cotton and silk-on-silk carpets.

The towns of Hereke and Kayseri are each famous for producing a certain type of carpet. **Hereke** (heh-reh-keh) carpets are denser, require much more workmanship, and are more expensive. Authentic Hereke carpets are becoming rare, and cheap imported knock-offs are in the market nowadays; watch out. **Kayseri** (kay-seh-ree) wool-on-cotton and silk-on-silk carpets generally have floral designs. Their wool-on-wool carpets are favored for their unique patterns and lively colors.

Kilims (kee-leem) feature a flat weave without the pile, similar to a Navajo rug. These also have traditional designs and natural colors. Used in the past as blankets and bedspreads, they're mainly popular now as decorative items (and can be used as wall hangings). Kilims are generally inexpensive, but old and rare pieces can cost several thousand dollars. For a wearable, affordable kilim, consider a vest made out of the material; you see these at the Grand Bazaar and elsewhere.

Tiles and Ceramics

A Turkish specialty is *çini* (chee-nee), which is usually translated in English as "tile" (or "quartz tile"). The word *çini* can be used to describe flat tiles used for architectural decoration, and also functional items such as bowls, vases, cups, and so on. While English-speakers might sometimes use the word "ceramic" to describe these functional items, *çini* technically has a higher quartz content than ceramic, and is therefore more difficult to work. Strictly speaking, while "tiles" *(çini)* are very traditional in Turkey, "ceramics" (*seramik;* seh-rah-meek) don't have much of a history here—though you will find them sold in markets. You'll also see pottery (*çömlek;* chom-lehk): simple, fired earthenware objects shaped on a wheel, usually without any design or glaze.

Many stores sell copies of old, authentic tiles, as well as new designs, both in a range of qualities. When comparing tiles, keep these tips in mind: Recycled clay has a creamy, darker look, and costs much less than the higher-quality white clay. To check the clay and glaze for cracks, hold the item up from the center on your fingertips (or your hand, if it's heavy), and flick the edge with your finger. If the sound is clear and the piece rings like a bell, it's free of cracks. The value is determined by the quality of the workmanship, combined with the chemical formula of the glaze, clay, and dyes. Superior-quality tile or ceramic has quartz (or kaolin) in the clay, little or no lead in the glaze, and metal oxide dyes. Also check whether colors have smeared over one another. Designs that are intricate, multi-colored, and hand-drawn are the most valuable.

High-quality items are often too costly for regular stores to carry. If you are seriously interested in the best ceramics and tile, try the İznik Foundation, which carries on Turkey's long-estab-lished tile tradition. Their main store is in the Kuruçeşme neigh-borhood, north of the New District, by the Bosphorus Bridge at Öksüz Çocuk Sokak.

If you're looking for something simple, you'll find plenty of inexpensive, pretty pieces at souvenir stores all around the Old Town and Grand Bazaar.

Gold

Gold is a good buy in Turkey. Prices change with the daily rate of gold; when you ask the price of a piece, the shopkeeper will weigh it for you. The Grand Bazaar's many displays of 22-carat gold brace-lets reflect Turkey's distrust of banks—many people literally wear their life's savings on their sleeves in the form of these bracelets. These simple bangles often cost little more than the gold itself.

Most mass-produced jewelry is made from molds with 14-carat gold, as it is harder and cheaper. Handmade items are the most expensive; in some pieces, the fine workmanship is more valuable than the gold itself. While the cheaper items cost around $14–20 per gram, the price can go as high as $35–50 for finely crafted ones. Precious and semi-precious stones are generally paired with 18-carat gold.

Silver Jewelry and Beads

Silver jewelry, with or without semi-precious stones, is a good and affordable alternative to fancy gold jewelry. As with gold, silver pieces usually won't have a price tag, but are sold by weight. Look around a bit in the Grand Bazaar to get an idea of what's avail-able and the range of prices. The government-managed Dösim shop, located behind Hagia Sophia (just before you go through the Imperial Gate into Topkapı Palace), carries traditional tribal designs.

You can also find beads to make your own jewelry. A few shops in the Grand Bazaar (in and near Cevahir Bedesten) carry silver jewelry and semi-precious stone beads.

Souvenirs and Trinkets

The Grand Bazaar is filled with stalls hawking endless mountains of junk, most of it made outside Turkey. This stuff sells well, as it's cheap and looks "Oriental." Those hats with tiny circular mirrors are common not because they're crafted by local artisans (they are made outside of Turkey), but because the merchants know tourists will buy them. Fortunately, the bazaar is also filled with plenty of affordable, authentically Turkish trinkets that make wonderful gifts.

You can't miss the **"evil eyes"** (*nazarlık;* nah-zahr-luhk)—blue-and-white glass beads that look like eyes. Traditionally thought to ward off negative energy from jealous eyes, these are a kind of good-luck charm popular among Turks. You'll see them on doorways, hanging down from a car's rear-view mirror, or anywhere else people want protection. Babies wear them, adults wear them, and teenage girls braid them in their hair. *Nazarlık*s are authentically and uniquely Turkish, which makes them good gifts. They come in various sizes—some with a metal frame, others on a hooked pin, still others embedded in tiles.

Small Turkish **tea glasses,** made of clear glass and shaped like a tulip blossom, are easy to find. Buy them toward the end of your trip, to minimize the risk of breaking them as you carry them around.

Machine-made textiles with traditional designs make good tablecloths, pillowcases, bedspreads, and sofa throws. Some are velvet, with silky-looking, colorful embroideries.

Coffee and pepper grinders don't break easily, since they're made of brass or wood.

The same goes for **backgammon sets** and **inlaid wooden boxes.** The best are inlaid with mother-of-pearl, while the cheapest are inlaid with plastic.

If you decide to buy a glass **water pipe** (*nargile;* nahr-gee-leh), get the kind that separates into parts and is easily re-assembled. For more on water pipes, see page 64.

Mined in central Turkey, **onyx** is plentiful, affordable, and popular in decorative objects such as vases and bowls, as well as chess sets (but not so common in jewelry).

Gifts for children are more limited. Consider Halloween **costumes.** You'll find tiny, colorful Turkish princess outfits for girls, with coins adorning the sleeves and trousers. Cheap knock-off **soccer jerseys** also abound.

ENTERTAINMENT

Lively Istanbul is a happening place, with thousands of nightclubs and bars, regular stage performances, and several annual world-class festivals. But if you're expecting nightlife full of shimmying belly dancers, you may be disappointed. Belly dancing in Istanbul is as popular as square dancing in New York City. Until very recently, belly dancing was looked down upon by modern Turks, though its presence on TV and in competitions is growing.

So rather than seeking out cultural clichés, spend your Istanbul evenings enjoying modern-day, international activities... with a Turkish flair, of course.

CONCERTS AND PERFORMANCES

Opera, Ballet, Symphony, and...Riverdance

From October through the end of May, the Atatürk Cultural Center (AKM) at Taksim Square hosts top-notch performances by the Istanbul State Opera, Ballet, and Symphony. Since they're state-subsidized, tickets are dirt cheap; front-row tickets can cost as little as 20 YTL (ask for a front-row seat). Season programs and tickets are available at the ticket office at the Atatürk Cultural Center (as you face the building, the ticket office is at the right-front corner), as well as online. The dress code is rather casual, but steer clear of shorts and sandals.

Opera and Ballet: Tickets are released 30 days prior to the event. For details, see www.idobale.com (tel. 0212/251-5600). Performance times vary.

Symphony: Tickets are released one week in advance of the event. For specifics, call 0212/243-1068 (or try their website, www.idso.gov.tr, to see if its English version is up and running). Performances are held weekly on Fridays at 19:30 and Saturday mornings at 11:00.

Fire of Anatolia: This well-promoted, high-energy show is set in a beautiful venue. Many visitors interested in a Turkish folk show may be tempted to choose this over a touristy restaurant show. But while advertised as a "folk show," it's really a Turkish "Riverdance," painfully similar to the Irish stomper with recorded music.

Whirling Dervishes

Touristy, fake "Whirling Dervish" performances spin through many of Istanbul's theaters and restaurants. But to see the authentic two-hour religious ritual performed by the Mevlevi, followers of the Muslim mystic Rumi, visit the Galata Dervish Monastery (Galata Mevlevihanesi) in the New District. For details on the performance (scheduled every Sunday), see page 51 in the Sights chapter.

Festivals

The Istanbul Foundation of Culture and Arts organizes several city-wide festivals every year, including the International Music Festival (June), the International Jazz Festival (early to mid-July), and the International Film Week (mid-Oct). Every other year in the fall, Istanbul also hosts Turkey's largest contemporary art show, the International Istanbul Biennial (next in 2011). Schedules for these festivals vary from year to year, and tickets can go fast, so it's worth checking the foundation's site at www.iksv.org/english.

The music and jazz festivals are worthwhile, partly for their venues. The jazz concerts take place in lively music clubs and outdoor stages, while music events are often held at historic monuments. Past festival performers have included members of Milan's La Scala Opera House and the New York Philharmonic.

NIGHTLIFE

Low-Key Evenings on the Golden Horn and the Bosphorus

Warm, clear evenings in Istanbul are perhaps best enjoyed with a short walk across the **Galata Bridge** to watch the sun go down. Take in the Old Town's magnificent skyline, dominated by floodlit domes and minarets. After sunset, head to the lower level of the Galata Bridge, where you'll find several moderately priced tavern-style restaurants (*meyhane;* mehy-hah-neh) and seafood restaurants.

Restaurants, bars, and clubs along the Bosphorus tend to be

Buying Tickets

To avoid an unnecessary trek out to a venue's box office, consider buying tickets online. Biletix (www.biletix.com) sells tickets for most events, including movies and soccer games. If you buy your ticket online, you pick it up at the ticket office on the day of the performance—just show the credit card you used for the online purchase. The deadline to pick up your ticket is usually an hour prior to the start of the event.

TicketTurk (www.ticketturk.com) concentrates on theater tickets, but also provides tickets to alternative events not available through Biletix.

For popular events, tickets can sell out fast. Still, if you're interested in a performance that's sold out, try going to the ticket office the day of the show to see if there have been any returns—your chances of scoring a ticket are fairly decent.

expensive, but some areas—such as Ortaköy—are more affordable than others. The **Ortaköy neighborhood,** by the European side of the Bosphorus Bridge, is a pedestrian area with many bars, tea-houses, and restaurants. In nice weather, especially on weekends, the area is packed with hundreds of people strolling its streets and alleys. Even on the warmest evenings, you'll want to bring along a sweater or shawl, as a cool breeze blows along the Bosphorus at night (in bad weather, the area is often empty). If you're on a tight budget, get a baked potato or a sandwich from one of the numerous summertime food stalls. Grab a drink from a grocery store, and enjoy your evening picnic on a bench by the Bosphorus, watching the boats pass by, with the bridge lit up like a pearl necklace and the Ortaköy Mosque as its backdrop. A couple of teahouses with good views of the Bosphorus are usually packed with Turks playing backgammon or a tile game called OK. To get to Ortaköy from Taksim Square in the New District, catch bus #40 or #40T (passes only, no tokens accepted).

İncisu Boats offers dinner cruises that include a pleasant evening ride on the Bosphorus, a decent seafood dinner, and a mediocre, touristy belly-dancing show. Evening cruises usually run on Tuesdays and Saturdays, and start and end in Kabataş (last stop of the tram in the New District). Figure around €60 per person, including drinks and a shuttle from your hotel. Their website is only in Turkish, so call to book your cruise (tel. 0216/418-5932 or 0216/344-5066, www.bogazturu.net).

Partying on İstiklal Street, in the New District

In the evenings, the neighborhood surrounding İstiklal street is transformed into a vast entertainment center. The street itself has several bars, jazz clubs, and *meyhanes* (taverns), all popular among the locals. Be warned that there's no such thing as a "non-smoking" section. Cigarette smoke is considered a visual effect, helping to create a more atmospheric experience—and Istanbul's citizens work hard to contribute to it.

Fasıl Music

Many visitors enjoy *fasıl* (fah-suhl) music, often performed in the inviting ambience of a *meyhane*. *Fasıl* is live, old-time Istanbul songs or classical Turkish tunes, performed by a small trio of musicians. Locals sing along as they drink *rakı* (firewater) and nibble on *mezes* (appetizers; see Eating chapter). You won't have to pay a cover charge for the music, but it's customary to tip the musicians—watch locals and imitate.

Cumhuriyet Meyhanesi is a popular and historic *fasıl* place just off İstiklal street (see listing in Eating chapter, page 304). Another good venue nearby is **Şahika** (shah-hee-kah), in a narrow townhouse on Nevizade Sokak (enter the fish market by the corner of Flower Passage/Çiçek Pasajı, then take the first right). A different style of music, including *fasıl* and contemporary, is played on each of its five floors. If you're a solo male, they may not let you in, so find a fellow traveler to come along.

Note that some of the restaurants in the Flower Passage (Çiçek Pasajı) and others on İstiklal street feature "Gypsy music," which is louder, faster, and more danceable than *fasıl*.

Clubs and Nightspots

If you're serious about nightlife, dip into one of the many nightspots on or near İstiklal street. These generally get rolling late in the evening, around 23:00 or later, and hit their peak around 1:00 to 2:00 in the morning. Quite a few clubs stay open until 4:00. To get tickets in advance for big-name shows, see the sidebar on the previous page.

Babylon, near Tünel, is a popular club where international bands and performers perform. It usually features jazz and ethnic music, but it's not unusual to see reggae or percussion bands. Its box office opens at noon, but for more popular performances, you might want to buy tickets in advance (Seyhbender Sokak 3, tel. 0212/292-7368).

Hayal Kahvesi is a bar and rock-music venue with daily live performances. It's an institution on the Turkish rock scene; almost all of Turkey's famous rock bands and singers have taken the Hayal Kahvesi stage at least once (Büyükparmakkapı Sokak 19, just off İstiklal street, tel. 212/244-2558).

ENTERTAINMENT

TRANSPORTATION CONNECTIONS

The following directions will get you from Istanbul's main airport, train stations, and bus station to the main tram line that connects all of central Istanbul. For specifics on using this local tram system, see page 30.

The following website has good information about transportation within and from Istanbul: www.turkeytravelplanner.com/go/Istanbul/Transport.

Atatürk Airport

Istanbul's main airport, Atatürk, is used by most international flights (except for charter flights from Europe, which use Sabiha Gökçen Airport—described in the sidebar on next page). Located to the west of the city center on the European side, Atatürk Airport is a 30- to 60-minute taxi ride (depending on traffic) to either the Old Town or the New District.

Atatürk Airport has an international terminal and a domestic terminal, which are located across from each another and connected by an indoor corridor on the upper level. Both terminals occupy two floors, with arrivals on the ground level and departures on the upper level. The international terminal has a TI desk on the arrivals level, where you can pick up a free map and brochures. Each terminal also has an airport information desk, a pharmacy, car-rental agencies, exchange offices, and ATMs (located mainly on the arrivals level). The phone numbers for Istanbul's airports and major airlines are listed on page 354.

Arriving at Atatürk Airport

When you arrive at the international terminal, signs and airport staff will direct you to passport control. Before going through this checkpoint, you'll have to buy a visa (windows are next to passport

Flying in Turkey

Atatürk Airport is the hub for Turkish Airlines (www.thy.com), the country's major airline. Smaller, private carriers—which fly from Atatürk Airport to other major Turkish cities, such as Ankara, İzmir, and Trabzon—include Atlasjet Airlines (www. atlasjet.com), Pegasus Airlines (www.pegasusairlines.com), and Onur Air (www.onurair.com.tr, in Turkish only).

Istanbul's other airport, Sabiha Gökçen Airport, is on the Asian side. It's served mainly by budget airlines—but the added expense of getting across the Bosphorus bridge to your Old Town or New District hotel might negate your savings (figure 75-85 YTL for a taxi, 1–2.5 hours depending on traffic).

For a domestic economy flight within Turkey, estimate 75–250 YTL one-way (about $50–170). You can buy your ticket in Turkey from a local travel agent, or book online through the airline's website. Flights book up more quickly in high season (May–Sept).

control, pay exact change: Americans pay $20, Canadians pay $60 in US dollars; for more information on the visa, see page 7). After getting your visa, go through passport control, then baggage claim, then Customs into the arrivals lounge.

From here, you have several options for getting to the Old Town or the New District. A taxi is easiest for any location; otherwise, the airport shuttle bus (described later) is convenient for the New District, while public transportation is easier for the Old Town.

By Taxi: The taxi stand is right outside the arrivals (ground) level of the terminal. Airport cabs are yellow; as long as they're in the line, you know that they work for the official airport-taxi service. It takes 30–60 minutes to get to your hotel in the Old Town or the New District; expect to pay roughly 35–55 YTL ($25–40). Up to four people can fit into a cab—share to save money. For taxi tips, see page 29.

By Airport Shuttle Bus: Airport shuttle buses are usually white, and are marked with *Havaş* (hah-vahsh) signs. As you exit the arrivals level, go past the taxi stand to the *Havaş* stop. Shuttles leave on the half-hour from 6:00 to 1:00 in the morning (10 YTL, 50 percent more after 24:00). The shuttle bus is especially handy if you're heading for the New District. It takes roughly an hour to get to Taksim Square; if your hotel is located in the Galata district, or near the southern end of İstiklal street, get off at Tepebaşı (teh-peh-bah-shuh; the stop before Taksim), which is a few minutes' walk from either location. For hotels near Taksim Square and the northern end of İstiklal street, get off at the Taksim (tahk-seem) stop. If you're heading to the Old Town, get off at Aksaray (ahk-sah-ray), then take a taxi or tram (described next) to the core of the Old Town.

If you're heading from the Old Town to the airport, you'll probably notice that local travel agencies have signs out front advertising their shuttle-bus service (charging as little as €5 per person, get details per agency). If you go this route, note that you need to catch the bus at the travel agency; buses don't pick up at hotels.

By Public Transportation (Light Rail and Tram): Public transportation from the airport into Istanbul is cheap (2.80 YTL to the Old Town, 4.20 YTL to the New District) but complicated, involving at least one transfer—no fun if you're packing heavy. From the international terminal's arrivals level, take the stairs (located midway along the terminal) to the light rail platform; trains leave from the airport every 5–15 minutes (6:00–24:00). Take the light rail to Zeytinburnu or to Aksaray (last stop)—you can catch the tram from either stop (look for signs to the tram, or ask). To reach the Old Town, take this tram to the Sultanahmet stop. To go all the way to the New District, stay on the tram and take it across the Golden Horn; get off at the Karaköy stop (near Tünel funicular) for Galata district hotels, or the Kabataş stop (near the Taksim Square funicular) for Taksim Square hotels. Remember that any time you change between the light rail, tram, Metro, or funicular, you'll need to pay 1.50 YTL (all these transportation systems use the same tokens, which you can buy at ticket booths at any major stop). For more on Istanbul's rail network, see page 30.

Departing from Atatürk Airport
To take a flight out of Turkey, enter the airport's international terminal after first going through a security checkpoint. Once inside, check the screens for the check-in desk for your flight. After checking in, you'll go through a second security checkpoint to reach the gate area.

Buses
Arriving by Bus
Buses arrive at the city's **main bus terminal** (*otogar;* oh-toh-gar), located in the Esenler (eh-sehn-lehr) district on the European side. Some bus lines stop at other points in the city, which may be closer to your hotel—ask when you buy your ticket. Some bus companies offer a free transfer to alternate locations in the city.

From the main *otogar,* it's about a 30-minute taxi ride to either the Old Town or the New District. You can also catch the light rail from the *otogar* to Aksaray, where you can take the tram to your

TRANSPORTATION

destination in the Old Town (Sultanahmet stop) or in the New District (Karaköy stop for Galata district hotels or the Kabataş stop for Taksim Square hotels).

Traveling by Bus Within Turkey

Turkey has a good network of highways, and the bus system is easy to figure out. Every major city or town in Turkey has a bus terminal *(otogar)*, usually located close to the city center and lined with small ticket offices run by competing companies. Additional, centrally located offices are linked to the *otogar* by shuttle. Service and prices are similar—just take whichever bus leaves soonest for your destination.

Bus rides cost about 15–20 YTL for every 60 miles. Turkish buses are quite comfortable, and they usually have WCs and tea/coffee/snack service aboard. Buses stop every two hours or so for breaks, giving passengers time to use the restroom, buy food, or stretch. Most bus lines make local stops. A few companies have non-stop express services to major destinations; these don't make local stops and usually have an attendant on board.

Certain bus companies stand out for their good service, including Ulusoy (www.ulusoy.com.tr/eng), Varan (www.varan.com.tr/english), Boss, Kamil Koç, and Pamukkale. While you'll pay up to 50 percent more than on the cheaper bus companies, these carriers are more convenient since they have private, more centrally located bus terminals in the city (and may not stop at the main *otogar*).

Trains

Arriving by Train

Istanbul has two train stations, one on each side of the Bosphorus.

If you enter Istanbul from Europe, you'll arrive at the **Sirkeci** (seer-keh-jee) **Train Station,** located on the Old Town side of the Golden Horn, just a few steps from the Galata Bridge. Go out the main entrance; across the street, you'll see the Sirkeci stop on the tram line, which you can take either to the core of the Old Town (Sultanahmet stop) or to the New District (Karaköy or Kabataş stop). This station was once the terminus of the fabled Orient Express.

If you enter Istanbul from Asian Turkey (or elsewhere in Asia), you'll arrive at the train station called **Haydarpaşa Garı** (high-dar-pah-shah gah-ruh). To reach the European side of the city, take the ferry (the port is just outside the train station) to Karaköy in the New District; the ferry will dock near the Galata Bridge on the Golden Horn. The Karaköy tram stop is just a block from this ferry port.

Traveling by Train Within Turkey

Since most train destinations in Turkey are in the Asian part of the country, you'll most likely use the Haydarpaşa Garı station if you take a train from Istanbul. But you can buy train tickets at either station—and Sirkeci Train Station at the edge of the Old Town is more convenient to most of Istanbul's main attractions.

To Ankara: From Istanbul's Haydarpaşa Garı station, several trains a day run to the capital city of Ankara (about $20–25 one-way, 6.5–9 hrs). If you take an overnight train, you'll pay about $20–25 for a seat or berth in a shared compartment. But for more privacy, consider taking the new, convenient Ankara Ekspresi (ahn-kah-rah ehks-preh-see; "Ankara Express"; about $65 for a private one-person sleeping compartment, $90 for two people, departs nightly at 22:30, arrives at Ankara around 8:00).

Boats

Arriving by Boat

The passenger port of Istanbul, where cruise ships arrive, is in the Karaköy neighborhood in the New District, at the mouth of the Golden Horn (across from the Old Town). This centrally located port is just a few blocks from the Karaköy tram stop, where you can catch the tram to various points around town  (Sultanahmet stop for the Old Town, Kabataş stop for the Taksim funicular).

TRANSPORTATION

TURKISH HISTORY AND CULTURE

Anatolia is the timeless term for the geographical baklava that makes up most of modern Turkey. This fertile peninsula has nourished civilizations for thousands of years. The oldest city in the world—dating from 7500 B.C.—is thought to be Çatalhoyuk, near modern-day Konya.

Geographically, the terms "Anatolia" and "Asia Minor" both describe the Asian portion of Turkey—the part of the country east of the Bosphorus Strait. (European Turkey, west of the Bosphorus, is called "Thrace.") Istanbul itself straddles the continents; the oldest, most historic portion of the city (including most of what's covered in this book) is located west of the Bosphorus, on the European side.

Here at the crossroads of continents, Turkish history has played out against a backdrop of the greatest empires of East and West. As Turkey has entered the 21st century, the empires of the past have given way to a proud democracy with a secular government and a predominantly Muslim population.

TURKISH HISTORY

Hittites in Anatolia, 2000–1180 B.C.

Anatolia, which quietly coasted through the Neolithic and Bronze Ages, was easily conquered in 2000 B.C. by the Hittites, an Indo-European people. The Hittites' records indicate an advanced legal system. By uniting all of Anatolia, the Hittites created a superpower that rivaled Egypt. In 1180 B.C., the Hittites abruptly—and mysteriously—fell.

After the Hittites, 1180–334 B.C.

Anatolian unity passed with the Hittites, and the land became filled with small, unrelated, and relatively unimportant groups.

The Lycians lived in city-states fringing Anatolia's southern coast. The Phrygians (FRIJ-ee-ans) settled in the middle of Anatolia, and were known for their bravery, artistic talents, and intricately designed tombs. Their King Midas was endowed with the touch of gold (in legend only). The Lydians (not to be confused with the Lycians), known for their creativity, invented numerous musical instruments (such as the lyre and harp). More significantly, they invented coinage. During this period, Greek city-states such as Smyrna (today's Izmir) hugged Anatolia's western coast—an area the Greeks called Ionia. These cities existed as separate entities, united only by their Greek culture.

Among those city-states was one called **Byzantium**—today's Istanbul. It was founded in 659 B.C. by Greek colonists (led by a man named Byzas), who built a hill city surrounded by ramparts at the tip of a peninsula (today's Old Town). It had a port and a sheltered cove, and prospered due to its key geopolitical position: Byzantium not only had strategic water access, but also was located on the busy trade route to Greek colonies around the Black Sea.

Then, around 600 B.C., the Persians swept in from the east. Cyrus the Great conquered all of Anatolia and began a 300-year period of Persian rule. It was during this time that people first attempted to bridge the Bosphorus Strait, which is only a half-mile wide at its narrowest point. In 490 B.C., the Persian emperor Darius the Great ordered his men to build a bridge for the safe passage of his troops. Boats were tied to one another, allowing thousands of troops to cross the strait.

Hellenistic and Roman Anatolia (334 B.C.–A.D. 330)

After conquering Greece in the late fourth century B.C., Alexander the Great, a Macedonian, turned his eye to the east. Alexander beat back Persia and conquered Anatolia in 334 B.C. Wherever he went, he founded new "Hellenistic" cities (patterned after the Greek city model and based on the Greek culture and language). Trade and prosperity increased.

After Alexander's death in 323 B.C., his generals fought over an empire that stretched from Italy to India. Anatolia got chopped up. The biggest chunk, called the Pergamon Kingdom, struck up an alliance with Rome. Byzantium struggled to preserve its autonomy, cutting deals with the Romans over the centuries to avoid an invasion. But in A.D. 73, Roman armies under Emperor Vespasian marched through the gates of Byzantium, making the city part of the Roman Empire. Eventually Rome took over most of Anatolia,

A City of Many Names

Istanbul has had several names through its history, including Byzantium, Nova Roma, Constantinople, Konstantiniye, and finally, Istanbul.

Byzantium, which means "the city of Byzas," was named for its legendary Greek founder. When Constantine proclaimed Byzantium as the new capital of the Roman Empire, the official name was changed to Nova Roma, or New Rome. However, the people of the city called it Constantinople, or "the city of Constantine." That name survived during the period of the Ottoman Empire as Konstantiniye, the Arabic interpretation of Constantinople.

So, when did the city's name become Istanbul? Actually, Constantinople was always Istanbul. The word "Istanbul" comes from the Greek phrase *"(i)stinpoli(n),"* which means "to the city." So when people used this phrase, it meant that they were going into the city...that is, to Constantinople. The Turks kept using the adopted version of this phrase, and called the city Istanbul.

and over the next 300 years, Rome's "Province of Asia" prospered.

When Septimius Severus claimed the throne of Rome in A.D. 193, his rival, Pescennius Niger, had the support of Byzantium. Severus and his armies crushed Niger's forces and reduced Byzantium to ashes in A.D. 196. Soon realizing the city's strategic importance, Severus had Byzantium rebuilt on an even grander scale. But even Severus' walls couldn't protect the city against Goth raids during the third century.

Just a few decades later, fortune would again smile on Byzantium, when Constantine the Great became the emperor of Rome.

Constantinople and the Byzantine Empire (A.D. 330–1453)

Constantine decided to move the capital of his far-flung empire from a declining Rome to a more strategic, powerful position in the east. After considering Troy, he instead chose Byzantium, a city that linked Europe and Asia. In A.D. 330, Constantine declared Byzantium to be the "New Rome" (Nova Roma).

Thus began the Eastern Roman Empire, later known as the Byzantine Empire: a synthesis of Greek culture, Roman politics, and Christian religion that would survive for more than a thousand years. Constantine kicked things off by converting to Christianity, hastening the demise of traditional Roman gods and culture. Even the Roman language, Latin, was eventually abandoned (Greek became the official language when the Byzantine Empire was reorganized in A.D. 620). The word "Byzantine" comes from Byzantium, the original name of the ancient city—another reflection of the area's traditional roots in Greek language and culture.

Theodosius (ruled 379–395) was the last Roman emperor to rule a united Roman Empire from Constantinople. After his death, the eastern part of the empire permanently broke away from the western part. While the last western Roman emperor submitted to a barbarian king within a hundred years, the Byzantines to the east continued to thrive for a millennium.

From across the sweep of a thousand years of Byzantine history, one emperor stands out: Emperor Justinian (ruled 527–565). Under Justinian, the Byzantine Empire expanded its borders and reconquered some of the empire's lost Roman territories in the west, including most of Italy; his vast holdings also included the Balkans, Egypt, and North Africa. Justinian's code of law, the Codex Justinianus, regulated public and private affairs and business dealings. Also known as Corpus Juris Civilis (Body of Civil Law), it later provided a foundation for the legal system of the West. Justinian's most recognizable contribution was the construction of Hagia Sophia, the Great Church of Constantinople.

Although Justinian's 38-year reign marks the zenith of the empire, he left behind a crippled state. Ambitious building projects drained the treasury. Farms were deserted, as owners lacked the income to pay the taxes. Soon after Justinian died, Italy was lost to Germanic invaders. And so the Byzantines began their slow and steady decline (800–1453)—partly because of their own political mistakes, and partly because of an upstart religion on their doorstep: Islam.

The Selçuks (1037–1243)

In the 11th century, Selçuk Turks from Central Asia rode a wave of Islam into Anatolia, where they established a Selçuk kingdom. After taking over present-day Iran and Iraq, the Selçuks fought Byzantine forces, winning control of nearly all of Anatolia but leaving Constantinople to the Christians. The Selçuks created a wealth of beautiful architecture, ornate tiles, and poetry.

In the 13th century, the Selçuks' greatest philosopher was born. A religious leader and mystic, Rumi (or Mevlana) inspired an Islamic sect in Konya known for its Whirling Dervishes. Rumi's words were simple and profound. He said, "Love lies out of the reach of dogma. In all mosques, temples, churches, I find one shrine alone. The lovers of God have no religion but God alone."

Meanwhile, Constantinople limped along as its rulers fought over succession. From 1202 to 1204, during the Fourth Crusade, crude Crusaders sacked the Christian city and carried off its wealth. They stuck around for 50 years as the "Latin Empire" before the Byzantines regained control. With friends like these, the Byzantines hardly needed enemies. But look out...

Ottoman Empire (1299–1918)

The Mongols trampled through Anatolia in 1243, scattering the Turks and ending Selçuk rule. The Turks formed small principalities, or city-states. Osman was one of the rulers. His subjects took his name and called themselves Osmanlı. The Europeans mangled the pronunciation of "Osmanlı" into "Ottoman."

Over the years, Osman's principality grew in size and power, taking over Bursa as its capital and capturing Byzantine territories in Anatolia as early as the 11th century. However, the Byzantine presence—centered in Constantinople and nearby towns—lasted for another 400 years, as the continuing Mongolian raids from the east helped preserve the status quo.

By the mid-1400s, the Ottomans had grown strong enough to challenge Constantinople, the eastern stronghold of Christendom. Leading the charge was a young Ottoman sultan, Mehmet II (ruled 1451–1481). Mehmet II became sultan when he was only 12 years old, after his father retired. A military crisis soon broke out, and Mehmet II asked his father to lead the army one last time. When his father refused, the enraged Mehmet II proclaimed, "If I am the sultan, I order thee to command the armies"...and, sure enough, his father returned to the throne. Upon his father's death, Mehmet II resumed the throne at the age of 19.

Two years later, Mehmet II laid siege to Constantinople. The Orthodox Byzantines looked for help in the Catholic West, but their pleas were in vain, due to the longstanding conflicts between these two branches of the divided Church. Giving up, the Byzantine clergy reportedly said, "We would rather be ruled by the Ottoman turban than by the Latin miter" (referring to the tall, skinny hat worn by a Roman Catholic bishop).

The siege lasted for almost two months. Constantinople was the best-fortified city of its time, with the world's strongest city walls. The Byzantines stretched a large chain across the entrance of the Golden Horn to keep enemy fleets from sailing into the heart of the city. Mehmet II knew he must gain control of this inlet if he was to conquer Constantinople. But instead of trying to break through the chain, he went around it. In just one night, his troops pulled their ships out of the Bosphorus Strait on greased logs, slid them up over the hills past the entrance of the Golden Horn, and then deposited them back into the Horn. The next morning, the Ottoman cannons—still relatively new weapons—bombarded the city's western walls. Constantinople—and with it, Byzantine and Christian rule in the region—fell on May 29, 1453.

Top 10 Figures in Istanbul History

Byzas (seventh century B.C.): Greek colonist who founded a namesake city on the Bosphorus: Byzantium.

Constantine the Great (ruled 306–337): Roman emperor who legalized Christianity and moved the capital of his vast empire from Rome to Byzantium (which became known as Constantinople).

Justinian (ruled 527–565): Byzantine emperor who expanded the empire to its greatest extent, codified law, and built Hagia Sophia.

Rumi, a.k.a. **Mevlana** (1207–1273): Great Selçuk philosopher and mystic who inspired the order of Whirling Dervishes.

Osman I (1258–1326): Founder of a small Anatolian principality that eventually grew into a 600-year-long empire, which bore a modified version of his name—"Ottoman."

Sultan Mehmet II, the Conqueror (ruled 1451–1481): Successfully laid siege to Constantinople, putting the Ottoman Empire on the map as a world power.

Sultan Süleyman the Magnificent (ruled 1520–1566): With his wife Roxelana, vastly expanded Ottoman territory and financed many fine buildings. See page 222.

Mimar Sinan (1489–1588): Süleyman's magnificent architect, whose grand but tastefully restrained buildings and monuments still rank among Istanbul's best. See page 225.

Kösem (1590–1651): "Favorite" of Sultan Ahmet I, who ran the empire through her sultan sons as the most significant figure in a 150-year-long "reign of the ladies." See page 78.

Mustafa Kemal Atatürk (1881–1938): The "Grand Turk" who liberated his people from Western invasion at the end of World War I, founded the modern Turkish Republic, and enacted sweeping reforms that made Turkey more European than Asian. See page 112.

TURKISH HISTORY

Mehmet the Conqueror made Constantinople the new capital of his Islamic empire, and Turk-ified its name to "Konstantiniye." Although Mehmet was a soldier at heart, he was also a man of intellect. He spoke six languages fluently and appreciated art and science. He assembled both Christian and Muslim scholars in his court, beginning a practice of religious tolerance that was continued by succeeding sultans.

Mehmet II transformed the Ottoman state into a formidable empire. However, it was one of his descendants, Süleyman the Magnificent (ruled 1520–1566), who made it into a world power. Süleyman triggered an explosion of architecture (with the help of his master architect, Sinan) and expanded his territory as far west as Hungary and as far south as North Africa. Under Süleyman, one-third of Europe's population lived within the borders of the Ottoman Empire, and Istanbul was the largest and most prosperous city in the world. (For more on Süleyman, see the sidebar on page 222.)

The titles of Süleyman's successors—such as Selim the Sot and İbrahim the Mad—tell a story of decay. Incompetent sultans, over-taxation, corruption, and technological advances in the West would eventually combine to bring down the mighty Ottomans.

Decline of the Ottomans and Westernization Struggles (1700s–1914)

By the 1700s, sultans and state administrators agreed that the Ottoman Empire had to be reorganized in order to function effectively. The empire sought inspiration from the West.

The Ottoman Empire's first Westernization attempt was the so-called Tulip Era (1718–1730), but due to the sultan's extravagant lifestyle and increased taxes, it ended in riots (see page 156). A century later, the 1839 Reformation Decree—which promoted social, political, and economic reform—marked the empire's first serious attempt to Westernize. The concept of citizenship entered the political jargon, and while the sultan still had authority, bureaucrats were given more power. In 1876, under pressure from within the empire as well as from Western powers, the sultan established a parliament, with representatives elected by popular vote. But shortly thereafter, the Ottoman-Russian War provided a good excuse for the sultan to abolish the parliament.

The strongest opposition to the sultan's limitless authority came from intellectuals known as the Young Turks (or New Ottomans). Agitating for civil rights, they printed papers and periodicals in Europe and distributed them in Istanbul. Their efforts came to fruition in 1908, when the sultan issued a decree limiting his executive power and reinstating the parliament. But this parliament would last only a decade, and was abolished by the Allies as they invaded Istanbul in 1918. Most of the Young Turks fled Istanbul at the close of World War I. To some Turkish people, they were heroes; to others, they were traitors. Although they didn't succeed in creating a lasting Western-style government, their contribution to democracy in Turkey was significant.

In spite of the various attempts at reform, the Ottoman Empire continued to decline. Rotten from within, and stifled by palace intrigue and infighting, by the late 1800s the Ottoman Empire became known as the "Sick Man of Europe"...and World War I finally took it off life support.

World War I (1914–1918)

In the early 20th century, the clueless Ottoman Empire sided with Germany. The sultan hoped the war would help the empire regain lost territories in the Balkans and the Middle East, and unify the various ethnicities of the empire. Instead, the war only hastened the empire's demise.

The Ottomans fought valiantly despite their limited resources. While the bloody Gallipoli battle on the Dardanelles Strait cost heavy human losses on both sides, it ultimately triggered the process of independence for three nations: Australia, New Zealand, and the Turkish Republic.

World War I also saw a controversial chapter in Turkish history. In 1915, the Ottoman government decided to relocate its independence-minded Armenian population in the east, some of whom had staged armed uprisings. During the course of this relocation, hundreds of thousands of Armenians died. Some say this was due to inter-ethnic fighting and disease, while others say it was a concerted government campaign of ethnic cleansing. Today, many Armenians (and many other people outside Turkey) consider it genocide. But most Turks—including the government—don't accept that it was state-sponsored, and maintain that such claims lack historical evidence.

From the ashes of that same tragic war rose the greatest hero of the Turkish people: Atatürk.

Atatürk and the Turkish Republic (1923–present)

When Germany surrendered at the end of World War I, so did the Ottomans. The sultan signed a disarmament truce, and Allied

troops marched through the streets of Istanbul. The eager vultures of Europe—France, Britain, and Italy—could hardly wait for the feast to begin. The Allies drew up a treaty that would carve up Turkey among the victors.

But even as the sultan was capitulating to Allied demands, Turkish nationalists and ex-army officers were mobilizing to fight back. One of them was Mustafa Kemal (1881–1938), a former army officer who had shown great success and bravery in Gallipoli and on other fronts during the war. Kemal—later bestowed with the honorary last name "Atatürk" ("The Grand Turk") by the Turkish parliament—led a three-year-long liberation movement to repel the invading armies. He eventually prevailed, and established the Turkish Republic in 1923.

Atatürk enacted a series of sweeping reforms to propel Turkey into the 20th century, and orient it towards Europe rather than Asia. State administration, education, lifestyle, dress, language—every aspect of Turkish life was affected. The new parliament abolished all of the old Ottoman institutions—the sultan was history, and the royal family was sent into exile. Constantinople was officially renamed Istanbul, but lost its capital-city status to Ankara, which was then a small town. Atatürk, who saved Turkey from dissolution, remains revered by the Turkish people. For more on Turkey's greatest visionary leader, see the sidebar on page 112.

After Atatürk's death in 1938, Turkey floundered as it searched for a leader and experimented with democracy. İsmet İnönü, the second president of the Turkish Republic, managed to keep Turkey neutral during World War II, but immense financial losses due to the war led to friction and new political movements.

Ongoing political clashes resulted in three military interventions, the last one in 1980. Each time, the military returned control of the country to the people. In 1982, a new constitution abolished the Senate and made the National Assembly the sole legislative body. The current political system is based on the concept of a strong administration, rather than fractured coalitions.

Istanbul Today

Today, Turkey is a member of NATO, with aspirations to join the European Union. Although Istanbul is no longer the capital, it remains the financial and cultural center of Turkey. With over 15 million people, Istanbul is also the biggest city in Turkey (one out of every five citizens lives here), and one of the largest cosmopolitan areas in the world.

Several issues power Turkey's politics today: the privatization of state enterprises, the country's increasing loans, and ongoing regional conflicts in the east. Visitors to today's Turkey will encounter three hot-button issues in particular.

First, Turkey is making a strong drive to join the European Union. The idea of admitting this Texas-size country (with 70 million people, 98 percent of whom are Muslims) presents Europe with some challenges. Demographic trends are clear: Europe is becoming a geriatric old folks' continent, and if the population is not infused with fresh immigrant blood, it will start to wither away. But the inability of white Europe and its Muslim minorities (10 percent of the Continent's population) to assimilate comfortably is a serious problem that won't just disappear. While Turkey is enthusiastic about joining the European club, the EU is split on whether Turkish membership is in its best interest.

Second is the issue of the hundreds of thousands of Armenians who died in Turkey during World War I (explained on previous page). Was it genocide—or the casualties of war? Most Turks would prefer if this question were debated by historians, rather than politicians. But outside observers see it as a formidable obstacle in Turkey's race to join the EU. Around Europe, parliaments are voting on whether or not to recognize it as genocide. Meanwhile, the newly independent country of Armenia lies just northeast of Turkey, while many of Armenia's historic treasures lie ruined and desolate in eastern Turkey.

Finally, Turkey has a huge Kurdish population of about 10 million people, located mostly in the southeast. The Kurdish people also occupy land in Iraq and Iran. While Turkey's persistent Kurdish insurgency was pretty much quelled in the last decade, the prospect of Iraq falling apart—and its Kurds forming an autonomous nation—reignites this prickly issue. One thing is for sure: Turkey doesn't want to share a border with an independent Kurdistan.

Despite these challenges, Turkey and Istanbul are undeniably enjoying a period of unprecedented stability and wealth. There's no better time than now to visit one of Europe's most dynamic cities, Istanbul...and make your own history.

TURKISH LANGUAGE

Without a doubt, Turks speak more English than Americans speak Turkish. The younger generation is particularly fluent, and most learn a foreign language (usually English, German, or French) at school. Even if they don't speak English, most Turks will do their best to communicate with you. Still, it helps to know a few words of the local language. The Turkish people love visitors, and a friendly greeting in their language is an easy icebreaker. Give it your best shot. The locals will appreciate your efforts.

To hurdle the language barrier, bring a phrase book (or use the Turkish Survival Phrases on page 361), a small English/Turkish dictionary, and a good supply of patience. In transactions, a small notepad and pen minimize misunderstandings about prices: Have vendors write down the price.

Since Turkish is pronounced exactly as it's spelled, it's easy to sound things out—once you know a few key rules. Most notably, some letters are pronounced differently than in English, and Turkish includes a few diacritics—little markings below and above the letters that change their sound:

Vowels
A / a sounds like "ah" as in "call"
E / e sounds like "eh" as in "egg"
I / ı (with no dot) sounds like "uh" as in "the"

İ / i (with a dot) sounds like "ee" as in "email"
O / o sounds like "oh" as in "old"
Ö / ö sounds like "uhr" as in "urn" (the same as the German Ö / ö)
U / u sounds like "oo" as in "ooze"
Ü / ü sounds like "ew" as in "dew" (the same as the German Ü / ü)

Consonants

Most consonants are pronounced just as they are in English. Here are the exceptions:

C / c sounds like "j" as in "jet"
Ç / ç sounds like "ch" as in "church"
G / g sounds like a hard "g" as in "good"
Ğ / ğ is almost silent, and makes the preceding vowel longer (so the word *Ağa* is pronounced "aah-ah")
J / j sounds like "zh" as in "leisure"
Ş / ş sounds like "sh" as in "shoe"
V / v usually sounds like "v" as in "viper," but sometimes like "w" as in "wiper"

The letters q, x, and w don't currently exist in the Turkish alphabet. The "q" sound isn't used. The letter x in borrowed words is spelled as "ks," as in the Turkish word for taxi, *taksi*. And, with the increase in foreign words entering Turkish, the Turks are now considering adding w to the alphabet...but only if it behaves itself.

Turkish is usually pronounced rather flatly, without much emphasis on certain syllables—unless you're asking a question. If you want to invite someone to coffee *(kahve)*, you'd say, "kah-VEH?" (accent on the second syllable).

Also note that the verb-noun order in Turkish can be different from English. For instance, to ask for a beer, you'd say, *"Bira lütfen"* (bee-rah lewt-fehn; "Beer, please"). But to ask where the toilet is, you'd say, *"Tuvalet nerede?"* (too-vah-leht neh-reh-deh; literally "Toilet where is?").

Adding -*lar* or -*ler* to the end of a word makes it plural (which one you add depends on which vowel comes last). Words in Turkish don't have a gender, and the language doesn't use articles (such as "the" or "a").

If you master only four phrases, learn and use these: To say hello, say *merhaba* (mehr-hah-bah). Please is *lütfen* (lewt-fehn). Thank you is *teşekkür* (teh-sheh-kewr). For goodbye, say *hoşçakal* (hohsh-chah-kahl).

A few common phrases you may hear: *inşallah* (een-shah-lah; God willing), *maşallah* (mah-shah-lah; may God keep it so), *kolay gelsin* (koh-lay gehl-seen; may it be easy), and *rastgele* (rust-geh-leh; may you receive some).

It's All Turkish to Me

The Turkish language—a distant relative of Hungarian, Finnish, and Mongolian—is very unfamiliar to American ears. Yet Turkish is spoken by over 200 million people worldwide, and is also the native language of some areas of Cyprus, Bulgaria, and Greece.

For a millennium, the people of today's Turkey spoke a confusing mix of languages—Turkish, Persian, and Arabic—depending on the subject and the speaker. Turkish was written in the Arabic alphabet. But in 1928, when modern-day Turkey was founded, the reforms that swept the country included an overhaul of the language. The Arabic script was abandoned in favor of the Latin alphabet. Not only did this nudge the country further toward Europe, but it was also more effective for conveying Turkish sounds than Arabic had been. As a result, more and more Turks became comfortable with their written language; today, illiteracy is less than 3 percent.

GLOSSARY

ablution: The ritual self-cleansing that Muslims do before entering a mosque for the five daily prayer services

aigrette: Spray of gems used on a turban

alem: Bronze or brass minaret tops (see "minaret")

Allah: Muslim name for the one God

bedesten: Commercial building, also known as a *han*

Bosphorus Strait: Waterway running through the middle of Istanbul, separating Europe from Asia; most of this book's sights are on the European side

Byzantine Empire: Eastern branch of the Roman Empire (A.D. 330–1453), with its capital at Constantinople, now Istanbul

caddesi: Street

caftan: Man's traditional outer garment, made of silk, velvet, or wool

caliph: Muhammad's successors as head of Islam; during Ottoman times, the sultan also held this title

caliphate: Government based on Islamic law

çini: Quartz tile (see "tile")

concubine: Female slave kept in a harem

Constantinople: Capital city of the Eastern Roman, Byzantine, and Ottoman Empires; now called Istanbul

Dervish: Member of the Sufi religious order; the Mevlevi sect practices whirling to reach enlightenment

Divan: Chamber where the sultan's advisors (viziers) met during Ottoman times

TURKISH HISTORY

Eastern Orthodox: Branch of Christianity established in the 11th century, after splitting from the Roman Catholic Church

emir: Ruler or leader in an Islamic country

eunuch: Castrated slave; often served in a harem

fasıl: Traditional Turkish tunes performed live by a trio of musicians

favorite: Favored concubine (see "haseki")

Golden Horn: Inlet separating Istanbul's Old Town from its New District

Grand Vizier: Prime minister to the sultan in Ottoman times

hadith: Recorded works and words of the Prophet Muhammad

hajj: Once-in-a-lifetime pilgrimage to Mecca required of Muslim people (*hac* in Turkish)

hamam: Turkish bath

harem: Part of the home that was off-limits to male strangers; also refers collectively to the sultan's wives, favorites, and concubines

haseki: Favorite concubine of the sultan, who, if she bore his child, became known as a "haseki sultan" (and was treated more like a wife)

hat: Artistic calligraphy using Arabic script, often used to decorate a mosque

hattat: Calligrapher who creates hat (elaborate Arabic script)

henna: Green powder commonly sold in the Spice Market, used to dye hair and to decoratively stain the palms of young brides

imam: Muslim cleric or prayer leader, like a Christian priest or Jewish rabbi

Islam: The Muslim faith (see "Muslim")

İznik tiles: The most prized of all Turkish tiles, typically with a blue-and-white pattern, most famously produced in the 16th and 17th centuries in the city of İznik

janissary: An elite professional soldier for the sultan; usually a non-Muslim who was taken from his family, converted to Islam, and raised and trained at the palace school

Kaaba: Black cube-like temple in Mecca and focal point for Islamic prayer services

kathisma: Grandstand for royals to watch chariot races

kese: Raw-silk mitten used by an attendant at a Turkish bath to scrub the skin of bathers

kilim: Reversible rug that differs from a carpet in that it features a flat weave, without a raised pile

kiosk: Turkish pavilion

kontör: Credit, as on a prepaid telephone card

Kufic script: Early form of Arabic script

kuruş: Currency sub-unit; 1/100th of one New Turkish Lira

Latin Empire: Brief Roman Catholic empire (1204–1261) formed when Crusaders sacked Constantinople in 1204

lokum: See "Turkish delight"

madrassa: School of theology, attached to a mosque

meydanı: City square or neighborhood

meyhane: Tavern-style restaurant

meze: Appetizer

mihrab: Prayer niche in a mosque, always oriented toward Mecca

mimber: Small, symbolic staircase near the front of a mosque, used as a pulpit

minaret: Skinny tower adjacent to a mosque, used for call to prayer

mosque: Islamic house of worship

mother sultan: Ottoman sultan's mother, who directed the harem

muezzin: Person who announces call to prayer

muezzin mahfili: A mosque's elevated choir loge

mufti: Islamic lawyer

Muhammad: The central figure of Islam, a sixth- and seventh-century A.D. prophet who received revelations from God (Allah), which were recorded in the Quran

Muslim: A person who follows the Islamic faith

nargile: Water pipe

nazarlık: "Evil eye"; blue-and-white beads thought to ward off bad luck

Ottoman Empire: Powerful Turkish dynasty that ruled present-day Turkey and huge swaths of the Middle East, Africa, and Europe (lasted from 1299–1922; conquered Constantinople in 1453)

peştemal: Large cotton wrap used at Turkish bath

Quran: Islam's holy book, which collects God's revelations to the Prophet Muhammad

rahle: Holder for a Quran or other large book

Ramadan: One-month Islamic fasting observance (see "Ramadan" sidebar, page 62)

satrap: Persian governor, akin to a viceroy ruling in the emperor's name

Şeker bayramı: Breaking-of-fast celebration at end of Ramadan

Selçuk Empire: Pre-Ottoman Turkish dynasty that ruled much of today's Turkey, Middle East, and Iran (11th–14th centuries)

sıcaklık: Hot, steamy room at the center of a Turkish bath

stele: Carved stone pillar used to mark important events

sufi: Muslim mystic, including Whirling Dervishes

sultan: Sovereign Ottoman ruler, equivalent to an emperor; also known as Padişah or Han in Turkish

sultana: Ottoman emperor's wife, in Western languages

sultan's loge: A mosque's elevated prayer section for the sultan

sultan's paste: Herbal energy-booster and reported aphrodisiac, more recently known as "Turkish Viagra"

tile: The word that Turks use to describe high-quality decorative tiles and functional vessels (like bowls or vases) made with high quartz content; also known as *çini*

tuğra: Calligraphy representing the sultan's signature, often marking a building

tumulus: Ancient Phrygian burial mound

türban: Muslim woman's head covering (*hijab* in Arabic)

türbe: Mausoleum for a sultan

Turkish delight: Sweet cube of gelatin dusted with powdered sugar and often embedded with nuts (*lokum* in Turkish)

vizier: High executive officer in Ottoman times

Whirling Dervish: See "Dervish"

yalı: Expensive waterfront mansion along the Bosphorus

UNDERSTANDING ISLAM

Turkey offers Western visitors a unique opportunity to explore a land that's fully Muslim, moderate, and welcoming. This chapter, written by the Turkish Muslim authors of this book, explains the practice of Islam in Turkey to help travelers from the Christian West understand and respect a very rich but often misunderstood faith.

"Islam" is an Arabic word meaning "to surrender"—to submit to God's will. The word "Muslim" refers to a person who surrenders to God in all things.

Over 98 percent of Turks identify themselves as Muslims, mostly of the Sunni denomination. But the decision to practice Islam, and to what degree, is strictly an individual choice—a freedom protected by the secular state. Turks don't talk much when it comes to religion, considering it a private matter. An old saying goes, "You never know who's got the faith, and who's got the money." There is a great diversity in the way Islam is practiced among Turkish people, with many different sects or paths tending to focus on Islam's spiritual side. Turks, who have a tradition of tolerance, accept the various sects, as long as none tries to impose its individual interpretation on others.

The Roots of Islam

The Prophet Muhammad (A.D. 570–632) was born in Mecca (in today's Saudi Arabia), in a community he believed was in the throes of moral decadence. Most of the Arab people at the time were pagans who worshipped idols.

Muhammad sought a new way. He retired to a cave for a whole month every year to meditate and seek truth. When Muhammad was 40 years old, the Archangel Gabriel appeared to him in the cave and said that God had chosen Muhammad to be God's prophet.

His first revelation was, "Read in the name of Allah who created you." Revelations kept coming over the next 21 years. Muhammad's followers memorized and wrote down the revelations, and compiled them in a book called the Quran, which Muslims believe is a faithful recounting of God's word.

Muhammad didn't introduce a new religion. Rather, he invited people to return to the religion of Abraham: submitting to one God. That alone was enough to cause trouble, as Muhammad's words clashed with the personal interests of local community leaders and even Muhammad's own tribe. Early converts to Islam had a difficult time in Mecca, where they were persecuted. Seeking freedom to practice their beliefs, a group of Muhammad's followers migrated to the city of Medina in 622. This event and date mark the beginning of the Muslim calendar.

For more on the history of Islam, see the Turkish History and Culture chapter on page 322.

The Five Pillars of Islam

Most Muslims largely accept these five fundamentals, or "pillars," of Islam as the basis of their faith:

1. Say and believe, "There is no other God but Allah, and Muhammad is his Prophet." This is called *şehadet* (sheh-hah-deht) in Turkish, which means to declare, witness, or accept. A Muslim bears witness by accepting and declaring the fundamentals of the faith.

2. Pray five times a day. *Namaz* (nah-mahz) is the word for daily ritual prayers. It means to pray, to recite "Allah," and to prostrate oneself before God. For more on prayer, see the next page.

3. Give to the poor. Charity, or *zekat* (zeh-kaht), is required of Muslims who can afford a decent living for their family. They should give away one-fortieth (about 2.5 percent) of their annual income to help the needy. Their giving should be discreet—undertaken without boasting and with care not to hurt the feelings of the receiver.

4. Fast during Ramadan. Devout Muslims in good health are required to fast (*oruç*; oh-rooch), from sunrise to sunset during the month of Ramadan. If for some reason a believer cannot fast, he must instead feed the poor. Fasting is not just about staying away from food and drink all day; it is about self-discipline and becoming closer to God. (For more, see the sidebar on page 62.)

5. Make a pilgrimage to Mecca. Muslims who can afford it, and who are physically able, are required to go on a pilgrimage,

An Essential Part of Prayer

Fatiha (fah-tee-hah) means "the opening"—specifically, the opening chapter of the Quran. *Fatiha* is an important part of Muslim worship—no spiritual contact, or prayer, is complete unless it is recited. On Turkish tombstones, you'll often see the phrase *"Ruhuna El Fatiha"* (*"fatiha* for the soul"). People praying at shrines with open hands recite the words of the *fatiha:*

> *In the name of Allah, the Beneficent, the Merciful.*
> *Praise be to Allah, Lord of the Worlds, the Beneficent, the Merciful.*
> *Owner of the Day of Judgment,*
> *Thee (alone) we worship; Thee (alone) we ask for help.*
> *Show us the straight path,*
> *The path of those whom Thou hast favored; not the (path) of those who earn Thine anger, nor of those who go astray.*

called a *hac* (hahdge) to the sacred sites in Mecca and Medina at least once in their lifetimes. The highlight of this journey to Islam's holiest places is a visit to the Kaaba, the iconic cube-like building in Mecca. Muslims believe the Kaaba was built by the Prophet Abraham, and is dedicated to the worship of the one God, Allah.

God requires more than these five elements from those who truly "submit." To Turks, God's will is recorded in the Quran—giving believers a more extensive code of ethics governing daily conduct. Muslims also follow the works and life of the Prophet Muhammad, known as the *sünnet* (sew-neht), "the path," which appear in the *hadith*, the recorded works and words of the prophet.

Components of Islam

Prayer

Mainstream Islam asks believers to perform *namaz* (ritual prayer) five times each day: morning, noon, afternoon, evening, and night. The exact times of prayers change each day according to the position of the sun, and are announced by the call to prayer, or *ezan* (eh-zahn). This very Eastern-sounding chant warbles across Istanbul's rooftops five times daily. However, you won't see Turks in shops, restaurants, and on the streets suddenly prostrate themselves in prayer; people pray mainly in mosques.

No matter where they are in the world, Muslims face Islam's holy city of Mecca when they pray. Muslims are not required to go to a mosque to pray, except for the Friday noon prayer, which the Quran tells believers to perform with their congregation. But

Friday is not a day of rest like the Christian or Jewish Sabbath, because the Quran says Muslims should go back to work when the service is over.

The Mosque

The English word "mosque" comes from the Arabic *masjid* (mahs-jeed), meaning "place for prostration." The Turkish word for mosque is *cami* (jah-mee), meaning "place for congregation." Turks also use the word *mescit* (mehs-jeet; from the Arabic *masjid*) for a small mosque, or a simple chamber to perform *namaz*.

The mosque grew from the need to provide a safe place for Islamic congregations to practice their religion, protected from the world and the blazing desert sun. Mosques are not described in the Quran, so there is no proscribed architectural form. A building's function is what makes it a mosque.

Even within the predominantly Muslim world, religious architecture varies according to place and time. Istanbul's older mosques, to a great extent, were built in the Ottoman style. The classical Ottoman architecture in the Old Town gives way in the New District to a more eclectic style with Western influences.

The most common form of mosque (exemplified by the Blue Mosque and the Mosque of Süleyman the Magnificent, both covered by self-guided tours in this book) has a central dome, with cascading semi- and quarter-domes. The concept of a massive central dome supported by pillars was first used at Hagia Sophia, which was built originally as an Eastern Orthodox Christian church. In the centuries since, Turkish architects have refined this traditional design, which is still reflected in many contemporary mosques.

Because early Muslims were turning away from the pagan worship and idolatry of the time, Islamic tradition prohibits portrayals of humans in places of worship. It was believed that icons could distract followers from worshipping Allah as the only God—and mainstream Islam continues this tradition today. Mosques are instead decorated with fine calligraphy, and floral and geometric patterns—often displayed on colored tiles.

Minarets—the tall, skinny towers near a mosque—were originally functional: From here, the call went out five times a day to let people know it was time for prayer. Even though the call to prayer is now usually broadcast electronically, minarets remain a symbolic fixture of mosque architecture, like bell towers on Christian churches in Europe.

Prayer services in a mosque are generally segregated, with women and men in different parts of the mosque or separated by a screen. This is for practical reasons: Islamic prayer involves different body positions, such as kneeling with one's forehead on the

UNDERSTANDING ISLAM

floor—and early believers thought it could be distracting to have members of the opposite sex doing this in close proximity.

For details on the proper protocol for visiting a mosque, see page 61.

Ablution

Ablution (*abdest;* ahb-dehst) is the physical—and spiritual—cleansing proscribed for a Muslim before prayer. It involves ritual washing of certain parts of the body: hands and arms to the elbows, feet and lower legs, face, nose, ears, and so on. The fountains and water taps you'll see outside of every mosque are for ablution.

The Imam

In Turkey, the imam (ee-mahm) is the Muslim counterpart of a Christian priest or Jewish rabbi. His primary role is to lead the service in a mosque, five times a day. In the past, the imam was more active in Turkish society, in both religious and social matters. Though the imams' influence has waned in urban areas, villagers in rural Turkey usually go to their imam when they need advice.

The imam is usually responsible for calling the congregation to prayer, but at large mosques, this duty is delegated to a second person, called a muezzin (muh-ehz-zeen). The muezzin is chosen for his talent in correctly voicing the call to prayer.

Although Turkey is a secular country, both imams and muezzins in Turkey are civil servants, appointed and paid by the state's Religious Affairs Directorate. To become an imam, you have to complete a four-year university degree in theology (to study Islam as well as other religions) and pass a rigorous final exam. The government regulates the rotation of imams, but there is no hierarchy among them (such as with the bishops and cardinals in the Catholic Church).

Islam, Christianity, and Judaism

The Quran refers to Muslims, Christians, and Jews as "People of the Book," and to people in general as "believers" and "non-believers." Just as the word "catholic" can mean "universal," the words "Islam" and "Muslim" can have a wider meaning in the verses: "Muslim" can be taken to mean all those who have faith in the one God, and "Islam" as all those who submit to God's will. For instance, in a verse related to "People of the Book," the Quran says, "There are good Muslims among them."

The Quran recognizes 28 prophets by their names, including Abraham, Noah, Moses, Jesus, and Muhammad. According to the Quran, Allah sent hundreds of prophets to take his message to humankind.

The Quran speaks of an afterlife (heaven and hell), but no

eternal punishment and no original sin. There is no confession in Islam—faith and repentance are strictly between God and the believer.

Muslim Women

Islam advises modesty for both men and women in attire and attitude. Some Muslims interpret this as an order for women to cover

their bodies from head to toe. Veils or black coveralls are not traditionally a part of Turkish culture—but you'll sometimes see these trends borrowed from Arab Muslim cultures farther east.

The majority of Turkish Muslims prefer a more liberal interpretation of modesty; in fact, the way a woman dresses is left to individual choice. On the streets of Istanbul, you'll mostly

see women dressed in contemporary styles, ranging from conservative dresses to miniskirts. But you'll also see many women wearing headscarves, as well as some women wearing head-to-toe coverings.

How does a woman decide how to dress? Her particular community, personal beliefs, family, status, age, education, and profession all play a role. For example, wearing a head covering or scarf does not always have religious significance. Some women simply feel more comfortable in public wearing a scarf—or maybe they're just having a bad hair day.

In poorer and more rural areas, women tend to dress more conservatively. The young women generally dress however they like, as long as they are modest, but elderly women typically wear a scarf in public, often accompanied by a cloak that looks like a long raincoat. In the countryside, it's traditional for women to wear a simple white or colorful scarf—not only as part of their religion, but also as practical protection from the sun and dust.

APPENDIX

CONTENTS

RESOURCES

Tourist Information Offices

In the US

Turkey's national tourist office has three helpful branches in the US. Before your trip, get the free general information packet, and request any specifics you may want, such as city maps and festival schedules. The offices are in **New York** (info.ny@tourismturkey .org, tel. 212/687-2194, fax 212/599-7568, 821 United Nations Plaza, New York, NY 10017); in **California** (info.la@tourism turkey.org, tel. 323/937-8066, fax 323/937-1271, 5055 Wilshire Blvd., #850, Los Angeles, CA 90036); and in **Washington, DC** (info.dc@tourismturkey.org, tel. 202/612-6800, fax 202/319-7446, 2525 Massachusetts Ave. NW, Washington, DC, 20008).

Several brochures can be downloaded from their website at www.tourismturkey.org. The Turkish Ministry of Culture and Tourism website at www.kultur.gov.tr is also helpful and has short movie clips about Istanbul's main sights—great for pre-trip viewing.

In Istanbul

While Istanbul's city tourist information office often misses the mark, it's worth stopping in to pick up a free map. For the locations of the branches, see page 24 in the Orientation chapter.

Resources from Rick

Guidebooks and Online Updates

We've done our best to make sure that the information in this book is up-to-date—but things change. For the latest, visit www.rick steves.com/update. Also at the website, you'll find a valuable list of reports and experiences—good and bad—from fellow travelers (www.ricksteves.com/feedback).

This book is one of more than 30 titles in a series on European travel, which includes country guidebooks, city and regional guidebooks, and a budget-travel skills handbook, *Rick Steves' Europe Through the Back Door*. Rick's phrase books—for German, French, Italian, Spanish, and Portuguese—are practical and budget-oriented. Rick's other books are *Europe 101* (a crash course on art and history, newly expanded and in full color), *European Christmas* (on traditional and modern-day celebrations), and *Postcards from Europe* (a fun memoir of Rick's travels). For a complete list of *Rick Steves* books, see the inside of the last page of this book.

Public Television and Radio Shows

The TV series *Rick Steves' Europe* covers European destinations in 80 shows, including four different episodes that explore Turkey. The weekly public radio show, *Travel with Rick Steves*, features interviews with travel experts from around the world, including Tankut, Lale, and other Turkish friends. All the TV scripts and radio shows (which are easy and free to download to an iPod or other MP3 player) are at www.ricksteves.com.

Free Audiotours

If your travels take you beyond Turkey to Italy or France, you could take advantage of the free, self-guided audiotours we offer of the major sights in Venice, Florence, Rome, and Paris. The audiotours, produced by Rick Steves and Gene Openshaw (the co-author of seven books in the Rick Steves series) are

Begin Your Trip at www.ricksteves.com

At our travel website, you'll find a wealth of free information on European destinations, including fresh monthly news and helpful tips from thousands of fellow travelers.

Our **online Travel Store** offers travel bags and accessories specially designed by Rick Steves to help you travel smarter and lighter. These include Rick's popular carry-on bags (wheeled and rucksack versions), money belts, totes, toiletries kits, adapters, other accessories, and a wide selection of guidebooks, planning maps, and DVDs.

Choosing the right **railpass** for your trip—amidst hundreds of options—can drive you nutty. We'll help you choose the best pass for your needs, plus give you a bunch of free extras.

Rick Steves' Europe Through the Back Door travel company offers **tours** with more than two dozen itineraries and about 450 departures reaching the best destinations in this book...and beyond. Our 13-day Best of Turkey tour begins in the ancient city of Istanbul and ends in seaside Kuşadası. Along the way you'll walk in the footsteps of the Greeks, Romans, Byzantines, and Ottomans, and get to know some of today's Turkish people. You'll enjoy great guides, a fun bunch of travel partners (with small groups of generally around 26), and plenty of room to spread out in a big, comfy bus. You'll find European adventures to fit every vacation length. For all the details, and to get our Tour Catalog and a free Rick Steves Tour Experience DVD (filmed on location during an actual tour), visit www.ricksteves.com or call the Tour Department at 425/608-4217.

available through iTunes and at www.ricksteves.com. Simply download them onto your computer and transfer them to your iPod or other MP3 player. (Remember to bring a Y-jack and extra set of ear buds for your travel partner.)

Maps

The black-and-white maps in this book, designed by Rick's well-traveled staff, are concise and simple. The maps are intended to help you locate recommended places and get to local TIs, where you can pick up a more in-depth map of the city or region (usually free). Better maps are sold at newsstands and bookstores—take a look before you buy to be sure the map has the level of detail you want.

Other Guidebooks

If you're like most travelers, this book is all you need. But if you'll be exploring beyond this book's recommended neighborhoods and destinations, $40 for extra maps and books is money well-spent. Especially for several people traveling by car, the extra weight and expense of a few books are negligible.

The following books are worthwhile, though not updated annually; check the publication date before you buy.

Lonely Planet's *Turkey* and the more in-depth *Istanbul* are thorough, well-researched, and packed with good maps and hotel recommendations for low- to moderate-budget travelers.

Older travelers enjoy guides from Frommer's, even though, like the Fodor's guide, they ignore alternatives that enable travelers to save money by dirtying their fingers in the local culture. My readers have found Cadogan's *Turkey* to be useful for advance planning.

The Eyewitness series—which covers Turkey and Istanbul—is popular for great, easy-to-grasp graphics and photos, 3-D cutaways of buildings, aerial-view maps of historic neighborhoods, and cultural background. But written content in Eyewitness is relatively skimpy, and the books weigh a ton. You can simply borrow them for a minute from other travelers at certain sights to make sure you're aware of that place's highlights.

Those staying longer in Istanbul might consider the pocket guides by Insight or Berlitz. The British entertainment publication *Time Out* sells a well-researched annual magazine with up-to-date coverage on Istanbul, including the latest on hotels, restaurants, and nightlife (look for it at newsstands and at bookstores, www .timeout.com).

Recommended Books and Movies

To get the feel of Istanbul (and Turkey) past and present, consider these books and films.

Non-Fiction

To learn about the rise and fall of Constantinople, read *A Short History of Byzantium* (1998, Norwich) or *Sailing from Byzantium* (2007, Wells). *Suleiman the Magnificent* (2004, Clot) introduces the most celebrated of Ottoman sultans, while *Osman's Dream: The History of the Ottoman Empire* (2006, Finkel) traces the empire from medieval times to modernity.

For an overview of modern Turkish history and current affairs, try *Crescent & Star* (2002, Kinzer), or *The Turks Today* (2006, Mango). *Atatürk: The Biography of the Founder of Modern Turkey* (2002, also by Mango) is the most comprehensive biography of Atatürk since Lord Kinross's 1967 *Atatürk: A Biography of Mustafa Kemal.*

Orhan Pamuk won the 2006 Nobel Prize in literature; one of his works is the melancholy memoir *Istanbul: Memories and the City.* *Memoirs of an Exile* (2001, Nesin) is the sad and funny story of the Turkish satirist's forced banishment to Bursa.

In *Turkish Reflections* (1992), Mary Lee Settle recounts two visits to Turkey, 15 years apart. *Istanbul: The Imperial City* (1998, Freely) is both a brief history and a travel guide. *Turkish Odyssey* (1999, Serif Yenen) is a handbook to Turkish society and culture. *Tales from the Expat Harem* (2006, Ashman and Gökmen) compiles 29 personal stories from foreign women living in Turkey. *Eat Smart in Turkey* (2004), by Joan Peterson, describes the fascinating history and culture of Turkish cuisine and includes delicious recipes.

Karen Armstrong's *Muhammad: A Biography of the Prophet* (2001) and *Muhammad: A Prophet for Our Time* (2006) explore the foundations of the Islamic faith. *The Pleasantries of the Incredible Mullah Nasrudin* (Shah, 1993) collects stories told by Sufi mystics, and *The Drop That Became a Sea* (Emre, 1999) is a compilation of Sufi poetry.

Fiction

One for Sorrow is the first of six mysteries set in a vividly Byzantine Constantinople (2000, Reed and Mayer). *Birds Without Wings* (2005), by Louis de Bernieres of *Corelli's Mandolin* fame, sets a village tragedy amid the fall of the Ottoman Empire, while Irfan Orga's *Portrait of a Turkish Family* (2007) looks at a moneyed family over the same time period. For portraits of contemporary Turkey, with all its religious, ethnic, and political contradictions, try Elif Shafak's *The Bastard of Istanbul* (2007) or O. Z. Livaneli's *Bliss* (2007).

Memed, My Hawk (1955, Kemal) is a dramatic tale of a bandit hero, seeking justice in the Turkish countryside. Poet and author Nazim Hikmet wrote *Human Landscapes from My Country*—a novel in verse—while being held in a Turkish prison in the 1940s.

Film

Peter Ustinov won an Oscar for his supporting role in *Topkapi* (1964), a crime caper worth seeing for its grand tour of 1960s Istanbul. Sean Connery sneaks around Istanbul as James Bond in *From Russia with Love* (1963), with a great scene filmed inside the Underground Cistern. *Gallipoli* (1981) tells the story of the famous battle from the perspective of two Australian soldiers (including a very young Mel Gibson). In the Golden Globe–nominated drama *Yol* (1982), five political prisoners are given a week's leave. In *Hamam* (1997)—also titled *Steam: The Turkish Bath*—an Italian inherits a traditional public bath in Istanbul. A photographer and his unemployed cousin try to connect in snow-covered Istanbul in *Distant* (2004), which won awards at the Cannes and Toronto International Film Festivals. Among documentaries, *Crossing the Bridge: The Sound of Istanbul* (2005) stands out for its fascinating musical portrait of modern Istanbul.

TELEPHONES, EMAIL, AND MAIL

Telephones

Smart travelers learn the phone system and use it daily to book or reconfirm rooms, get tourist information, reserve restaurants, confirm tour times, or phone home.

Types of Phones

You'll encounter various kinds of phones in Turkey.

Card-operated phones—public pay phones into which you insert a locally bought phone card—are common.

Coin-operated phones, the original kind of pay phone (but growing increasingly rare), require you to have enough change to complete your call.

Hotel room phones are sometimes cheap for local calls (confirm at the front desk first), but pricey for long-distance calls unless you use an international phone card (described later). Incoming calls are free, making this a cheap way for friends and family to stay in touch, provided they have a good long-distance plan for calls to Turkey. Hotels often charge for calls to "toll-free" 800 numbers; ask before you dial.

American mobile phones work in Turkey if they're GSM-enabled, tri-band or quad-band, and on a calling plan that includes international calls. They're convenient, but pricey. For example, with a T-Mobile phone, you'll pay $2 per minute for calls and about $0.35 for text messages. If your American phone works in Europe, ask about getting it "unlocked" so you can buy a Turkish SIM card (a fingernail-sized chip that holds the phone's information, available at mobile-phone stores) to make calls cheaply abroad.

Turkish mobile phones are usually quite expensive, and work affordably only in Turkey. The Turkish word for a mobile phone is *cep* (jehp; meaning "pocket phone"). These phones are loaded with prepaid calling time that you can recharge as you use up the minutes. As long as you're not "roaming" outside the phone's home country, incoming calls are free.

If you're traveling to multiple countries within Europe, make sure your phone—whether brought from home or purchased in Turkey—is electronically "unlocked," so that you can swap out its SIM card for a new one in other countries. For around $25 more, you can buy an unlocked phone that allows you to use different SIM cards in different countries—which saves money if you'll be making lots of calls.

Using a Turkish mobile phone or SIM card, you'll pay about $0.75 per minute to call the US (or $2 per minute to call a mobile phone in the US). The main mobile-phone providers in Turkey—with stores everywhere—are Turkcell, Vodafone, and Avea. Turkcell calls its SIM card Hazır Kart (hah-zur kahrt; "ready card"), while Vodafone sells MyCep (my-jehp; "my pocket"). For more information on mobile phones, see www.ricksteves.com/phones.

Using Phone Cards

Get a phone card for your calls. Prepaid cards come in two types: international phone cards (usable from any phone) and insertable phone cards (usable only in pay phones). The company that sells both kinds of cards is Türk Telekom (TT). Look for these cards at post offices, Türk Telekom shops, mobile-phone dealers (that also sell tram and bus tickets), most newsstands, and at food kiosks near phone booths.

Prepaid **international phone cards** (TT Kart; teh-teh kahrt) are the cheapest way to make international calls from Europe—and they also work for domestic calls. Cards come in three denominations: 5, 10, and 25 YTL, and work only in Turkey.

You can use these cards from any phone, including those in hotel rooms (check to make sure that your phone is set on tone instead of pulse, and ask at the desk about hidden fees for toll-free calls).

To use a card, scratch off the back to reveal your PIN (Personal Identification Number) code. After you dial the access phone number, the message tells you to enter your code and then dial the phone number you want to call. Before you dial, a voice may announce how much is left in your account. If the prompts start out in Turkish, just wait a moment for English.

To call the US, see "Dialing Internationally," later. To make calls within Turkey, dial the area code plus the local number; when

European Calling Chart

Just smile and dial, using this key:
AC = Area Code, LN = Local Number.

European Country	Calling long distance within ...	Calling from the US or Canada to ...	Calling from a European country to ...
Austria	AC + LN	011 + 43 + AC (without the initial zero) + LN	00 + 43 + AC (without the initial zero) + LN
Belgium	LN	011 + 32 + LN (without initial zero)	00 + 32 + LN (without initial zero)
Bosnia-Herzegovina	AC + LN	011 + 387 + AC (without initial zero) + LN	00 + 387 + AC (without initial zero) + LN
Britain	AC + LN	011 + 44 + AC (without initial zero) + LN	00 + 44 + AC (without initial zero) + LN
Croatia	AC + LN	011 + 385 + AC (without initial zero) + LN	00 + 385 + AC (without initial zero) + LN
Czech Republic	LN	011 + 420 + LN	00 + 420 + LN
Denmark	LN	011 + 45 + LN	00 + 45 + LN
Estonia	LN	011 + 372 + LN	00 + 372 + LN
Finland	AC + LN	011 + 358 + AC (without initial zero) + LN	999 + 358 + AC (without initial zero) + LN
France	LN	011 + 33 + LN (without initial zero)	00 + 33 + LN (without initial zero)
Germany	AC + LN	011 + 49 + AC (without initial zero) + LN	00 + 49 + AC (without initial zero) + LN
Greece	LN	011 + 30 + LN	00 + 30 + LN
Hungary	06 + AC + LN	011 + 36 + AC + LN	00 + 36 + AC + LN
Ireland	AC + LN	011 + 353 + AC (without initial zero) + LN	00 + 353 + AC (without initial zero) + LN

European Country	Calling long distance within...	Calling from the US or Canada to...	Calling from a European country to...
Italy	LN	011 + 39 + LN	00 + 39 + LN
Montenegro	AC + LN	011 + 382 + AC (without initial zero) + LN	00 + 382 + AC (without initial zero) + LN
Netherlands	AC + LN	011 + 31 + AC (without initial zero) + LN	00 + 31 + AC (without initial zero) + LN
Norway	LN	011 + 47 + LN	00 + 47 + LN
Poland	LN	011 + 48 + LN (without initial zero)	00 + 48 + LN (without initial zero)
Portugal	LN	011 + 351 + LN	00 + 351 + LN
Slovakia	AC + LN	011 + 421 + AC (without initial zero) + LN	00 + 421 + AC (without initial zero) + LN
Slovenia	AC + LN	011 + 386 + AC (without initial zero) + LN	00 + 386 + AC (without initial zero) + LN
Spain	LN	011 + 34 + LN	00 + 34 + LN
Sweden	AC + LN	011 + 46 + AC (without initial zero) + LN	00 + 46 + AC (without initial zero) + LN
Switzerland	LN	011 + 41 + LN (without initial zero)	00 + 41 + LN (without initial zero)
Turkey	AC (if no initial zero is included, add one) + LN	011 + 90 + AC (without initial zero) + LN	00 + 90 + AC (without initial zero) + LN

- The instructions above apply whether you're calling a land line or mobile phone.
- The international access codes (the first numbers you dial when making an international call) are 011 if you're calling from the US or Canada, or 00 if you're calling from virtually anywhere in Europe (except Finland, where it's 999).
- To call the US or Canada from Europe, dial 00, then 1 (the country code for the US and Canada), then the area code and number. In short, 00 + 1 + AC + LN = Hi, Mom!

using an international phone card, the area code must be dialed even if you're calling across the street.

To make numerous, successive calls with an international phone card without having to redial the long access number each time, press the keys (see instructions on card) that allow you to launch directly into your next call. Remember that you don't need the actual card to use a card account, so it's shareable. You can write down the access number and PIN in your notebook and share it with friends. If you have a still-lively card at the end of your trip, give it to another traveler.

Insertable phone cards (TT Smart Cards or Smart Telefon Kartı; teh-leh-fohn kahr-tuh) are a convenient way to pay for calls from the new, card-operated pay phones. The cards come in four denominations of units *(kontörs):* 50 units (3.75 YTL), 100 units (7.50 YTL), 200 units (15 YTL), and 350 units (19 YTL). To make a call with this card, find a public phone with a display screen, which you'll use to pick your language. Simply take the phone off the hook, insert the prepaid card, wait for a dial tone, and dial away. The price of the call (local or international) is automatically deducted while you talk. Insertable phone cards are a good deal for calling within Turkey, but calling the US can be more expensive than if you use an international phone card.

Using Hotel-Room Phones, VoIP, or US Calling Cards

Calling from the phone in your **hotel room** is convenient...but expensive (unless you use an international phone card, described above). While incoming calls (made by folks back home) can be the cheapest way for you to keep in touch, charges for *outgoing* calls can be a very unpleasant surprise. Before you dial, get a clear explanation from the hotel staff of the charges, even for local and (supposedly) toll-free calls.

If your family has an inexpensive way to call Europe, either through a long-distance plan or prepaid calling card, have them call you in your hotel room. Give them a list of your hotels' phone numbers before you go. Then, as you travel, send them an email or mobile-phone text message, or make a quick pay-phone call to set up a time for them to give you a ring.

If you're traveling with a laptop, consider trying **VoIP (Voice over Internet Protocol).** With VoIP, two computers act as the phones, allowing for a free Internet-based call. The major providers are Skype (www.skype.com) and Google Talk (www.google.com/talk).

US Calling Cards (such as the ones offered by AT&T, MCI, and Sprint) are the worst option. You'll nearly always save a lot of money by paying with a phone card (described previously).

APPENDIX

How to Dial
Calling from the US to Turkey, or vice versa, is simple—once you break the code. The European calling chart on the next page will walk you through it. Remember that Turkey is seven/ten hours ahead of the East/West Coasts of the US.

Dialing Within Turkey
Turkey, like much of the US, uses an area-code dialing system. Turkish phone numbers are seven digits, preceded by a four-digit area code. If you're dialing within an area code, you just dial the local number to be connected; but if you're calling outside your area code, you have to dial both the area code (which starts with a 0) and the local number.

Istanbul has two different area codes: European Istanbul is 0212, and Asian Istanbul is 0216. So if you're calling within European Istanbul, you need only dial the seven-digit number; but if you're calling from European to Asian Istanbul, dial 0216, then the number. The number for one of our recommended hotels (on the European side) is 0212/517-7173. To call it from within European Istanbul, just dial 517-7173. But to call it from Asian Istanbul—or anywhere else in Turkey—dial 0212/517-7173. To call a mobile phone number, you'll always dial the entire 11-digit number (no matter where you're calling from).

Dialing Internationally
If you want to make an international call, follow these three steps:

Dial the international access code (00 if you're calling from Turkey, 011 if you're calling from the US or Canada).

Then dial the country code of the country you're calling (see chart on next page).

Then dial the area code (*without* its initial 0) and the local number.

For example, to call the Istanbul hotel from the US, dial 011, 90 (Turkey's country code), 212 (Istanbul's area code without the initial zero), and 517-7173.

To call my Edmonds, Washington office from anywhere in Turkey, I dial 00 (Europe's international access code), 1 (the US country code), 425 (Edmonds' area code), and 771-8303.

Europeans often write their phone numbers with + at the front—it's just a placeholder for the international access code (again, that's 011 from the US or Canada, 00 from Europe).

Useful Phone Numbers
For the phone numbers answered in Turkish, ask a local person (such as your hotelier) to make the call for you.

Consulates

US Consulate: 24-hour emergency assistance tel. 0212/335-9000, recorded information tel. 0212/335-9200, passport services Mon–Thu 8:00–11:30 & 13:30–15:00, closed Fri–Sun (İstinye Mahallesi, Kaplıcalar Mevkii Sokak 2, http://istanbul.usconsulate.gov)

Canadian Consulate: General info tel. 0212/251-9838, passport services Mon–Thu 9:30–12:30 & 13:30–17:30, Fri 9:30–12:30, closed Sat–Sun (İstiklal Caddesi 189/5, http://geo.international .gc.ca/canada-europa/turkey)

Emergency Needs

Police (Turkish-language only): tel. 155
Fire (Turkish-language only): tel. 110
Emergency Medical Assistance (Turkish-language only): tel. 112
Med-line Ambulance: tel. 0212/444-1212
American Hospital: In the New District at Güzelbahçe Sokak 20, Nişantaşı, tel. 0212/444-3777
International Hospital: Close to Atatürk Airport at İstanbul Caddesi 82, Yeşilköy, hospital tel. 0212/663-3000, ambulance service tel. 0212/444-4505

Dialing Assistance

Directory Assistance for Istanbul (Turkish-language only): tel. 118
Collect Calls to the US (Turkish-language only): tel. 115

Airline Offices in Istanbul

Air France: tel. 0212/310-1919 (www.airfrance.com)
Alitalia: tel. 0212/315-1990 (www.alitalia.com)
American Airlines: tel. 0212/251-1315 or 0212/251-1316 (www .aa.com)
Atlasjet: tel. 0212/465-5364 (www.atlasjet.com)
British Airways: tel. 0212/317-6600 (www.britishairways.com)
Delta: tel. 0212/310-2000 (www.delta.com)
Emirates: tel. 0212/334-8888 (www.emirates.com)
KLM: tel. 0212/310-1900 (www.klm.com)
Lufthansa: tel. 0212/315-3434 (www.lufthansa.com)
Onur Air: tel. 0212/662-9797 (www.onurair.com.tr)
Turkish Airlines: tel. 0212/444-0849 or 0212/225-0556 (www .thy.com)

Istanbul Atatürk Airport

Airport Services: General info tel. 0212/465-5555; TI tel. 0212/465-3547 or 0212/465-3451; Airport clinic tel. 0212/663-6400, ext. 707
Air France: tel. 0212/465-5491 or 0212/465-5492

Alitalia: tel. 0212/465-3575
Czech Airlines: tel. 0212/465-4895 or 0212/465-5766
Delta: tel. 0212/465-4011 or 0212/465-4012
Emirates: tel. 0212/465-3000 or 0212/465-1966
Iberia: tel. 0212/469-8020
KLM: tel. 0212/465-4287
Lufthansa: tel. 0212/465-4650
Malev: tel. 0212/465-4344
Olympic Airlines: tel. 0212/465-3388
Turkish Airlines: tel. 0212/444-0849

Car-Rental Agencies—International Terminal
Avis: tel. 0212/465-3455 or 0212/465-3456
Hertz: tel. 0212/465-5999
Sixt: tel. 0212/465-3645 or 0212/465-4422

Car-Rental Agencies—Domestic Terminal
Avis: tel. 0212/465-4645 or 0212/465-4488
Budget: tel. 0212/465-5479 or 0212/465-5806
National: tel. 0212-465-3545 or 0212-465-3546

Sabiha Gökçen Airport (on the Asian side of the Bosphorus)
Airport Information: tel. 0216/585-5000
Turkish Airlines: tel. 0216/585-5850 or 0216/585-5851
Pegasus Airlines: tel. 0216/585-5970 or 0216/585-5971
Avis: tel. 0216/585-5154
Hertz: tel. 0216/585-5179

Email and Mail
Email: Many travelers set up a free Web-based email account with Yahoo, Microsoft (Hotmail), or Google (Gmail). Internet cafés are easy to find in Istanbul, especially in the New District. Look for the places listed in this book, or ask your hotelier for suggestions. Some hotels have a computer for guests' email needs—sometimes free, sometimes for a fee, and generally with a slow Internet connection. Small places are accustomed to letting clients (who've asked politely) sit at their desk for a few minutes just to check their email.

Internet access for those with their own laptops is becoming more commonplace at Istanbul hotels, especially in the New District. Most hotels that offer this do so for free, but some charge by the minute. You'll either access the hotel's wireless Internet (Wi-Fi, sometimes called "WLAN" in Europe), often using a password provided by the hotelier; or plug your computer directly into an Internet wall socket (they can usually loan you a cable). In this book's hotel listings, "Internet access" means there's a public terminal in the lobby for guests to use. "Wi-Fi" means you can access it in your room, but only if you have your own laptop.

Turkish keyboards include many unfamiliar letters. Most of these are on the right part of the keyboard (where you'd find the punctuation keys on an English keyboard). To type an "@" symbol, press two keys at the same time: "alt gr" (a special shift key to the right of the space bar) + Q. When typing passwords or addresses, be careful to select the right version of the two Turkish letters equivalent to the English "i (I)." One is undotted: ı (I). The other is dotted: i (İ). Notice that this means an English capital I and lowercase i are actually on different keys.

Mail: You can only buy stamps at Turkish post offices, which are usually marked with yellow *PTT* signs (for "Post, Telephone, and Telegraph"). Most are open Monday–Friday 9:00–17:00, and are closed on weekends. It costs about 0.80 YTL to mail a postcard to the US. Phoning and e-mailing are so easy that you could dispense with mail stops altogether.

HOLIDAYS AND FESTIVALS

This is a partial list of holidays and festivals in Istanbul—note that holidays may strike without warning. On the days preceding national and religious holidays, many businesses close for the afternoon, if not the entire day.

Dates for Muslim holidays are set according to a lunar calendar, so the specific dates vary from year to year. Even though Christian holidays (such as Easter, Ascension, and Christmas) are not celebrated in Istanbul, the city is especially crowded during these times with visiting Europeans.

Jan 1	New Year's Day (Yılbaşı, national holiday)
Late March–mid-April	International Film Festival (April 3–18 in 2010, www.iksv.org/film/english)
Easter	April 4 in 2010 (Christian holiday; Western and Orthodox Easters fall on the same day in 2010)
April 23	National Sovereignty and Children's Day (national holiday)
April	Turkey Grand Prix (likely April 23–25 in 2010)
Ascension	May 13 in 2010 (Christian holiday; Western and Orthodox Ascensions fall on same day in 2010)

May 19	Atatürk Commemoration and Youth Day (national holiday)
June	International Music Festival (www.iksv.org /muzik/english)
Early July	International Jazz Festival (www.iksv.org /caz/english)
Aug 30	Victory Day (national holiday)
Sept	International Istanbul Biennial (four weeks, www.iksv.org/bienal/english)
Ramadan	Aug 11–Sept 8 in 2010 (Muslim holy month)
Seker Bayramı	Sept 9–11 in 2010 (national holiday)
Mid-Oct	October Film Week (www.iksv.org)
Oct 29	Republic Day (national holiday)
Kurban Bayramı	Nov 16–19 in 2010 (Muslim festival)
Dec 24–Jan 1	Christmas Week (Christian holiday)

CONVERSIONS AND CLIMATE

Numbers and Stumblers

- Europeans write a few of their numbers differently than we do. 1 = 1, 4 = 4, 7 = 7.
- In Europe, dates appear as day/month/year, so Christmas is 25/12/10.
- Commas are decimal points and decimals commas. A dollar and a half is 1,50, and there are 5.280 feet in a mile.
- When counting with fingers, start with your thumb. If you hold up your first finger to request one item, you'll probably get two.
- What Americans call the second floor of a building is the first floor in Turkey. The entrance level is generally called the *zemin* or *zemin kat* (zeh-meen kaht) in Turkey, and marked as "0" on elevators, or "L" (lobby) at hotels.
- On escalators and moving sidewalks, Europeans keep the left "lane" open for passing. Keep to the right.

Metric Conversions (approximate)

1 foot = 0.3 meter	1 square yard = 0.8 square meter
1 yard = 0.9 meter	1 square mile = 2.6 square kilometers
1 mile = 1.6 kilometers	1 ounce = 28 grams
1 centimeter = 0.4 inch	1 quart = 0.95 liter
1 meter = 39.4 inches	1 kilogram = 2.2 pounds
1 kilometer = 0.62 mile	32°F = 0°C

Climate Chart

The first line is the average daily high; the second line, the average daily low. The third line shows the average number of days without rain. For more detailed weather statistics for destinations in this book (as well as the rest of the world), check www.worldclimate .com.

J	F	M	A	M	J	J	A	S	O	N	D
48°	49°	53°	63°	70°	79°	82°	82°	77°	68°	60°	52°
35°	36°	39°	45°	53°	60°	65°	66°	60°	53°	45°	39°
13	14	17	21	23	24	27	27	23	20	16	13

Temperature Conversion:
Fahrenheit and Celsius

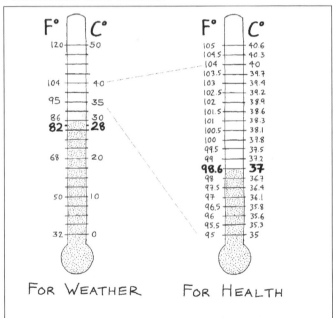

Europe takes its temperature using the Celsius scale, while we opt for Fahrenheit. For a rough conversion from Celsius to Fahrenheit, double the number and add 30. For weather, remember that 28°C is 82°F—perfect. For health, 37°C is just right.

Essential Packing Checklist

Whether you're traveling for five days or five weeks, here's what you'll need to bring. Remember to pack light to enjoy the sweet freedom of true mobility. Happy travels!

- ❏ 5 shirts
- ❏ 1 sweater or lightweight fleece jacket
- ❏ 2 pairs pants
- ❏ 1 pair shorts
- ❏ 1 swimsuit (women only—men can use shorts)
- ❏ 5 pairs underwear and socks
- ❏ 1 pair shoes
- ❏ 1 rain-proof jacket
- ❏ Tie or scarf
- ❏ Money belt
- ❏ Money—your mix of:
  - ❏ Debit card for ATM withdrawals
  - ❏ Credit card
  - ❏ Hard cash in US dollars
- ❏ Documents (and back-up photocopies)
- ❏ Passport
- ❏ Airplane ticket
- ❏ Driver's license
- ❏ Student ID and hostel card
- ❏ Railpass/car rental voucher
- ❏ Insurance details
- ❏ Daypack
- ❏ Sealable plastic baggies
- ❏ Camera and related gear
- ❏ Empty water bottle
- ❏ Wristwatch and alarm clock
- ❏ Earplugs
- ❏ First-aid kit
- ❏ Medicine (labeled)
- ❏ Extra glasses/contacts and prescriptions
- ❏ Sunscreen and sunglasses
- ❏ Toiletries kit
- ❏ Soap
- ❏ Laundry soap (if liquid and carry-on, limit to 3 oz.)
- ❏ Clothesline
- ❏ Small towel
- ❏ Sewing kit
- ❏ Travel information
- ❏ Necessary map(s)
- ❏ Address list (email and mailing addresses)
- ❏ Postcards and photos from home
- ❏ Notepad and pen
- ❏ Journal

Hotel Reservation

To: _____   _____
              hotel   *email or fax*

From: _____   _____
              name   *email or fax*

Today's date: _____ /_____ /_____
                    day   *month*   *year*

Dear Hotel _____ ,
Please make this reservation for me:

Name: _____

Total # of people: _____   # of rooms: _____   # of nights: _____

Arriving: _____ /_____ /_____   My time of arrival (24-hr clock): _____
              day   *month*   *year*   (I will telephone if I will be late)

Departing: ____ /____ /____
                day   *month*   *year*

Room(s): Single____   Double ____   Twin ____   Triple ____   Quad____

With: Toilet _____   Shower _____   Bath _____   Sink only ____

Special needs: View____ Quiet____ Cheapest____ Ground Floor____

Please email or fax confirmation of my reservation, along with the type of room reserved and the price. Please also inform me of your cancellation policy. After I hear from you, I will quickly send my credit-card information as a deposit to hold the room. Thank you.

_____
Name

_____
Address

_____
City   *State*   *Zip Code*   *Country*

Before hoteliers can make your reservation, they want to know the information listed above. You can use this form as the basis for your email, or you can photocopy this page, fill in the information, and send it as a fax (also available online at www.ricksteves.com/reservation).

INDEX

▸ Plan Your Trip

Browse thousands of articles and a wealth of money-saving tips for planning your dream trip. You'll find up-to-date information on Europe's best destinations, packing smart, getting around, finding rooms, staying healthy, avoiding scams and more.

▸ Eurail Passes

Find out, step-by-step, if a rail p[ass] makes sense for your trip—and how to avoid buying more than need. Get a bunch of free extras

▸ Graffiti Wall & Travelers' Helpline

Learn, ask, share—our online community of savvy travelers is a great resource for first-time travelers to Europe, as well as seasoned pros.

Rick Steves

www.ricksteves.com

TRAVEL SKILLS
Europe Through the Back Door

EUROPE GUIDES
Best of Europe
Eastern Europe
Europe 101
European Christmas
Postcards from Europe

COUNTRY GUIDES
Croatia & Slovenia
England
France
Germany
Great Britain
Ireland
Italy
Portugal
Scandinavia
Spain
Switzerland

CITY & REGIONAL GUIDES
Amsterdam, Bruges & Brussels
Athens & The Peloponnese
Budapest
Florence & Tuscany
Istanbul
London
Paris
Prague & The Czech Republic
Provence & The French Riviera
Rome
Venice
Vienna, Salzburg & Tirol

PHRASE BOOKS & DICTIONARIES
French
French, Italian & German
German
Italian
Portuguese
Spanish

RICK STEVES' EUROPE DVDs
Austria & The Alps
Eastern Europe
England
Europe
France & Benelux
Germany & Scandinavia
Greece, Turkey, Israel & Egypt
Ireland & Scotland
Italy's Cities
Italy's Countryside
Rick Steves' European Christmas
Spain & Portugal
Travel Skills & "The Making Of"

PLANNING MAPS
Britain, Ireland & London
Europe
France & Paris
Germany, Austria & Switzerland
Ireland
Italy
Spain & Portugal

JOURNALS
Rick Steves' Pocket Travel Journal
Rick Steves' Travel Journal

NOW AVAILABLE

RICK STEVES APPS FOR THE iPHONE OR iPOD TOUCH

With these apps you can:

➤ Spin the compass icon to switch views between sights, hotels, and restaurant selections—and get details on cost, hours, address, and phone number.

➤ Tap any point on the screen to read Rick's detailed information, including history and suggested viewpoints.

➤ Get a deeper view into Rick's tours with audio and video segments.

Go to iTunes to download the following apps:

Rick Steves' Louvre Tour

Rick Steves' Historic Paris Walk

Rick Steves' Orsay Museum Tour

Rick Steves' Versailles

Rick Steves' Ancient Rome Tour

Rick Steves' St. Peter's Basilica Tour

Once downloaded, these apps are completely self-contained on your iPhone or iPod Touch, so you will not incur pricey roaming charges during use overseas.

Rick Steves books and DVDs are available at bookstores and through online booksellers.
Rick Steves guidebooks are published by Avalon Travel, a member of the Perseus Books Group.
Rick Steves apps are produced by Übermind, a boutique Seattle-based software consultancy firm.

CREDITS

Contributor

Cameron Hewitt

Cameron helped to road-test, rewrite, and revise the first edition of this guidebook. He has co-authored two guidebooks and led tours through Eastern Europe with Rick Steves. When offered the opportunity to work on this book, he snapped it up like a gooey Turkish delight. When he's not on the road, Cameron lives in Seattle with his wife, Shawna, and edits guidebooks at Rick Steves' Europe Through the Back Door.

Rick Steves' Guidebook Series

Country Guides

Rick Steves' Best of Europe
Rick Steves' Croatia & Slovenia
Rick Steves' Eastern Europe
Rick Steves' England
Rick Steves' France
Rick Steves' Germany
Rick Steves' Great Britain
Rick Steves' Ireland
Rick Steves' Italy
Rick Steves' Portugal
Rick Steves' Scandinavia
Rick Steves' Spain
Rick Steves' Switzerland

City and Regional Guides

Rick Steves' Amsterdam, Bruges & Brussels
Rick Steves' Athens & the Peloponnese
Rick Steves' Budapest
Rick Steves' Florence & Tuscany
Rick Steves' Istanbul
Rick Steves' London
Rick Steves' Paris
Rick Steves' Prague & the Czech Republic
Rick Steves' Provence & the French Riviera
Rick Steves' Rome
Rick Steves' Venice
Rick Steves' Vienna, Salzburg & Tirol

Rick Steves' Phrase Books

French
German
Italian
Spanish
Portuguese
French/Italian/German

Other Books

Rick Steves' Europe Through the Back Door
Rick Steves' Europe 101: History and Art for the Traveler
Rick Steves' Postcards from Europe
Rick Steves' European Christmas

(Avalon Travel)

Avalon Travel
a member of the Perseus Books Group
1700 Fourth Street
Berkeley, CA 94710

Text © 2009 by Rick Steves
Cover © 2009 by Avalon Travel. All rights reserved.
Maps © 2009 by Tankut Aran and Europe Through the Back Door
Printed in the USA by Worzalla. Second printing October 2009.

For the latest on Rick Steves' lectures, guidebooks, tours, public radio show, and public
television series, contact Europe Through the Back Door, Box 2009, Edmonds, WA 98020,
tel. 425/771-8303, fax 425/771-0833, www.ricksteves.com, rick@ricksteves.com.

ISBN(13) 978-1-59880-215-3
ISSN: 1936-7112

Europe Through the Back Door Senior Editor: Jennifer Madison Davis
ETBD Editors: Tom Griffin, Cathy McDonald, Sarah McCormic
ETBD Managing Editor: Risa Laib
Avalon Travel Senior Editor and Series Manager: Madhu Paşa
Avalon Travel Project Editor: Kelly Lydick
Copy Editor: Amy Scott
Proofreader: Ellie Behrstock
Indexer: Carl Wikander
Production & Typesetting: McGuire Barber Design
Cover Design: Kimberly Glyder Design
Maps & Graphics: David C. Hoerlein, Laura VanDeventer, Lauren Mills, Mike
    Morgenfeld, Brice Ticen, Chris Markiewicz, Kat Bennett, Hank Evans
Photography: Lale Surmen Aran, Tankut Aran, Cameron Hewitt, Rick Steves, Carol Ries,
    Laura VanDeventer, Rudi Nisargand
Front Matter Color Photo: p. i, Turkish Delight at the Spice Market © Laura
    VanDeventer
Cover Photo © Keren Su / Danita Delimont Agency / DRR.net

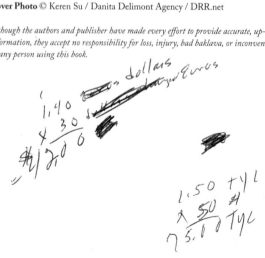